FROM
IBSEN'S WORKSHOP

NOTES, SCENARIOS,
AND DRAFTS OF THE MODERN PLAYS

FROM
IBSEN'S WORKSHOP

NOTES, SCENARIOS,
AND DRAFTS OF THE MODERN PLAYS

TRANSLATED BY
A. G. CHATER

EDITED AND
WITH AN INTRODUCTION BY
WILLIAM ARCHER

NEW FOREWORD BY
JOHN GUARE

A DACAPO PAPERBACK

Library of Congress Cataloging in Publication Data

Ibsen, Henrik, 1828-1906.
　From Ibsen's workshop.

　(A Da Capo Paperback)
　Reprint of the 1913 ed. published by Scribner, New
York, in series: The collected works of Henrik Ibsen,
copyright ed,
　I. Archer, William, 1856-1924. II. Title.
PT8854.A68 1978　　839.8'2'26　　　　78-16738
ISBN 0-306-80090-X

ISBN: 0-306-80090-X

First Paperback Edition 1978

This Da Capo Press paperback edition of *From Ibsen's Workshop*
is an unabridged republication of the first edition published by
Charles Scribner's Sons in 1911 as Volume 12 of *The Collected
Works of Henrik Ibsen*. The present edition contains a new foreword by John Guare, and is reprinted by arrangement with the
original publisher.

Published by Da Capo Press, Inc.
A Subsidiary of Plenum Publishing Corporation
227 West 17th Street, New York, New York 10011

FOREWORD TO THE 1978 EDITION

John Gassner stunned our playwrighting class in the early sixties with the heresy that Henrik Ibsen would live longer than Chekhov for the simple reason that that dour Norwegian constructed in iron while the Russian of our dreams built his plays out of molasses. Gassner emphasized the word "wright" in "playwright," speaking of it as a craft. Plays with titles like *A Glass of Water* and *A Scrap of Paper.* And *A Doll House.* Scribe. Sardou. and Ibsen. First, you have this *donnée*, this premise, this problem—syphilis, divorce, et al. A series of conflicts brings the hero/ine down to his/her lowest ebb. Then you bring on the *peripeteia*, the reversal of fortunes which rise until the inevitable *scène à faire*, that ultimate scene in which illusions are stripped bare, hypocrisies revealed. Tosca dies. Nora walks out the door. Curtain. Applause. House lights up. Were we in drama school only to learn how to create some wind-up toy that could crank out a laugh, yank out a tear, contrive scenes, manipulate emotions, and at the finale pop out a moral that would also insult us by telling us what to think after an evening of telling us what to feel? Didn't Shaw write a well-made *Devil's Disciple* (a trifle cynically) after the failure of his three *Plays Unpleasant*—using the formula to give *them* what *they* wanted?

As a kid I saw *Raisin in the Sun*, highly praised as a black play but which seemed to me like any white ethnic (Jewish, Irish) well-made classroom play of the thirties updated to the fifties. Except for one extraordinary moment when the young daughter with the unforgettable name of Beneatha imagined her African past. The play burst out of its four-walled naturalism. Poetry breathed on that stage. They were in Africa. The play gave me an image that let me understand them with a dream-like clarity. I swore that when I became a playwright I would never settle for a single brief moment of lightning. My plays would *live* in that lightning. The violent fabric of my dream life would not be forced into any pre-existing mold. Like Konstantin, the fabulously-doomed playwright in *The Seagull*, I dreamed of finding new forms. Of doing away with form. Of letting my life determine its own form.

Years go by. I become a playwright. I realize that the play does not take place solely on the stage. Nor does it take place in the audience's response to the play. I learn that the dramatic event takes place in that invisible space between the stage and the audience. The role of the artist is to charge the air with dreams made visible. And if the audience cannot enter the dream world of the artist, then we are talking not so much about failed art as we are about schizophrenia. The audience enters the atmosphere of the play by understanding the design of the play. The play reveals itself through its patterns. "Designs"? "Patterns"? Aren't these other words for "Structure"? Are we back at that fork in the road again? Did those divergent paths of Ibsen and Chekhov merge all these miles later?

I stumbled onto a biography of Ibsen remaindered at a local bookstore.

In one's life one has a few great reading experiences. For me, *Remembrance of Things Past*. The Leon Edel biography of Henry James. Add this third: Michael Meyer's biography of Henrik Ibsen. Because as I got to each play in Meyer's work, I put down the life and picked up the play. Why were the plays so disturbing? What had happened to the impenetrable thesis plays one only picked up to cram for a test? What trolls had sneaked in, leaving the words the same, but swapping the spirit?

In our time, Mark Rothko wrenched, out of the simplest secular forms of shape and color, a reverberance, a religious power. This force possessed the plays of Ibsen. Where was the well-made politeness? Why did the individual scenes of the play move in great Stonehenges of energy? Why didn't the plays of Ibsen seem like the plays of Ibsen? These seemed to be all about furies and one's relation to those furies. Nora walks out the door not just to get to some Moscow, not just to find some freedom, but to go out and pursue furies that belong to her maturity, Hedda kills herself to find furies that have passed her by. Ellida, the Lady from the Sea, makes peace with her furies and moves on. Solness, driven on by one fury, climbs a steeple to find another fury. The artist, Rubek, at the end of *The Resurrection Day*—the last play, which James Joyce calls the greatest play—goes up the mountain to meet that fury.

I can't reconcile this imagined abyss between Chekhov and Ibsen. I try to find images for them in my head so I can grab onto them. Chekhov is easy. Isn't Chekhov Renoir given speech? Surely Madame Ranevskaya is caught by Renoir in a plump, rosy instant—smiling at us from the canvas as she turns around from that lacy window, the orchard there in the nacreous distance.

Ibsen doesn't seem half so attractive or accessible. Henry James calls him "talent without glamour." Ibsen's people always seem to be returning from a mountain, going to a mountain, climbing that mountain. The image of that mountain. Is

Ibsen Cézanne? Cézanne spending the bulk of his life in Provence painting Mont Sainte-Victoire? Ibsen never spiritually leaving Norway. James Joyce in a letter refers to Ibsen as an "egoarch." "He never broke with his set." Ibsen spent the rest of his life trying to get back to the Ice Palace he created for Brand. The stillness. Always the great stillness.

Paul Klee wrote an essay in which he tries "to give you a glimpse of the painter's workshop." He could be writing about Ibsen, and the notes, drafts and scenarios you hold in your hands.

Chosen are those artists who penetrate to the region of that secret place where primaeval power nurtures all evolution.

There, where the powerhouse of all time and space —call it brain or heart of creation — activates every function; who is the artist who would not dwell there?

In the womb of nature, at the source of creation, where the secret key to all lies guarded?

But not all can enter. Each should follow where the pulse of his own heart leads.

So, in their time, the Impressionists—our opposites of yesterday—had every right to dwell within the matted undergrowth of everyday vision.

But our pounding heart drives us down, deep down to the source of all.

What springs from this source—whatever it may be called, dream, idea or fantasy—must be taken seriously only if it unites with the proper creative means to form a work of art.

(From *Paul Klee on Modern Art*, translated by Paul Findlay, 1948, Faber and Faber).

For Ibsen, the proper creative means were the tools of a well-made play. But he made these tools serve him in the way

Cézanne used his paints and brushes to find the energy lying hidden in that mountain, or that bowl of apples. (Would Eve ever have been tempted by an apple of Cézanne's? I don't think so. His apples contain too many harsh judgments; they will explode into the forms of Braque and Picasso.) Ibsen uses the machinery of Scribe and Sardou not to pander to the audience like some android, some R2D2, but to drill down to those secret springs in all our souls.

These notebooks, read in tandem with the plays, show us a great artist in the intense throes of making a play happen. In the first draft of *Hedda Gabler*, to pick one example, Hedda is a weak woman dominated by the powerful Mrs. Elfsted. We see Hedda suggesting to her husband that they burn Lövborg's manuscript—in effect, asking his permission and approval before the fact. Here Hedda is a pathetic, clawing creature who mewls her way to suicide. Compare this Hedda with the Hedda of the finished play. Ibsen takes qualities away from Mrs. Elfsted and invests them in Hedda until she dominates the play like some suburban Clytemnestra. The vine leaves Hedda dreams about in Lövborg's hair are also not in this first draft. We see Ibsen's application of imagery as he works on the plays.

Compare the first draft of the scene between Allmers and his sister in *Little Eyolf* with its final version. In the draft, Ibsen lays out a careful, well-ordered scene between brother and sister. In the final version, the sister is not the sister. Their relationship, horrifyingly to him, can go anywhere. Ibsen has so charged the play with a fierce poetry that the scene never becomes melodramatic, but he needs the steel of his construction to contain the shifting moral sands of the play. The absence of the prime images of the play, Little Eyolf's crutches floating out to sea, his eyes looking out from under the water, illuminate Ibsen's searching out of the images that will make the inner life of the play visible, the images that will haunt us *after* the form of the play has been roughly set.

It's not that I say, "Ah yes, my professor in school was right and Ibsen in the final round got Chekhov on a TKO." We must realize that Chekhov's roots are in the loose form of the short stories, where the themes for his plays have all appeared. The short stories are Chekhov's workshop. Ibsen writes only plays. All the energies go into the plays. These notebooks, drafts, scenarios contain the bold action, that stab as in a dream, that Ibsen does not fully understand at first but will work out in the final writing of the plays. He uses the form of Scribe the way that Shakespeare used the tight form of the sonnet. The strictness of the form does battle with the size of the poet's soul.

The American playwright has been at war with the sense of form for the past twenty years, not out of ignorance of the form, or spite for it. We're products of the same forces that made Jackson Pollack throw down his brushes and passionately sprawl the paint onto the canvas. The forms of the theatre have been too chewed over to taste.

But one slowly learns that forms are there not only to constrain but also to liberate. Pollack leaped into his canvas and had nowhere to go out of the brilliance he found there.

In Boston, Trinity Church was designed and built by Henry Hobson Richardson at roughly the same time Ibsen was writing the plays. In the 1970s, I. M. Pei built the Hancock Tower across the street from that church and designed it so that the mirrored skyscraper captures the church in its glass and re-creates it. It forces us to re-examine the beauty of the Richardson creation. In the same way, it is time, on this one hundred and fiftieth anniversary of his birth, to re-invent Ibsen.

George Bernard Shaw wrote that the highest function a man can perform is this: "to pick out the significant incidents from the chaos of daily happenings and arrange them so that their relation to one another becomes significant, thus changing us from bewildered spectators of a monstrous confusion to men intelligently conscious of the world and its destinies." These notes and drafts and scenarios sanctify the chaos of preparation. The final drafts of the plays sanctify the role of the artist.

Ibsen kept a portrait of Strindberg over his desk. He said he needed the eyes of that madman burning into him.

We've been mad.

We need the eyes of this poet to burn into us.

These notebooks are a talisman.

JOHN GUARE
New York City
May 1978

CONTENTS

FROM IBSEN'S WORKSHOP

INTRODUCTION

THIS volume contains all the notes, sketches, drafts, and other "foreworks" (as he used to call them) for Ibsen's plays from *Pillars of Society* onwards. They were published in Scandinavia and Germany in 1909, under the editorship of those learned and devoted Ibsen scholars, Halvdan Koht and Julius Elias. They occupied somewhat less than one-half of the three volumes of the poet's *Efterladte Skrifter*, or (to use the consecrated but somewhat unfortunate English phrase) his *Literary Remains*. The other contents of these three volumes are of great interest for special students of Ibsen's biography; but not until the period of his modern plays is reached do his drafts and jottings assume what may be called world-wide importance. The papers here translated throw invaluable light upon the genesis of his ideas and the development of his technique. They are an indispensable aid to the study of his intellectual processes during that part of his career which made him world-famous.

The first volume of the Norwegian edition is very varied in its contents. About half of it is occupied by early poems, including the boyish verses to Hungary and to King Oscar, written about 1848, which were probably the "first heirs of his invention." Most of the contents of this section are occasional pieces—prologues,

3

student songs, etc.—but in some of the lyrics we find the germs of ideas to which he afterwards gave more finished form.   Then come some miscellaneous prose pieces, ranging from one or two of his school themes, which have somehow been preserved, to the singularly laconic and unrhetorical speeches of his later years.[1]   The remaining pages are given up to hitherto unpublished plays and dramatic fragments, dating from the 'fifties and early 'sixties.   The most important of these is the romantic comedy *St. John's Night*, produced in Bergen, January 2, 1853.   This very youthful but not uninteresting play was known to exist in manuscript, and had been described by Ibsen's biographers; but, during his lifetime, he had not suffered it to be printed.   It is a vivacious and really imaginative piece of work, containing foretastes both of *Love's Comedy* and of *Peer Gynt*.   Its culminating scene is a midnight revel of fairy folk, which is witnessed by two pairs of mortal lovers.   The pair who are really in touch with nature and with things elemental, see it as it is, while the conventional and affected romanticists take it for a dance of peasants around a bonfire.   We have here the germ of several passages in the poet's maturer work.   Another item of interest in the first volume is a fragment entitled *Svanhild*, being the first sketch, in prose, of what afterwards became *Love's Comedy*.[2]   Ibsen said that he abandoned this form because he had not yet the art of writing modern prose dialogue.   I should rather be disposed to say that he had not a theme adapted

[1] Even his entries in the complaint-book of the Scandinavian Club in Rome are piously included.
[2] See Professor Herford's introduction to that play.

for treatment in prose. There is practically no action in the play—none of that complex interweaving of the past with the present, and of event with character, which afterwards formed the substance of his art. We have only a group of people expressing certain ideas on life and love—ideas which naturally tend to shape themselves in lyric or satiric verse. The form, in short, was indicated by the lack of substance. The theme was a very thin one, which needed the starch of metre.

The second volume of the Norwegian edition opens with the so-called "epic *Brand*"—the fragment of a narrative version of *Brand*, which is described by Professor Herford in his Introduction to that play.[1] Then come sundry chips from the workshop in which *Brand* and *Peer Gynt* were wrought to perfection. In the *Peer Gynt* fragments there are one or two points of interest, to which I have alluded in my Introduction.[2] The preliminary sketches for *The League of Youth* are of small importance, except in so far as they show that the play grew and developed very little in the course of incubation. Far more interesting are the long scenarios and drafts which preceded the final form of *Emperor and Galilean*. A pretty full account of them may be found in my Introduction to the "world-historic drama."[3] This brings us down to *Pillars of Society* and to the sketches and drafts included in the present volume.

Whatever he may have been in youth, Henrik Ibsen, in maturity and age, was the most reticent of artists. It is said, I believe with truth, that even his wife and son knew nothing of what he was meditating and hatching

[1] Vol. II., p. 4.　　[2] Vol. IV., p. 14.　　[3] Vol. V., p. 13.

out, until each new play was polished to the last syllable. In the Introduction to *An Enemy of the People* may be found an anecdote of his apparently disproportionate anger when he learned that some loose scrap of paper had revealed the fact that the hero of the play on which he was then engaged was to be a doctor. In his correspondence he never indicates or discusses the themes which are occupying him, except when he is asking for historical material to be used in *Emperor and Galilean*. So far as my own experience went, he never said more of his work than that he was "preparing some devilment for next year." I remember, too, that, when he was engaged on *When We Dead Awaken*, he told me that he thought of describing it as "An Epilogue."

It seems like an irony of fate that this ultra-secretive craftsman, so jealous of the privacy of his workroom, should, after death, have all his pigeon-holes ransacked, and even the contents of his waste-paper basket, one might say, given to the world. At first sight this may seem like a profanation; but on looking into the matter we find no just cause for sentimental regret. If Ibsen had been violently averse from any posthumous study of his methods, he had safety in his own hands—he could always have destroyed his papers. He seems, on the contrary, to have treasured them with considerable care. The drafts and experiments for his romantic plays (*Lady Inger*, *The Vikings*, and *The Pretenders*) were scattered in a sale of his effects after he left Norway, in 1864, and have not yet been recovered. He was very angry when he heard of their dispersal; but he was probably not thinking of the loss to posterity. What he re-

sented at the time, no doubt, was the thought that unknown and irreverent persons might be prying into his
secrets while he lived. Was he, perhaps, recalling this
experience when he made Lövborg, in *Hedda Gabler*,
speak so bitterly of the possible profanation of his lost
manuscript? Be this as it may, we find that not even
the wandering life which he led for so many years inter-
fered with his habit of treasuring up the chips from his
workshop. It will be seen that this volume contains
"foreworks" of more or less importance for all his plays
from *Pillars of Society* onwards, with the single exception
of *An Enemy of the People*. We do not know what has
become of the sketches and studies for this play. He
produced it in half the time that he usually gave to the
ripening of a dramatic creation, and seems, indeed, to
have thrown it off with unusual facility and gusto. Still,
it is difficult to suppose that he dispensed altogether with
preliminary notes and jottings. We must rather conclude
that they have been accidentally lost or destroyed.

As he carefully preserved his papers, and as he left his
executors a free hand to deal with them as they thought
fit, they would have done the world a great wrong had
they decided to suppress documents of such unique interest. Nowhere else, so far as I am aware, do we obtain
so clear a view of the processes of a great dramatist's
mind. There is something of the same interest, no
doubt, in a comparison of the early quartos of *Romeo
and Juliet* and *Hamlet* with the completed plays; but
in these cases we cannot decide with any certainty how
far the incompleteness of the earlier versions represents
an actual phase in the growth of the plays, and how far

it is due to the bad stenography of the playhouse pirates. In Ibsen's manuscripts we can actually follow the growth of an idea in his mind; distinguish what is original and fundamental in his conception from accretions and after-thoughts; see him straying into blind alleys and trying back again; and estimate the faultless certainty of taste with which he strengthened weak points in his fabric, and rejected the commonplace in favour of the rare and unforgettable. Not once, I think, is a scene or a trait suppressed which ought to have been preserved; not once is a speech altered for the worse. Sometimes, in-deed, we find him using absolutely commonplace ideas and phrases which he must have known to be tempo-rary makeshifts, awaiting transfiguration at a later stage. How much he relied upon the final revision of his work is apparent from a curious expression of which he makes use in a letter to Theodor Caspari, dated Rome, 27th June, 1884. "I have just completed a play in five acts," he says; and then adds: "that is to say, the rough draft of it; now comes the elaboration, the more ener-getic individualisation of the persons and their modes of expression." The play in question was *The Wild Duck*. Any one who compares the draft in the follow-ing pages with the finished play will see that what Ibsen called "elaboration" amounted, at some points, almost to reinvention.

In the Introductions to the various plays, in the Sub-scription edition, I have pretty fully compared the earlier with the final forms. As the reader has now before him the complete text of the sketches and drafts, and can make the comparison for himself, it will be sufficient if I briefly direct his attention to some of the most significant features of these "foreworks."

PILLARS OF SOCIETY

Of this play we have three brief and fragmentary scenarios, two almost complete drafts of the first act, an almost entirely rejected draft of the beginning of the second act, and large fragments of a draft of the fourth act.

Here we at once discover that Ibsen was not one of the playwrights who have their plays clearly mapped out before they put pen to paper. Even in the second draft of the first act, he is still fumbling around after his characters and their relations. That the actual plot was still obscure to him while he was writing the first draft appears from several indications. It is only in the second draft that the reappearance of Johan and Lona causes Bernick to display any uneasiness. Moreover we find in the first draft that " Madam Dorf," Dina's mother, is still alive, and that Dina is in the habit of paying her surreptitious visits; whence we may assume that the light to be thrown on Bernick's past was in some way intended to proceed from her. While she was alive, at any rate, Bernick would scarcely try to suppress the scandal by sending Johan and his documents to sea in a coffin-ship. This could not occur to him while the best witness to the true state of affairs was living at his very doors. Thus we see that the actual intrigue of the play was a rather late after-thought.

A prominent character in both drafts of the first act is Bernick's blind mother, who has disappeared from the

finished play.   Mads Tönnesen, nicknamed "the Badger," the father of Mrs. Bernick, Johan and Hilmar,
was destined to drop out of this play, and to reappear,
under the name of Morten Kiil, in *An Enemy of the
People*.   The business of the railway is taken up at a
much later stage in the completed play than in the drafts
—a good instance of the condensation to which Ibsen
invariably subjected his work.   Another instance may be
found in the treatment of Johan Tönnesen and Lona
Hessel.   In the first draft they are not half brother and
sister, but only, it would seem, distant cousins;   they
have not been together in America;   and it is by pure
chance that they arrive on the same day.   The farcical
scene at the end of the first act in this draft may perhaps
be taken as showing that Ibsen at first thought of giving
the whole play a lighter tone of colouring than that which
he ultimately adopted.   Perhaps he conceived it rather
as a companion-piece to *The League of Youth* than as a
new departure on the path that was to lead him so far.

A DOLL'S HOUSE

Of *A Doll's House* we possess a first brief memorandum, a fairly detailed scenario, a complete draft, in quite
actable form, and a few detached fragments of dialogue.
The complete draft is perhaps the most valuable of all
the documents contained in this volume, since it shows
us how, at a point at which many dramatists would have
been more than content to write "Finis," the most characteristic part of Ibsen's work was only about to begin.
It is scarcely an exaggeration to say that all the traits

which have most deeply impressed themselves on the public mind, and which constitute the true individuality of the play, prove to have been introduced during the process of revision. This assertion the reader must verify for himself, by a comparison of the texts: I will merely enumerate a few of the traits of which the draft contains no indication. In the first act, the business of the macaroons is not even suggested; there is none of the charming talk about the Christmas tree and the children's presents; no request on Nora's part that her present may take the form of money, no indication on Helmer's part that he regards her supposed extravagance as an inheritance from her father. It is notable throughout that neither Helmer's æstheticism nor the sensual element in his relation to Nora is nearly so much emphasised as in the completed play; while Nora's tendency to small fibbing—that vice of the unfree— scarcely appears at all. In the first scene with Dr. Rank, there is no indication either of the doctor's ill health or of his pessimism: it seems as though he had at first been designed as a mere confidant. In the draft, Nora, Helmer, and Rank discuss the case of Krogstad in a dispassionate way before Nora has learnt how vital it is to her. An enormous improvement was effected by the suppression of this untimely passage, which discounted the effect of the scene at the end of the act. That scene is not materially altered in the final version; but the first version contains no hint of the business of decorating the Christmas tree, or of Nora's wheedling Helmer by pretending to need his aid in devising her costume for the fancy-dress ball. Indeed this ball has not yet

entered Ibsen's mind.   He thinks of it first as a children's party.

In the second act there is no scene with Mrs. Linden
in which she remonstrates with Nora for having (as she
thinks) borrowed money from Dr. Rank, and so suggests to her the idea of applying to him for aid.   In the
scene with Helmer, we miss, among other characteristic
traits, his confession that the ultimate reason why he
cannot keep Krogstad in the bank is that Krogstad, as
an old schoolfellow, is so tactless as to *tutoyer* him.
When Rank enters, he speaks to Helmer and Nora together of his failing health: it is an immeasurable improvement which transfers this passage, in a carefully
polished form, to his scene with Nora alone.   Of the famous silk-stocking scene—that curious side light on Nora's
relations with Helmer—there is not a trace.   There is
no hint of Nora's appeal to Rank for help, nipped in the
bud by his declaration of love for her.   All these elements we find in the second draft of the scene.   In this
draft, Rank says, " Helmer himself might quite well know
every thought I have ever had of you; he shall know them
when I am gone."   If Ibsen had retained this speech it
might have saved much critical misunderstanding of a
perfectly harmless episode.   Even when the end of the
second act is reached, Ibsen has not yet conceived the
idea of the fancy-ball and the rehearsal of the tarantella.
It is not a very admirable invention, but it is at any rate
better than the strained and arbitrary incident which, in
the draft, brings the act to a close.

Very noteworthy is the compression and simplification
to which Ibsen has subjected the earlier scenes of the

third act. In the draft, they are clumsy and straggling.
The scene between Helmer, Nora and Rank has absolutely none of the subtlety and tragic intensity which
it has acquired in the finished form. To compare the
two versions is to see a perfect instance of the transmuta-
tion of dramatic prose into dramatic poetry. There is in
the draft no indication either of Helmer's being warmed
with wine, or of the excitement of the senses which gives
the final touch of tragedy to Nora's despair. The process of the action in the final scene is practically the
same in both versions; but everywhere the revision has
given a sharper edge to things. In the draft, for instance,
when Krogstad's letter has lifted the weight of appre-
hension from Helmer's mind, he cries, "You are saved,
Nora, you are saved!" In the revised form, Ibsen has
cruelly altered this into "I am saved, Nora, I am saved!"
Finally, we have to note that Nora's immortal repartee,
"Millions of women have done so," was an after-thought.
Was there ever a more brilliant one?

GHOSTS

Of the studies for *Ghosts* only a few brief fragments
have been preserved. The most important of these are
mere casual memoranda, some of them written on the
back of an envelope addressed to "Madame Ibsen, 75
via Capo le Case, Città (that is to say, Rome). These
memoranda fall into six sections, of which the fourth and
fifth seem to have as much bearing on other plays—for
instance, on *An Enemy of the People* and *The Lady from
the Sea*—as on *Ghosts*. I should take them rather for

detached jottings than for notes specially referring to that play.

THE WILD DUCK

The drafts of *The Wild Duck*, though rather fragmentary, are very interesting and important. They show that the general outline of the play was pretty well established from an early stage; but they also show it to have been enormously enriched in detail in the final revision. This is particularly notable in the character of Hedvig. In the drafts, she is a quite commonplace girl ; all the delicacy and beauty of the character, which make her fate so heart-rending, was added during that process of "energetic individualisation" to which the poet refers in his letter to Caspari. It is worth noting, too, that in all these drafts there is no allusion either to old Werle's weak eyes or to Hedvig's threatened blindness: that idea, which at once helped out the plot of the play, added to the pathos of Hedvig's figure, and illustrated Hialmar's selfishness in allowing her to strain her eyes over the retouching which he himself ought to have done, was entirely an afterthought. An idea which presents itself in a rudimentary form in the first draft is that of Hialmar Ekdal's "invention"—here called his "problem." The later development of this wonderful "invention" forms a very good specimen of Ibsen's method. Everywhere, on a close comparison of the texts, we see an intensive imagination lighting up, as it were, what was at first somewhat cold and colourless. In this case, as in many others, the draft suggests a transparency before the electricity has been switched on.

ROSMERSHOLM

We can trace this play to its completion from a very embryonic form. It is clear that, when the poet jotted down the earliest memorandum, he had as yet no idea of the tragedy of Rebecca's relation to Beata; for he could scarcely have described as "somewhat unscrupulous" a woman who, under the mask of friendship, goaded another to suicide. Rosmer, we see, was to have had two daughters; but they soon disappeared from this play, to reappear as Boletta and Hilda Wangel in *The Lady from the Sea.*

The drafts of *Rosmersholm* afford a good example of the way in which Ibsen almost always fumbled around for the names of his characters. It is fortunate that Rebecca did not eventually retain the name of "Miss Badeck," which would have lent itself, in English, to somewhat too facile pleasantries of the type in vogue among "Anti-Ibsenite" critics of the 'nineties. At one stage in the incubation of the play, we find Rebecca figuring as "Mrs. Rosmer"; but she very soon, so to speak, comes unmarried again. The student of technique may learn a valuable lesson in noting the improvement effected in the finished play by the transference of Rosmer's confession of his change of faith from the second act to the first. Another point worth noting is the fact that in the first draft of the first Brendel scene we find Brendel coming forward as a champion of land-nationalisation, and greatly disappointed on learning that he has been anticipated in a well-known book—an allu-

sion, no doubt, to Henry George's *Progress and Poverty.*
Ibsen showed his usual fine instinct in abandoning
this idea.

THE LADY FROM THE SEA

The sketches and drafts of *The Lady from the Sea*
show that the theme was a good deal modified in the
course of incubation. Wangel, as at first conceived,
was entirely different, both in character and in profession, from the Wangel of the finished play. Several characters appear in the original jottings who have disappeared from the play as we know it: among them one
who was treasured up for seventeen years, to come to
life ultimately as the delightful Foldal of *John Gabriel
Borkman.* The story of Ellida was much more commonplace in its original conception than it eventually
became—it "suffered a sea change Into something rich
and strange." But the most remarkable fact which the
"foreworks" bring to light is that Arnholm and the
Stranger were formed by the scission, so to speak, of
one character, denominated the "Strange Passenger"—
possibly not without a certain reference to the person-
age of that name in *Peer Gynt.*

HEDDA GABLER

Almost the first germs of *Hedda Gabler* seem to have
come to the poet in the form of scraps of dialogue, roughly
jotted down. In his original conception, Tesman was
to have been much more of an active intermediary between Hedda and Lövborg than he became in the end.
It was Tesman who, at her instigation, was to lure

Lövborg to Brack's orgy; and it was apparently Tesman who was actually to make away with, or misappropriate, Lövborg's manuscript. Both Tesman and Mrs. Elvsted were to have known much more of the former "comradeship" between Lövborg and Hedda than they do in the play. There is no hint of any "Mademoiselle Diana" in the draft: when Hedda asks Mrs. Elvsted who the woman is whom Lövborg cannot forget, she replies point-blank, "It is yourself, Hedda." Mrs. Elvsted's luxuriant hair and Hedda's jealousy of it are afterthoughts; so is the famous conception of Lövborg "with vine-leaves in his hair." In the stage-direction for the burning of Lövborg's manuscript, the allusion to the "white leaves" and "blue leaves" evidently belongs to some phase in the working-out of the play of which no other trace remains. It is interesting to speculate on what may have been in the poet's mind; but I am not aware that any satisfactory solution of the problem has as yet been offered.

THE MASTER BUILDER

The preliminary studies for this play are scanty and of slight interest. They nowhere indicate any considerable change of plan. Perhaps the most noteworthy trait in them occurs where Solness is giving Hilda an account of his progress in his profession. His work is in demand, he says, far and wide; "and now, of late years, they are beginning to take an interest in me abroad." Probably this touch was struck out because it showed too clearly the identity of Solness and his creator.

LITTLE EYOLF

In spite of several gaps, the draft of *Little Eyolf* may be called fairly complete. Here again revision amounted almost to reinvention; and it was the reinvention that determined the poetic value of the play. The poet's original idea (though he doubtless knew very well that this would not be final) was simply to study a rather commonplace wife's jealousy of a rather commonplace child. The lameness of Eyolf proves to have been an after-thought; and as Eyolf is not lame, it follows that the terrible cry of "The crutch is floating" was also an after-thought, as well as the almost intolerable scene of recrimination between Allmers and Rita as to the accident which caused his lameness. We find, in fact, that nearly everything that gives the play its depth, its horror and its elevation came as an after-thought. The suggestion of the "evil eye" motive is of the very slightest. Instead of the exquisite beauty of the final scene in its ultimate form, we have a page of almost conventional sentimentalising over Eyolf's continued existence in the hearts of his parents. Instead of telling her the wonderful tale of his meeting with Death in the mountains, Alfred reads to Rita the poem of which Ibsen had written as a first hint for *The Master Builder*. In no case, perhaps, did revision work such a transfiguration as in *Little Eyolf*.

JOHN GABRIEL BORKMAN

Only brief and unimportant fragments of the preliminary studies for this play have been preserved. They tell us nothing more noteworthy than that Borkman at first bore the incurably prosaic name of Jens, and that he was originally conceived as occupying his leisure by playing Beethoven on the violin, to a pianoforte accompaniment provided by Frida Foldal.

WHEN WE DEAD AWAKEN

In the preliminary studies for *When We Dead Awaken* there are several curious features, but nothing of very great significance. We look in vain for the note referred to in the following anecdote, related in the Christiania *Aftenpost*, for April 16, 1911, by the dramatist Gunnar Heiberg. The Norwegian actress who played Irene in the original production gave her a rather juvenile appearance,—with Ibsen's approval, it was reported. "Tell me, Dr. Ibsen," Heiberg said to him one day, "how old is Irene?" He replied, "Irene is 28 years old."

"That is impossible," said I.

He looked at me, measured me up and down, and said with crushing quietness, "You naturally know better, don't you?"

"Yes, I do," I answered. And I set to work to prove that Irene must be at least 40 years old. . . .

"Irene is supposed to be 28," Ibsen interrupted me. "And why do you ask, since you know all about it?"

He went away annoyed.

Next day, I received a letter from him, which ran thus:

"Dear Gunnar Heiberg, You were right and I was wrong. I have looked up my notes.   Irene is about 40 years old.

"Yours,

HENRIK IBSEN."

The note determining Irene's age does not seem to have been preserved; but it ought to have been sufficient to refer to the text.

WILLIAM ARCHER.

PILLARS OF SOCIETY

ARGUMENT

First Act

An open garden-room in the house of "the great leader of industry." The ladies of the place are met together, doing needlework for the benefit of the "Lapsed and Lost." The schoolmaster has been reading an edifying book to the ladies. In the background the manufacturer talking business to influential men belonging to the town and neighbourhood. Violent scene with Valborg, who finds it unbearable here and wishes to go home to her mother. The merchant enters in triumph, because it appears that the projected new railway can be carried through. The dialogue brings out information about all kinds of antecedent circumstances. "The Old Badger" comes in with news of the damaged ship. Who is the captain? Arrival of the steamer. The captain enters and is recognised. Olaf comes from school; announces that Aunt Lona is on the steamer. General surprise and mixed feelings. She shows herself at the garden gate just as the curtain falls.

Second Act

The new arrivals upset things considerably in the town. Rumours of the captain's great wealth and of the former scandal with Valborg's mother. The schoolmaster begins to think of becoming engaged to Valborg. Beginning of conflict between the manufacturer and the captain.

THIRD ACT

We hear of irregularities in the repairing of the ship. The engagement is announced and celebrated. The captain decides to leave the country. Fresh reports from the yard. The manufacturer undecided; it is to be kept quiet for the time being.

FOURTH ACT

Secret understanding between the captain and Valborg. The railway scheme assured. Great ovations. Flight of Olaf with the departing couple. Thrilling final catastrophe.——

PERSONS

BENNICK, a merchant, owner of forests and factories.
MRS. BENNICK, his wife.
MRS. COLONEL BENNICK, his mother.
MARGRETE, her daughter.
MADS TÖNNESEN, a ship-owner and builder.
EMIL (HILMAR) TÖNNESEN, his son.
RÖRSTAD, a schoolmaster.
MADAM DORF, a former actress.
DINA, her daughter.
MISS HASSEL.
CAPTAIN JOHN TENNYSON.
EVENSEN, a private tutor.

FIRST ACT

Introductory scene. Hints of Bernick's numerous plans. The former worldly life of the town. Lona Hassel's departure. The ladies go out into the verandah to take coffee. Exchange of words between the schoolmaster and Dina, who on the previous evening has secretly visited her mother. Hilmar Tönnesen enters. Mr. Bernick and old Tönnesen come in from the left together with some of the best men of the town, all involuntarily struck by Bernick's plan of setting on foot a railway project. Great scene of conflict between different points of view. Bernick propounds his superior view and the duties of the individual to society. Arrival of the steamer. Olaf enters with Miss Hassel, who brings the news that Captain John Tennyson is (was) on board.

SECOND ACT

A part of the garden of Bernick's house, with the street and a row of houses at the back. Dina in the garden; Hilda and Netta come along the street; they question her about the American; fantastic rumours in circulation. Bernick and Knap enter in front from the left; the master-carpenter is to be sent for; Knap goes out through the garden gate. Sandstad passes; dialogue with B. Rumours of the purchase by an English company of all the large properties in the surrounding district. Sandstad off. Old Tönnesen enters with both his sons. These three go up the garden steps to the ladies. Bernick and Aune, the master-carpenter. Aune off. The Tönnesens re-enter with all the ladies and the schoolmaster, also Miss Hessel. The schoolmaster proposes to Dina;

NOTES

Mrs. R. and Mrs. H. are at first thinking of the schoolmaster for their daughters; after his engagement they turn their attention to the American.

PILLARS OF SOCIETY

1st Act

Introductory scene: The Ladies' Union assembled in the merchant's house; the schoolmaster present.

Hilmar Tönnesen enters; Dina sent for the coffee-things; the ladies one by one go out on to the balcony.

Old Tönnesen enters; he and Hilmar go out.

Bernick and business men enter; the business men off.

1st Act

(Room in Bernick's House.)

The situation with regard to Aune is prepared. Meeting of the ladies. Dina and the schoolmaster. Hilmar, and later old Tönnesen. The merchant and the magnates of the town; the railway affair; Bernick's explanation of proposals. Return home of the American captain and Miss Hessel, etc.

2nd Act

(Bernick's garden.)

Bernick and his wife in the garden. Afterwards the ladies. Aune has been degraded. Rumours of the great purchases of property in the neighbourhood. The schoolmaster enters. Old Tönnesen and both his sons. Lona Hessel. Johan and his million. Conflict. The schoolmaster proposes to Dina.

3rd Act

(The walk by the shore.)

Johan, Olaf and the girls, also Martha. Johan and Marta; explanation between them. Johan and Bernick; the old affairs are touched upon. The head of the office confides to Bernick what he has noticed at the ship-yard; Bernick wishes to see for himself. The great rustic festival is decided upon; difficulties in the way of the railway.

4TH ACT
(*In the park.*)

The great rustic festival is held. Many people from the town and neighbourhood. Bernick about to report Aune to the police. Johan threatens to disclose the affairs of his young days.

I

FIRST ACT

(*An elegant and spacious garden-room in* BERNICK'S *house. In front, to the left, a door leads into* BERNICK'S *office; farther back, in the same wall, a similar door. In the middle of the opposite wall is a large entrance door. The back wall is almost entirely composed of plate-glass, with an open doorway leading to a broad flight of steps, over which a sun-shade is let down. Beyond the steps a part of the garden can be seen, enclosed by a railing with a little gate. Beyond the railing, and running parallel with it, is a street of small, brightly painted wooden houses. It is summer, and the sun shines warmly. Now and then people pass along the street: they stop and speak to each other: customers come and go at the little shop nearly opposite, and so forth.*)

(*In the garden-room a number of ladies are gathered round
a long table.   In an armchair at the end of the table
on the left*, MRS. BERNICK, *widow of the* Amtmand,[1]
*a handsome old lady with white hanging curls and
green glasses, busy with knitting.   Next to her sits
her daughter*, MARTHA BERNICK; *then* MRS. RUM-
MEL, *the younger* MRS. BERNICK, MRS. SALVESEN,
MRS. HOLT, *besides* MISS NETTA HOLT *and* MISS
HILDA RUMMEL.   DINA DORF, *for whom there is no
room at the table, sits on a low stool behind the elder*
MRS. BERNICK.   *All the ladies are busy sewing.   On
the table lie large heaps of half-finished and cut-out
linen, and other articles of clothing.   Farther towards
the back, at a little table on which are two flower-pots
and a glass of* eau sucrée, *sits* DOCTOR RÖRLUND *with
a handsomely bound book with gilt edges, from which
he has just been reading.*)

DR. RÖRLUND.   Well, ladies, with this chapter I think
we may conclude for to-day.
    (*He places a marker in the book and closes it with a
    bang.*)
MRS. RUMMEL.   Oh, how delightful it is with books
like that, that one doesn't quite understand——
DR. RÖRLUND.   I beg your pardon?
MRS. RUMMEL.   Well, I mean—that one doesn't see
the meaning of at once——
MRS. SALVESEN.   —and that one has to think over——
MRS. HOLT.   —and that one has to read several
times.
MRS. BERNICK JUNIOR (*with a fixed look*).   Yes
[H'm]; such a book gives us indeed much to think about.
DR. RÖRLUND (*moving his chair nearer to the ladies*).

---

[1] A superior magistrate.

It is, one may say, a book for all. It is neither wholly poetry nor wholly philosophy; nor yet is it altogether a book of devotion. It is in a way something of all these. [It touches upon the most various spheres of existence.] And the whole is inspired by a gentle religious spirit. I consider that such books ought to be found in the palace as in the cottage, and in the cottage as in the palace. And they are found there, too. Heaven be praised— our people are still steadfast enough for that.

MRS. BERNICK JUNIOR. I'm sure it would have lain a long while on our shelves, if you had not——

DR. RÖRLUND. Your husband does not read much, I believe?

MRS. BERNICK JUNIOR. Oh, how should he find time for it?

MRS. BERNICK SENIOR. You can't say that Karsten doesn't read much, Betty——

MRS. BERNICK JUNIOR. He doesn't read that kind of book, I meant.

MRS. BERNICK SENIOR. My son reads enormously, Dr. Rörlund. But mostly works on political economy and other things that may be useful to him.

MRS. BERNICK JUNIOR. Yes, and that doesn't do *us* any good. So it's really more than kind of you to give up your spare time to us.

DR. RÖRLUND. But could I better apply a leisure hour? I consider that needlework should always be seasoned with good reading, especially when the work has such an object as here.

MRS. BERNICK JUNIOR. Ah, but it is a sacrifice on your part all the same, Dr. Rörlund.

DR. RÖRLUND. Pray don't speak of it, dear lady. Do not all of you make sacrifices for a good cause? And do you not make them willingly and gladly? That is as it should be. The Lapsed and Lost, for whom we are working, are like wounded soldiers on a battlefield; you, ladies, are the Red Cross Guild, the Sisters of Mercy, who pick lint for these unhappy sufferers, tie the bandages gently round the wounds, dress, and heal them——

MRS. BERNICK SENIOR. It must be a great blessing to see everything in so beautiful a light.

DR. RÖRLUND. The gift is largely inborn; but it can in some measure be acquired. Tribulation and affliction are a good school. I am sure that you, Mrs. Bernick, have become aware of a purer and more beautiful light even as your bodily eyes grew dim.

MRS. BERNICK SENIOR. Ah, do not speak of that, Dr. Rörlund! I must confess I am often worldly enough to want to exchange the inner light, if I could recover the outer light instead.

DR. RÖRLUND. We have all such moments of temptation. But we have to be on our guard. And, in truth, Mrs. Bernick, what have you really lost? Have you not much rather gained a barrier between yourself and the world? Are you not at your ease here in a circle of kind and sympathetic friends? Do you really find so much to attract you in the life you hear surging outside? Look at the people in the sweltering sunshine, toiling and moiling over their paltry affairs and paltry sorrows. Ours, surely, is the better part, sitting here in the pleasant shade, and turning our backs toward the quarter from which disturbance might arise.

MRS. BERNICK SENIOR. Yes, no doubt you are quite right——

DR. RÖRLUND. And in a house like this, in a good and pure home, where the Family is seen in its fairest shape, where peace and unity reign— (*To* MRS. BERNICK JUNIOR.) What are you listening to, Mrs. Bernick?

MRS. BERNICK JUNIOR (*who has turned towards the door of her husband's room*). How loudly they are talking in there!

DR. RÖRLUND. Is anything particular going on?

MRS. BERNICK JUNIOR. I don't know. There is evidently someone with my husband.

MRS. BERNICK SENIOR. Who can it be?

MRS. BERNICK JUNIOR. I don't know in the least——

MRS. BERNICK SENIOR. Why, that's your father who is talking so loudly, Betty!

MRS. BERNICK JUNIOR. Yes, I believe it is——

(HILMAR TÖNNESEN, *with a cigar in his mouth, comes in by the door on the right, but stops on seeing so many ladies.*)

HILMAR. Oh, I beg your pardon——

(*Turning to go.*)

MRS. BERNICK JUNIOR. Come in, Hilmar, come in. You are not disturbing us. Do you want anything?

HILMAR. No, I just happened to be passing. Good-morning, ladies. (*To his sister.*) Is he here still?

MRS. BERNICK JUNIOR. Who?

HILMAR. The old man.

MRS. BERNICK JUNIOR. Yes, I can hear father in Bernick's room. I didn't know——

HILMAR. I wish I could guess what they want with *him*——

MRS. BERNICK JUNIOR. But what is it at all——?

HILMAR. Don't you know?

MRS. BERNICK JUNIOR. No, I know nothing.

HILMAR. Don't you know that Bernick has called a railway meeting?

MRS. BERNICK JUNIOR. Has he?

MRS. BERNICK SENIOR. Has Karsten?

MRS. RUMMEL. A railway meeting?

Mrs. Salvesen. Is Mr. Bernick going to build a railway?

Mrs. Holt. Only think, if we were to have a railway here!

Dr. Rörlund. Oh, let us hope that is a very distant prospect.

Mrs. Bernick Junior. But what did father say to it?

Hilmar. Do you think *he* said anything? I don't suppose he had any idea of what they were going to talk about. But I heard it from Knap. They've sent a list round to Sandstad, to Rasmussen—Rasmussen on the hill—and to Vigeland—and to the old man as well. Goodness knows why *he* should be in it.

Mrs. Rummel. But they are our capitalists, Mr. Tönnesen!

Hilmar. Yes, if capital could do it, it might perhaps succeed; but you want intelligence as well, and that's a class of goods of which there is no great supply here—I mean in trading circles, of course!

Mrs. Rummel. No, I hardly think I can imagine it, Mrs. Holt!

Mrs. Holt. That we should have a railway here!

Hilda Rummel. Then we should be able to go by train on Sundays!

Dr. Rörlund. On Sundays?

Hilda Rummel. No, I meant on week-days.

Mrs. Bernick Senior. Would you then really consider it harmful if we had a railway here, Dr. Rörlund?

Dr. Rörlund. No, I should by no means consider it absolutely harmful. Its harmfulness would depend upon so much else. Nor can one in our days cut one's self off, even if one wished it. And even at the present time this town is connected in such manifold ways with the outer world and in contact with much that is not as it should be. It is not indeed a question of a temptation more or less, Mrs. Bernick! Of such we have enough already— both here and elsewhere. No, we must seek a shield and buckler in our own mind; but first and foremost, of course, with—; well, that is understood.

HILMAR. Well, I should be very glad if they could build us [if they would begin to squabble about] a railway. It would be a variety at least.

DR. RÖRLUND. Oh, I think there is quite enough variety here as it is.

HILMAR. Possibly. But here I am smoking. I really beg your pardon, ladies.

(*Going towards the back.*)

MRS. BERNICK SENIOR. By all means smoke; I think it is a good cigar——

HILMAR. No, it's a very bad cigar; there isn't such a thing as a good cigar to be got in the whole town. That's another of the pleasures of provincial life. (*Turning over the leaves of* RÖRLUND'S *book.*) "Hours of Repose in the Bosom of Nature." What rubbish is this!

MRS. BERNICK JUNIOR. Oh, Hilmar, you mustn't say that! You have surely not read the book.

HILMAR. No, and don't intend to.

MRS. BERNICK JUNIOR. You seem out of sorts to-day.

HILMAR. Yes, I am.

MRS. BERNICK JUNIOR. Perhaps you didn't sleep well last night?

HILMAR. No, I slept very badly. I went a walk yesterday evening, by my doctor's orders, and came across Evensen. Then we went up to [looked in at] the club and stayed there till half past twelve. Evensen was telling me about a polar expedition. An extraordinary imagination that man has.

MRS. RUMMEL. Well, it doesn't seem to have agreed with you.

HILMAR. No, I lay tossing all night half asleep, and dreamt I was being chased by a horrible walrus. Ugh, there he is shouting again!

THE LADIES. Who is shouting?

HILMAR. Old Tönnesen, of course. He never can moderate his voice, and it always makes me so nervous.

DR. RÖRLUND. The others are not whispering either, it seems to me. I fear Mr. Bernick is being sorely tried.

MRS. BERNICK SENIOR. When my son has resolved upon anything, he is capable of carrying it out, Dr. Rörlund!

MRS. RUMMEL. Yes, indeed, he has shown that many a time. We have to thank Mr. Bernick for our water supply and the new street lamps——

MRS. HOLT. —and proper paving and trees in the market-place!

MRS. BERNICK SENIOR. Dear me, yes! what a great change there has been in this town! When I think of the time when I was young——

MRS. BERNICK JUNIOR. Oh, you needn't go back more than twelve or fourteen years. And it is not only outwardly that things have changed, but inwardly almost more so. Heavens, what a life it was people led here! There was a dancing club and a music club——

MARTHA. And the dramatic club—I remember it quite well.

MRS. RUMMEL. Yes; it was there your play was acted, Mr. Tönnesen.

[HILMAR. Oh, nonsense——!]

MRS. SALVESEN. Mr. Tönnesen's play? Wasn't it in that play you told me you played the heroine, Mrs. Rummel?

MRS. RUMMEL (*glancing at* RÖRLUND). I? I really don't remember, Mrs. Salvesen. But I remember too well all the noisy gaiety that went on among families.

MRS. HOLT. Yes; I actually know houses where there were two great dinner-parties in one week.

MRS. BERNICK JUNIOR. And in the summer we had picnic parties both on sea and land——

DR. RÖRLUND. And that on Sundays too, from what I have been given to understand.

MRS. BERNICK JUNIOR. Yes, at that time we knew no better. We even thought it extremely amusing.

DR. RÖRLUND. Well, to unaided human nature such things are amusing. But we have to overcome that, Mrs. Bernick!

MRS. BERNICK SENIOR. I must say, though, that there were many circumstances which in a way excused us.

DR. RÖRLUND. Excused——?

MRS. BERNICK SENIOR. Or, if they didn't excuse us, at any rate—well, the men at that time had little to do, and we women still less. We had our housekeeping and nothing else. None of our societies had then been started. Until you came here no one thought of anything of the kind.

MRS. BERNICK JUNIOR. And yet there were serious people among us even then.

DR. RÖRLUND. Were there really? And who were they?

MRS. BERNICK JUNIOR. Oh, there were several.

MRS. BERNICK SENIOR. Betty is no doubt thinking of Lona Hessel in particular.

Dr. Rörlund. Hessel? Is that the Miss Hessel who lives abroad?

Mrs. Bernick Junior. Yes; she has lived abroad a long while; ever since——

Dr. Rörlund. How long, do you say?

Mrs. Bernick Junior. No, I can't remember exactly.

Mrs. Rummel. Oh, Mrs. Bernick, can't you remember, she went away just at the time you were married?

Mrs. Bernick Junior. No, I really don't remember that.

Mrs. Holt. She is probably roving about all over the place, in Germany, France, Italy.

Mrs. Bernick Senior. We have not heard from her for several years. She was a very distant relative of my late husband, Dr. Rörlund. But she never writes. Heaven knows whether she has found peace anywhere.

Dr. Rörlund. I doubt it, Mrs. Bernick! That peace which we lack within ourselves can scarcely be found outside. And least of all abroad. We see every day, both in newspapers and books, how matters stand there. Doubt and fermenting unrest on every side; the soul at war with itself, insecurity in every relation of life; disintegration of family life and a spirit of subversion in the great communities. No; we ought to thank God that our lot is ordered as it is. A tare, alas! will now and then spring up among the crop; but we live upon a soil where things *can* grow, whether they turn to good or evil.—Therefore, as I was saying, I should very much doubt that Miss Hessel has found peace far from home, if it was *that* she went to seek.

Martha. Perhaps we shall see sooner than anyone thinks.

Mrs. Holt. Yes, who was it said that she was coming home this summer?

MRS. BERNICK JUNIOR. Oh, that has been said so many times. I don't suppose anything will come of it.

MARTHA. But this time it may come true.

MRS. BERNICK SENIOR. Surely you know something, child; one can tell that from the way you speak.

MARTHA. No, indeed I know nothing; but I think——

DR. RÖRLUND. Telegraph secrets! We must not enquire more closely.

MRS. RUMMEL. Well, if she comes home this summer, she will find great changes indeed! She left just when things were at their worst,· and the town was upsidedown. That was the winter Möller's comedy company was here. Don't you remember, Mrs. Bernick, they played in Holm the sailmaker's hall?

MRS. BERNICK. Yes, very likely.

MRS. HOLT (*with a glance at* MRS. RUMMEL). H'm —h'm.

MRS. RUMMEL (*without noticing it*). No, there's no doubt about it. I remember it as clearly as if it were to-day. Yes, that winter there were fine doings in the town. Wasn't it that year that——?

MRS. HOLT (*as before*). H'm——!

MRS. RUMMEL (*noticing her*). No, of course—. I don't know what I'm saying——

MRS. BERNICK JUNIOR. But don't you think we'd better——?

MRS. SALVESEN. But what was the real truth of all the wild stories of that time? I am so new to the town that I don't know what happened——

MRS. RUMMEL. Oh, it was really nothing after all, Mrs. Salvesen!

MRS. HOLT. Dina, dear, hand me that piece of linen, please.

MRS. BERNICK JUNIOR (*at the same time*).   Dina, my love, will you go and ask Katrina to bring the coffee into the verandah.

MARTHA.   I will help you, Dina.

(DINA *and* MARTHA *go out by the second door on the left.*)

MRS. BERNICK JUNIOR.   And now we may put aside our work for to-day.   Come, let me help you, mother dear!   Will you come, ladies?

(*She and* RÖRLUND *lead* MRS. BERNICK SENIOR *out to the verandah.   The other ladies have risen and are arranging their work on the table in the room.*)

MRS. RUMMEL (*softly*).   Oh dear, Mrs. Salvesen, how you frightened me!

MRS. SALVESEN.   I?

MRS. HOLT.   Ah, but you began it yourself, Mrs. Rummel.

MRS. RUMMEL.   I?   Oh, how can you say so, Mrs. Holt?   Not a single word passed my lips.

MRS. SALVESEN.   But what is the matter?

MRS. RUMMEL.   How could you talk about—?   Only think—didn't you see that Dina was in the room?

MRS. SALVESEN.   But, mercy on us, what *is* the matter?

MRS. HOLT.   Here, in this house, too!   Don't you know that it was Mrs. Bernick's brother——?

MRS. SALVESEN.   What about him?   I know nothing at all; remember I am quite new to the town——

MRS. RUMMEL.   Then you haven't heard that—?   H'm; don't wait for us, Hilda.

MRS. HOLT.   You go too, Netta.   And be sure you are very kind to Dina when she comes.

(HILDA *and* NETTA *go out into the verandah.*)

Mrs. Salvesen. Well, what about Mrs. Bernick's brother?

Mrs. Rummel. Don't you know, he was the hero of the scandal?

Mrs. Salvesen. Mr. Hilmar the hero of a scandal!

Mrs. Holt. No, not he, Mrs. Salvesen! It was the other brother——

Mrs. Rummel. The prodigal brother——

Mrs. Holt. Old Tönnesen's youngest son; one who was a sailor. He ran away to America.

Mrs. Salvesen. And there was a scandal about him?

Mrs. Rummel. Yes, there was a sort of—what shall I call it?—a sort of a—with Dina's mother.

Mrs. Salvesen. Oh, no! how unfortunate that I knew nothing——

Mrs. Rummel. Hush, there she comes. (*Loud.*) Yes, as you say, Dina is really quite a clever girl—What, are you there, Dina? We are just finishing our work here.

Mrs. Holt. Ah, how nice your coffee smells, my dear Dina. It will be a treat to take a little cup of it.

(Martha *and* Dina *have meanwhile helped the servant to bring in the coffee things. The ladies go out and sit down; they vie with each other in talking kindly to* Dina. *After a time she comes into the room and looks for her sewing.*)

Mrs. Bernick Junior (*on the verandah*). Dina, don't you want——?

Dina. No, thanks; I haven't nearly finished.

(*She takes her sewing and sits down on the right, with her back turned towards the end of the table.* Mrs. Bernick Junior *and* Rörlund *exchange a few words; a moment after, he comes into the room.*)

RÖRLUND (*goes up to the table, as if looking for some thing, and says in a low voice*). Dina!

DINA. Yes!

RÖRLUND. Why will you not come out?

DINA. You know very well.

RÖRLUND. Do you think that anyone is speaking ill of—of one who is absent?

DINA. I am sure they are not *speaking* of one who is absent.

RÖRLUND. Well, what then?

DINA (*quivering*). I know that they are thinking about her—all of them.

RÖRLUND. Thinking evil?

DINA. No!

RÖRLUND. There, you see!

DINA. They do what is worse.

RÖRLUND. What is worse, then?

DINA. Oh, I know well enough; they pity her.

RÖRLUND. Do you call that worse?

DINA. Yes.

RÖRLUND. Yours is a rebellious nature, Dina.

DINA (*softly*). Yes.

RÖRLUND. What makes it so?

DINA. It has never been otherwise.

RÖRLUND. But could you not try to change?

DINA. No.

RÖRLUND. Do you not think it would be of any use?

DINA. No.

RÖRLUND. And why don't you think it would be of any use?

DINA. You know quite well why.

RÖRLUND. No, I do not. Tell me.

DINA (*looks up at him firmly*). Because I belong to the Lapsed and Lost.

RÖRLUND. Fie!

DINA. Mother and I belong to the Lapsed and Lost.

RÖRLUND. I am sure no one in this house has ever said that to you.

DINA. No, but they think it.

RÖRLUND. I have often seen signs of this distrust in you. Has it anything to do with your sometimes concealing your movements?

DINA. What do you mean by that?

RÖRLUND. Where were you late yesterday evening, Dina?

DINA (*bending over her work*). Do you know *that* too?

RÖRLUND. Where were you?

DINA. At home.

RÖRLUND. At home? I suppose you mean with your mother?

DINA. Yes.

RÖRLUND. I thought your home was here?

DINA. Yes, they have taken me into their house.

RÖRLUND. On condition that you do not visit your mother.

DINA. Yes.

RÖRLUND. And you promised that?

DINA. Yes.

RÖRLUND. And nevertheless you do visit her?

DINA. Yes.

RÖRLUND. In spite of your promise?

DINA. Such is my nature.

RÖRLUND. Why do you do it?

DINA. It is more amusing with her.

RÖRLUND. Indeed? Then what do you think it is here?

DINA. They are all good to me.

RÖRLUND. And these serious occupations and endeavours of ours—do you like taking part in them?

DINA. Yes.

RÖRLUND. For what reason?

DINA. Because *you* wish it.

RÖRLUND. Do you like doing something for my sake?

DINA. Yes, I do.

RÖRLUND. Why?

DINA. Because you are so much more perfect than
the others.

RÖRLUND. What makes you think that, Dina?

DINA. Because you have taught me so much that is
beautiful.

RÖRLUND. Beautiful? Do you call the truths of religion beautiful?

DINA. Yes.

RÖRLUND. What do you understand, then, by a beautiful thing?

DINA. I have never thought of that.

RÖRLUND. Then think of it now. What do you understand by a beautiful thing?

DINA. A beautiful thing is something great—and far
away.

RÖRLUND. H'm. Listen, Dina, I want to say to
you—. Oh, here they come.

(*He goes up towards the verandah. At the same
moment* OLD TÖNNESEN *comes noisily out of* MR.
BERNICK'S *room.*)

MADS TÖNNESEN (*in the doorway*). No, no, no, I
say! It's no use, I say! I'm off now, as sure as my
name's Mads Tönnesen!   (*Slams the door.*)

HILMAR TÖNNESEN (*at the same time, to* MRS. BER-
NICK JUNIOR). There he is. Good-bye!

(*Is hurrying off to the right.*)

MADS TÖNNESEN. Hilmar! My son Hilmar, wait, we'll go together. You ought to have been in there, listening to your brother-in-law. I'm damned if I ever heard anything so mad!

HILMAR. Hush; don't swear so horribly. Can't you see Mrs. Bernick sitting out there?

MADS. What, is the old lady there? (*Approaching.*) Good morning, ma'am.

HILMAR. Come on; come on!

MRS. BERNICK SENIOR. Good morning, Tönnesen. What is going to be done about the railway?

MADS. It won't come to anything, ma'am; he wants to build it with our money; I never heard anything so unreasonable!

MRS. BERNICK SENIOR. But I suppose he will build it with his own as well.

MADS. Yes, he can do what he likes with his own money; he has plenty of it; and he earned it easily enough. But I, ma'am, who began with two empty fists——

HILMAR (*still at the door*). Hands——

MADS. *I* say fists, my son Hilmar! Yes, ma'am, I can tell you, they were empty then, and dirty too——

HILMAR. Ugh!

MADS. But that's the glory of labour, ma'am, and with those fists I hold on to what I've sweated so hard for——

HILMAR. Ugh, ugh, ugh!

MADS. Yes, I know very well people here give me nicknames and call me the Badger; but the Badger will show them that he has claws! Isn't that so, my son Hilmar?

HILMAR. Yes, only do come; come on!

MADS. Railway! As if I didn't know all about railways. When a young man over in America gets on board a railway, he's never seen again.—But why the devil can't you come, Hilmar! I'm sure the dinner's on the table long ago, and you stand here wasting my time talking!—Good-bye, ma'am; good-bye, Betty; good-bye, all!

(OLD TÖNNESEN *and his son go out to the right.* At *the same moment* SANDSTAD, RASMUSSEN *and* VIGELAND *enter from the room on the left, followed by* BERNICK, *who has a bundle of papers in his hand.*)

BERNICK. Well, gentlemen, I shall not regard this as a final refusal. At any rate take the papers home with you and try to make yourselves better acquainted with my calculations.

SANDSTAD. To tell the truth, I don't think that would be of any use, Mr. Bernick. According to my best convictions I cannot advise private individuals to venture their money in this; and still less can I be a party to voting any public funds.

RASMUSSEN. Nor I either.

VIGELAND. To me it is evident that a railway project of this kind would be opposed to the most important interests of the town. Think of all our steamships in the coasting trade. What should we do with them?

RASMUSSEN. Yes, what should we do with the steam-ships?

VIGELAND. And another thing. If *we* get a railway round here, then the neighbouring towns will also have a railway. No one can tell what changes this will bring about in the shipping trade.

RASMUSSEN. No, no one can tell that.

BERNICK. But, gentlemen, what are you talking about? The country districts round here have produce

enough both for us and for the neighbouring towns, if
we only provide the means of communication.

RASMUSSEN. Yes, that's right.

BERNICK. Just think of our great tracts of forest,
which are now inaccessible. Think of the minerals it
would allow us to work. Think of our water-power,
with one waterfall above another;—what rare advantages for manufactures of all kinds!

RASMUSSEN. Yes, there are.

VIGELAND. But all this would not benefit the town,
Mr. Bernick!

BERNICK. My dear Mr. Vigeland, it would benefit
society; and what benefits society, would also benefit us.
Therefore we ought, as enlightened citizens, to support
the affair with all the powers that are at our disposal.
But we must hold together; that is all-important! Take
the draft prospectus home with you; go carefully through
all my calculations; help me, if you find any error in the
estimates;—here is one for you, Mr. Sandstad.

SANDSTAD. Well, there's no harm in taking them——

RASMUSSEN. No, there's no harm in that.

SANDSTAD. But I don't think anything will come of it.

RASMUSSEN. No, I don't either.

BERNICK. Well, well, gentlemen, sleep on it first.
Perhaps something will come of it after all. Men like
yourselves cannot possibly be blind to all the prosperity
and progress that lies behind this undertaking. It is only
the novelty of the thing that takes you by surprise. And
this disinclination to throw one's self at once into anything new and untried is very estimable, very honourable; it is a good and a characteristic side of our nation;
I even venture to say, it is one of the best pillars of our
society. But when we have once convinced ourselves of
the desirability and opportuneness of a measure, then it

is just as much our duty not to draw back, but to go through with it. Am I not right, we are all agreed on that?

VIGELAND. Well, I won't say either one way or the other, but——

RASMUSSEN. No, I won't either; but——

SANDSTAD. Then I'll take the estimates with me, Mr. Bernick?

BERNICK. Yes, do so, my dear Mr. Sandstad. Discuss the matter among yourselves. And when we have got so far as to be able to lay it before the public in due form, you will see that the difficulties are not nearly so great as you now think.—Well, good-bye, gentlemen. I will not detain you any longer. I should greatly dislike to appear a schemer in your eyes; therefore I wish you as soon as possible to see the affair in its true light. Good day, Mr. Sandstad. Your children are quite well, I hope? Good-bye, my dear Mr. Vigeland. Good-bye, Mr. Rasmussen. Remember me to Mrs. Rasmussen. Good-bye, gentlemen; remember me very kindly at home!

(*The three men take their leave and go out to the right.*)

BERNICK (*who has accompanied them to the door*). Phew! that's the first victory.

RÖRLUND. Do you call *that* a victory, Mr. Bernick?

BERNICK. Getting them to take the papers home? Yes, Dr. Rörlund, that was a great victory. I don't expect anything more to begin with.

MRS. BERNICK JUNIOR (*approaching*). My dear Karsten, what is the meaning of it?

BERNICK. Oh, my dear Betty, it can't possibly interest you.

MRS. BERNICK SENIOR (*on the verandah*). Yes, Karsten, you must come and tell us——

BERNICK.   No, my dearest mother, it is something you and Betty don't understand.

RÖRLUND.   There is some talk of a railway, so far as I could gather.

BERNICK.   Yes, you shall hear about it, Dr. Rörlund. You are a man of intelligence, and a man who stands outside local interests——

RÖRLUND.   I am certainly far removed from the material interests.

BERNICK.   But still you keep pace with public affairs —do you not?

RÖRLUND.   Yes, I read the papers, so far as my time permits; and of course one hears one thing and another.

BERNICK.   Good, then of course you know that there is talk of making a line of railway through the hills?

RÖRLUND.   Yes, one that will not come down to our town.

BERNICK.   It won't touch any of the coast towns about here—if it is carried out.   But *that* is what we are not going to permit!

MRS. BERNICK SENIOR.   But, Karsten, why are you mixing yourself up in all this?

BERNICK.   H'm, my dear mother, it would take too long to explain——

RÖRLUND.   Well, I am not a business man, of course; but still I too think that such things might be left to the Government.

BERNICK.   You do?   Well, that is a view that we often hear expressed.   But do you not really feel in yourself a call, a need, an impulse to support society in its striving for development and welfare?

RÖRLUND.   Yes, I do; within the sphere that is allotted to me.

BERNICK.   Yes, within *that* sphere you are [.   You

are] certainly a pillar of spiritual society among us. But I am now thinking [more particularly] of practical life. And that is just where the Government is found wanting, Dr. Rörlund. The Government has the best intentions, but it sees no further than the needs of the moment; it is lacking in foresight; and it is for this reason that we practical men have to step in. We have been educated in the school of experience; we are—I think I may say so with all modesty—we are the best pillars of civil society; for by pillars of society I do not mean those men who support existing institutions, but those who promote reasonable and necessary progress.

Mrs. Rummel (*in the doorway to the verandah*). Oh, how amusing it is——

Bernick. Do you call it amusing, Mrs. Rummel?

Mrs. Rummel. Yes, I think it is so amusing to hear men speaking.

Bernick. Then you can look forward to a good deal of amusement, for we shall have plenty of speaking and writing, and quarrelling and wrangling. But it *shall* go! Ay, if I have to risk all I possess in the affair, I am determined to see it through.

Mrs. Salvesen. Do you think butter will be cheaper if we have a railway, Mr. Bernick?

Bernick. It will bring prosperity to the whole community; that is all I can tell you for the moment. But, ladies, you must not mix yourselves up with the questions of the day; you must leave them to us men. Your place is in the home; there you must bring peace and comfort to those nearest and dearest to you, as my dear Betty, and my dear old mother bring peace and comfort to me and to Olaf. Why, where is Olaf?

Mrs. Bernick Junior. He is not back from school yet.   (Knap *enters from the right.*)

KNAP. A ship for repairs, Mr. Bernick.

BERNICK. Bravo! Who is it?

KNAP. A big American. Sprang a leak in the North Sea.

BERNICK. And can we take her in?

KNAP. I really don't know what to say. Things are going badly at the yard, Mr. Bernick. To-day the drilling-machine is out of order again; and the steam-plane won't work either.

BERNICK. H'm, h'm; I don't believe Aune will ever learn to work with machines.

KNAP. I don't believe he *wants* to learn; he has set himself against the machines ever since we put them in.

BERNICK. Oh, we shall be able to get over that. But under any circumstances—we mustn't lose the American. What kind of ship is she?

KNAP. The barque *Indian Girl* of New York, with dye-wood from Brazil to St. Petersburg.

BERNICK. And the captain?

KNAP. The captain went overboard in the North Sea, and the mate has delirium tremens. But a sailor, who was on board as a passenger, took command and brought the ship into Rægehavn.

BERNICK. Then you haven't spoken to him?

KNAP. Yes, I have; he was on the steamer.

BERNICK. Oh, then the steamer's in?

KNAP. Yes, and he has come in here with the crew to get more hands and to charter a tug. Here is his card.

BERNICK (*reads*). "John Rawlinson, New Orleans." Then he's from the Southern States. Well, you must see that you give him all the help you can, Mr. Knap.

KNAP. I'll do so, Mr. Bernick.

(*He goes out again to the right.*)

MRS. BERNICK JUNIOR (*calls from outside*). Good news, Karsten?

BERNICK. Business, my dear! You must be prepared to receive an American captain to dinner.

(OLAF BERNICK, *with a knapsack of school-books on his back, comes running up the street and through the garden-gate.*)

OLAF. Mamma, mamma, I've been down seeing the steamboat! Do you know who was on board?

MRS. BERNICK JUNIOR. Yes, child; I expect it was an American captain.

OLAF. How do you know that, mamma?

MRS. BERNICK JUNIOR. I guessed it.

OLAF. Then can you guess that Aunt Lona was on board too?

MRS. BERNICK JUNIOR. What are you saying?

OLAF. Yes, she was, mamma; I've seen her and spoken to her.

BERNICK. Now you're not telling the truth, Olaf!

OLAF. Yes, I am telling the truth.

BERNICK. No, you're not; for you don't know her.

OLAF. No, but Evensen was down on the pier, and *he* knew her.

MRS. BERNICK JUNIOR (*aside*). So then——!

MRS. RUMMEL. Only think—then she has come home after all!

MRS. HOLT. Well, what did I tell you, Mrs. Rummel? (*Many travellers come up the street.*)

MRS. RUMMEL. Look, look! Well, I never—there she is, as large as life!

(MISS HESSEL, *in an elegant travelling costume, with a satchel and a plaid over her shoulder and a knapsack in her hand, comes up the street.*)

MRS. BERNICK JUNIOR. Yes, there she is! (*Runs down to the garden-gate.*) Lona, Lona! Welcome home!

LONA. Why, yes—good morning, Betty! (*Calls up to the verandah.*) Good morning, old auntie!

MRS. BERNICK JUNIOR. But do come inside!

LONA. Thanks, presently, presently; I must go up to the hotel first and wash myself clean from top to toe; on the steamer you get as dirty as a pig. Au revoir!

(*She goes on up the street.*)

MRS. BERNICK SENIOR. She hasn't changed, has she, Betty?

MRS. BERNICK JUNIOR (*looking after her*). No,—and yet she has.

RÖRLUND. That lady appeared to me somewhat un-womanly.

MRS. HOLT. How funnily her dress was cut, Mrs. Rummel!

MRS. RUMMEL. Yes, but did you notice her hat, Mrs. Holt?

OLAF. Hurrah, mamma, here come all the Americans!

MRS. RUMMEL. No, look at these wild people; they've got a great flag——

MRS. HOLT. Ugh, I believe there are brown and black ones among them.

MRS. SALVESEN. The captain is almost the ugliest; he has a regular pirate's face.

RÖRLUND. Yes, that fellow is capable of anything.

BERNICK. Foreigners, Dr. Rörlund; we mustn't be so particular.

(CAPTAIN RAWLINSON *and his crew, with the American flag at their head, come up the street, followed by a crowd of children and grown-up people.*)

BERNICK (*waves his hand from the steps and calls out:*) Good morning, Mr. Rawlinson! This way, if you please, sir! I am Mr. Bernick!

CAPT. RAWLINSON (*waves his handkerchief and cries:*) Very well, Karsten; but first three cheers for the old Badger! (*The Americans and the whole crowd go past.*)

BERNICK (*starting back*). Ah!

MRS. BERNICK SENIOR (*with a cry*). Who spoke then?

MARTHA (*involuntarily takes a step forward and cries:*) Johan!

MRS. BERNICK JUNIOR. Heavens—it was my brother!

MRS. RUMMEL. Well, as I'm alive, I think so too——

BERNICK (*has composed himself and says calmly*). It was Johan Tönnesen. What of it?

MRS. HOLT. Oh, what a surprise! And how well he looked.

MRS. SALVESEN. And how well that beard suited him, Mrs. Bernick!

MRS. BERNICK JUNIOR (*aside*). Johan and Lona—on the same day——

BERNICK. Well, now we shall have turbulent spirits among us.

RÖRLUND. I hope no one will succeed in introducing a disturbing element here. With the place in its present state—a home of peace and good order and domesticity——

MRS. RUMMEL'S SERVANT-GIRL (*enters through the garden-gate*). Master sent me to say, ma'am, that you must please come home; Gurine has burnt the fish to a cinder.

MRS. RUMMEL. Oh, these servants, these servants; one can never leave anything to them! Good-bye, good-bye; we shall meet to-morrow!

(*She and the servant hurry off down the street.*)

Mrs. Salvesen. Yes, that's what you can expect if you trust your house to the servants.

Mrs. Salvesen's Two Little Girls (*come out of the chemist's shop, run to the garden-gate and call out:*) Mamma, mamma, you must come and see; Nicholas has fallen into the wash-tub!

Mrs. Salvesen. What do you say, children! And he had his new blouse on!

The Little Girls. Oh, he is in a filthy mess!

Mrs. Salvesen. Oh, these children, these children! Good day! I must run as fast as I can.

(*She and the little girls hurry into the chemist's shop.*)

Mrs. Holt. Yes, that's what happens if you leave everything lying about. I make it my rule to lock things up; and the keys (*slaps her pocket*) I carry about with me.

The Postman (*comes running down the street to the garden-gate*). Oh, heavens, ma'am, you must hurry home; we shall miss the steamer.

Mrs. Holt. Miss the steamer?

Postman. Yes, the second bell's gone already, and the postmaster can't take the mails on board till you come, ma'am.

Mrs. Holt. What are you talking about? Can't the mails go on board without me?

Postman. No, ma'am; you've locked up the postmaster's trousers in the wardrobe.

Mrs. Holt. Mercy on us! Good-bye, good-bye till to-morrow! Oh, these men, these men, they never can do anything for themselves.

(*She and the* Postman *run up the street.*)

Rörlund. People here make too great demands on woman's time and energies.

MARTHA (*aside*). Come home——!

MRS. BERNICK JUNIOR (*aside*). Both of them——!

OLAF (*in the garden*). Mamma, now the Americans are shouting hurrah outside grandpapa's!

> (*Noise and cries are heard far off; people appear at the windows; many people run up the street.*)

MRS. BERNICK SENIOR (*who has risen and is groping for the door*). Karsten—don't you think as I do—that it is like ghosts from old times?

BERNICK (*starts up from his thoughts*). Oh, come—ghosts? Yes, to you, dear mother—you in the dark, with your poor eyes—(*kisses her*) but I, you see, I am in the full light of day!

SECOND ACT

> (*Part of the garden outside* MR. BERNICK'S *house. The house itself, which is not seen, is supposed to lie to the left. At the back is the garden railing with the street beyond; on the right an open arbour, in which is the ladies' work-table.*)
>
> (BERNICK, *dressed to go out, with gloves, stick and cigar, is walking in the garden. After a little while* MRS. BERNICK JUNIOR *comes from the house with a quantity of sewing, which she places on the table.*)

MRS. BERNICK JUNIOR. Are you there, Karsten?

BERNICK. Yes, of course I'm here.

MRS. BERNICK JUNIOR. I thought you had gone to the office.

BERNICK. I am waiting for somebody.

MRS. BERNICK JUNIOR. Oh, perhaps it is Johan?

BERNICK. No.

MRS. BERNICK JUNIOR. Ugh, then it must be this railway business again?

BERNICK. No, it's a man I've sent for here. Why, what can it matter to you?

MRS. BERNICK JUNIOR. Oh, there's nothing strange in my asking.

(DINA *enters with the rest of the sewing.*)

BERNICK. Are you going to work out here to-day?

MRS. BERNICK. Yes, Dr. Rörlund proposed that we should sit here.

BERNICK. I see, it's more public here.

MRS. BERNICK JUNIOR. I'm sure he didn't intend any ostentation by it.

BERNICK. I didn't mean that either. There are loafers enough here who might take a lesson from seeing all these industrious ladies.

MRS. BERNICK JUNIOR. Ah, you're not much in sympathy with this cause, Karsten!

BERNICK. Yes, indeed I am! Sew away—so long as domestic concerns are not neglected—. Isn't Martha at home to-day?

MRS. BERNICK JUNIOR. No, Martha of course is on duty.

BERNICK. That was a great piece of folly of hers, going into the telegraph service.

MRS. BERNICK JUNIOR. Yes, I'm really afraid she hasn't strength enough for it.

BERNICK. Oh, as far as strength goes, she can do it well enough. But it is unpleasant for *me*. It looks as if I, her brother, were unwilling to support her.

MRS. BERNICK JUNIOR. Well, but it isn't always so pleasant to be supported—even by one's nearest relations.

BERNICK. A woman has to put up with that sort of thing. Why has she never wanted to marry? No, she is self-willed and stiff-necked, like most— Oh, now they're beginning to arrive [here come Mrs. Rummel and her daughter].

MRS. BERNICK JUNIOR.   Here is Mrs. Holt and Netta too.

BERNICK.   What a hurry they're in; I'm inclined to think those two good ladies have designs——

MRS. BERNICK JUNIOR.   How do you mean?

BERNICK.   Why do they always drag the daughters with them?

MRS. BERNICK JUNIOR.   Oh, you know we agreed that these two nice, well-brought-up girls were to be examples for Dina.

BERNICK.   H'm; a couple of mothers with marriageable daughters are sure to have little designs of their own——

MRS. BERNICK JUNIOR.   Really, Karsten, can you imagine it is because *he*——

BERNICK.   Yes, he, he, he; all the women in the place speak of him as *he*,—and then they know at once who is meant.

(MRS. RUMMEL *with* HILDA, *and* MRS. HOLT *with* NETTA *meet at the garden-gate and come in. At the same moment* MRS. BERNICK SENIOR *comes from the house, led by* DINA, *who has* RÖRLUND'S *book in her hand. There are greetings, all talking at once. During this* MRS. SALVESEN *joins them.*)

BERNICK.   Your punctuality really compels my admiration, ladies!   Never a minute behind time——

MRS. RUMMEL.   Oh, I can't tell you how I long for these cosy hours of work——

MRS. BERNICK SENIOR.   Did you bring the book, Dina?

DINA.   Yes.

MRS. RUMMEL.   Oh, he's sure not to come to-day.

MRS. HOLT.   No, he's sure not to——

BERNICK. Why not? It is holiday time, you know——

MRS. R. Yes, that's true; but aren't you taking a holiday too, Mr. Bernick?

BERNICK. You mean because I was taking a walk here with my wife? Dear me, one isn't a mere man of business and nothing else; one is also the head of a family——

MRS. H. Yes, you may truthfully say that of yourself, Mr. Bernick——

BERNICK. And one wants to enjoy the society of one's own circle; it is not a large one, but for that reason it is all the more closely bound together, Mrs. Holt.

MRS. RUMMEL. Ah, but now it is a little enlarged, isn't it?

BERNICK. Yes, since my brother-in-law has come home, you mean.

MRS. R. They say he has become a perfect gentleman, as it is called——

BERNICK. He has improved a good deal—the life over there on a large scale, you see—in the war he served in the Navy as a lieutenant——

MRS. R. No, did he indeed? and how does he like being at home——

BERNICK. Oh, we said so little about that.

MRS. B. JR. He was only in here for a minute——

MRS. BERNICK SENIOR. And then Lona Hessel came just after——

MRS. R. Oh, then she was here too——

MRS. B. SR. Yes, and she has changed, to be sure——

[Here is inserted some dialogue to the effect that Johan will stay at home to take over the management of Bernick's ship-yard, etc. MRS. B. JR. asks what is to become of poor Aune. BERNICK: That is a thing that my little Betty must leave to us men.]

MRS. SALVESEN. Oh, look, there he is——

BERNICK. He? No, not at all, it's—— Oh, *he*, yes—— of course—— (DR. RÖRLUND *enters.*)

RÖR. Good morning, good morning, ladies! Good morning, Mr. B.

THE LADIES. Good morning——

MRS. B. JR. How late you are, Dr. Rörlund.

RÖR. Yes, I sincerely ask your pardon, ladies; but I have been in a place where my presence was more necessary than here——

BERNICK. You have just come from the harbour, I see——

RÖR. Yes, I come from there.

MRS. B. JR. And no doubt you had some unpleasantness——?

RÖR. Well, it was not exactly pleasant.—Will you just imagine——

BERNICK. Excuse me—here is someone I want to speak to——

(*During this* AUNE *has come in through the garden-gate.* BERNICK *goes towards him.*)

BERNICK. You're late, Aune! I've been waiting here for you.

AUNE. You must excuse me, sir; but we had to get the American warped in first.

BERNICK. And do you think now you can get her repaired at once? [The ship has to be at St. Petersburg in a fortnight——]

AUNE. I'd get her repaired all right, if I was allowed to work in my own way.

BERNICK. At once—I asked you. In your own way? We can't hear of that. I haven't provided all these expensive machines to let them stand idle, and it won't do for a foreign ship to lie here for months and then perhaps be badly repaired after all.

AUNE. No, no, I dare say that's true.

BERNICK. Listen to me, Aune; I suppose you can guess why I sent for you?

AUNE. Well, it might be several things, I dare say.

BERNICK. Yes, it is several things; but still in a way they are all the same. In the first place—what was that address you gave last Saturday evening at the Workmen's Club?

AUNE. It was about the harm that is done to the workmen by all these new machines——

BERNICK.

II

FROM THE FIRST ACT

AUNE. Mr. Bernick wouldn't have said it like that, Mr. Krap! But I know well enough who it is I've got to thank for this. I can thank you for it, Mr. Krap! You've never been able to forget a certain occasion——

KRAP. Occasion—occasion? I don't know what you're referring to with occasions. But I have told you Mr. Bernick's wishes, and that is enough. Now you had better go down to the yard again; you're sure to be wanted; I shall be down myself presently.—I beg your pardon, ladies!

(*He bows, and goes out through the garden and down the street.* AUNE *goes quietly out to the right.* DOCTOR RÖRLUND, *who during the foregoing has continued reading, presently closes the book with a bang.*)

RÖRLUND. There, my dear ladies, that is the end.

MRS. RUMMEL (*drying her eyes*). Oh, what a beautiful tale!

MRS. HOLT. And so moral.

MRS. BERNICK JUNIOR. Such a book really gives one a great deal to think over.

RÖRLUND. Yes, it shows us in what wonderful ways providence sometimes furthers its designs. This little Christian congregation [community] takes refuge in the primeval forests of the far west in order to live in peace and unity as brothers and sisters together. Then worldly-minded speculators come and lay down a railway straight through the quiet region. With intercourse, temptations and corruption find an inlet. But then it is that this convulsion of nature takes place at a far distant spot, and renders it necessary to transfer the railway to quite another line of valley. And as the last locomotive puffs away, the little congregation [community] feels that it is freed from noisy and sinful toil and can now breathe again in peace and sabbath stillness.

DINA. But what happens to the people in the other valley?

RÖRLUND. My dear child, we must suppose that the other valley was uninhabited.

MRS. BERNICK SENIOR. H'm; that about the railway reminds me of the danger we were in last year. We only escaped having the railway here by a hair's-breadth. But Karsten managed to put a stop to that.

RÖRLUND. Providentially, Mrs. Bernick! You may be sure your son was an instrument in a higher hand when he refused to support that scheme.

MRS. BERNICK JUNIOR. Yes, everything is wonderfully linked together in this world. It is difficult to see the working of it. If we had not you, Dr. Rörlund—!

It is really more than kind of you to sacrifice your leisure time to us.

RÖRLUND. Oh, not at all—in holiday-time, you know——

MRS. BERNICK JUNIOR. Yes, yes; but it's a sacrifice on your part, nevertheless.

RÖRLUND (*drawing his chair nearer to the ladies*). Pray don't speak of it, dear lady. Do not all of you make sacrifices for a good cause? And do you not make them willingly and gladly? That is as it should be. The Lapsed and Lost, for whom we are working, are like wounded soldiers on a battlefield. You, ladies, are the Red Cross Guild, the Sisters of Mercy, who pick lint for these unhappy sufferers, tie the bandages gently round the wounds, dress, and heal them——

MRS. BERNICK SENIOR. It must be a great blessing to see everything in so beautiful a light.

RÖRLUND. The gift is largely inborn; but it can in some measure be acquired. Tribulation and affliction are a good school. I am sure that you, Mrs. Bernick, have become aware of a purer and more beautiful light even as your bodily eyes grew dim.

MRS. BERNICK SENIOR. Ah, do not speak of that, Dr. Rörlund! I must confess I am often worldly enough to want to exchange the inner light, if I could recover the outer light instead.

RÖRLUND. Yes, yes; that is temptation, dear Mrs. Bernick! It is like the railway trains that bring noisy passengers to the little congregation in the far west. But you must bar the door against such an unquiet guest. And, in truth, what have you really lost? Have you not much rather gained a barrier between yourself and the world? Do you not feel secure here, where you form one of the pillars of our little charitable society? Do you really find so much to attract you in the life you hear surging outside? Look at the people in the sweltering sunshine, toiling and moiling over their paltry affairs and paltry sorrows. Ours, surely, is the better part, sitting here in the pleasant shade, and turning our backs toward the quarter from which disturbance might arise.

HILMAR TÖNNESEN. Oh, it is this railway nonsense again.

MRS. BERNICK JUNIOR. No! is it?

MRS. BERNICK SENIOR. Poor Karsten, is he to have all that worry over again——?

RÖRLUND. I really thought that affair was dead and buried.

HILMAR. Well, if it wasn't before, it's sure to be to-day.

MRS. BERNICK JUNIOR. Did father say so?

HILMAR. *He?* Do you think *he* had any idea of what it was all about? But I met Krap just now and he told me that Bernick had sent to Sandstad, and Rasmussen—"Rasmussen on the hill"—and to Michael Vigeland—"Holy Michael," as they call him——

RÖRLUND. H'm——

HILMAR. I beg your pardon, Doctor!—And then he sent for old Tönnesen. Goodness knows why *he* should be in it.

MRS. RUMMEL. They are the town council, Mr. Tönnesen.

HILMAR. Old Tönnesen is no longer on the town council.

MRS. HOLT. No, but they are the men who stopped the scheme last year.

MRS. BERNICK SENIOR. It was my son who put a

stop to it last year, Mrs. Holt! I should think that when anything is to be done or left undone in this town, it depends upon Karsten.

MRS. HOLT. Yes, of course; there is no doubt about that, but——

HILMAR. For that matter, I shouldn't mind their beginning their twaddle again; it would be a variety at least.

RÖRLUND. I think we can dispense with that sort of variety.

HILMAR. Well, it depends upon how one takes it.—But here I am smoking. I really beg your pardon, ladies—— (*Going towards the verandah.*)

MRS. BERNICK SENIOR. By all means smoke; I think it is a very good cigar——

HILMAR. No, it's a very bad cigar; there isn't such a thing as a good cigar to be got in the whole town. That's another of the pleasures of provincial life.—(*Turning over the leaves of* RÖRLUND'S *book.*) "The Forest Community." What rubbish is this?

RÖRLUND. The others are not whispering either, it seems to me.

MRS. BERNICK SENIOR. It must be very annoying for Karsten to have this tiresome affair up again.

RÖRLUND. Let us hope he will send the schemers about their business, so that they will keep quiet in future.

MRS. RUMMEL. Yes, indeed, Mr. Bernick has always been the good spirit of the place——

MRS. HOLT. You may well say that, Mrs. Rummel! Ever since he came home from abroad as a young man——

MRS. BERNICK SENIOR. Ah, yes, those were disorderly times.

MRS. SALVESEN. Were things really so bad here?

MRS. RUMMEL. They were as bad as bad could be, Mrs. Salvesen! You may thank your stars that you didn't live here then; and you too, Dr. Rörlund!

MRS. BERNICK SENIOR. Yes, what changes I can remember! When I think of the time when I was young——

MRS. BERNICK JUNIOR. Oh, you needn't go back more than twelve or fourteen years. Heavens—what a life it was—! Everything ended in dissipation. There was a dancing club and a music club——

MARTHA. And the dramatic club—I remember it quite well.

MRS. RUMMEL. Yes; it was there your play was acted, Mr. Tönnesen!

HILMAR (*at the back*). Oh, nonsense——!

RÖRLUND. Mr. Tönnesen's play?

MRS. SALVESEN. Wasn't it in that play you told me you played the heroine, Mrs. Rummel?

MRS. RUMMEL (*glancing at* RÖRLUND). I? I really don't remember, Mrs. Salvesen. But I remember too well all the noisy gaiety that went on among families.

MRS. HOLT. Yes; I actually know houses where there were two great dinner-parties in one week.

MRS. BERNICK JUNIOR. And in the summer, when the foreign officers were here with the training-ship——

MRS. HOLT. Ugh, the horrid officers!

MRS. BERNICK JUNIOR. Then we had picnic-parties both on sea and land——

—————

MRS. HOLT. You see, Madam Dorf was one of Möller's company——

Mrs. Rummel. And one evening Dorf came home very late——

Mrs. Holt. —and quite unexpectedly——

Mrs. Rummel. And there he found—no, really, I don't think I can tell you.

Mrs. Holt. But—only think!—young Tönnesen had to jump out of the window!

Mrs. Rummel. Yes, and it was an attic window too! And that was why he ran away to America.

Mrs. Salvesen. Oh, no! how unfortunate that I knew nothing——

Mrs. Holt. Well, now you can see how careful we have to be. Poor Dina can't help her mother being a person like that. She was then a child of six or seven——

Rörlund. Oh, you cannot possibly realise the thousand considerations—. When a man is singled out as a pillar of the society he lives in—. Sh! here they come.

(*She looks at him for a moment, then goes out to the verandah;* Rörlund *also goes towards the back. At the same moment* Old Tönnesen *comes noisily out of* Mr. Bernick's *room.*)

Mads Tönnesen (*in the doorway*). No, no, no, I say! Never while I'm alive, I say! I'm off now, as sure as my name's Mads Tönnesen! (*Slams the door.*)

Hilmar (*at the same time, to* Mrs. Bernick Junior). There he is. Good-bye! (*Is hurrying off to the right.*)

Mads Tönnesen. Hilmar! My son Hilmar, wait, we'll go together. Now we shall see signs and wonders, Hilmar! I'm damned if I ever heard anything so mad!

Hilmar. Hush; don't swear so horribly. Can't you see who is sitting out there?

MADS. What, is the old lady there? (*Approaching.*)
Good morning, ma'am!

HILMAR. Come on; come on!

MRS. BERNICK SENIOR. Good morning, Tönnesen.
Well, is it all over?

MADS. Yes, it'll soon be all over with the whole of
us. I never heard anything so unreasonable. Now he
wants to build the railway after all!

RÖRLUND. What do you say?

MRS. BERNICK SENIOR. Who?

MADS. Your son, of course!

MRS. BERNICK JUNIOR. But, my dear father——?

THE THREE LADIES. No, can it be possible——!

MADS. No, it's quite impossible! It won't come off;
for he wants to build it with our money——

RÖRLUND. But this is quite contrary to what Mr.
Bernick last year——

MRS. BERNICK SENIOR. Your father must be mistaken, Betty.

MRS. BERNICK JUNIOR. Yes, I can't suppose anything else.

(SANDSTAD, RASMUSSEN [RUMMEL] *and* VIGELAND
enter from the room on the left, followed by BERNICK,
who has a bundle of papers in his hand.)

BERNICK. Well, gentlemen, I shall not regard this as
a final refusal. At any rate take the papers home with
you and try to make yourselves better acquainted with
my calculations.

SANDSTAD. I'm a plain-spoken man, Mr. Bernick,
and I say the same this year as I said last——

BERNICK. But the case is not the same this year as
last.

RASMUSSEN. No, it is not——

SANDSTAD. Well, be that as it may, I cannot advise private individuals to venture their money in this; and still less can I be a party to voting any public funds.

RASMUSSEN. Nor I either.

VIGELAND. And then I am afraid it will lead us into worldliness, Mr. Bernick! The minds of all serious people are now intent upon the building of the new meeting-house. And we must think of spiritual needs before all else.

BERNICK. Of course, of course, Mr. Vigeland; but——

SANDSTAD. Yes, you've chosen your time as unfortunately as you could have, Mr. Bernick! Excuse my plain-speaking; but just think of the severe storm we had in the North Sea last week. Nobody can tell how heavy the losses of the town may be; damaged ships are putting in here every day——

RASMUSSEN. Yes, it was a severe storm.——

BERNICK. All that is admitted; but you know that the main line is under construction, and unless we are quick in arriving at a decision now, it will be too late; we shall not be able afterwards to get a branch line brought here. You must bear that in mind, gentlemen.

SANDSTAD. Well, then we shall have to do without.

BERNICK. And you are really prepared to take such a moral responsibility upon yourselves? Are our great tracts of forest to remain inaccessible? Remember all the rich mineral-seams it would allow us to work! Think of our water-power, with one waterfall above another! What rare advantages for manufactures of all kinds!

RASMUSSEN. Yes, there are.

VIGELAND. But all this would benefit the inland districts more than the town, Mr. Bernick!

RASMUSSEN. Yes, that is true.

BERNICK. My dear Mr. Vigeland, it would benefit society; and what benefits society, would also benefit us. Therefore we ought, as enlightened citizens, to support the affair with all the powers that are at our disposal. Men like yourselves cannot possibly be blind to all the prosperity and progress that lies behind this undertaking. Take the draft prospectus home with you. Go carefully through all the calculations. Tell me if you find any error in the estimates. Here is one for you, Mr. Sandstad.

SANDSTAD. Well, there's no harm in taking them——

RASMUSSEN. No, there's no harm in that.

VIGELAND. I for my part won't say either one way or the other——

RASMUSSEN. I won't either.

BERNICK. Well, well, gentlemen, at any rate, sleep on it first. We may perhaps come to an agreement after all. Discuss the matter as it affects your own interests and those of society; and when we have got so far as to be able to lay it before the public in due form, you will see that the difficulties to be met are not nearly so great as you now think.—Well, good-bye, gentlemen. I must not detain you any longer. You know we have not much time for arriving at a decision. Good day, Mr. Sandstad. Good-bye, my dear Mr. Vigeland. Good-bye, Mr. Rasmussen. Good-bye, good-bye; remember me very kindly at home!

(*The three men take their leave and go out to the right.*)

BERNICK (*who has accompanied them to the door*). Phew! we've got so far at least.

RÖRLUND (*at the back*). Yes, you have certainly gone farther than last year, Mr. Bernick.

MRS. BERNICK JUNIOR (*also at the back*). But, my dear Karsten, what is the meaning of it all?

BERNICK. Oh, my dear Betty, it can't possibly interest *you*.

MRS. BERNICK SENIOR. Yes, Karsten, you must come and tell us——

BERNICK. No, my dearest mother, it is something you and Betty don't understand.

RÖRLUND. So you want to bring a branch line here after all, Mr. Bernick?

BERNICK. Yes, you shall hear about it. You are a man of intelligence, Dr. Rörlund, and you know, of course, what has already been done in the matter——

RÖRLUND. Yes, I know that an inland line was chosen in preference to a coast line.——

BERNICK. Quite right!

RÖRLUND. —and that you and the other leading men of the town refused last year to contribute to a branch line.

BERNICK. Exactly! The proposal that was before us last year was inadmissible. It would have cost an unreasonable amount of money; we should have had to make tunnels and bridges and a great deal besides. And now we can avoid all that and get our line at an unusually low cost.

RÖRLUND. But how will you do that, Mr. Bernick?

BERNICK. Ah, *that's* what I'm going to tell you!— Yes, you may listen too, ladies!—Now, can you remember, Doctor, that I was away for a week last spring on a journey up-country?

RÖRLUND. Yes; it was at Whitsuntide.

BERNICK. Precisely! The spring floods were, as you know, extraordinarily heavy this year and did a great deal of damage. Thus I heard amongst other things that the Trangdal River had overflowed its banks and that it ran out into the Trangdal Water along its old bed. It struck me like a flash of lightning! I went up there; and what did I find? Just as they told me—the whole Trangdal ravine lying dry as a high-road—the Trangdal ravine, you understand, which had been the vital natural obstruction to the branch line——

RÖRLUND. That was indeed most remarkable.

BERNICK. It was more than remarkable, Doctor! I arrived there one Sunday morning, and as in an instant my eyes were thus opened to the immense bearing of this occurrence, a feeling almost of devotion came upon me. This convulsion of nature just at the eleventh hour—; was it not evident that providence itself had intervened?

RÖRLUND. Ah, it is so difficult to pronounce upon——

BERNICK. I am, I regret to say, not a remarkably religious man; but still I have at times my deeper moments and that moment was one of them. I saw before me the thousand happy homes which might be created in this wilderness; I saw our town, which hitherto has been almost isolated on the land side, suddenly brought into communication with flourishing inland districts. Life, prosperity, progress on all sides! You will see, you will not be able to recognise the place after the first railway train has rolled in. Am I not right?

MRS. BERNICK SENIOR. Yes, Karsten, indeed you are!

MRS. BERNICK JUNIOR. And you have kept all this secret!

BERNICK. Oh, my dear, you would not have been able to see—; one ought never to speak of business matters before the decisive moment. But now I have the engineers' report—all the estimates;—now we have only to get the necessary contribution subscribed. And that must and shall be done! Ay, if I have to risk all I possess in the affair, I am determined to see it through!

MRS. BERNICK SENIOR. You are a man, Karsten!

Mrs. Rummel. Yes, we were just saying that you were like a good spirit to the town [were the good spirit of the town, Mr. Bernick].

Mrs. Holt. Only think, if we should have a railway here!

Netta [Dina]. Then we should be able to go by train on Sundays!

Rörlund. On Sundays?

Mrs. Rummel. Dina means on week-days, no doubt.

Mrs. Salvesen. Do you think butter will be cheaper if we have a railway, Mr. Bernick?

Bernick. The railway will bring prosperity to the whole community; that is all I can tell you for the moment. But that is just what we all have to work for. Don't you agree with me, Dr. Rörlund?

Rörlund. H'm; I am not a man of business, Mr. Bernick; and the restricted community to which I belong——

Bernick. It will suffer no injury from the railway, I can assure you of that! Our busy little town is built, heaven be thanked, on a sound moral foundation. We men will ward off the shock, and our wives and daughters will continue to occupy the place that nature has assigned them. Believe me, the purity of our homes is not so easily disturbed, if only our women remain what they ought to be. Proceed unwearied in your charitable labours, ladies, and be a support and comfort to those nearest and dearest to you, as my dear Betty and my dear old mother are to me and Olaf—(Looks around.) Why, where is Olaf to-day?

Mrs. Bernick Junior. Oh, in the holidays it's impossible to keep him at home.

Bernick. Then he's certain to have gone down to the water again. You'll see, this will end in a misfortune.

(Krap enters from the right.)

KRAP. A ship for repairs, Mr. Bernick.

BERNICK. Oh? Is she owned here?

KRAP. No, a big American; sprang a leak in the North Sea——

BERNICK. Bravo! But, I say—(*coming forward with* KRAP). Can we take her in?

KRAP. Don't know what to say. Things are going badly at the yard, Mr. Bernick. To-day, drilling-machine out of order again. Steam-plane won't work either.

BERNICK. H'm, h'm; I don't believe Aune will ever learn to work with machines.

KRAP. Doesn't want to learn; has set himself against the machines ever since we put them in.

BERNICK. Oh, we shall be able to get over that. But under any circumstances—we mustn't lose the American. What kind of ship is she?

KRAP. The barque *Indian Girl* of New York. Bound from Brazil to Glasgow with dye-wood; driven out of her course towards Jutland;—boisterous weather, Mr. Bernick!

BERNICK. And the captain?

KRAP. Captain went overboard—drunk. The mate's in his bunk—with delirium tremens. A passenger took command—a sailor. She was towed in just now by the Hamburg steamer.

BERNICK. Is the Hamburg steamer in already?

KRAP. Just this moment. Here is the American's card.

BERNICK (*reads*). "Captain John Tennyson. New Orleans." Then he's from the Southern States. Well, you must see that you give him all the help you can, Mr. Krap.

KRAP. I'll do so, Mr. Bernick.

BERNICK. And, look here—one other thing: do you know whether Mr. Busk, the lawyer, has come back?

KRAP. Not yet. (*He goes out to the right.*)

MRS. BERNICK SENIOR. Yes, is it not like ghosts of old days? Listen, now they're singing. How it fills the air. How it sounds over our quiet town——

RÖRLUND. And just at dinner-time too! While grace is being said in every quiet home. Look, look, serious men are running to the windows with their napkins under their chins——

OLAF (*in the garden*). Mamma, now the Americans are shouting hurrah outside grandpapa's!

RÖRLUND. Hurrah? Yes, it is true! So this is the prodigal son's return. Not with contrition; not with the tears of repentance, but with impudent bawling, with ribald songs—! My dear friends, we ought not to witness this. Let us go back to our work!

MRS. BERNICK JUNIOR. Yes, come, come!

(*All the ladies go into the front room and take their places at the table.*)

RÖRLUND (*shutting the garden door*). There; a barrier between us and frivolity——

MRS. RUMMEL. Don't look out, Hilda!

MRS. HOLT. Nor you either, Netta!

RÖRLUND. —and a veil before indecorousness——

(*He draws the curtains so that the room becomes half dark.*)

BERNICK. You are giving yourself too much trouble, Doctor! We are so much accustomed to the disturbances of foreign sailors——

RÖRLUND. Foreigners—yes, that is another thing. But he who has now suddenly reappeared among us, and who announces his return in so significant a way—; well, in an ordinary house I would not express myself so openly, but I know that within these walls considerations are entertained which outweigh a casual relationship——

BERNICK. Well, well, well, don't be alarmed;—our little society has its pillars, Dr. Rörlund!

RÖRLUND. Pillars that have stood the test, Mr. Bernick! I know it, I know it. Once before you put a stop to excesses here——

(*The door on the right is thrown open and* LONA HESSEL *enters quickly.*)

LONA. No, I couldn't wait any longer! Here I am, dear friends!

MRS. BERNICK JUNIOR. Lona!

MRS. BERNICK SENIOR. Lona—my dear girl!

MRS. HOLT and MRS. RUMMEL. Miss Hessel!

LONA. Yes, but don't look at me; for the big wash didn't come off. As soon as I heard who the American was—; but you don't know, it seems?

MRS. BERNICK JUNIOR. Ah, we do, unfortunately!

LONA. Unfortunately? Has anything gone wrong? You are sitting here in this twilight? And sewing at something white? There hasn't been a death in the family?

RÖRLUND. This is a meeting, Miss Hessel, of the Society for the Moral Regeneration of the Lapsed and Lost.

LONA. What? These nice-looking, well-behaved ladies, can *they* be——?

MRS. RUMMEL. Oh, this is too much——!

LONA. Ah, I see, I see! But look here, the Lapsed and Lost will have to wait for one day; they'll be none the worse for it; on a joyful occasion like this——

RÖRLUND. A joyful occasion? Don't you know that old Tönnesen's prodigal son has returned?

LONA. Is the prodigal son to be received with long faces? How do you read your Bible, Pastor?

RÖRLUND. I am not a clergyman.

LONA. Oh; then you will be one, for certain.—But, pah!—all this linen smells like a shroud. Come and help me, Cousin Karsten; we must have the doors and windows open.

MRS. BERNICK JUNIOR. But, Lona, what are you doing——?

RÖRLUND. But, Mr. Bernick——?

BERNICK. Yes, excuse me; it is really rather oppressive in here.

LONA (*drawing up the Venetian blinds*). And then broad daylight. So! Now we are out of the sepulchral vault. Look, look; the whole town is on its feet! And listen, how they play and sing in the sunshine, these foreigners! They are real human beings—full of sun like southern fruits. Oh, my dear aunt, what a pity it is that with your bad eyes you can't see all this beautiful life——

MRS. BERNICK SENIOR. Tell me about it, my dear girl, then I shall see it.

RÖRLUND (*picking up his book, hat and gloves*). I do not think, ladies, that we are quite in the mood for doing more work to-day; but we shall meet again to-morrow.

LONA (*as the visitors rise to go*). Yes, by all means— I shall be here.

RÖRLUND. You? Allow me to ask, Miss Hessel, what *you* will do in our Society?

LONA. Open all the doors and windows wide, Pastor!

III

FROM THE FOURTH ACT

Dina, you will.

DINA. I am your wife from this hour.

JOHAN. Oh, say that once more.

DINA. Your wife.

JOHAN. And all that lies—that you think lies behind us——

DINA. I know nothing about it; I only know that I must love you——

JOHAN. Then I'll burn my boats—this community of hypocrites shall never see us again.

LONA. On board—on board—Johan——

JOHAN. Yes, on board—Ah, but—Lona—my dear— come here—(*he leads her up to the back and talks rapidly to her*).

MARTHA. Dina—happy girl! Let me look at you and kiss you once more—for the last time.

DINA. Not the last time; no, my dear, dear aunt—we shall meet again.

MARTHA. Never! Promise me, Dina, never to come back again. What are you doing here? This is no place for you; here they deprive one of the courage to wish to be happy——

DINA. Oh, now I have courage enough for anything; now I defy them all.

MARTHA. Yes, out there in the great free world, when you are alone with him, without all these terrifying considerations, without the oppression of all this deadly respectability——

DINA. Yes, yes; that is it!

MARTHA. My dear child! Now go to your happiness —over the sea. Oh, how often have I sat in the school-room and longed to be over there. It must be beautiful there; the heaven is wider; the clouds sail higher than here; a purer air sweeps over the heads of the people——

DINA. Oh, Aunt Martha,—why do you not come with us?

MARTHA. I? Never! Now my position is fixed. Heaven be praised that I was able to see clearly; now I think I can give myself wholly to what I have to do.

DINA. I cannot imagine being parted from you.

MARTHA. Ah, one can part from so much, Dina. (*Kisses her.*) But you will not have to learn that lesson, my dear child! Promise me to make him happy.

DINA. Promise? I know of nothing to promise, will promise nothing—here I have learnt to hate the very word promise.

MARTHA. You shan't promise anything either; you have to remain as you are, true and faithful to yourself.

DINA. That I will, Aunt Martha; for I must remain so.

MARTHA. Yes, yes, yes; I know that well enough.

LONA (*to* JOHAN). Good, good, my dear boy; that's the way. And now on board!

JOHAN. Yes, there's no time to be lost. Good-bye, Lona! thanks, thanks for all you have been to me. Good-bye, Martha; thanks to you too. Be happy; the single state, you see——

MARTHA. Oh, that that should be your last word! No, no, no; but go; good-bye, Johan; good-bye, Dina —and happiness be over all your days!

(*She and* LONA *hurry them towards the door in the background; hand-shakings and farewells;* JOHAN *and* DINA *go quickly out;* LONA *shuts the door after them.*)

LONA. Now we are alone, Martha. You have lost her and I him.

MARTHA. You—him?

LONA. What am I to him now? An old step-sister—what can he want with her? An encumbrance. Men break many a tie when happiness beckons to them.

MARTHA. That is true, sometimes.

LONA. Now we two must hold together, Martha.

MARTHA. Can I be anything to you?

LONA. Who more? We two foster-mothers. Have we not both lost our children? Now we are alone.

MARTHA. Yes, alone. So now I will tell you this; I have loved him more than you.

LONA. Martha!—Is this the truth?

MARTHA. My whole life lies in the words. I have loved him, and waited for him. And then he came; but he did not see me.

LONA. Loved him! And it was you that with such self-sacrifice gave his happiness into his hands.

MARTHA. How could I love him, if I were not willing to give him his happiness? Yes, I have loved him; I have lived my whole life for him, ever since he went away. Oh, it was really a happy life, though a life of longing and impatience——

LONA. And you call yourself impatient who have waited all these years?

MARTHA. Yes, that was the misfortune, that I did not notice how the years were going by. When he went away we were of the same age; and when I saw him again—Oh, that horrible moment—I realised that I was ten years older than he. He had lived out there in the bright, quivering sunshine, and drunk in health at every breath; and here sat I the while, spinning and spinning——

LONA. —the thread of his happiness, Martha.

MARTHA. Yes, it was gold I spun. No bitterness; the problem is not how to be happy, but how to deserve happiness.

LONA. That is true, Martha—would that certain others thought the same.

(CONSUL BERNICK *comes out of the room on the left.*)

BERNICK (*speaking off*). Yes, yes, settle it as you please; when the time comes, I shall be ready—(*Shuts the door.*) Oh, are you there? Now, Martha, you might as well look to your dress a little; and tell Betty to do the same. Nothing out of the way, of course; just a certain note of festivity—but be quick——

LONA. And you must look bright and happy, Martha; your brother forgot that.

MARTHA. I will tell Betty.

(*She goes out by the second door on the left.*)

LONA. Well, so the great and solemn hour has come.

BERNICK. Yes, it has come.

LONA. Now you must feel proud and happy, no doubt.

BERNICK (*looks at her*). H'm!

LONA. The whole town is to be illuminated, I hear.

BERNICK. Yes, I believe there is some such idea.

LONA. All the guilds will turn out with their banners; Hilmar has written a song and Pastor Rörlund is going to make a speech. To-night it will be telegraphed to every corner of the country—"Surrounded by his happy family, Consul Bernick received the homage of his fellow citizens as one of the chief pillars of society——"

BERNICK. So it will; and the crowd in the street will shout and hurrah, and insist on my coming forward to the window—and I shall have to bow and thank them——

LONA. Have to—? that's hardly the right expression.

BERNICK. Do you think I feel happy at this moment?

LONA. No, *I* do not think that you can feel altogether happy.

BERNICK (*after a pause*). Lona, you despise me.

LONA. Not yet.

BERNICK. And you have no right to. And yet—yes, yes, after all, there are times when I despise myself. But you cannot conceive how unspeakably alone I stand, here in this narrow, hypocritical society—you cannot conceive how, year by year, I have had to put a tighter curb on my ambition for a full and satisfying life-work. What have I accomplished, for all the show it makes?—scrap-work, odds and ends—there is no room here for other and larger work. If I tried to go a step in advance of the views and ideas of the day, all my influence was gone. Do you know what we are, we, who are reckoned the pillars of society? We are the slaves of society, neither more nor less.

LONA. And why do you only see this now?

BERNICK. Do you think there have not been moments, when this has been uppermost in me? But then the lukewarm currents of everyday life came over me again. And so lonely as I was! Lona—why did I not know you through and through then?

LONA. What then?

BERNICK. I should never háve given you up; and, with you by my side, I should not have stood where I stand now.

LONA. And are you so certain of what she might have been to you, she, whom you chose in my stead?

BERNICK. I know, at any rate, that she has not been anything that I required. You will say that the fault is mine—but how does that help? And yet she might have met me, might have shared my interests, might now and then have thrown upon me a ray of that disconnected, spasmodic way of looking at things, which a man cannot exactly make use of in his work, but which nevertheless has an inspiring and purifying effect on his whole course of conduct. It is this power that the women among us are not allowed to exercise; most of them do not even possess it; Lona—not one in a thousand has the courage to be like you——

LONA. That is to say—to be herself.

BERNICK. Yes, and to be what a man most profoundly needs. That is why I never felt satisfaction when fortune was with me, never felt the stimulating increase of strength which may result from adversity; my whole life has been a series of petty annoyances or petty, stale triumphs—like the one we are going to have now——

LONA. This too?

BERNICK. I have not sunk so low that empty glitter can smother what I have to say to myself in secret.

LONA. Then why not break with all this hollowness?

BERNICK. You don't understand. You don't know the inner force that drives a man to work and accomplish something in this world. It is different with you women; you must have something to love, a cat or a dog or a canary, if you have nothing else. You think I am working for my own profit, but that is not so; what I have done has brought me profit, it is true, but it is not for that I have been working—I have wanted to be the first—but I know that this is also to the advantage of society.

LONA. And yourself? What satisfaction does this give you?

BERNICK. None; the whole of this generation of shams must go under. But a new generation will grow

up after us; it is my son that I am working for; it is
for him I am preparing a foundation; there will come
a time when truth will make its way into our social order, and upon it he shall found a happier life than his
father's——

LONA. With a lie for its groundwork? Think what
it is you are giving him for an inheritance——*

---

* Here a couple of lines have been omitted in copying
Ibsen's MS. In the published play they read:—

BERNICK (*with suppressed despair*). I am giving him
an inheritance a thousand times worse than you know
of. But, sooner or later,——

---

the curse must pass away. I have gone a hundred times
further than you suspect, but good can turn to evil, and
so too can evil—; why did you come here? I shall not
give way; cannot give way; you shall not succeed in
crushing me——

HILMAR (*enters quickly from the right*). Why, this is—
Betty, Betty!

BERNICK. What now? Are they coming already?

HILMAR. No, certainly not; but I must speak to
some one at once——

(*Goes out by the second door on the left.*)

LONA. Bernick, you say we came to crush you. Then
let me tell you what he is, this prodigal son whom your
moral society shrinks from as if he were plague-stricken.
He can do without you all; he has gone away.

BERNICK. But he will come back.

LONA. He will never come back; and you know nothing. He has gone for ever, and Dina with him.

BERNICK. Gone? And Dina with him?

LONA. Yes, as his wife, without clergy or wedding;

that is how he strikes your society in the face, as I once—
No matter!

BERNICK. Gone; she too in the *Indian Girl*——

LONA. No; he dared not entrust such a precious
freight to those scoundrels; he has sailed in the *Olive
Leaf*——

BERNICK. Ah; then it was—to no purpose—(*calls
into his room*) Krap—stop the *Indian Girl*—she mustn't
sail to-night——

KRAP (*inside*). The *Indian Girl* is already standing
out to sea, Consul.

BERNICK. Too late—and all for nothing.

LONA. What do you mean?——

BERNICK. Nothing, nothing—leave me alone, you
spirit of vengeance.

LONA. H'm! Listen, Bernick; Johan told me to tell
you that he makes you a present of the good name he
once lent you; see, I hold in my hand your letters——

BERNICK. You have them! And now—now you will
—this very night perhaps—when the procession——

LONA. How far you are from knowing me through
and through, Karsten—see—I tear your letters to shreds;
now, there is nothing to bear witness against you—except
your own conscience; now you are safe—be happy too—
if you can——

BERNICK. Lona—why did you not do this before; it
is too late now—you have spoilt my whole life now—I
cannot live after to-day——

LONA. What has happened?

BERNICK. Don't ask me! Not live! Yes, I will—
live, live—work—I have bought it dearly enough.

LONA. Karsten!

HILMAR (*enters hurriedly from the left*). No one to be
found; all away! not even Betty!

BERNICK.   What is it?

HILMAR.   I can't tell you——

BERNICK.   Speak, I tell you——

HILMAR.   Well then—Olaf has run away in the *Indian Girl*.

BERNICK.   Run away—and in the *Indian Girl*—no, no——

LONA.   Ah, yes—now I understand—he went through here a little while ago and——

BERNICK (*at the door on the left*).   Krap—stop the *Indian Girl* at any cost!

KRAP.   Impossible, Consul—she's already at sea——

BERNICK.   And my son is on board.

KRAP.   What?

RUMMEL.   Run away; impossible——

SANDSTAD.   They'll send him back.

HILMAR.   No, no, he writes that he'll hide among the cargo until they are fairly out to sea.

BERNICK.   I shall never see him again.

RUMMEL.   Oh, nonsense; a good stout ship, newly repaired——

VIGELAND.   —and in your own yard, too, Consul——

BERNICK.   I shall never see him again, I tell you.— (*Listens.*)   What is that?

RUMMEL.   Music.   The procession is coming.

BERNICK.   I cannot, I will not see any one.

RUMMEL.   What are you thinking of?   It's impossible.

SANDSTAD.   Impossible, Consul—the scheme is not yet firmly established—think how much you have at stake.

BERNICK.   What does it all matter to me now? Whom have I now to work for?

LONA.   Society, brother-in-law, society.

RUMMEL. Yes, very true.

SANDSTAD. And us others; you won't forget, Consul, that——

MARTHA (*from the left*). Here they come; but Betty is not at home——

BERNICK. Not at home? There, you see, Lona; on an evening like this; no support either in joy or sorrow——

RUMMEL. Up with the curtains; more candles; up with all the curtains; help me, Mr. Sandstad!

BERNICK. And now to come to the chief point in my settlement with society and with my conscience. Betty, collect yourself to bear what is coming.—It has been said that elements of evil have left us this evening—; I can add what you do not know; the man thus alluded to did not go alone—with him went, as his wife——

LONA. Dina Dorf!

RÖRLUND. What? (*Great sensation among the crowd.*)

RÖRLUND. Fled?—run away, impossible!

BERNICK. As his wife, without either clergyman or wedding ceremony, and yet I tell you that I regard this marriage as higher than many another among us, in which all forms have been observed—and I will add more—honour to that man, for he has nobly taken upon himself another's sin—my fellow citizens, I will get clear of the lie—you shall know all—fifteen years ago, it was I who sinned——

MRS. BERNICK. Oh, Karsten, thanks, thanks.

LONA. At last you have found your true self!

(*Astonished whispering among the crowd.*)

BERNICK. There; now we are on a fair footing with each other; now we shall see whether fifteen years' activity can wipe out a youthful aberration—let him who knows himself to be pure cast the first stone; but do not decide this evening; I ask every one of you to go home —to collect himself—away with all this show!—you will feel that it is out of place here——

RÖRLUND. Assuredly it is—well, I thank God—it would have been a sacrifice in vain—Yes, gentlemen, I think we had better——

(*The announcement is whispered from mouth to mouth; the crowd retires noiselessly.*)

BERNICK. Betty, this was a heavy blow for you.

MRS. BERNICK. This is the happiest occasion for fifteen years.

BERNICK. How so? Did you——?

MRS. BERNICK. I knew all.

BERNICK. Knew——?

MRS. BERNICK. The evening before our wedding-day. That was her revenge.

BERNICK. Knew—and yet said nothing?

MRS. BERNICK. Oh, why have you been silent, Karsten? Why have you never thought me worthy of forgiving a moment of aberration?

BERNICK. Because I have never known you until this evening. But now let him come!

MRS. BERNICK. Yes, yes; you shall have him.—Mr. Krap—(*whispers to him in the background; he goes out by the garden door*).

BERNICK. Thanks, Lona; you have saved what is best in me.

LONA. What else did I intend?

BERNICK. How then? not hatred;—not revenge?

LONA. Old love does not rust.

BERNICK. Lona!

LONA. Mona!

BERNICK. Oh, how little has a pitiful coward like me deserved——

LONA. Yes, if we women always asked for deserts, Karsten——   (AUNE *and* OLAF *enter from the garden.*)

BERNICK. Olaf!

OLAF. Father, I'll never——

BERNICK. Never do it again? Yes, you shall—but not secretly—listen, boy—In future you shall be allowed to be yourself——

OLAF. Not a pillar of society?

BERNICK. No, no; yourself, do you hear? whatever may happen. And you, Aune——

AUNE. I know it, Consul—I am dismissed——

BERNICK. We will not part company, Aune—; forgive me——

AUNE. What? the ship can't get away.

BERNICK. Heaven be thanked for that; and—forgive me—to-morrow she must be overhauled—perhaps fresh repairs may be necessary——

AUNE. Perhaps.

BERNICK. Yes, yes, there is much here that needs overhauling. Good-night, Aune!

AUNE. Good-night, Consul—and thank you heartily.
(*Goes out to the right.*)

MRS. BERNICK. Now they are all gone.

BERNICK. And we are alone. All the lights are out in the windows——

MRS. BERNICK. Would you have them lighted again?

BERNICK. Not for all the world. Oh, come nearer, closer around me—I have grown young again! Come, Betty—come, Olaf—and you, Martha—it seems as though I had never seen you during all these years—our society is a society of bachelor-souls—we have no eyes for

womanhood—and you, Lona—it is settled, is it not?—
you won't leave us——

LONA. No; how could I think of going away and
leaving you young people, just beginning life? Am I
not your foster mother? You and I, Martha, we are
the two old aunts—what are you looking at?

MARTHA. How the sky is clearing—; how the clouds
are lifting—the *Olive Leaf* has fortune with it.

LONA. And happiness on board——

BERNICK. And we, we have a long, earnest day of
work before us—I most of all—but let it come—gather
close around me, you strong and true women—one thing
I have learnt to-day: it is you women who are the pillars
of society——

LONA. Then you have learnt a poor wisdom, brother-
in-law. (*Grasps his hand.*)—the spirits of Truth and
Freedom—*these* are the Pillars of Society.

A DOLL'S HOUSE

NOTES FOR THE MODERN TRAGEDY

Rome, 19. 10, 78.

There are two kinds of spiritual law, two kinds of conscience, one in man and another, altogether different, in woman. They do not understand each other; but in practical life the woman is judged by man's law, as though she were not a woman but a man.

The wife in the play ends by having no idea of what is right or wrong; natural feeling on the one hand and belief in authority on the other have altogether bewildered her.

A woman cannot be herself in the society of the present day, which is an exclusively masculine society, with laws framed by men and with a judicial system that judges feminine conduct from a masculine point of view.

She has committed forgery, and she is proud of it; for she did it out of love for her husband, to save his life. But this husband with his commonplace principles of honour is on the side of the law and regards the question with masculine eyes.

Spiritual conflicts. Oppressed and bewildered by the belief in authority, she loses faith in her moral right and ability to bring up her children. Bitterness. A mother in modern society, like certain insects who go away and die when she has done her duty in the propagation of the race.[1] Love of life, of home, of husband and children and family. Here and there a womanly shaking-off of her thoughts. Sudden return of anxiety and terror. She

[1] The sentence is elliptical in the original.

91

must bear it all alone. The catastrophe approaches, inexorably, inevitably. Despair, conflict and destruction.

(Krogstad has acted dishonourably and thereby become well-to-do; now his prosperity does not help him, he cannot recover his honour.)

PERSONS

STENBORG, a Government clerk.
NORA, his wife.
MISS (MRS.) LIND (, a widow).
ATTORNEY KROGSTAD.
KAREN, nurse at the Stenborgs'.
A PARLOUR-MAID at the Stenborgs'.
A PORTER.
THE STENBORGS' THREE LITTLE CHILDREN.
DOCTOR HANK.

SCENARIO

FIRST ACT

A room comfortably, but not showily, furnished. In the back, on the right, a door leads to the hall; on the left another door leads to the room or office of the master of the house, which can be seen when the door is opened. A fire in the stove. Winter day.

She enters from the back, humming gaily; she is in outdoor dress and carries several parcels, has been shopping. As she opens the door, a Porter is seen in the hall, carrying a Christmas-tree. She: Put it down there for the present. (Taking out her purse) How much? Porter: Fifty öre. She: Here is a crown. No, keep

the change. The Porter thanks her and goes. She continues humming and smiling with quiet glee as she
opens several of the parcels she has brought. Calls off,
is he at home? Yes! At first, conversation through the
closed door; then he opens it and goes on talking to her
while continuing to work most of the time, standing at
his desk. There is a ring at the hall-door; he does
not want to be disturbed; shuts himself in. The maid
opens the door to her mistress's friend, just arrived in
town. Happy surprise. Mutual explanation of the position of affairs. He has received the post of manager
in the new joint-stock bank and is to enter on his duties
at the New Year; all financial worries are at an end.
The friend has come to town to look for some small
employment in an office or whatever may present itself.
Mrs. Stenborg gives her good hopes, is certain that all
will turn out well. The maid opens the front-door to the
debt-collector. Mrs. Stenborg terrified; they exchange
a few words; he is shown into the office. Mrs. Stenborg
and her friend; the circumstances of the debt-collector
are touched upon. Stenborg enters in his overcoat; has
sent the collector out the other way. Conversation about
the friend's affairs; hesitation on his part. He and the
friend go out; his wife follows them into the hall; the
Nurse enters with the children. Mother and children
play. The collector enters. Mrs. Stenborg sends the
children out to the left. Great scene between her and
him. He goes. Stenborg enters; has met him on the
stairs; displeased; wants to know what he came back
for? Her support? No intrigues. His wife cautiously
tries to pump him. Strict legal answers. Exit to his
room. She (repeating her words when the collector
went out) But that's impossible. Why, I did it from
love!

SCENARIO

SECOND ACT

The last day of the year. Midday. Nora and the old Nurse. Nora, impelled by uneasiness, is putting on her things to go out. Anxious random questions of one kind and another give a hint that thoughts of death are in her mind. Tries to banish these thoughts, to turn it off, hopes that something or other may intervene. But what? The Nurse goes off to the left.—Stenborg enters from his room. Short dialogue between him and Nora. —The Nurse re-enters, looking for Nora; the youngest child is crying. Annoyance and questioning on Stenborg's part; exit the Nurse; Stenborg is going in to the children.—Doctor Hank enters. Scene between him and Stenborg.—Nora soon re-enters; she has turned back; anxiety has driven her home again. Scene between her, the Doctor and Stenborg. Stenborg goes into his room.—Scene between Nora and the Doctor. The Doctor goes out.—Nora alone.—Mrs. Linde enters. Scene between her and Nora.—Krogstad enters. Short scene between him, Mrs. Linde and Nora. Mrs. Linde goes in to the children.—Scene between Krogstad and Nora.—she entreats and implores him for the sake of her little children; in vain. Krogstad goes out. The letter is seen to fall from outside into the letter-box.—Mrs. Linde re-enters after a short pause. Scene between her and Nora. Half confession. Mrs. Linde goes out.— Nora alone.—Stenborg enters. Scene between him and Nora. He wants to empty the letter-box. Entreaties, jests, half playful persuasion. He promises to let business wait till after New Year's Day; but at 12 o'clock midnight—! Exit. Nora alone. Nora (looking at the

Note: No tarantella in Act 2 scenario!

clock:) It is five o'clock. Five;—seven hours till midnight. Twenty-four hours till the next midnight. Twenty-four and seven—thirty-one. Thirty-one hours to live.——

THIRD ACT

(A muffled sound of dance music is heard from the floor above. A lighted lamp on the table. Mrs. Linde sits in an armchair and absently turns the pages of a book, tries to read, but seems unable to fix her attention; once or twice she looks at her watch. Nora comes down from the dance; uneasiness has driven her; surprise at finding Mrs. Linde, who pretends that she wanted to see Nora in her costume. Helmer, displeased at her going away, comes to fetch her back. The Doctor also enters, but to say good-bye. Meanwhile Mrs. Linde has gone into the side room on the right. Scene between the Doctor, Helmer and Nora. He is going to bed, he says, never to get up again; they are not to come and see him; there is ugliness about a death-bed. He goes out. Helmer goes upstairs again with Nora, after the latter has exchanged a few words of farewell with Mrs. Linde. Mrs. Linde alone. Then Krogstad. Scene and explanation between them. Both go out. Nora and the children. Then she alone. Then Helmer. He takes the letters out of the letter-box. Short scene; goodnight; he goes into his room. Nora in despair prepares for the final step; is already at the door when Helmer enters with the open letter in his hand. Great scene. A ring. Letter to Nora from Krogstad. Final scene. Divorce. Nora leaves the house.——

I

FIRST ACT

(*A room, comfortably and tastefully, but not expensively,
furnished. In the back, on the right, a door leads to
the hall; on the left another door leads to* STENBORG'S
*study. In the middle of the left wall a door to the
nursery; in front on the same side, a sofa, table and
armchairs. In the right wall, somewhat to the back, a
door, and, further forward, a white porcelain stove; in
front of it a couple of armchairs and a rocking-chair.
It is a winter day. Carpet. A fire in the stove.*
(*A bell rings in the hall outside. Presently the outer door
of the flat is heard to open. Then* MRS. STENBORG
*enters, humming gaily. She is in outdoor dress, and
carries several parcels, which she lays on a chair on
the right. As she opens the door, a* PORTER *is seen
in the hall, carrying a Christmas-tree and a basket,
which he gives to the* MAID-SERVANT *who has opened
the door.*)

MRS. STENBORG (*to the* MAID). Hide the Christmas-
tree carefully, Christina; the children must on no account see it before to-morrow. (*To the* PORTER, *taking
out her purse.*) How much?

PORTER. Fifty öre.

MRS. STENBORG. There is a crown. No, keep the
change.

(*The* PORTER *thanks her and goes.* MRS. STENBORG
*shuts the door. She continues humming and smil-
ing in quiet glee as she takes off her outdoor things.*)

MRS. STENBORG (*listening at her husband's door*). Yes;
he is at home. (*Begins humming again.*)

STENBORG (*within*). Is that my lark twittering there?

MRS. STENBORG (*busy opening some of her parcels*). Yes, it is.

STENBORG. Is it the squirrel frisking around?

MRS. STENBORG. Yes.

STENBORG. When did the squirrel get home?

MRS. STENBORG. Just this minute. Come here, Thorvald, and see what I've been buying.

STENBORG. Don't interrupt me. (*A little later he opens the door and looks in, pen in hand.*) Buying, did you say? What! All that? Has my little spendthrift been making the money fly again?

MRS. STENBORG. Why, Thorvald, surely we can afford to launch out a little now. It's the first Christmas we haven't had to pinch.

STENBORG. Come, come; we can't afford to squander money.

MRS. STENBORG. . Oh yes, Thorvald, do let us squander a little now! You know you'll soon be earning heaps of money.

STENBORG. Yes, from New Year's Day. But there's a whole quarter before my first salary is due.

MRS. STENBORG. Never mind; we can borrow in the meantime.

STENBORG. Nora! (*He enters the room.*) You know my principles on these points. No debts! No borrowing! That must be understood between us. (*He puts his arm round her.*) It's a sweet little lark, but it gets through a lot of money. No one would believe how much it costs a man to keep such a little bird as you.

MRS. STENBORG. For shame! How can you say so? Why, I save as much as ever I can.

STENBORG (*laughing*). Very true—as much as you *can*—but that's precisely nothing.

MRS. STENBORG (*hums and smiles with covert glee*). H'm! If you only knew, Thorvald, what expenses we larks and squirrels have!

STENBORG. You're a strange little being, Nora! Sitting here often and often till late at night, slaving away at your copyist's work, to earn the few crowns you can get for it; and then—at the same time—the money often seems to slip through your fingers, without your knowing what becomes of it. But that's going to come to an end, Nora. The copying, I mean. That sort of thing is not good for merry little larks; and now there is no need of it either.

MRS. STENBORG (*clapping her hands*). No, there isn't, Thorvald, is there? Oh, how delightful it is to think of! (*Takes his arm.*) And now I'll tell you how I think we ought to manage, Thorvald. As soon as Christmas is over— (*The hall-door bell rings.*) Ouf, there's a ring! That's somebody come to call. How tiresome!

STENBORG. I'm "not at home" to callers; remember that.   (*He goes into his study and shuts the door.*)

(MRS. STENBORG *arranges the room. The* MAID-SERVANT *opens the door to the hall.*)

MAID-SERVANT. A lady to see you, ma'am.

MRS. STENBORG. Please come in.

(MISS [MRS.] LIND, *in travelling costume, comes into the room. The* MAID *shuts the door.*)

[(*The bell rings again. Brief exchange of words with the* DOCTOR.)]

MISS [MRS.] LIND (*embarrassed and hesitating*). How do you do, Nora?

MRS. STENBORG. How do you do?

MISS [MRS.] LIND. I see you don't recognise me.

MRS. STENBORG. No—oh yes!—I believe— (*Suddenly brightening.*) What, Christina! Is it really you?

MISS LIND. Yes; really I!

MRS. STENBORG. Christina! And to think I didn't know you! But how could I— How changed you are, Christina!

MISS LIND. Yes, no doubt. In eight long years——

MRS. STENBORG. Is it really so long since we met? Yes, so it is. Oh, it has been a happy time, I can tell you! And now you have come to town?

MISS LIND. I arrived this morning.

MRS. STENBORG. To have a merry Christmas, of course. Oh, how delightful! Yes, we *will* have a merry Christmas. Do take your things off. Aren't you frozen? (*Helping her.*) There; now we'll sit cosily by the fire. No, you take the armchair; I shall sit in this rocking-chair. (*Seizes her hands.*) Yes, now I can see the dear old face again. It was only at the first glance— But you're a little paler, and perhaps a little thinner.

MRS. LIND. And much, much older, Nora!

MRS. STENBORG. Yes, perhaps a little older—not much—ever so little. (*She suddenly checks herself; seriously.*) Oh, what a thoughtless wretch I am! Here I sit chattering on, and— Dear, dear Christina, can you forgive me!

MRS. LIND. What do you mean, Nora?

MRS. STENBORG (*softly*). Poor Christina! I forgot: you are a widow.

MRS. LIND. Yes; my husband died three years ago.

MRS. STENBORG. I know, I know; I saw it in the papers. Oh, believe me, Christina, I did mean to write to you; but I kept putting it off, and something always came in the way.

MRS. LIND. I can quite understand that, Nora dear.

MRS. STENBORG. No, Christina; it was horrid of me. Oh, you poor darling! how much you must have gone through!—And he left you nothing?

MRS. LIND. Nothing.

MRS. STENBORG. And no children?

MRS. LIND. None.

MRS. STENBORG. Nothing, nothing at all?

MRS. LIND. Not even a sorrow or a longing to dwell upon.

MRS. STENBORG (*looking at her incredulously*). My dear Christina, how is that possible?

MRS. LIND (*smiling sadly and stroking her hair*). Oh, it happens so sometimes, Nora.

MRS. STENBORG. So utterly alone! How dreadful that must be! I have three of the loveliest children. I can't show them to you just now; they're out with their nurse. But now you must tell me everything.

MRS. LIND. No, no; I want you to tell me——

MRS. STENBORG. No, you must begin; I won't oe egotistical to-day. To-day I'll think only of you. Oh! but I must tell you one thing—perhaps you've heard of our great stroke of fortune?

MRS. LIND. No. What is it?

MRS. STENBORG. Only think! my husband has been made manager of the Joint Stock Bank.

MRS. LIND. Your husband! Oh, how fortunate!

MRS. STENBORG. Yes; isn't it? Now he'll leave that tiresome Government office, where they pay him so badly. For he is to enter on his new position at the New Year, and then he'll have a large salary, and percentages. In future we shall be able to live quite differently—just as we please, in fact. Oh, Christina, how happy I am! It's delightful to have lots of money, and no need to worry about things, isn't it?

MRS. LIND. Yes; at any rate it must be delightful to have what you need.

MRS. STENBORG. No, not only what you need, but heaps of money—*heaps!*

MRS. LIND (*smiling*). Nora, Nora, haven't you learnt reason yet? In our schooldays you were a shocking little spendthrift.

MRS. STENBORG (*quietly smiling*). Yes; that's what Thorvald says I am still. (*Holding up her forefinger.*) But "Nora, Nora" is not so silly as you all think. Oh! we haven't had the chance of being spendthrifts. We have both had to work.

MRS. LIND. You too?

MRS. STENBORG. Yes, light work: copying, and embroidery, and things of that sort. But not so much as he of course. In the first year after our marriage he overworked himself terribly. Then the doctors declared he must go to the South.

MRS. LIND. You spent a whole year in Italy, didn't you?

MRS. STENBORG. It was a wonderful, delicious journey, you may imagine! And it saved Thorvald's life. But it cost a frightful lot of money, Christina.

MRS. LIND. So I should think.

MRS. STENBORG. Twelve hundred dollars! Isn't that a lot of money?

MRS. LIND. How lucky you had the money to spend.

MRS. STENBORG. We got it from father, you must know.

MRS. LIND. Ah, I see. He died just about that time, didn't he?

MRS. STENBORG. Yes, Christina, just then. And only think! I couldn't go and nurse him! I had to stay here with Thorvald, of course; he was ill too. Dear, good father! I never saw him again, Christina. Oh! that's the hardest thing I have had to bear since my marriage.

MRS. LIND. But then you went to Italy?

MRS. STENBORG. Yes; you see, we had the money, and the doctors said we must lose no time. We started three weeks later.

MRS. LIND. And your husband came back completely cured?

MRS. STENBORG. Sound as a bell. [MRS. LINDE. But wasn't that the doctor—?] He has never had an hour's illness since that time. Only he has to be careful, the doctor says, and avoid any kind of excitement. And I shall take good care of that. Oh, it will be so easy now. He shall have no anxiety and no annoyance. I and the children will make things so comfortable for him. (*Jumps up and claps her hands.*) Oh, Christina, Christina, what a wonderful thing it is to live and to be happy!— Oh, but it's really too horrid of me! Here am I talking about nothing but my own concerns. (*Seats herself upon a footstool close to* CHRISTINA, *and seizes her hands.*) Oh, don't be angry with me!— Now tell me, is it really true that you didn't love your husband? What made you marry him, then?

MRS. LIND. My old mother was still alive, you see, bedridden and helpless, and then I had my two younger brothers to think of. I didn't think it would be right for me to refuse him.

MRS. STENBORG. Perhaps it wouldn't have been. I suppose he was rich then?

MRS. LIND. Very well off, I believe. But his business was 'uncertain. It fell to pieces at his death, and there was nothing left.

MRS. STENBORG. And then——?

Mrs. Lind. Then I had to fight my way by keeping a shop, a little school, anything I could turn my hand to. My whole life since that time has been one long, weary struggle. My old mother no longer needs anything, for she is at rest, as perhaps you know. But my heaviest years for the two boys are still to come; they are now getting into the higher classes; their school fees and all their requirements are increasing. (*Stands up restlessly.*) It can't be done any longer in that out-of-the-way corner, Nora! That is why I came here. They say that here things are better than they used to be for us women. I must try to get some office work—some settled employment——

Mrs. Stenborg. But, Christina, that's such drudgery, and you look worn out already. It would be ever so much better for you to go to some watering-place and rest.

Mrs. Lind. I have no father to pay my travelling expenses, Nora!

Mrs. Stenborg (*rising*). Oh, don't be vexed with me.

Mrs. Lind. My dear Nora, don't you be vexed with me. The worst of a position like mine is that it makes one so bitte . You become selfish; you have to be always on the strain. When I heard of the happy change in your fortunes—can you believe it?—I was glad not for your sake, but for my own.

Mrs. Stenborg. How do you mean? Ah, I see! You think my husband can perhaps do something for you.

Mrs. Lind. Yes; I thought so.

Mrs. Stenborg. And so he shall, Christina. I'm sure he will. I'll keep at him, you see. He shan't have any peace until he has hit upon something or other.

Mrs. Lind. How good of you, Nora, to stand by me

so warmly! Doubly good in you, who know so little of the troubles and burdens of life.

Mrs. Stenborg. I? I know so little of——?

Mrs. Lind (*smiling*). Oh, well—a little copying, and so forth.—You're a child, Nora.

Mrs. Stenborg (*tosses her head and paces the room*). Oh, come, you mustn't be so patronising!

Mrs. Lind. No?

Mrs. Stenborg. You're like the rest. You all think there's nothing serious about me——

Mrs. Lind. Well, well——

Mrs. Stenborg. You think I've had no troubles in this world.

Mrs. Lind. My dear Nora, you've just told me all your troubles.

Mrs. Stenborg. Those trifles! (*Softly.*) I haven't told you the great thing.

Mrs. Lind. The great thing? What do you mean?

Mrs. Stenborg. You look down upon me. You are proud of having worked so hard and so long for your old mother.

Mrs. Lind. I'm sure I don't look down upon you; but it's true I am proud and glad when I remember that I was able to keep my mother's last days free from care.

Mrs. Stenborg. And you will be both proud and glad too when once you have got your brothers into a good position.

Mrs. Lind. Have I not the right to be?

Mrs. Stenborg. Yes indeed. But now let me tell you, Christina—I, too, have something to be proud and glad of.

Mrs. Lind. No doubt;—but what do you mean?

Mrs. Stenborg. Hush! Not so loud. Thorvald is

in there. He mustn't for the world— No one must
know about it, Christina—no one but you.

Mrs. Lind. Why, what can it be?

Mrs. Stenborg. Come over here. (*Takes her over
to the stove.*) I, too, have something to be proud and
glad of. I saved my husband's life.

Mrs. Lind. Saved his life?

Mrs. Stenborg. I told you about our going to Italy.
Thorvald would have died but for that.

Mrs. Lind. Well—and your father gave you the
money.

Mrs. Stenborg (*smiling*). Yes, so Thorvald and
everyone believes; but——

Mrs. Lind. But——?

Mrs. Stenborg. Father didn't give us one penny.
It was I that found the money.

Mrs. Lind. You? All that money?

Mrs. Stenborg. Twelve hundred dollars. What do
you say to that?

Mrs. Lind. My dear Nora, how did you manage it?
Did you win it in the lottery?

Mrs. Stenborg. No, indeed I didn't.

Mrs. Lind. Then where ever did you get it from?

Mrs. Stenborg (*smiling and humming gaily*). H'm;
tra-la-la-la!

Mrs. Lind. Of course you couldn't borrow it.

Mrs. Stenborg. No? Why not?

Mrs. Lind. Why, a wife can't borrow without her
husband's consent.

Mrs. Stenborg (*tossing her head*). Oh, when one has
some idea of business—and knows how to set about
things——

Mrs. Lind. But, Nora, I don't understand——

Mrs. Stenborg. Well, you needn't. I never said I

borrowed the money. There are many ways I may have got it. That's beside the point, you see. But——

MRS. LIND. Listen to me, Nora dear: haven't you been a little rash?

MRS. STENBORG. Is it rash to save one's husband's life?

MRS. LIND. No, but without his knowledge——

MRS. STENBORG. But it would have been fatal for him to know! He wasn't even to suspect how ill he was. The doctors came to me privately and told me his life was in danger—that nothing could save him but a journey to the South. Do you think I didn't try diplomacy first? I told him how I longed to have a trip abroad, like other young wives; and then I hinted that he could borrow the money. But then, Christina, he got almost angry with me. He said I was frivolous and understood nothing at all about serious matters and that it was his duty as a husband not to yield to my whims and fancies —so I think he called them. Well, I had to save him, you see; and then I found the way to do it.

MRS. LIND. And was there never any explanation between him and your father?

MRS. STENBORG. No, never. Father died at that very time; I thought of telling him all about it and coaching him in what to say; but as he lay ill—unhappily, it wasn't necessary.

MRS. LIND. And you have never confessed to your husband?

MRS. STENBORG. Good heavens! What can you be thinking of? Tell him, when he has such a loathing of debt! No, this thing is my grand secret, Christina. Oh, you may believe it has been no joke to meet my engagements punctually. You must know that in business there are things called instalments, and quarterly interest, that are terribly hard to provide for. So I've had to pinch a little, wherever I could. I couldn't save out of the housekeeping, for of course Thorvald had to live well. And I couldn't let the children go about badly dressed; all I got for them, I spent on them, the blessed darlings!

MRS. LIND. So it had to come out of your own pocket-money, Nora?

MRS. STENBORG. Yes, of course. After all, the whole thing was my doing; so it was my finery and my amusements that had to suffer. When Thorvald gave me money for clothes, and so on, I never spent more than half of it; I always bought the simplest things. Oh, it was often very hard, Christina dear; for it's nice to be beautifully dressed. (*Smiling.*) And with all that he calls me a spendthrift, and says the money seems to melt away in my hands.

MRS. LINDE. How much have you been able to pay off?

MRS. STENBORG. Well, I can't precisely say. It's difficult to keep that sort of business clear. But it doesn't matter much now. There will be so many resources open to me now; for we are going to live quite differently from the way we have been doing. Oh, Christina, how glorious it is to think of! Free from all anxiety! Free, quite free. To be able to play and romp about with the children; to have things tasteful and pretty in the house. And then the spring will soon be here, with the great blue sky. Perhaps then we shall be able to travel, on railways and great steamships, and see foreign countries again. The first time I saw so little, for I was so anxious about Thorvald then. Oh, what a wonderful thing it is to live and to be happy! And you shall be happy too, Christina; as happy as you *can* be, poor dear, without

either husband or children— (*A bell rings outside.*)
Who can that be?

Mrs. Linde (*rising*). Perhaps I had better go.

Mrs. Stenborg. No; do stay. It's sure to be someone who wants to see Thorvald; he won't come through
here.

Maid-Servant (*in the doorway*). If you please,
ma'am, Mr. Krogstad insists on seeing Mr. Stenborg——

Mrs. Stenborg (*springing up*). My husband——!

Mrs. Linde (*starts*). Who is it?

Maid. But I didn't know, as the Doctor is in there——

Mrs. Stenborg (*in the doorway*). What do you want
to see my husband about?

Krogstad (*in the hall*). Only about things that are
of no interest to anyone else. (*Seeing* Mrs. Linde.)
But—surely that can't be——

Mrs. Stenborg. Mrs. Linde—from the west country. Well, go into my husband's room; I dare say he
can see you. (*To the maid.*) Open the door for Mr.
Krogstad. (*Shuts the door into the hall and goes back to*
Mrs. Linde.) Do you know that man, Christina?

Mrs. Linde. I used to know him—before I was married. He was in a lawyer's office in our town.

Mrs. Stenborg. Yes, so he was.

Mrs. Linde. How he has changed!

Mrs. Stenborg. I believe his marriage was unhappy.

Mrs. Linde. And he is a widower now?

Mrs. Stenborg. With a lot of children.

Mrs. Linde. And his business is not of the most
creditable, they say?

Mrs. Stenborg. No, they say it isn't. But don't let
us think of business. It's so tiresome.

(Doctor Hank *comes out of* Stenborg's *room.*)

The Doctor (*still in the doorway*). No, no; I'd

rather go; I'll have a chat with your wife. (*Shuts the door and sees* MRS. LINDE.) Ah, I beg your pardon——

MRS. STENBORG (*introduces them*). Doctor Hank— Mrs. Linde.

HANK. Oh, indeed? Your old friend—or rather, your friend of old days. I think I saw you as I came in, Mrs. Linde. And now you've come up for Christmas? Quite right, too. One ought to enjoy life as well as one can.

MRS. STENBORG. Yes, oughtn't one, Doctor?

HANK. Then we're agreed upon that? But, I say, you've got a new carpet! Congratulate you! Yes, and a very handsome carpet, too. Now, is that a luxury? I say, no, it isn't. A carpet like that gives you a good return for your money, ladies; with a carpet like that under one's feet one has higher and finer thoughts, nobler feelings, than one would have in an uncomfortable room with cold, creaking planks under one. And especially where there are children. [The race is ennobled in beautiful surroundings.]

MRS. STENBORG. Oh, how often I have felt the same; but I have never been able to give it expression.

HANK. No, I dare say not. You see, it belongs to psychological statistics; and that is a science that is not much developed at present. But it is possible to show a connection between such things. For instance, if that fellow who is with Stenborg——

MRS. STENBORG. Mr. Krogstad?

HANK. Yes, if Krogstad had been brought up in a home which, so to speak, was on the sunny side of life, with all its spiritual windows facing the light, instead of the cursed cold, damp north—I know it—I'll undertake to say that he would have turned out a decent person, like the rest of us.

Mrs. Linde. Then he is not one?

Hank. He can't be one. Impossible. His marriage was not such that he could be one. An unhappy marriage is like the small-pox; it leaves marks on the soul!

Mrs. Stenborg. And what does a happy marriage do?

Hank. It acts like a course of baths; it drives out all the noxious humours and encourages the growth of all that is good and useful in a man. What would have become of Stenborg, I wonder, if he hadn't found his little song-bird——?

Mrs. Stenborg. What? How can you think that Thorvald should require——?

Hank. I know him. He would have become a bit of a slave to duty, a bit of a drudge, a bit of a pedant—in a good sense.

Mrs. Stenborg. Fie, Doctor, now I'm angry with you.

Hank. But don't you think it's true? (*Sees* Stenborg *coming.*) Then ask him yourself.

Mrs. Stenborg. No, no, no, leave off. (*To* Stenborg.) Has he gone?

Stenborg. Yes, this moment.

Mrs. Stenborg. Thorvald, let me introduce you—this is Christin——

Stenborg. Ah, Mrs. Linde! Welcome. I have just heard from Krogstad that you were here.

Mrs. Linde. From Krogstad——?

Mrs. Stenborg. What has it to do with him?

Stenborg. Well, he connected it with what he had to say to me.

Mrs. Linde. My being here?

Stenborg. Yes, he thinks he can see a design behind everything.

MRS. STENBORG. But what did he want with you?

STENBORG. It's really a tiresome story. (*To* DR. HANK.) I dare say you know that for the last year or so Krogstad has had a little place in the Joint Stock Bank?

HANK. Yes; what of it?

STENBORG. When I accepted the post of manager I made it one of my conditions that there should be a weeding-out of the staff.

HANK. And that was by no means unnecessary, from what one hears.

STENBORG. More necessary than people suppose. Jobbery and routine had got the upper hand in an altogether unwarrantable way. I can't put up with that; I mean to begin with a staff that I can depend upon in everything. I have therefore seen to it that all the undesirables have received notice.

HANK. You were quite right there.

MRS. LINDE. And Krogstad is among them?

STENBORG. Yes, I'm sorry to say so, he above all. He is altogether untrustworthy.

MRS. STENBORG. Oh but, Thorvald, you've known him for years.

STENBORG. For that very reason I must be all the more strict. I wish indeed I could spare him; but it is impossible. You must not think me hard-hearted, Mrs. Linde. I am certainly not that; but I have a duty and a regard for the institution I am to manage. I obtained my post by opposition to the existing system, by a pamphlet, by a series of newspaper articles and by decisive action at the last general meeting. And am I to begin by contradicting myself?

HANK. No, I hope you'll do nothing of the sort.

STENBORG. I simply can't do so. My task is before

all things to restore public confidence in the bank; and therefore there must be a weeding-out.

MRS. LINDE. And yet I'm sorry for the people who will be hit.

MRS. STENBORG. So am I.

STENBORG. And I no less.

HANK. There we have it! This damned humanity! Excuse me if I express myself rather strongly. But it makes me wild when I hear—. Who are the people who will suffer? Incapable or disorderly individuals, drunkards many of them, persons who take advantage of the weakness of their superiors to obtain advances or loans that they can never repay.

STENBORG. Yes, you're not far from the truth.

HANK. And then, who is it that will suffer next? Why, the shareholders, myself and a lot of other honest men. We are the people who are robbed by incapacity and irregularity and apathy, so that we never see a penny of our deposits. But nobody pities us. No, of course not; we are not failures, we are not drunkards, forgers, discharged convicts; and these are the sort of fellows who have a monopoly of pity in our humane age.

MRS. LINDE. And I suppose they are the ones who most need it.

HANK. But we don't need the degenerate specimens of the race; we can do without them. Study the natural sciences, ladies, and you will see how there is one law pervading everything. The stronger tree deprives the weaker of the conditions of life and turns them to its own use. The same thing happens among animals; the unfit individuals in a herd have to make way for the better ones. And that is how nature progresses. It is only we human beings who forcibly retard progress by taking care of the unfit individuals.—But, bless my soul!

I'm standing here talking and forgetting all about a patient I ought to look up. The brute is quite capable of slipping through my hands.

MRS. LINDE. Is that another specimen of the unfit, Doctor?

HANK. A drunken scoundrel of a miner; got his right hand blown off while tipsy. If he survives it, he'll be fit for nothing——

MRS. LINDE. But then it would surely be best to get rid of him.

HANK (*putting on his coat*). Yes, you're perfectly right there; that is a thought that often forces itself upon us doctors, especially when we're practising among the poor. But who is going to take such a responsibility? Not I. I won't say anything about its being punishable by law; but even if it were not—. No, Mrs. Linde, our development has not yet gone far enough for that. Well, good-bye, good-bye, ladies.

STENBORG. Wait, I'll go with you.

MRS. LINDE. Yes, it's time I was going too, Nora. Where is the post office?

STENBORG. I'll show you. We'll go together.

MRS. LINDE. Thanks. (*Aside, as she puts on her things.*) Not a word to your husband about me——

MRS. STENBORG. Oh, but Christina!

MRS. LINDE. You can see it would be of no use.

MRS. STENBORG. Poor Christina. But come back this evening.

(*They go towards the door, talking, and out into the hall. Outside on the stairs are heard children's voices.*)

MRS. STENBORG. There they are! There they are! (*She runs to the outer door and opens it. The nurse enters the hall with the three children.*)

MRS. STENBORG. Come in; come in; oh, my sweet darlings! Do you see them, Christina?

HANK. Don't let us stand here chattering in the draught.

STENBORG. Come, Mrs. Linde, only mothers can stand such a temperature.

(DR. HANK, MRS. LINDE *and* STENBORG *go out.* MRS. STENBORG, *the nurse and the children enter the room.*)

MRS. STENBORG. How fresh and red you look! Have you had great fun?—Oh, really! You've been giving Emmy and Bob a ride on your sledge; why, you're quite a man, Alf. Oh, give him to me a little, Anna. (*Takes the smallest one on her arm and dances with him.*) Yes, yes; I'll dance with you too—What! Did you have a game of snowballs? Oh, I should have liked to be there. No, let me take their things off, Anna. Go to the nursery; you look frozen. You'll find some hot coffee there.

(*The* NURSE *goes out to the left.* MRS. STENBORG *takes off the children's things and throws them down anywhere, while the children all talk together.*)

MRS. STENBORG. Really! A big dog ran after you? But he didn't bite you? No, he doesn't bite good children. Don't peep into those parcels, Emmy. What is it? Wouldn't you like to know? Take care—it'll bite! What? Shall we have a game? What shall we play at? Hide-and-seek? Yes, let's play hide-and-seek. Alf shall hide first. Am I to? Yes, let me hide first.

(*She and the children play, with laughter and shouting, in the room and the adjacent one to the left. At last* MRS. STENBORG. *hides under the table; the children come rushing in, look for her, but cannot find her, hear her half-choked laughter, rush to the table, lift up the cover and see her—loud shouts;*

she creeps out as though to frighten them. Fresh shouts. Meanwhile there has been a knock at the door leading into the hall; no one has heard it. Now the door is half opened and KROGSTAD *puts his head in.*)

KROGSTAD. I beg your pardon, Mrs. Stenborg——

MRS. STENBORG (*with a slight cry, half jumps up*). Ah, what do you want?

KROGSTAD. Excuse me. The hall door was ajar—somebody must have forgotten to shut it——

MRS. STENBORG (*standing up*). My husband is not at home, Mr. Krogstad.

KROGSTAD. I know it. I saw him go down the street.

MRS. STENBORG. Then what do you want here?

KROGSTAD. To speak to you.

MRS. STENBORG. To me? (*To the children, softly.*) Go in to Anna. And mind you are quiet and good. What? No, the strange man won't hurt mamma. When he's gone we'll go on playing. (*She leads the children into the left-hand room, and shuts the door behind them. Softly, in suspense.*) It is to me you wish to speak?

KROGSTAD. Yes, to you.

MRS. STENBORG. To-day? But it's not the first yet——

KROGSTAD. No, Mrs. Stenborg; it's two days to Christmas. It will depend upon yourself what sort of a Christmas you will have.

MRS. STENBORG. What do you want? I'm not ready to-day——

KROGSTAD. Never mind that for the present. I have come about another matter. You have a minute to spare——?

MRS. STENBORG.   Oh, yes, I suppose so; although——

KROGSTAD.   Good.   I was sitting in Olsen's restaurant opposite, and I saw your husband go down the street——

MRS. STENBORG.   Well?

KROGSTAD.   —with a lady——

MRS. STENBORG.   It was Mrs. Linde.

KROGSTAD.   I used to know that lady.

MRS. STENBORG.   She told me so.

KROGSTAD.   Did she tell you no more?

MRS. STENBORG.   No; nothing at all.

KROGSTAD (*suspiciously*).   H'm;—as I was saying, she has crossed my path once, and now it seems that she is going to do so again.

MRS. STENBORG.   But I don't understand at all——

KROGSTAD.   Will you give me a straightforward answer to a question?   Did Mrs. Linde come here to look for employment?

MRS. STENBORG.   Yes, she did.

KROGSTAD.   I suppose it wasn't a place in the Joint Stock Bank that she——

MRS. STENBORG.   But I don't see——

KROGSTAD.   I suppose it wasn't the situation that I'm to be turned out of?

MRS. STENBORG.   Mr. Krogstad, I don't see that I am bound to give you an account——

KROGSTAD.   We will speak of our account presently.— You are perhaps aware that I have had notice.

MRS. STENBORG.   Yes.

KROGSTAD.   By your husband's directions?

MRS. STENBORG.   Yes.

KROGSTAD.   Mrs. Stenborg, you must see that I retain my position in the Bank.

MRS. STENBORG. I? How can you imagine that I should have any such influence over my husband?

KROGSTAD. Oh, I don't suppose Mr. Stenborg is any more inflexible than other husbands.

MRS. STENBORG. If you talk disrespectfully of my husband, I must request you to leave the house.

KROGSTAD. You are bold, madam.

MRS. STENBORG. I am afraid of you no longer. When New Year's Day is over, I shall soon be out of the whole business.

KROGSTAD. Listen to me, Mrs. Stenborg. If I fight as though for my life to keep my place in the Bank, it is not for the sake of the salary.

MRS. STENBORG. Why then?

KROGSTAD. It is because this place is a kind of position of confidence; it is the only situation that any one has entrusted to me. Of course you know, like every one else, that some years ago I—got into trouble?

MRS. STENBORG. I've heard something of the sort.

KROGSTAD. The matter never came into court; but from that moment all paths were barred to me. Then I took up the business you know about. I had to turn my hand to something; and I don't think I've been one of the worst. But now I must get clear of it all. My sons are growing up; for their sake I must try to recover my character as well as I can. This place in the Bank was the first step; and now your husband comes and kicks me off the ladder, and I am back in the mire.

MRS. STENBORG. But I assure you, Mr. Krogstad, I have no power to help you.

KROGSTAD. I can compel you.

MRS. STENBORG. You won't tell him that I owe you money?

KROGSTAD. Suppose I were to?

MRS. STENBORG. It would be shameful of you. (*Bursts into tears.*) This secret is my joy and pride. I had been looking forward so eagerly to getting it all paid off by saving and working, and one day telling my husband that it was I——. And you can have the heart to—! (*Hotly.*) But just do it! And then you *will* lose your place! It would involve me in all sorts of unpleasantness; but then my husband will see what a bad man you are; and then you certainly won't keep your place.

KROGSTAD. Nothing but unpleasantness?

MRS. STENBORG. My husband will of course pay what I owe you.

KROGSTAD. Either your memory is defective, or you don't know much about business. I must make the position a little clearer to you.

MRS. STENBORG. How so?

KROGSTAD. When your husband was ill, you came to me to borrow twelve hundred dollars.

MRS. STENBORG. I knew of nobody else.

KROGSTAD. I promised to find you the money.

MRS. STENBORG. And you did find it.

KROGSTAD. I promised to find you the money, on certain conditions. You were so much taken up at the time about your husband's illness, and so eager to have the wherewithal for your journey, that you probably did not give much thought to the details. Allow me to remind you of them. I promised to find you the amount in exchange for a note of hand, which I drew up.

MRS. STENBORG. Yes, and I signed it.

KROGSTAD. Quite right. But then I added a few lines, making your father security for the debt. Your father was to sign this.

MRS. STENBORG. Was to—? He did sign it!

KROGSTAD. I had left the date blank. That is to

say, your father was himself to date his signature. Do
you recollect that?

Mrs. Stenborg. Yes, I believe——

Krogstad. Then I gave you the paper to send to
your father, by post. Is not that so?

Mrs. Stenborg. Yes.

Krogstad. And of course you did so at once; for
within eight or ten days you brought me back the document with your father's signature; and I handed you the
money.

Mrs. Stenborg. Well? Have I not made my payments punctually?

Krogstad. Fairly—yes. But to return to the point:
you were in great trouble at the time, Mrs. Stenborg?

Mrs. Stenborg. I was indeed.

Krogstad. Your father was very ill, I believe?

Mrs. Stenborg. He was on his death-bed.

Krogstad. And died soon after?

Mrs. Stenborg. Yes.

Krogstad. Tell me, Mrs. Stenborg: do you happen
to recollect the day of his death? The day of the
month, I mean?

Mrs. Stenborg. He died on the 29th of September.

Krogstad. Quite correct. I have made inquiries.
And here comes in the remarkable point—(*produces a
paper*) which I cannot explain.

Mrs. Stenborg. What remarkable point? I don't
know——

Krogstad. The remarkable point, madam, that your
father signed this paper five days after his death!

Mrs. Stenborg. What! I don't understand——

Krogstad. Your father died on the 29th of September. But look here: he has dated his signature October
4th! Is not that remarkable, Mrs. Stenborg? (Mrs.

STENBORG *is silent.*) Can you explain it, madam?
(MRS. STENBORG *continues silent.*) It is noteworthy,
too, that the words "October 4th" and the year are not
in your father's handwriting, but in one which I believe
I know. Look there. Well, this may be explained;
your father may have forgotten to date his signature,
and somebody may have added the date here. There is
nothing wrong in that. Of course it is genuine, Mrs.
Stenborg? It was really your father himself who wrote
his name here?

MRS. STENBORG (*after a short silence, throws her head
back, looks him firmly in the face and says proudly and
defiantly*). No, it was not. It was I who copied his
signature.

KROGSTAD. Ah!—Are you aware, madam, that that
is a dangerous admission?

MRS. STENBORG. How so? You will soon get your
money.

KROGSTAD. May I ask you one more question? Why
did you not send the paper to your father?

MRS. STENBORG. It was impossible. My father was
very ill. Had I asked him for his signature, I should
have had to tell him why I wanted the money; but he
was so ill I really could not tell him that my husband's
life was in danger. It was impossible.

KROGSTAD. Then would it not have been better to
have given up your tour?

MRS. STENBORG. I couldn't do that; my husband's
life depended on that journey. I couldn't give it up.

KROGSTAD. Did it never occur to you that you and
your husband might die on the journey, and that I should
then be defrauded of my money?

MRS. STENBORG. That was nothing to me. I didn't
care in the least about you. I couldn't endure you for

all the cruel difficulties you made, although you knew how ill my husband was.

KROGSTAD. Mrs. Stenborg, you evidently do not realise what you have been guilty of. Let me tell you it was nothing more nor worse that made me an outcast from society.

MRS. STENBORG. You? You want me to believe that you did anything to save your wife's life?

KROGSTAD. The law takes no account of motives.

MRS. STENBORG. Then it must be a very bad law.

KROGSTAD. Bad or not, the judges must follow it.

MRS. STENBORG. I don't believe that. Do you mean to tell me that a daughter has no right to spare her invalid father?—that a wife has no right to save her husband's life? I don't know much about the law, but I'm sure you'll find, somewhere or another, that that is allowed. And you don't know that—you, a lawyer! You must be a bad one, Mr. Krogstad.

KROGSTAD. Allow me, madam——

MRS. STENBORG. I don't want to hear any more—. You think you can frighten me, but you haven't succeeded. I'm not so foolish as you imagine.

KROGSTAD. Very well. I may tell you once more: you are on the edge of the precipice; you have everything to lose; your whole future; everything, I tell you. If I am flung into the gutter a second time, you shall keep me company. (*Bows and goes out through hall.*)

NORA (*stands a while thinking, then reassured*). Oh, nonsense! (*Begins folding the children's clothes, but pauses in the middle:*) But—? No, it's impossible! Why, I did it for love!

CHILDREN (*at the door, left*). Mamma, has the strange man gone?

NORA.   Yes; but don't tell papa that any one has been here.

CHILDREN.   No, and now will you play with us again.

NORA.   No, no; not now, children.

CHILDREN.   Oh, do, mamma; you know you promised.

NORA.   Yes, but I can't just now.   Run to the nursery. I have so much to do.   Run along, run along, and be good, my darlings!   (*She closes the door behind them; then takes up her knitting, but lets it drop again, then knits hurriedly and says in a spasmodic voice:*)   No, it's quite impossible!

Enter STENBORG *from the hall.*

NORA.   Oh, you're back already?

STENBORG.   Yes, Has anybody been here?

NORA.   Here? No.

STENBORG.   Are you sure? That's odd. I saw Krogstad come out of the house.

NORA.   Did you?   Oh, yes, by-the-bye, he was here for a minute.

STENBORG.   Nora, he has been begging you to put in a good word for him?

NORA.   Yes.

STENBORG.   And you were to say nothing to me of his having asked you?   You were to do it as if of your own accord?

NORA.   Yes.

STENBORG.   Nora, Nora! And you could agree to that!   To condescend to intrigue with such a person! And to tell me an untruth!

NORA.   An untruth!

STENBORG.   Didn't you say that nobody had been here?   My little bird must never do that again!   A song-bird must sing clear and true; no false notes—.   Well, well, well, it was the first time; let's say no more about it.

(*Sits down before the fire.*)   Oh, how warm and quiet it is here!

NORA (*busy with her parcels*).   Thorvald!

STENBORG.   Yes.

NORA.   Was it anything so very dreadful that poor Krogstad got into trouble about?

STENBORG.   Forgery.   Don't you know what that means?

NORA.   But mayn't he have been driven to it by need?

STENBORG.   Yes; or, like so many others, he may have done it in pure heedlessness.   I am not so hard-hearted as to condemn a man absolutely for a single fault.

NORA.   No, surely not, Thorvald.

STENBORG.   I have seen examples of such men retrieving their character, when their crime has been discovered at once and they have taken the punishment.

NORA.   Punishment——?

STENBORG.   Yes, there's imprisonment for forgery. But that didn't happen with Krogstad.   His crime was not discovered till long afterwards, and that is what has morally ruined him.

NORA.   How——?

STENBORG.   Just think how such a man must be always lying and canting and shamming.   Think of the mask he must wear even towards those who stand nearest him—towards his own wife and children.   The effect on the children—that's the most terrible part of it, Nora.

NORA.   Why——?

STENBORG.   Because in such an atmosphere of lies home life is poisoned and contaminated in every fibre; every breath the children draw contains some germ of evil.

NORA (*behind him*).   Are you sure of that, Thorvald?

STENBORG.   I have absolute statistical proof of it.   I

have studied these questions a good deal and I have found that nearly all cases of early corruption may be traced to lying mothers.

NORA. Mothers——?

STENBORG. Yes, mothers in particular; but of course the father's influence may act in the same way; and Krogstad knew that only too well. And yet he has been poisoning his own children for years past by a life of untruthfulness and hypocrisy. That is why I call him morally ruined. So my sweet little Nora must promise not to plead his cause. Shake hands upon it. Come, come, what's this? Give me your hand. That's right. Then it's a bargain. I assure you it would have been impossible for me to work with him; it gives me a sense of discomfort to come in contact with such people. (NORA *draws her hand away, and moves towards the table.*) Well, what is it?

NORA. It is so warm. Oh, I have so much to do.

STENBORG (*rising*). Yes, and I must try to get through my business. And then the Christmas-tree shall be decorated, and we'll bring the children in—and then we'll have a joyful and happy Christmas Eve, my precious little song-bird! (*He goes into his room and shuts the door.*)

NORA. No, no, no—! It can't be. I will decorate the Christmas-tree. No; not with my hands!

ANNA (*at the door, left*). The children are asking if they may come in, ma'am?

NORA. No, no, don't let them come to me! Keep them with you, Anna.

ANNA. Very well, ma'am. (*Goes back into the nursery.*)

NORA (*pale with terror*). Corrupt them? Poison—! No! Yes; yes!—But it's impossible! It must be impossible! Why, I did it for love!

SECOND ACT

The same room

NORA *is putting on her hat and cloak; her muff and gloves are on the table.*

NORA (*anxiously, at the hall door*). Is somebody coming?—Nobody. No, of course, he won't come to-day; it's New Year's Eve; nor to-morrow either.—Stuff and nonsense! Of course he won't come at all. He won't do it. It won't happen. It's impossible.—O God, O God, put something in Thorvald's mind, so that he won't irritate that terrible man. O God, O God, I have three little children. Oh, do it for the sake of my little children!

NURSE (*at the door, left*). Now I have everything ready, if you would—. Oh, I see, you're going out, ma'am?

NORA. Yes, I must go out. Isn't it fearfully close in here? I feel as if I should be stifled.

NURSE. But there's a keen wind out-of-doors. Do be careful, ma'am; you might easily make yourself ill.

NORA. Well, what does that matter? Do you count it a misfortune to be ill?

NURSE. Yes, that I do.

NORA. But people are sympathetic towards those who are ill. No one will do any harm to a person who is ill.—Oh yes, though, there is somebody who would do it.

NURSE. Oh, but, ma'am——

NORA. Listen, Lena, if anything should happen to me, will you promise to take care of the children——

NURSE. But you make me so terribly frightened, ma'am. Is anything the matter?

NORA. No, no, but nobody can tell what may happen. Oh, Lena, you must never desert them, so long as they need you. Will you promise me that?

NURSE (*in tears*). Didn't I look after Nora when she was little and had no mother? Can Nora think that I should desert her little children?

NORA. No, of course not, I know that very well, Lena. Oh, the little darlings will still be well, if I am not—. But it isn't certain that anything will happen. So many strange things happen in the world; so many people are saved from great misfortunes. Very often it turns out to be only a dream. Oh, how splendid it would be to wake up and come to one's senses and cry out, I've been dreaming, I've been dreaming!

NURSE. But, in heaven's name, ma'am——

NORA. You mustn't look so frightened. I had so little sleep last night.

NURSE. Yes, that's the fault of all these parties. Oh, ma'am, is it wise?—out every single evening the whole Christmas week; out till late at night.

NORA. Ah, but it's lovely, Lena—there's music and lights, and beautiful clothes—and so much amusement; one forgets; one doesn't think—Oh, but it's lovely to live, Lena—to be young—to be really alive. Look, how the sun is shining—the snow is dripping off the roofs; it is not cold, as you said—it's spring weather—we shall soon have spring—and—Spring!

NURSE. What is it, ma'am? You're as white as a sheet.

NORA. Oh, it was fearful.

NURSE. What? What was it?

NORA. I was thinking of the terrible story you told me when I was little.

NURSE. I?

NORA. Don't you remember the girl who lived near us, who had helped to murder her father and was executed? When they came to fetch her she screamed: No, not now in the spring-time! Not now in the sunshine!— Yes, it is terrible to die in the spring-time and in the sunshine.

NURSE. As I'm alive, as soon as the Doctor comes I'll——

NORA. You're not to say a single word to the Doctor. You silly old Lena—(*laughing*) how could you be so frightened—ha, ha, ha—can't you guess that I was joking——

NURSE. Well, then God forgive Nora——

NORA. Yes, yes, it was horrid of me. (*Petting her.*) Don't be angry; I'll never do it again. Oh, now you're laughing! That's right; go in to the children——

NURSE. Yes, I'll go. But I'll never forget how frightened I was.   (*She goes into the nursery.*)

NORA. There, there. Now I'll go out. Only not to think. Only not to think.—What a delicious muff! Beautiful gloves! Beautiful gloves!—To forget!—One, two, three, four, five, six— (*With a scream.*) Ah, who's that?

STENBORG (*at the hall hoor*). Heavens! what's happening?

NORA. Oh, is it you?

STENBORG. Of course. Is that anything to be frightened of, silly little girl? But how worn-out you look, my dear Nora. What is the matter with you?

NORA. You know, we were up very late last night.

STENBORG. Much too late. But we'll make an end of that.

NORA. Yes, there will soon be an end of that.

STENBORG. Fortunately. After New Year's Day, work will begin.

NORA. New Year's Day;—why, that's to-morrow.

STENBORG. And the day after to-morrow, business. Are you going out——?

NORA. Yes.

STENBORG. What, again? You've already been out once to-day.

NORA. If you would rather, I will stay at home.

STENBORG. No, go if you like; it will bring the roses back into your cheeks. They suit you so well. My little elf mustn't have such pale cheeks and tired eyes. I must have you about me, well and fresh and lively, to make me feel happy and comfortable. (*Kissing her.*) There, now go; I'll get on with my work. I've been down to the Bank and brought home these papers.

NORA. To the Bank? Have you already——?

STENBORG. It's only some details that I want to make myself more familiar with. Good-bye; go now; but don't catch cold.

NORA. Thorvald.

STENBORG. Yes.

NORA. If your little squirrel were to beg you for something so prettily?

STENBORG. Well?

NORA. Would you do it?

STENBORG. I must first know what it is.

NORA. The squirrel would skip about and play all sorts of tricks if you would do it.

STENBORG. Out with it.

NORA. Your lark would twitter from morning till night——

STENBORG. Nora——

NORA. Your elf would dance for you, Thorvald——

STENBORG. I understand. Have you really the courage to ask me that again——?

NORA. I beg and implore you, Thorvald!

STENBORG. You have done that every single day this week.

NORA. Yes, but to-day you will do what I ask.

STENBORG. I shall not. What has put it into your head to be so frightened of this person, to be afraid I shall make an enemy of him, that he will write against me in the newspapers? It is an insult to me, Nora, a double insult, first to think that I am weak and then that I am afraid.

NORA. No, no, no, it's not an insult. Oh, we could live so quietly and happily now, in our cosy, peaceful home, you and I and the children.—The children, the children, Thorvald!

STENBORG. The children? What about them?

NORA. Oh, Thorvald, you must do what I ask. Remember, it is the last day of the year. This is the last thing I shall ask of you this year.

STENBORG. And you would end the year by carrying through a wilful fancy? Yes, you are wilful, Nora; you have never learnt to overcome your whims. That is your father's fault. He was too indulgent with you. I'm sure he was never able to deny you anything. And I haven't been able to, either. I am partly to blame. But this must be changed; it is for your own good.

NORA. Yes, after this! Be strict, Thorvald—be as strict as you like; but do what I ask just this once. Do you hear, Thorvald——

STENBORG. We'll put an end to this. (*Rings the bell by the door to the hall.*)

NORA. What do you want?

STENBORG. To settle the thing. (THE MAID *enters*.)
Here; take this letter; give it to a messenger. See that
he takes it at once. The address is on it. Here's the
money.

MAID. Very well, sir. (*Goes out.*)

STENBORG. There, my little song-bird.

NORA. Thorvald, what was in the letter?

STENBORG. It was a business letter.

NORA. What was in the letter, Thorvald.

STENBORG. Krogstad's dismissal.

NORA. Call it back again, Thorvald! There's still
time.

STENBORG. There is no time; he must have it before
the year is out.

NORA. Oh, call it back again, Thorvald! For my
sake. For your own sake. For the children's sake.
Oh, Thorvald, you don't know what you're doing.

STENBORG. Have I deserved this of you—this anxiety?
Yes, Nora, it is a slur upon me. I understand very well
what you are thinking of. You remember all the accusations and denunciations and newspaper attacks that your
father in his time was exposed to, and that caused him so
many bitter hours. And now you are afraid that I—;
that is what offends me, Nora. But you ought to know
that I am unimpeachable, while your father was not.

NORA. Thorvald!

STENBORG. No, your father was not a methodical
official, Nora. I can give you an example; I have never
cared to tell you before, but now you shall know it. The
twelve hundred dollars that he gave you when you in-
sisted on going to Italy were never even entered in his
accounts; it is quite impossible to find out where he got
them from.

NORA. My poor, poor father.

STENBORG. My dearest Nora, I'm not saying that to hurt you, but to make you understand what a difference there is between him and me. I make no reproach against your father; he was the kindest-hearted man, much too good; and he was on his death-bed at the time.

NORA. Oh, what a good thing it was that father died!

STENBORG. There, there, there, my little song-bird! We won't have any of that. What are you saying? That it's a good thing to die? Is that the sort of thing for little song-birds, who are just beginning to live? Now then, a cheerful face, to give me light and warmth. Isn't that what you're for?

NORA. Who's that coming?

STENBORG. What, anxious again?

(DOCTOR RANK *comes in from the hall.*)

RANK. Good-day to you. All well?

STENBORG. Oh, fairly.

NORA. Yes, thanks, Doctor.

STENBORG. But you don't look too well yourself.

RANK. I am running down hill; there's no help for it.

STENBORG. Oh, but, my dear friend.

RANK. Yes, yes—why lie to one's self? In these last days I have been auditing my life-account. A confoundedly wretched result. I may be tolerably certain that this is the last New Year's Eve I shall see. A year hence I shall lie rotting in the churchyard.

NORA. Ugh, that's frightful——

RANK. Well, one has to go some day. But to suffer thus for another's sin! Where's the justice of it? And yet you can trace in every family an inexorable retribution. It is my father's wild oats that my poor spinal marrow must do penance for.

STENBORG. Oh, you'll last a long while yet with that spinal marrow.

RANK. Like a Lazarus; it isn't a very tempting prospect. Ah, for a healthy, happy person it must be a desperate thing to have to go. For one who has a home, a circle of dear ones around him——

NORA. Good-bye.

RANK. Are you going out?

NORA. Yes, yes; I must have some fresh air. Good-bye. (*She goes out.*)

RANK. Is anything the matter with her?

STENBORG. I don't know what to say; she has been like that all the week, in an unnaturally excited condition; she has all kinds of needless anxieties; it seems as if she was not at ease in the house; she no longer plays with the children——

RANK. It is the great change in your position——

STENBORG. Yes, it must come from that. She seems to be constantly tormented by the idea that it will not last.

RANK. I see, I see.

STENBORG. At first she was so exuberantly happy about it. You can imagine—with her light-hearted disposition, how she felt on being suddenly placed in a position free from care and even opulent. My poor little Nora; I blame myself for not having prepared her more cautiously.

RANK. Yes, perhaps you ought to have done so.

STENBORG. But I couldn't guess—and besides, I couldn't deny myself the pleasure of seeing her so radiantly happy. (NORA *re-enters.*) What? Are you back already?

NORA. Yes, I couldn't stand it. I had such a feeling of anxiety; one never knows what may happen when one is out. I must see the children—(*Goes to the door and lays her hand on the handle, but quickly withdraws it.*)

STENBORG. Why don't you go in?

NORA. No, no, I won't go to them. There's no need to; I can hear that everything is quiet; I will stay here with you.

STENBORG. Well, you must dispense with my society for half an hour, my dear Nora.

NORA. Oh, no, no, Thorvald, don't go out.

STENBORG. I don't intend to; I must do some work in my room. But Rank will stay a little while—(*Signs to him.*) Won't you? I think you said——

RANK. Yes, I shall be glad to walk about a little on your new carpet.

STENBORG. And I'll make fast my door. No one is to come in; no disturbers of the peace; no squirrels among my papers—

(*Goes into his room and bolts the door.*)

NORA (*taking off her hat and cloak*). Don't you think it's frightfully warm, Doctor?

RANK. No, on the contrary.

NORA. You're cold, perhaps?

RANK. Not that either. You keep a pleasant temperature as usual. That is one of the wonderful gifts that many women have—when one enters their rooms, one is permeated, as it were, by a gentle sense of well-being.

NORA. Oh, yes, it is pleasant here.

RANK. Yes, isn't it? We bachelors have a keen sense for such things. And we know how to appreciate them. The worthy husbands don't always do that. They get so used to it; they think that all these blessings are a matter of course, something that follows quite naturally from the fact that one is alive. It is the same as with a constant unremitting noise; one does not notice it until it ceases. I am almost certain that this is

the case with Stenborg.   Now that your circumstances
allow it, you ought now and then to leave him for a day
or two.

NORA (*after a short pause*).   Do you think he would
miss me much, if I were away?

RANK.   Try.

NORA.   Oh, no, no, no.   For heaven's sake, don't
speak like that.   Who would do such a thing voluntarily?
To leave him and the children!

RANK.   I knew it.   But *with* him, Mrs. Stenborg?
With him and the children too.

NORA.   Ah, that would be lovely.

RANK.   To get away a little; to see the great open
sea again—you who are so fond of the sea.

NORA.   Oh, yes, the sea, the sea!   Isn't the sea
splendid?

RANK.   And then, to see your home from a distance,
in a new light.

NORA.   And to come back again, to go round one's
own rooms, arranging all the beautiful things one has
brought home, to play with the children, to see them
growing strong and— (*In terror.*)   Ah!——

RANK.   What's the matter?

NORA.   Oh, it was nothing; it was something I just
remembered, something that had escaped my memory.

RANK.   May I feel your pulse?

NORA.   No, no, there's nothing wrong with me; I assure you——

RANK.   There is something on your mind, in any case.
Do you think it is any use denying that to me?   And why
do you wish to deny it?   Why hide anything from an
old friend?   For I am one, am I not?

NORA.   Oh, Doctor Rank!

RANK.   Well, what is it?

Nora. No, no, I can't.—Well, tell me this, Doctor; is Thorvald quite strong now?

Rank. Yes, certainly he is.

Nora. Are you quite sure that he could stand a great shock, a great grief, or anything of that sort?

Rank. What kind of a shock or grief are you talking about?

Nora. I can't tell; so many things might happen. At the time he was ill you said he must avoid any strong emotion.

Rank. Yes, at that time.

Nora. And do you think after all that Thorvald is so immoderately fond of me?

Rank. But, my dear Mrs. Stenborg——

Nora. Perhaps it would be well if he were not so. And yet I think he would surely be able to bear it, he would surely get over it.

Rank. What, Mrs. Stenborg? What?

Nora. If anything happened to me. Doctor, I am so fearfully anxious. My head is so confused. Suppose I went out of my mind?

Rank. What is the meaning of this? What makes you think of such things?

Nora. Oh, one never knows—. Or if something else happened to me; if I could not stay with him any longer——

Rank. What?

Nora. Oh, Doctor, he would surely be able to survive it.

Rank. My dear Mrs. Stenborg, these are fancies that you must struggle against with all your might.

Nora. Oh, yes; oh, yes; I shall do that. But tell me, don't you think that Thorvald would survive it, like other men, if he lost me?

RANK. Well, you see, this idea of a thing being the death of a person is in most cases nothing but a figure of speech, at any rate as far as the male sex is concerned. As a matter of fact, we survive everything, my dear Mrs. Stenborg. At the moment when the blow falls, it seems impossible to bear it. But time passes, day after day, and one learns to accept the inevitable, one makes fresh ties——

NORA. Fresh ties——!

RANK. Well, I mean——

NORA. Fresh ties—! I hadn't thought of that. But no, no, no!

RANK. I must speak to Stenborg.

NORA. What will you speak about?

RANK. About your condition.

NORA. You won't! You mustn't do that!

RANK. I must. All this is so inexplicable and so serious——

NORA. Oh, I beg you not to alarm him.

RANK. Don't be uneasy, I'll do it as gently as possible; but both for his sake and your own we must find some way——

NORA. Oh, there is no way of escaping from this.

RANK. From what?

NORA. From what is going to happen; I don't know, but I feel——

RANK. H'm— (*Knocks.*) Open the door, I must speak to you.

STENBORG (*opening his door*). Well?

RANK. Look here— (*Softly.*) Don't be uneasy, Mrs. Stenborg! (*He and* STENBORG *go into the room; the bolting of the door is heard.*)

NORA (*listening at the door*). What are they talking about? They are whispering. What are they saying

about me? What does he think? Oh, it isn't yet—.
In to the children. (*Stops before the door on the left.*)
No, no, mustn't see them. (Mrs. Linde *enters from
the hall.*) Oh, Christina, is that you? I'm so glad
you have come.

Mrs. Linde. I hear you called at my lodgings.

Nora. Yes, but you had just gone out. I'm so glad
you have come. I want so much to see you and speak
to you.

Mrs. Linde. And I have come to thank your husband——

Nora. Have you heard already?

Mrs. Linde. Yes, I have just got the letter. Perhaps he is not at home?

Nora. Yes, he is; but Doctor Rank is with him. Sit
down here with me till he comes. No, don't sit down.
I'm so restless. Let us walk up and down.

Mrs. Linde. Nora dear, you're not well, are you?

Nora. Oh, yes, oh, yes. So you've heard from him?
You got the letter, you said?

Mrs. Linde. Yes, just as I was going out. Oh, it
is a great kindness that your husband has shown me.

Nora. I hope it will bring you happiness.

Mrs. Linde. I feel happy already. In my position
there is no greater happiness than to feel one's self secure.

Nora. Yes, you're right there; it is a great happiness
to feel one's self secure.

Mrs. Linde. Ah, you can't appreciate the feeling as
I do; you have never been tortured by insecurity.

Nora. Haven't I? Have I not been tortured by
anxiety for my husband's life?

Mrs. Linde. That is true. Well, fortunately that
time is past.

NORA. Ah, secure, secure. That is a great thing indeed. There is no greater happiness in the world. (*Rings.*) But who can feel really secure? (THE MAID *appears at the door.*) Bring in tea.——

MRS. LINDE. So you're going to a dance overhead to-morrow?

NORA. To-morrow? Yes, of course. I shall go up to it. It's to be a children's party. I'm going for the sake of the children. (THE MAID *enters with tea.*) Thank you, move the table nearer the stove. And then bring us the lamp. (*Exit* MAID.) Now then, you must take a seat and make yourself comfortable.

MAID (*brings the lamp and puts it on the table by the sofa*). Is there anything else, ma'am?

NORA. No, thank you. (*Exit* MAID.) Now you shall taste real tea, Christina. I always have the best kind.

MRS. LINDE. And the best of tea-things too. How pretty and tasteful! And how well it all harmonises!

NORA. Yes, Thorvald will have everything like that; there must be style about it, he says, or it offends his eye. You see, the pattern on the cups corresponds to the pattern on the napkins.

MRS. LINDE. Yes, indeed you have pretty things.

NORA. And in future we shall have them still prettier. In future——!

MRS. LINDE. What is the matter, Nora?

NORA. Hush; it was nothing; it was only a pain in the side. Look here; take the footstool for your feet. Now we're comfortable; aren't we?

MRS. LINDE. Yes. You really have a talent for making one comfortable.

NORA. Thorvald says the same.

Mrs. Linde. Ah, what would become of your husband if he had not you?

Nora. If he had not—? What makes you think of that? Why shouldn't he have me?

Mrs. Linde. Oh, of course. I'm only saying, *if* he had not you.

Nora. Don't you think somebody could be found who would look after him just as well?

Mrs. Linde. Not in his eyes.

Nora. Yet one often sees a man able to forget his first wife.

Mrs. Linde. Yes, and many a wife can forget her first husband.

Nora. But can you understand that, Christina?

Mrs. Linde. Oh, well, it depends——

Nora. Ah, but divorce, now; I don't think I can understand that.

Mrs. Linde. No. But it happens nevertheless, my dear Nora; and it *must* happen.

Nora. Yes, yes, I know that; but it seems to me it must be so awful, so absolutely impossible to get over——

Mrs. Linde. Yes, it must be a hard struggle, no doubt.

Nora. To have to leave one's house, everything; never to be allowed to see it again; to know that everything is there, but that one is as it were dead to it—. Tell me, Christina, what is it that usually makes married people separate?

Mrs. Linde. It may be that they don't agree, or that one of them has brought shame upon the other.

Nora. Then the husband divorces his wife?

Mrs. Linde. Yes, in most cases, I suppose.

Nora. But sometimes he forgives her, doesn't he?

Mrs. Linde. No doubt; but do you think that would be better?

Nora. No, you are right. It would not be better.—And the children, an unhappy divorced wife would not be allowed to keep them either? Is that really so?

Mrs. Linde. Yes, I believe so; that is, if she is the guilty party.

Nora. Oh, guilty, guilty; what does it mean, being guilty? Has not a wife the right to love her husband?

Mrs. Linde. Precisely; her husband—and only her husband.

Nora. Yes, of course, who is thinking of anything else? But that law is unjust, Christina. It is easy enough to see that it was made by men.

Mrs. Linde. Aha! you are beginning to go in for Woman's Rights.

Nora. No, I don't care about them at all. Do you, perhaps?

Mrs. Linde. Not in the least. I leave that to others; I have enough to do in fighting my own battle.

Nora. So have I.

Mrs. Linde. You?

Nora. Well, I mean—I think of all the unhappy mothers and unhappy little children. Christina, to think of one's little children in the hands of strangers!

Mrs. Linde. That is better than that they should be with a criminal mother.

Nora. Oh, there are terrible things in the world.

(The Maid opens the door to Krogstad.)

Maid (softly). Madam——!

Nora (turns and starts; in a low and trembling voice). There he is!

Mrs. Linde (in the same tone). He! What does he want?

NORA (*to* THE MAID). It's all right; go.
(THE MAID *goes out.* KROGSTAD *approaches.*)
KROGSTAD. I'm afraid I'm disturbing you, ladies?
NORA. What do you want? My husband is not at home.
KROGSTAD. But I think he is in there.
NORA. Yes, but he can't see anyone.
KROGSTAD. He needn't either——
NORA. Go, Christina; go in to the children.
MRS. LINDE. Nora, what is this?
NORA. Go, go, Christina; I must speak to this man.
MRS. LINDE. I understand.
NORA. Oh, you don't understand anything.
MRS. LINDE. I understand. Krogstad—what have you come to?
KROGSTAD. To what—you drove me to.
MRS. LINDE. Ah——
KROGSTAD. It is too late now.
MRS. LINDE. Krogstad—we must talk by-and-bye.
KROGSTAD. Too late.
NORA. Go, go——
(MRS. LINDE *goes into the room on the left.*)
NORA (*in suspense*). Now?
KROGSTAD. Yes, now.
NORA. Mr. Krogstad, you won't do it.
KROGSTAD. Did he hesitate to do what he did?
NORA. Ah, but that was not my fault.
KROGSTAD. The wife must suffer for the husband's fault.
NORA. Oh, you don't know how I fought and pleaded your cause.
KROGSTAD. Did you do that from sympathy with me?
NORA. Oh, I've been fighting for my life these last days.

KROGSTAD. Bah, for your life! I too thought that
my life was at stake when I got into trouble—but you
see, Mrs. Helmer, I have survived it.

NORA. Yes, you—but how——?

KROGSTAD. How——?

NORA. But I can't live such a life as—as——

KROGSTAD. As I do, you mean——

NORA. Pardon me——

KROGSTAD. You'll see, you'll get along all right in
time.

NORA. Mr. Krogstad, think of my little children——

KROGSTAD. Did your husband think of my children,
when he closed my last road to recovery?

NORA. O God, O God, to die so young—to have to
leave my husband and children——

KROGSTAD. And you want me to believe that you have
the courage to die—ha, ha!——

NORA. You don't believe it?

KROGSTAD. Do you believe it yourself?

NORA. I have thought of nothing else the last few
days.

KROGSTAD. I dare say. But the means? Poison?
Not so easy to get. Shoot yourself? That wants some
practice, Mrs. Helmer. Hanging? Fie, there's something ugly about it—you get cut down; you would never
bring yourself to do that.

NORA. Do you hear it roaring?

KROGSTAD. The river? Yes, of course, that is what
you've been thinking of. But haven't you thought just
casually—Think now of putting it into execution—Out
of the house at night—down into the foaming black water
—to be carried along, dragged under the ice—to struggle,
be suffocated, and to be fished up—some day, from far
below—and in what a state——

NORA. Oh, it is horrible—oh, that I could not—Oh, it is horrible——

KROGSTAD. What, madam——?

NORA. You see it, don't you? It's no use concealing it; I have not the courage to die.

KROGSTAD. I thought you hadn't; but I wanted to make sure——

NORA. And then?

KROGSTAD. There is no need to, either. Nobody but your husband will know anything.

NORA. Oh, but he is the last person who must——

KROGSTAD. I dare say you have read in novels of villains whose only motive is revenge. Well, it might be very pleasant if everyone could say: Look, the wife of the bank manager is not a bit better than that pettifogger Krogstad, whom her husband dismissed——

NORA. But you won't reveal anything?

KROGSTAD. I can't afford to, Mrs. Helmer. In my first moments of despair I thought of doing so, but I can't afford it. I am not like the villains in romances; I have four children to support; they require food and clothing. For more than a year and a half I have been content with the most straitened circumstances, in order to retrieve my character. Now your husband has barred my way. Very well then, I will at any rate live, and live well, my children shall be well looked after—Here is the letter—this will tell him everything—and then he will have an avalanche hanging over him; he will be in my power, I can do what I like with him—make what demands I like; he won't dare to show fight; it will be the dismissed junior clerk that manages the bank——

NORA. You will do that?

KROGSTAD. That and nothing else.

NORA. That will be taking his future away from him.

KROGSTAD.   He has taken my future away from me.

NORA.   This bank represents his life's work.   And he is to give it up and become dependent on you.

KROGSTAD.   He will do that for love of you.

NORA.   The fault is mine.   And I did it for love of him.

KROGSTAD.   Our deeds all have offspring—but the progeny does not always turn out as it ought.

NORA.   And you can do this thing.

KROGSTAD.   I have four children.

NORA.   Mr. Krogstad, you won't do it.

KROGSTAD.   Here is the letter.

NORA.   Give it to me.

KROGSTAD.   To deliver?

NORA.   Yes, yes.

KROGSTAD.   Thanks; there is a letter-box at the door; it is perhaps safer——

NORA.   You don't know what this will bring in its train.

KROGSTAD.   The river?

NORA.   Yes, now there is nothing else for it.   If I do not go under, my husband will.

KROGSTAD.   I don't believe in romances, Mrs. Helmer.

NORA.   You are a wretch! Yes, you are a wretch. I'm not afraid of you any longer, for now I have no choice——

KROGSTAD.   Oh yes, you have—if only your husband yields——

NORA.   He will not—he shall never be tempted to do so.   Now I have courage for anything.

KROGSTAD.   Bah——

NORA.   Away from this home that you have ruined.

KROGSTAD.   I? Not you?

NORA. What I did was done for love of my father and my husband.

KROGSTAD. And what I am doing is done for love of my children.

NORA. This will bring no blessing upon your children.

KROGSTAD. You think not?

NORA. You will see what this deed brings in its train.

KROGSTAD. Bah!

NORA. You will see; you feel it yourself—you are cowardly—you dare not—you're going, you're taking the letter with you.

KROGSTAD (*at the hall door*). Bah! (*Goes out.*)

NORA. Wretch!—Ah—the letter. In the box.—There it lies.

(MRS. LINDE *enters from the room on the left.*)

MRS. LINDE. Hasn't he gone?

NORA. Yes.

MRS. LINDE. And he won't come back?

NORA. He will never come back any more.

MRS. LINDE. Nora, what is the matter with you? What is there behind all this?

NORA. Nothing at all; but don't tell my husband that he was here.

MRS. LINDE. Nora, you and he have some secret between you.

NORA (*smiling*). Yes, of course; a secret understanding.

MRS. LINDE. If you were really joking, you would not be so deadly pale.

NORA. Can you see that?

MRS. LINDE. Your husband will also be able to see it.

NORA. My husband shall not see anything; I have more faces than one.

MRS. LINDE. Nora, Nora, you are surrounding yourself with hollowness.

NORA. Oh, but isn't it beautiful here?

MRS. LINDE. Without truth?

NORA. Truth? We may not think of that.

MRS. LINDE. But would it not be better if you could?

NORA. We must not ask too much; we must be satisfied with a little; soon I shall have to be satisfied with——

MRS. LINDE. With——?

NORA. With nothing.

MRS. LINDE. Nora, it is no use concealing anything from me. I understand it all. What you told me the first time. This secret with Krogstad——

NORA. Well, what then?

MRS. LINDE. I—I used to know him long ago. I have reasons for wanting to know this. Is he a bad, a despicable person?

NORA. I don't know; I only know that he is terrible.

MRS. LINDE. From what do you know that?

NORA (*opening the door to the hall*). Look; there is a letter in the box.

MRS. LINDE. From him?

NORA. Yes.

MRS. LINDE. To your husband?

NORA. Yes.

MRS. LINDE. I must speak to Krogstad.

NORA. It is too late.

MRS. LINDE. Who knows?

NORA. Too late, I tell you—there lies the letter.

MRS. LINDE. Good-bye. (*Goes out at the back.*)

NORA. No, no; I'm dreaming. All this is a dream.

(*Looks out into the hall.*)   Yes, there it lies.   The whole story is in there.

(HELMER *and* DOCTOR RANK *enter from the room on the right.*)

NORA.   Are you coming at last, Thorvald?   I'm so glad you've come.   Shame on you, Doctor, for keeping him so long——

HELMER.   We had something to talk about.   How is my little song-bird?

NORA.   The song-bird is very well; you can see that, can't you?

HELMER.   Yes, I think so too—   (*To* RANK.)   But what can it be, then——?

RANK.   H'm——

NORA.   What?   Which?

HELMER.   Oh, nothing at all.

NORA.   Oh yes, I know.   Just think, Doctor Rank insists that I shall be ill.

HELMER.   Yes, that's it; it's all nonsense.   We be ill?   Would this be a time—now that we have everything we have wished for so long?   Now we are going to keep New Year's Eve in peace and harmony.   All business is to wait till the new year.

NORA.   Yes, isn't it, Thorvald?

HELMER.   Yes, I won't touch either pen or book to-night.   But, by-the-bye, I must just——

(*Going to hall door.*)

NORA.   Where are you going?

HELMER.   Just to see if there are any letters.

NORA.   No, no, Thorvald——

HELMER.   Why not?

NORA.   No, no, I beg you not to—there are none there——

HELMER.   Let me just see.

Nora (*plays a few chords at the piano*).

Helmer (*stops at the door*).   Aha!

Nora.   Do you know it?

Helmer.   Will you really?

Nora.   What shall I have for a reward?

Helmer.   What do you want?

Nora.   I'll tell you afterwards.

Helmer.   No, now.

Nora.   No, afterwards.   Do you promise me?

Helmer.   Is it something you have asked me before?

Nora.   No, never.   Now do you promise?

Helmer.   Yes, I promise.   (*To* Rank.)   Now listen to this.   But we must have cigarettes with it; real Turkish ones.

> (*He and* Rank *sit by the stove.* Nora *plays and sings Anitra's song from* Peer Gynt.)

Mrs. Linde (*enters from the hall*).   Oh, but what is this?

Nora.   Don't interrupt.

Helmer.   A picture of family life.   What do you say to it?

Rank.   Turkish, but pretty; is it not?

Nora.   Sit down to the piano, Christina; go on playing.   (*She drapes herself in shawls and dances.*)

Helmer.   How lovely she is, Rank.   Look at the fine curve of the neck.   What grace in her movements, and she is quite unconscious of it.

Rank.   A wife is a good thing.

Helmer.   A wife like her.

Nora.   Are you pleased?

Helmer.   Thanks!

Nora.   Was it pretty?

Helmer.   Thanks, thanks!

THE MAID (*enters from the right*). Dinner is ready.

HELMER. Good. But business first——

(*Opens the door to the hall.*)

NORA. Where are you going?

HELMER. To look in the letter-box.

NORA. No, no.

HELMER. There's a letter in it.

NORA. Don't take it out! Let it lie there.

HELMER. But, my dear Nora—; aha, it's from Krogstad.

NORA. Thorvald, if you take it out, I'll jump out of the window.

HELMER. But, Nora——

RANK. H'm, Helmer——

HELMER. What is it, Nora? What is the matter with you?

NORA. Oh, nothing, but I want you all to myself. No business this evening—oh, you know very well what he is writing about——

HELMER. Yes, exactly; but I should like to see all the same.——

NORA. You promised me what I asked. So now, you are not to open the letter-box this evening, nor to-morrow either——

HELMER. But, my dear little Nora——

NORA. He promised, Doctor, didn't he?

RANK. Yes, you are bound, Helmer.

NORA. No worries on holidays—and to-morrow you won't have any time for business; visits all day long, and the party upstairs in the evening——

HELMER. Very well, so be it. To-day and to-morrow I exist for you—but I give you notice—to-morrow, after midnight——

MRS. LINDE. Oh, you surely don't work after midnight——

HELMER. I am accustomed to it, Mrs. Linde. But now let us go to dinner and drink to the old year and to all our hopes in the new.

NORA. Lead the way. Help me to take off all this finery, Christina.

RANK (to HELMER, *as they go out*). You see, she is not at all normal.

HELMER. I assure you, it is nothing but anxiety about me; she has a foolish terror of that man.

(*They go out.*)

NORA. Well?

MRS. LINDE. He's gone away already.

NORA. I told you so.

MRS. LINDE. But he'll be back to-morrow.

NORA. How will that help? Thorvald has seen the letter.

MRS. LINDE. He does not know what is in it; we must get hold of it.

NORA. Krogstad will write another.

MRS. LINDE. Is it so bad then?

NORA. No, no, certainly not; it is silly of me. Don't let them see anything in your manner. Go in to them; I'll manage myself.

(MRS. LINDE *goes into the dining-room.*)

NORA (*taking off the shawls*). Thorvald in his power? no, thank you, I didn't save his life for that. But—no, no, there is no going back now. (*Looks at the clock.*) Five. Seven hours till midnight. Then twenty-four hours till the next midnight. Twenty-four and seven? Thirty-one hours to live. (*She goes out.*)

THIRD ACT

The same room. A lighted lamp on the table in front. Mrs. Linde sits by the table and absently turns the pages of a book. She tries to read, but seems unable to fix her attention; she frequently listens and looks anxiously towards the hall; then looks at her watch.)

Mrs. Linde (*jumping up*). What! Already? No, it is not——

Nora (*enters in evening dress*). What! Christina, are you here?

Mrs. Linde. Oh, is that you, Nora?

Nora. Are you sitting here, Christina?

Mrs. Linde. Yes, I wanted to see you dressed; but I came too late. It was cold at my rooms, and so I stayed sitting here.

Nora. I see; but you must go again——

Mrs. Linde. Why?

Nora. Yes, yes, you must go.

Mrs. Linde. Have you left the party so early?

Nora. Yes, I could not bear it; it was so hot and stifling. (Helmer *enters from the hall.*)

Helmer. But, my dear Nora, what is the meaning of this? Are you leaving the party so early? And without saying good-bye? Ah, good evening, Mrs. Linde!

Nora. Yes, I had to. I knew Christina was here. She came to see my new dress.

Helmer. Well, but come up again; it looks so bad——

Nora. Yes, yes, I'll go up and fetch the children— but then— Oh, I can't stay long, Thorvald; but you must stay; dance and amuse yourself—promise me that.

Helmer. Yes, yes—only do come. Good-night, Mrs. Linde—and excuse us.

NORA. Good-night, Christina—good-night, good-bye —you must not sit here any longer, with your weak eyes. Now you have seen my dress. Don't you think it suits me very well? When you think of me—then remember me as I am now. Good-night—good-bye, Christina—good-bye——

MRS. LINDE. Good-night, my dear Nora.

HELMER. Come, come, we must go.

NORA. Good-night, good-bye.

(HELMER *and* NORA *go out through the hall.*)

MRS. LINDE (*listens for a moment*). What terrible mental anguish! And he does not see it. He understands nothing.—But the time—if he should not— (*Listens.*) Ah——(*Opens the door into the hall; three soft knocks are heard on the outer door;* MRS. LINDE *opens it.* KROGSTAD *enters.*)

MRS. LINDE. Come in here. There is no one here.

KROGSTAD. You have written to me. What does it mean?

MRS. LINDE. Yes, I had to; I could not see you at my rooms—there is nobody at home here.

KROGSTAD. Have we anything to say to each other?

MRS. LINDE. A great deal.

KROGSTAD. I should not have thought so.

MRS. LINDE. You have never understood me.

KROGSTAD. What was there to understand that was not perfectly plain? So many men are thrown over when a better match offers.

MRS. LINDE. Do you think I broke with you lightly?

KROGSTAD. Did you not?

MRS. LINDE. Do you really think so?

KROGSTAD. Why then did you write me that letter?

MRS. LINDE. Could I do anything else? Was not everything to be broken off between us?

KROGSTAD. Yes, for the sake of profit.

MRS. LINDE. Do you forget that I had a helpless mother and two little brothers? You had no prospects at all.

KROGSTAD. Did that give you the right to cast me off?

MRS. LINDE. I don't know. I have often asked myself whether I had the right.

KROGSTAD. When I had lost you, I seemed to lose all firm footing in life. Look at me now. I am a shipwrecked man clinging to a spar.

MRS. LINDE. Rescue may be at hand.

KROGSTAD. You can say that, when you are helping to loosen my hold?

MRS. LINDE. Do you think I shall do that?

KROGSTAD. Are you not in league with my persecutors?

MRS. LINDE. Oh? And why do you think that?

KROGSTAD. It won't be the first time that hatred is felt for one who has been wronged.

MRS. LINDE. Krogstad, you don't think that of me?

KROGSTAD. Then what am I to believe? Are you not taking the place that I have lost?

MRS. LINDE. Yes.

KROGSTAD. And could you do that if——?

MRS. LINDE. I have learnt prudence; life and bitter necessity have schooled me.

KROGSTAD. And life has taught me not to trust fine speeches.

MRS. LINDE. Then life has taught you a very sensible thing. But deeds you will trust?

KROGSTAD. What do you mean?

MRS. LINDE. You said you were a shipwrecked man, clinging to a spar.

KROGSTAD. I have good reason to say so.

MRS. LINDE.   I too am shipwrecked, and clinging to a spar; I have no one to mourn for, no one to care for.

KROGSTAD.   You make your own choice.

MRS. LINDE.   Do not let us dispute about that; for me there was no choice left.

KROGSTAD.   Well, what then?

MRS. LINDE.   Nils, how if we two shipwrecked people could join hands?

KROGSTAD.   What do you mean?

MRS. LINDE.   Two on one raft have a better chance than if each clings to a separate spar.

KROGSTAD.   Christina!

MRS. LINDE.   What do you think brought me here?

KROGSTAD.   Could it be——?

MRS. LINDE.   I must have work, or I can't bear to live; I have worked all my life, and it has been my one great happiness.   Now I stand alone, aimless and forlorn.   There is no happiness in working for one's self. Nils, give me somebody and something to work for.

KROGSTAD.   I cannot believe in all this.   It is a woman's romantic craving for self-sacrifice.

MRS. LINDE (*smiling*).   H'm, I am the last person to be called romantic.

KROGSTAD.   And you could—?   Do you know all that is said about me?

MRS. LINDE.   You said that with me you would have been another man.

KROGSTAD.   Well——?

MRS. LINDE.   Is it too late?

KROGSTAD.   Christina, have you thought what you are doing?   Will you—?   Will you*——?

* Krogstad here changes from the formal *De* to the intimate *du* (thou).

MRS. LINDE. I need some one to be a mother to, and your children need a mother. You need me, and I need you. You told me you wanted to show the world that some one will trust you in a post of confidence. I will.

KROGSTAD. Now, Christina, I shall raise myself.— Ah, I forgot—; the whole thing is impossible——

MRS. LINDE. Why?

KROGSTAD. You don't know—; I have taken a step against this house——

MRS. LINDE. I know.

KROGSTAD. You know it?

MRS. LINDE. And I know to what lengths despair can drive a man.

KROGSTAD. Oh, if I could only undo it!

MRS. LINDE. You could. Your letter is still in the box.

KROGSTAD. Are you sure?

MRS. LINDE. Yes; but——

KROGSTAD. Now I understand. You want to save your friend at any price. Say it out—is that your idea?

MRS. LINDE. Nils, a woman who has once sold herself for the sake of others, does not do so again.

KROGSTAD. The letter shall be got back again.

MRS. LINDE. No, no.

KROGSTAD. There is still time. I shall wait here, ask for it, say that it is about my dismissal—but that I have accepted the situation——

MRS. LINDE. You must not recall it.

KROGSTAD. But wasn't it about the letter that you got me to come here?

MRS. LINDE. Yes, in my first moment of terror; but a day has passed since then. Helmer must know everything. This unhappy secret will undermine their marriage if it is allowed to remain. There must be perfect frankness. These shifts and subterfuges lead to ruin.

KROGSTAD. Christina, your friend has not told you everything.

MRS. LINDE. Is there more than the debt——?

KROGSTAD. H'm——

MRS. LINDE. Make haste! Go, go!—some one is coming downstairs. Wait for me at the door [in the street]; you must see me to my door.

KROGSTAD. I shall wait; and you will see. Oh, Christina, thanks, thanks, you have made a new man of me. (*He goes out quickly.*)

MRS. LINDE (*putting on her outdoor things*). He thanks me, and it is I—; now there is work to do——

(NORA *enters with the two elder children.* THE NURSE *has the youngest on her arm*).

NORA. What; are you still here?

MRS. LINDE. Good-night; I have a great deal to talk to you about to-morrow.

NORA. To-morrow——!

MRS. LINDE. Believe me, Nora, it is a good thing to speak out——

NORA. Yes, yes. Good-night.

MRS. LINDE. Good-night.

NORA. A thousand times good-night. Good-bye.

(MRS. LINDE *goes out.*)

NORA. Put them to bed, Anna—they are so tired and sleepy—Oh, look after them well. What do you say? Stay a little while with mamma? No, no—that won't do —you can't be with mamma—Good-night—oh, once more—Good-night—good-night—there—now you must go in—good-night, all of you——

(THE NURSE *goes out with the children.*)

NORA. Oh, never to see them again! Never—
never——

HELMER (*enters*). There—now it is over. Have
they gone to bed?

NORA. Yes, directly.

HELMER. You are tired?

NORA. Oh, yes, a little.

HELMER. After this my little Nora must take care of
herself. It will be good to take a long rest, won't it?

NORA. Yes, I almost think it will.

HELMER. Only "almost"?

NORA. Yes, yes, it will be good.

RANK (*enters*). May I come in so late as this?

HELMER. Oh, is it you? Yes, come in.

RANK. I didn't get a chance of saying good-bye to
you upstairs, and as I knew you were a pair of night-
birds——

HELMER. Yes, I have a couple of hours' work to do
yet. Well, you seemed to be enjoying yourself this
evening.

RANK. Yes, why not? One doesn't like to forego
one's last chance.

HELMER. Last? Why should it be the last?

RANK. Why? Ah, you must ask certain mysterious
powers about that. But it is the last, so far as I am concerned.

HELMER. But my dear Rank——

RANK. I feel it. There's no help for it. I'm going
home to bed now and shall not get up again. No, no,
it is so; I am perfectly clear upon it. That is why I
wanted to say good-bye——

HELMER. Oh, but of course I shall come and see you
every day——

RANK. You're not to do that—not on any account, I won't have it. There's something ugly about a death-bed. A sick-room is hideous; the poisoned air, the patient's failing strength, his altered appearance, his drawn, yellow skin, glassy eyes—. No, no, promise me you won't come, Helmer. I don't want to be associated in your memory with such impressions.

HELMER. Do you think it will be protracted?

RANK. Hardly. I was going to say, unfortunately. Yes, isn't it strange how we hang on to our wretched lives? I who am a doctor and could so easily put an end to the whole business; a few drops out of a bottle—; a slit with the lancet here over the artery——

HELMER. But, Rank—what are you thinking of——

RANK. I haven't the courage to do it; I swear I haven't the courage. I prefer to lie and suffer and die by inches. But at any rate there may be some interesting observations to be made. One can't very well experiment with other patients toward the end. There is never anything definite to be learnt from them. But on one's self—yes, my friends, that is the only thing I have left to look forward to. That, and my good cigars; I can smoke them. Well, good-bye now, and thanks for all your kindness. May you have a long life before you. Now, now, Mrs. Helmer—don't let us be sentimental, don't let us have any scenes—Good-bye——

HELMER. Rank, I shall come and see you.

RANK. You won't get in. Hang it, man, what have you got to do with death—at present? You are a healthy, happy man—no, no, it's not for you to see. Good-bye then, and may it be many years before you follow me. (*He goes out.*)

HELMER. This will be a hard blow for us, Nora!

NORA. Yes.

HELMER. He had so grown into our lives, I can't realise that he is gone. He and his sufferings and his loneliness formed a sort of cloudy background to the sunshine of our happiness. Well, perhaps it's best as it is. At any rate for him. And perhaps for us too. (*He goes into the hall and takes a key from his pocket.*)

NORA. Thorvald—what are you doing?

HELMER. Emptying the letter-box. Why, how is this? Has anyone been at the lock?

NORA. The lock——?

HELMER. I'm sure of it. What does it mean? I can't think that the servants—here is a bit of a hair-pin —Nora, it's one of yours——

NORA. It must have been the children——

HELMER. Yes, of course—you must break them of such tricks. H'm, h'm—there, I've got it open.—Just see how they've accumulated.

NORA. Are you going to work now?

HELMER. Yes, I must. I shall not be able to sleep anyhow—I can't get what Rank told us out of my head. There, there, my sweet little Nora; I see it has shaken you too. But you must struggle against it; it is not good for you. You must be happy and joyous, my little song-bird. Is not that what you were born for? It did not come upon us unexpectedly. We have long been prepared. And, as I said, perhaps it's best as it is—for us. Now we two are thrown entirely upon each other. There, there, don't be so moved, Nora; there is something unlovely in it. We will not let our happiness be taken from us. Now we have everything; an independent position. How I am looking forward to beginning my work; to be my own independent master —to work with free hands.

NORA. Yes, yes, you shall, Thorvald!

HELMER. I'll go into my room for a while. Good-night, my sweet little Nora; don't sit up too long. You are badly in want of rest.

NORA. Yes, I intend to—go now, Thorvald; good-night; I shall soon have finished.

HELMER. Good-night, my little lark. And to-morrow we begin a new life. Good-night; sleep well. Now I shall read my letters. (*He goes with the letters in his hand into his room.*)

NORA (*looks around with wild eyes; takes a step towards Helmer's room, but stops again; in a low voice.*) Thorvald, Thorvald, Thorvald! Never to see him again! The children; never to see them again. The black, icy water. Oh, can I do it! Oh, if it were over! What's that? Has he opened it? Is he reading it?—Good-bye, my home, my home, good-bye to him and my little ones!

> (*She has thrown a large shawl over her head and is hurrying out by the hall. At the same moment* HELMER *flings his door open, and stands there with an open letter in his hand.*)

HELMER. Nora!

NORA (*with a shriek*). Ah——!

HELMER. Nora, what is this——

NORA. I'm going—you see that I'm going.

HELMER (*holds her back*). Where do you want to go? Do you know what this wretch writes?

NORA. Yes, but kill me! Strike me!

HELMER. Nora!

NORA. Let me go—I'm going!

HELMER. Awful! Is what he writes true? No, no, it is impossible that this can be true.

NORA. What are you going to do to me?

HELMER. Wretched woman; what have you done!

NORA. Let me get away. Let me go.

HELMER (*locks the door*). I don't want any melodramatic airs. Here you shall stay and give an account of yourself.—Do you know what you have done?—Answer! Do you know?

NORA. Yes, now I know.

HELMER. Oh! what an awful awakening! During all these eight years—she who was my pride and my joy—a hypocrite, a liar—worse, worse—a criminal—oh, the unfathomable hideousness of it—ugh, ugh——

(NORA *says nothing.*)

HELMER. I ought to have foreseen it, guessed it. All your father's want of principle—be silent!—all your father's want of principle you have inherited. No religion, no morality, no sense of duty. How I am punished for screening him! I did it for your sake, and I am rewarded like this.

NORA. Yes,—like this.

HELMER. You have destroyed my whole happiness, my whole future. I am in the power of a scoundrel. He can do whatever he pleases with me, demand whatever he chooses; and I must submit.

NORA. When I am out of the world, you will be free.

HELMER. Oh, no fine phrases. Your father, too, was always ready with them. What good would it do, if you were gone? None. If he publishes the story, no one will doubt that I was in collusion with you. People will think I egged you on. You have undermined my whole position, my whole life's work. I must hold my tongue and serve him, or else I shall be ruined. Do you understand now what you have done to me?

NORA. Yes.

HELMER. The thing is so incredible, I can't grasp it. But we must come to an understanding. Take that shawl off! Take it off, I say. I must try to pacify him in one way or another—the matter must be hushed up. There must be no outward change in our way of life— no *outward* change, you understand. The children cannot be left in your care; I dare not trust them to you. Oh, to have to say this to one I have loved so tenderly! But that is a thing of the past; henceforward there can be no question of happiness, but merely of saving the ruins, the shreds, the show. (*A ring;* HELMER *starts.*) What's that? So late! Can it be the worst—! Can he—! Hide yourself——

(NORA *stands motionless. He goes to the door and opens it.*)

THE MAID (*in the hall*). Here is a letter for you, ma'am.

HELMER. Give it here. (*He seizes the letter and shuts the door.*) Yes, from him. Look there.

NORA. Read it.

HELMER. I have hardly the courage. I fear the worst. We may both be lost, both you and I. Ah! I must know. (*Hastily tears the letter open; reads a few lines; with a cry of joy.*) Nora!

(NORA *looks inquiringly at him.*)

HELMER. Nora!—Oh! I must read it again. Yes, yes, it is so. You are saved, Nora, you are saved.

NORA. How, saved?

HELMER. Look here. He sends you back your promissory note. He writes that he regrets and apologises, that a happy turn in his life—Oh, what matter what he writes. We are saved, Nora! There is nothing to witness against you. Oh, Nora, Nora—; but first to get rid of this hateful thing. I'll just see. (*Glances at the I. O. U.*) No, I will not look at it. The whole thing shall be nothing but a dream to me. (*Tears the I. O. U.*

and both letters in pieces; throws the pieces into the fire and watches them burn.) There! it's gone! Oh, Nora, Nora, what terrible days these must have been for you.

NORA. I have thought a great deal during these last few days, Thorvald.

HELMER. And in your agony you saw no other outlet but—no, no; we won't think of that horror. We will only rejoice and repeat—it's over, it's over! Don't you hear, Nora? You don't seem able to grasp it. Yes, it's over. What is this stony look on your face? Oh, Nora, I see what it is; you don't believe that I can forgive you. Everything is forgiven; I swear it. I know that what you did was all for love of me.

NORA. That is true.

HELMER. You loved me as a wife should love her husband. It was only the means that, with your lack of knowledge, you misjudged. Do you think I love you the less because you cannot do without guidance? No, no; lean on me; I will counsel you, and guide you. I should be no true man if this very womanly helplessness did not make you doubly dear in my eyes. You mustn't dwell upon the hard things I said in my first moment of terror, when the world seemed to be falling about our ears. I have forgiven you, Nora—I swear I have forgiven you.

NORA. I thank you for your forgiveness.

(Goes out through the open door on the right.)

HELMER. No, stay; where are you going?

NORA (*in the room at the side*). I must collect myself. Only a moment.

HELMER. Yes, collect yourself, my scared little songbird. I have broad wings to shield you. Our home is lovely and cosy, Nora; here you are safe; here I can have you for myself alone. You will be to me like a dove

that has escaped unhurt from the claws of the hawk;
I shall bring your poor beating heart to rest; believe me,
Nora, very soon. I shall not need to tell you again that
I forgive you. Soon you will feel for yourself that it is
true. Oh, this very thing has made you doubly dear to
me. How could I find it in my heart to drive you away,
or even to reproach you? Oh, you don't know a true
man's heart, Nora. There is something indescribably
sweet and soothing to a man in having forgiven his wife,
honestly forgiven her from the bottom of his heart. Has
she not become his property in a double sense? She
is as though born again. She has become, so to speak,
at once his wife and his child. That is what you shall
be to me in the future, my bewildered, helpless darling.
Don't be afraid, Nora; only open your heart to me, and
I will be both will and conscience to you.—Why, what's
this? You have changed your dress?

NORA (*in everyday dress*). Yes, Thorvald; now I
have changed my dress.

HELMER. But why?

NORA. I shall not sleep to-night.

HELMER. But, Nora dear——

NORA (*looking at her watch*). It's not so late yet. Sit
down, Thorvald; you and I have much to say to each
other. (*She sits at one side of the table.*)

HELMER. Nora, what does this mean? Your stony
look again.

NORA. Sit down. It will take some time. I have
much to talk over with you.

(HELMER *sits opposite to her.*)

HELMER. You alarm me, Nora. I don't understand
you.

NORA. No, that's just it. You don't understand me;
and I have never understood you—till to-night. No,

don't interrupt. Only listen to what I say.—We must come to a final settlement, Thorvald.

HELMER. How do you mean?

NORA. Does not one thing strike you as we sit here?

HELMER. What should strike me?

NORA. We have been married eight years. Does it not strike you that this is the first time we two, you and I, man and wife, have talked together seriously?

HELMER. Seriously! What do you call seriously?

NORA. During eight whole years, and more—ever since the day we first met—we have never exchanged one serious word about serious things.

HELMER. Was I always to trouble you with the cares you could not help me to bear?

NORA. I am not talking of cares. I say that we have never yet set ourselves seriously to get to the bottom of anything.

HELMER. Why, my dearest Nora, what have you to do with serious things?

NORA. There we have it! You have never understood me.—I have had great injustice done me, Thorvald; first by father, and then by you.

HELMER. What! By your father and me?—By us, who have loved you more than all the world?

NORA. Oh, you haven't ever loved me. You never loved anything but your own infatuation [only thought it amusing to be in love with me].

HELMER. Why, Nora, what a thing to say!

NORA. When I was a little girl of four or five, father said I had such an extraordinary desire to learn French; and he made me learn long pieces by heart; then he said I had a rare talent for writing verse, and I wrote many verses. But I had no wish either to learn French or to write verse; only I believed I had, because father had said so. Then he told me that his old-fashioned furniture and high-backed chairs with leather seats were the most handsome; and I thought they were. Then he said his high, white stock and his gold-headed cane gave him a distinguished appearance, and I thought they did so. Father used to tell me all his opinions, and I held the same opinions. If I had others I said nothing about them, because he wouldn't have liked it. He used to call me his doll, and played with me as I played with my dolls. Then I came to you, Thorvald——

HELMER. You came to me?

NORA. Well, I mean I passed from father's hands into yours. You didn't want me to have anything to do with French, because of all the immoral books; nor did you think it the right thing for women to write verse. But you were fond of music, and you liked me to recite monologues that we had heard at the theatre, and dress myself up in picturesque costumes. You arranged our house according to your taste, and I got the same tastes —or I pretended to, I don't know which; or both ways, perhaps; sometimes one and sometimes the other. You and father have done me a great wrong. It is your fault that I have got into the habit of lying and that my life has come to nothing.

HELMER. You are unreasonable and ungrateful, Nora! Have you not been happy here?

NORA. No. I thought I was; but I never was.

HELMER. Not—not happy!

NORA. No; only merry, cheerful. Our home has been a doll's house. Here I have been your doll, just as I used to be father's. And the children, in their turn, have been my dolls. And I thought it was amusing to be played with by you, just as I thought it amusing to play with them. That has been our marriage, Thorvald.

HELMER. There is some truth in what you say, exaggerated and overstrained though it be. But henceforth it shall be different. Play-time is over; now comes the time for education.

NORA. Whose education? Mine, or the children's?

HELMER. Both, my dear Nora.

NORA. Oh, Thorvald, you are not the man to teach me to be a fit wife for you.

HELMER. And you can say that?

NORA. And I—how have I prepared myself to educate our children?

HELMER. Nora!

NORA. Did you not say yourself just now, you dared not trust them to me?

HELMER. In my first excitement. Why should you dwell upon that?

NORA. You spoke the truth. That problem is beyond me. There is another to be solved first—I must try to educate myself. You are not the man to help me in that. I must set about it alone. And that is why I am leaving you.

HELMER (*jumping up*). What — do you mean to say——?

NORA. I must stand alone if I am ever to know myself and my surroundings; so I cannot stay here.

HELMER. Nora, Nora!

NORA. I am going this evening. It is no use postponing such things. I daresay Christina will take me in for to-night——

HELMER. You are mad. I shall not allow it. I forbid it.

NORA. It is of no use your forbidding me anything now. I shall take with me what belongs to me. From you I will accept nothing, either now or afterwards.

HELMER. What madness is this!

NORA. To-morrow I shall go home—I mean to what was my home. It will be easier for me to find some opening there.

HELMER. Oh, in your blind inexperience——

NORA. I must try to gain experience, Thorvald!

HELMER. To forsake your home, your husband, and your children! And you don't consider what the world will say?

NORA. I can pay no heed to that. I only know that I must do it.

HELMER. This is monstrous! Can you forsake your holiest duties in this way?

NORA. What do you consider my holiest duties?

HELMER. Do I need to tell you that? Your duties to your husband and your children.

NORA. Have I not other duties equally sacred?

HELMER. Not in the first rank. What duties do you mean?

NORA. My duties towards myself.

HELMER. Before all else you are a wife and mother.

NORA. That I no longer believe. I believe that before all else I am a human being—or that I should try to become one. I know that most people agree with you, Thorvald, or that they say something of that sort. But henceforth I can't be satisfied with what people say, and what is in books. I must think things out for myself, and try to get clear about them.

HELMER. Are you not clear about your place in your own home? Have you not an infallible guide in such things? Have you not religion?

NORA. Oh, Thorvald, I don't really know what religion is.

HELMER. What do you mean?

NORA. I know nothing but what Pastor Hansen told me when I was confirmed. He explained that religion was this and that. When I get away from all this and stand alone, I will look into that matter too. I will see whether what he taught me is right, or, at any rate, whether it is right for me.

HELMER. Oh, this is unheard of! And from so young a woman! But if religion cannot keep you right, let me appeal to your conscience—for I suppose you have some moral feeling? Or, answer me: perhaps you have none?

NORA. Ah, Thorvald, what shall I answer? [it's not easy to say]. I really don't know—I am all at sea about these things. I only know that I think quite differently from you about moral questions. I hear, too, that the law is on your side; but I can't believe it. I can't understand that the law is right in what concerns me. That a woman has no right to spare her dying father, or to save her husband's life!

HELMER. You talk like a child. You don't understand the society in which you live.

NORA. No, I do not. But now I shall try to learn. I must make up my mind which is right—society or I.

(*She goes into the room on the right and fetches her hat and cloak.*)

HELMER. Nora, you are ill; you are feverish; I almost think you are out of your senses.

NORA. I have never felt so much clearness and certainty as to-night.

HELMER. You are clear and certain enough to forsake husband and children?

NORA. Yes.

HELMER. Then there is only one explanation possible.

NORA. What is that?

HELMER. You no longer love me.

NORA. Yes, Thorvald, that is so.

HELMER. Nora! Oh, oh!

NORA. I will not hide it from you—I do not love you any longer. That is why I am going.

HELMER (*mastering himself with difficulty*). Are you clear and certain on this point too?

NORA. Yes, quite.

HELMER. And can you also make clear to me how I have forfeited your love?

NORA. (Ah, Thorvald, the point is: you have not forfeited). I can. You forfeited my love this evening, when I discovered that you had never loved me as I loved you. You forfeited it when I saw you were not the man I had imagined—when I could no longer look up to you as an exalted and superior being; for you are not one.

HELMER. And how did I disclose all this?

NORA. I will tell you. That which you call my crime, my forging my father's name to save your life, this secret has been my joy and pride, until my eyes were opened to the consequences that might result from it. I have gone through a week of deadly terror.

HELMER. I can well understand that.

NORA. But you do not understand why. Or can you tell me?

HELMER. Well, you had no need to fear punishment and disgrace. You must have known that I should employ every means of saving you; that I should have been compelled to submit to any conditions——

NORA. H'm. What then do you think it was that made me want to die?

HELMER. You were afraid of my anger.

Nora. No, Thorvald, I wanted to die in order to hinder what I so firmly believed your gratitude, your love and your manly spirit would prompt you to do. It never for a moment occurred to me that you would think of submitting to that man's conditions, that you would agree to direct your actions by the will of another. I was convinced that you would say to him, "Make it known to the whole world"; and that then——

Helmer. Well? I should give you up to punishment and disgrace.

Nora. No; then I firmly believed that you would come forward, take everything upon yourself, and say, "I am the guilty one"——

Helmer. Nora!

Nora. You mean I would never have accepted such a sacrifice? No, of course not. But what would my word have been worth in opposition to yours? I so firmly believed that you would sacrifice yourself for me —"don't listen to her," you would say—"she is not responsible; she is out of her senses"—you would say that it was love of you—you would move heaven and earth. I thought you would get Doctor Rank to witness that I was mad, unhinged, distracted. I so firmly believed that you would ruin yourself to save me. That is what I dreaded, and therefore I wanted to die.

Helmer. Oh, Nora, Nora!

Nora. And how did it turn out? No thanks, no outburst of affection, not a shred of a thought of saving me. Only reproaches—sneers at my father—petty terrors—tyrannical abuse of a defenceless victim.

Helmer. Yes, yes——

Nora. And then, the very moment the danger was over, it seemed to you as though nothing had happened. I was·again your lark, your doll, whom you would take twice as much care of in future, because she was so weak and fragile. Thorvald, in that moment you stood revealed to me as [it burst upon me that I had been living here with] a strange man; and with a strange man I cannot continue to live [that is what cannot continue].

HELMER. Yes, yes, yes, an abyss has opened between us. But, Nora, Nora, can it never be filled up?

NORA. As I now am, I am no wife for you.

HELMER. I have strength to become another man.

NORA. Perhaps—when your doll is taken away from you.

HELMER. To part—to part from you! No, Nora, no; I can't grasp the thought.

NORA. The more reason for the thing to happen!

(*She fetches her travelling-bag from the room on the right.*)

HELMER. Nora, Nora, [not now! Wait till to-morrow.

NORA. I can't spend the night in a strange man's house.

H. . . . brother and sister.

N. Phrases. You know very well—that wouldn't long be the case.]

NORA (*Putting on her outdoor things*). Good-bye, Thorvald. No, I won't go to the children. I know they are in better hands than mine. As I now am, I can be nothing to them.

HELMER. But some time, Nora—some time——?

NORA. How can I tell? I have no idea what will become of me.

HELMER. But you are my wife, now and always.

NORA. Listen to me, Thorvald—when a wife leaves her husband's house, as I am doing, I have heard that in the eyes of the law he is free from all duties towards her. At any rate, I release you from all duties. You must not feel yourself bound by any tie, any more than I shall. There must be perfect freedom on both sides. There, I give you back your ring. Give me mine.

HELMER. That too?

NORA. That too.

HELMER. Here it is.

NORA. Very well. Now it is all over. I lay the keys here. The servants know about everything in the house —better than I do. To-morrow, when I have started, Christina will come to pack up the things I brought with me from home. I will have them sent after me.

HELMER. All over! All over! Nora, will you never think of me again?

NORA. When a woman has lived with a man for eight years, I don't think he will ever become quite a stranger to her. I shall often think of you, and the children, and this house.

HELMER. Nora, may I write to you?

NORA. No,—never! You must not.

HELMER. But I must send you——

NORA. Nothing, nothing.

HELMER. I must help you if you need it.

NORA. Nothing, nothing, I say. I take nothing from strangers.

HELMER. I see it well; I have become a stranger to you.

NORA. You have, as I to you. And therefore, good-bye!

HELMER. Nora—can I never be more than a stranger to you?

NORA. Oh, Thorvald, then the miracle of miracles would have to happen——

HELMER. What is this miracle?

NORA. Both of us would have to change so that—Oh,
Thorvald, I no longer believe in miracles.

HELMER. But I believe in them. Tell me! We
must so change that——?

NORA. That communion between us shall be a marriage. Good-bye.

 (*She rapidly picks up her travelling-bag, nods and
  goes out.*)

HELMER (*sinks into a chair by the door*). Nora!
Nora!—The miracle of miracles——?!

II

FROM THE SECOND ACT

N. People are sympathetic towards those who are
ill.—What are the children doing?

A. Oh, poor mites, they're amusing themselves as
well as they can.

N. Ask for me. If I can't have them so much with
me in future——

A. Little children get used to anything.

N. If I went quite away from them, do you believe
they would forget me——

A. Gracious me quite away——

NORA. Hasn't your daughter become a stranger to
you——

A. How does Mrs. Nora know——

N. That you have had a child—I have known that
since I was twelve or thirteen—otherwise you could not
have been my nurse. Oh, it must be terrible to be torn
away from one's dear ones.

A.   We poor people don't look at it in that way.   My little Nora was like a child of my own——

N.   You must never leave the little ones, promise me that.

A.   Did I not look after Nora, when she was a little girl and had no mother but me.

N.   Yes, yes, they are in good hands with you.

No—   How kind of you to come.

Mrs. L.   I have come to thank your husband.

N.   Appointed.

Mrs. L.   Yes—Perhaps he is not at home.

N.   Is so busy.   But now you must help me.   Look here.   Fancy ball at Stenborg's overhead on third floor. I am to appear as a Neapolitan girl and dance the tarantella—learnt it on the spot—promised Torvald—Can you help——

Mrs. L.   Will try—But I've quite forgotten to thank you for the pleasant evening yesterday——

Nora.   Oh, Torvald has the art of making everything so pleasant.

Mrs. L.   You too—But tell me, is Doctor Rank always so serious as he was last evening——

N.   He suffers from a dreadful illness—But yesterday it was certainly marked——

Mrs. L.   He comes here very often.

N.   Every day—he is quite one of the family; I don't think he could get on without us.

N.   I assure you.   But, Doctor R. ?   I'm certain that if I asked him——

Mrs. L.   N. N. behind your husband's back—why don't you speak to your husband——

N. Oh, you don't understand it all, don't know Torvald.

Mrs. L. Not Dr. R. on any account.

N. Would never occur to me; although I am sure he would do it.

Mrs. L. But you must get clear of it. This secrecy is likely to undermine all truthfulness in your relations with your husband——

N. And you can say that. Yes, I must get clear of it. Tell me, when everything is paid, one gets back the paper?

Mrs. L. Yes, of course.

N. Oh, to have money, Christina——

Mrs. L. Would not your husband——?

N. Oh, there are many that he— (*Humming.*) But courage—leap into it, not creep——

Mrs. L. But no more secrets from your husband, N.

N. Pooh! a husband need not know everything. Hush, here he comes. [Go into the nursery, dear. Torvald doesn't like to see dressmaking.] (*Goes into the hall.*) Oh, is that you, Torvald dear—how cold you are. Haven't you been frozen at the Bank? Well, that's all right.

———

H. —If R. comes, he will find me in the inner office—
(*Goes into his room.*)

N. Doctor R—Yes, it's his time for coming—It must be. Now he will soon get the letter—There's a ring; that's he. No, it's not he—Ah, Doctor, it's you. Bring in the lamp, Ellen—Come here, Doctor; I think my husband has something to do——

———

R. One can't call an ugly thing by pretty names. Well, one has to go some day. But to suffer thus for another's sin. Where's the justice of it? And yet you can trace in every family an inexorable retribution. It is my father's wild oats that my poor spine must do penance for.

N. But, my dear Doctor R—You may live a long while yet.

R. H'm, I'm quite clear about it. This is the last Christmas I shall spend in this house. I wonder how things will look in a year's time——

N. Ah, if one could know that.

R—Well, the absent are soon forgotten——

R. You see, you see.

N. Only to put my costume in order. Now don't be angry, dear Dr. R. Fie, you were so unfriendly to her last evening. Do be good; you are our first and best friend, you know that—To-morrow you shall see how beautiful I shall be at the ball—R., now I'll show you something. Look here.

R. What is it.

N. Look.

R. Silk stockings.

N. Flesh-coloured—No, no, no, you must only look at the feet.—Oh, well, I suppose you may look at the rest too.

R. Do you think those stockings will fit you.

N. Why not——

R. Oh, I didn't know——

N. (*hits him lightly on the cheek with the stockings.*) For shame.

R. Nora—Mrs. Helmer—when one is going to die.

N. You mustn't die and leave us; you must go on being Torvald's and my best and dearest friend——

R.   Oh, I have never had an opportunity of proving my friendship to you.   I have only accepted what you have lavished upon me, comfort, kindness—I had almost said happiness——

N.   And if I were to ask you for—no——

R.   For what?

N.   For a great proof of your friendship?

R.   Oh, do so, N.; you don't know how gladly I would leave behind something—a remembrance; something that would keep me from oblivion.   But what is it?

N.   Oh, no, I cannot—Now that I am to say it, it seems to me an impossibility—I don't know how you will judge of me——

R.   Then I will tell you something.   You shall know now what you have never guessed; have never been able to guess—A dying man, as I am, may speak out; I have kept silence hitherto.

N.   Dr. R., keep silence still.

R.   No, you shall hear it; I have loved you, N., loved you ever since I have known you.   Every moment I have passed with you has been like a great indescribable happiness, the only happiness I have known.

N.   Not so loud—some one might hear you.

R.   Helmer himself may hear every single word I have addressed to you; when I am gone he shall know all; but you shall hear it now, so that you may turn to me with full confidence.   I will only tell you this.   No one has loved you more deeply than I.

NORA (*going to the door*).   Ellen, bring the lamp.

R.   Nora——

NORA.   Oh, my dear Dr. R—that was too bad of you——

R.   What?

N.   Why should you have told me that.   It was all so nice; it was so unnecessary——

R.   What do you mean? Did you know——

    (THE MAID *enters with the lamp.*)

NORA.   Thanks. Put it on the table there——

                       (*Exit* MAID.)

R.   Nora, I ask you, did you know——

N.   Oh, I don't know what I knew; one has an idea, or—no, I don't know at all——

R.   Well, you know now that you can count upon me— Now go on——

N.   Go on—now?

R—Oh, let me do for you whatever a man can.

N—You can do nothing for me now——

R.   Not now? Now that you know——

N—Above all, not now. Oh, Heaven, why can't a man understand——

R.   Yes, N., I ought to have understood.

N.   Too late.

R.   Ought I to go—for ever.

N.   No, you mustn't. You must come and go as you've always done. Torvald can't do without you.

R.   But you——

N.   Oh, I, I—but now you must go in to Torvald for a while——

R.   Are you angry?

N.   No; but now you must go to him. He's waiting for you in the inner office.

R.   When you remember what I have said to you, you must also bear in mind that I am a dying man.

             (*He goes into* HELMER'S *room.*)

N.   It was best thus. No obligation to anyone. He won't come. Nothing will happen.——

    (*She is going into the room on the left; at the same moment* THE MAID *opens the door into the hall.*)

MAID (*softly*). Please, ma'am.

N. What is it.

M. The gentleman who came to see Mr. Helmer yesterday——

N. What gentleman; there were so many——

M. He gave his card——

N. Ah—where is he——

M. He came up the back stair, he wanted to speak to you alone, ma'am.

N. Oh, Heaven, now; I—I can't——

M. He said he wouldn't go until he had spoken to you.

N. Then let him come in; Ellen, don't say anything; it's a surprise for my husband——

M. Oh, yes, ma'am, I understand——

N. Oh, this dreadful thing——

(*She slips the bolt of H.'s door.*) (THE MAID *opens the door for* K. *and shuts it after him.*)

KR. A money transaction of this kind with a minor is not even strictly speaking binding——

N. Is it not? Well, well, it's all the same, I shall pay nevertheless.

KR. Good, good; but what I was going to say was, if you have any desperate scheme in your head——

N. What if I have?

KR. Put all that out of your head. Were you perhaps thinking of going away secretly——

N. How do you know that? Who has told you——

KR. Or perhaps of something worse——

N. Oh, don't speak of it—that terrible——

KR. Yes, it must be terrible, especially for a lady so delicately brought up. The icy water, black, deep——

N. How do you know all this——

KR. And next spring when the ice melts to come up again—ugly, unrecognisable—I hadn't the courage, and it was in summer time, too—and now it is midwinter——

N. Never—I should never have courage to do it.

K. Besides, it would be very foolish. You have a happy home, a husband and children of whom you are fond. A number of good friends, respect from everyone —and your life before you.

N. Oh, yes, yes—, life might be so lovely——

KR. Therefore you must not throw it away thoughtlessly; I am afraid I frightened you too much yesterday, and so I want to talk to you now—to prepare you——

N. For what?

KR. I have been thinking more carefully over these matters. My position is not such that I can let go the hold I have now obtained over Helmer—I shall not abuse it, if he is reasonable.

N. What will you do.

K. This course is not my choice; it is your husband's. I would have preferred to content myself with regaining my position, step by step. That has not succeeded; very well; with this piece of paper I have my good friend T. H. in my pocket;

N. You never will;

K. I shall; within three months I 'shall be in the Bank's service again. Before a year is out I shall be the manager's right hand. He won't dare to show fight. It won't be T. H., but Nils K., that manages the Joint Stock Bank.

N. Do you know that this is his life's work; he will never give it up; he will have his liberty and no one over him.

K. Doesn't concern me—for your sake he will have to yield——

NORA. Very well; now I have courage enough for anything.

K. Bah—you haven't—I have seen that much—Drown yourself in the cold water?]

N. I shall do it——

K. What would be the use of it; I have him in my pocket all the same—I can hold your reputation over him.—Look, here is the letter.

N. Give it to me.

K. To deliver——

N. Yes, yes——

K. Thanks; but perhaps it will be safer if I——

N. You can't see him; you can't speak to him now—It is a relief to me to know that you won't do anything foolish——

N. He's going; he's changed his mind—ah—in the letter-box——

FROM THE THIRD ACT

H. What is it you won't have? There is nothing you may refuse, if I want it. Am I not your husband? What is it you won't have?

N. Nothing. Your wishes are mine.

H. Oh, what a brute—what a madman I am. But the thought of your being mine sometimes turns my head (*kisses her hands again and again*). Can you forgive me, my dearest Nora—can you—I swear to you—
                    (*A knock at the outer door.*)

N. (*with a scream*). Who is that coming?

GHOSTS

THE play is to be like a picture of life. Belief undermined. But it does not do to say so. "The Orphanage" --for the sake of others. They are to be happy—but this too is only an appearance—Everything is ghosts.——

A leading point: She has been a believer and romantic—this is not entirely obliterated by the standpoint reached later—"Everything is ghosts."

Marriage for external reasons, even when these are religious or moral, brings a Nemesis upon the offspring.

She, the illegitimate child, can be saved by being married to—the son—but then——?

He was dissipated and his health was shattered in his youth; then she appeared, the religious enthusiast; she saved him; she was rich. He was going to marry a girl who was considered unworthy. He had a son by his wife, then he went back to the girl; a daughter.——

These women of the present day, ill-used as daughters, as sisters, as wives, not educated according to their gifts, prevented from following their inclination, deprived of their inheritance, embittered in temper—it is these who furnish the mothers of the new generation. What is the result?

The key-note is to be: The prolific growth of our intellectual life, in literature, art, etc.—and in contrast to this: the whole of mankind gone astray.

185

The complete human being is no longer a product of nature, he is an artificial product like corn, and fruit-trees, and the Creole race and thoroughbred horses and dogs, the vine, etc.——

The fault lies in that all mankind has failed. If a man claims to live and develop in a human way, it is megalomania. All mankind, and especially the Christian part of it, suffers from megalomania.

Among us, monuments are erected to the *dead*, since we have a duty towards them; we allow lepers to marry; but their offspring——? The unborn——?

FROM THE FIRST ACT

PASTOR M. But one has a duty towards the society in which one lives. If one has a good and beneficial vocation to work at—and such we ought all to have, Mrs. Alving—then one owes it to that vocation and to one's self to stand before the eyes of society in as irreproachable a light as possible; for if one be not irreproachable, one can make no progress with one's aims.

MRS. A. Yes, you are perfectly right there.

PASTOR M. To say nothing of the difficulty—I may even say the painfulness—of the position. The serious Christians of the town take a lively interest in this Orphanage. It is, of course, founded partly for the benefit of the town, as well; and it is to be hoped it will, to a considerable extent, result in lightening our Poor Rates. But now, of course, every one in the town knows that I have been your adviser, and have had the business arrangements in my hands. My parishioners might therefore so easily be led to think that I, their clergyman——

MRS. A. Yes, it would undoubtedly be unpleasant for you.

PASTOR M. To say nothing of the fact that I have no idea of the attitude my superiors in the church would adopt towards the question.

MRS. A. Very well, my dear Pastor Manders; that consideration is quite decisive.

PASTOR M. Then we do not insure?

———

PASTOR M. That is a very disputable point, Mrs. Alving. A child's proper place is, and must be, the home.

Os. There I think you're quite right, Pastor Manders.

PASTOR M. Ah, you can hardly have any idea of what a home should be——

O. Oh, but anyhow I have seen other people's homes.

PASTOR M. I thought, however, that over there, especially in artistic circles, the life was a somewhat homeless one——

O. Well, most of the young men are forced to live so; they have no money, and besides they don't want to give up their precious freedom—they live frugally, I can tell you, a slice of ham and a bottle of wine.

PASTOR M. But in what company?

O. In very pleasant company, Pastor Manders. Sometimes a few models join them and then, as likely as not, there's dancing.

PASTOR M. Models—? What do you mean by that?

O. We painters and sculptors require models, I suppose. Otherwise how could we reproduce the tension of the muscles and the reflected lights on the skin—and all that sort of thing.

PASTOR M. But you don't mean to say that there are women who——

O. Who sit to us artists; yes, I can assure you there are.

PASTOR M. And such immorality is tolerated by the authorities?

O. The authorities tolerate worse kinds of immorality than that, Pastor, as you are doubtless not unaware——

PASTOR M. Alas, alas, that is only too true; but as to these models, it is even worse, for it takes place openly and is spoken about——

O. Yes, it would never occur to us to do otherwise. Oh, I can assure you, there are many fine figures among the models one doesn't often see here.

PASTOR M. Is it in such society you have been living abroad?

O. Sometimes too I visit my friends at their homes; one has to see what their domestic circle is like, play a little with the children.

PASTOR M. But you said most of the artists were not married.

O. Oh, that was a mistake—I meant wedded.

PASTOR M. But, good heavens——

O. But, my dear Pastor Manders, what are they to do? A poor painter, a poor girl; they can't afford to marry, it costs a great deal. What are they to do?

PASTOR M. I will tell you, Mr. Alving; they should remain apart.

O. That doctrine will scarcely go down with warm-blooded young people, full of the joy of life. Oh, the glorious free life out there.

PASTOR M. And, to make matters worse, such freedom is to be signalised as praiseworthy——

O. Let me tell you, sir, you may visit many of these irregular homes and you will never hear an offensive word there. And let me tell you another thing: I have never come across immorality among our artists over there—but do you know where I have found it——?

PASTOR M. No, I'm happy to say——

O. Well, then, I'm afraid I must inform you. I have met with it in many a pattern husband and father who has come to Paris to have a look round on his own account, one of these gentlemen with a heavy gold chain outside his waistcoat; do you know what is the first thing these gentlemen do? Why, they hunt up some poor artist or other, get on familiar terms with him, ask him to supper at a smart restaurant, make the champagne flow freely—and then take his arm and propose that they shall make a night of it—and then we artists hear of places we never knew of before, and see things we never dreamed of—But these are the respectable men, Pastor Manders, and on their return you can hear their praises of the pure morals of home in contrast to the corruption abroad—oh yes—these men know what's what—they have a right to be heard.

MRS. A. But, my dear Oswald, you mustn't get excited.

O. No, you're right; it's bad for me—I shall go for a little turn before dinner. Excuse me, Pastor, I know you can't take my point of view; but I had to speak out for once.

(*He goes out by the second door to the right.*)

PASTOR M. Then this is what he has come to!

FROM THE THIRD ACT

REG. You might have brought me up to be a lady, ma'am, it would have suited me better. And then I shouldn't have had to be so careful about money.

THE WILD DUCK

A PLAY IN FIVE ACTS

BY HENRIK IBSEN

1884

I

FIRST ACT

At WALLE'S *house. A richly and comfortably furnished smoking-room; upholstered sofas and armchairs; smoking-tables with pipes and cigar-boxes; lighted lamps and branching candlesticks. At the back, a large open door with curtains drawn back. Within is seen the billiard-room, also lighted up. In front, on the right (in the smoking-room), a small baize door leads into the office. On the left, in front, the fireplace with a fire, and beyond the fireplace a double door leading into the dining-room. From within is heard loud-voiced conversation and laughter of many guests. A glass is tapped with a knife; silence follows. A toast is proposed; then again a loud buzz of conversation.*

WALLE'S *servant, in livery, and two or three hired waiters in black are putting the smoking-room and billiard-room in order.*

WALLE'S SERVANT (*bends down to put more coal on the fire, while listening and saying to one of the hired waiters*). Hark to them, Jensen! now the old man's on his legs holding a long palaver about Mrs. Sörby.

HIRED WAITER (*lighting a candlestick*). Are they— very good friends, eh?

WALLE'S SERVANT. Lord knows.

HIRED WAITER. I've heard tell as he's been a lively customer in his day.

WALLE'S SERVANT.　May be.

　　　　　　　　　(*Puts down the fire-shovel.*)

ANOTHER HIRED WAITER (*in the doorway of the billiard-room*).　Pettersen, here's an old chap wanting——

WALLE'S SERVANT.　Now? They're just going to leave the table.

　　(OLD EKDAHL *appears from the right, in the billiard-room. He is white-haired, quiet in manner and stoops somewhat; he is dressed in an old-fashioned overcoat with a high collar; and carries in his hand a winter cap and a faded cotton umbrella. Under his arm a bundle of papers in a blue wrapper.*)

WALLE'S SERVANT.　Good Lord—what do you want here at this time of night?

EKDAHL.　I must get into the office——

WALLE'S SERVANT.　The office was closed an hour ago, and——

EKDAHL.　Yes, they told me so; but I'm sure Mr. Gråberg's in there still, and if you—if you * (*Points*

---

* Ekdahl here hesitates between the formal *De* and the familiar *du* (thou); Pettersen replies to him with *du*.

---

towards the baize door) would let me go this way——

WALLE'S SERVANT.　Well, you may go. (*Moving a table.*)　Oh, look here, Ekdahl, lend me a hand with this table.

EKDAHL (*involuntarily drawing himself up*).　I—!
(Meekly.)　Oh, I see, the table——

WALLE'S SERVANT.　Thanks. (*Opens the baize door.*) There, in with you, Ekdahl; but mind you go out again the other way, for we've got company.

EKDAHL.　Yes, I know——

　　　　　　　　　(*He goes into the office.*)

ONE OF THE HIRED WAITERS. Is he one of the office people?

WALLE'S SERVANT. No, he's only an outside hand that does odd jobs of copying. But he's been a tip-topper in his day, he has.

HIRED WAITER. Yes, he looked like it.

WALLE'S SERVANT. Ah, he's been a lawyer and deuce knows what. Lord, I know old Ekdahl well, I do. Many a nip of bitters and bottle of ale we two have drunk at Madam Eriksen's.

HIRED WAITER. He don't look as if he'd much to stand treat with.

WALLE'S SERVANT. Why, bless you, Jensen, it's me that stands treat. I always think there's no harm in being a bit civil to folks that have had a hard time.

HIRED WAITER. Did he go bankrupt then?

WALLE'S SERVANT. Worse than that. He went to prison.

HIRED WAITER. To prison!

WALLE'S SERVANT. Or perhaps it was the Penitentiary. (*Listens.*) Sh! They're leaving the table.

(*The dining-room door is thrown open from within, by a couple of waiters. The whole company gradually comes out.* WALLE *leads the way, with an elderly lady* [MRS. SÖRBY] *on his arm; he takes her out through the billiard-room and thence into an adjoining room on the right. Gentlemen of various ages enter in groups and scatter themselves in the smoking-room and billiard-room. Chamberlains* FLOR, KASPERSEN *and* SÆTHER *enter, conversing with* GREGERS WALLE. *Last comes* HALFDAN EKDAHL.)

FLOR. Whew! What a dinner!—It was no joke to do it justice!

KASPERSEN. Oh, with a little good-will one can get through a lot in three hours. What do you say, Sæther?

SÆTHER. It's the appetite that provides the motive power, he-he!

FLOR. Ah, if one had your stomach, Kaspersen.

KASPERSEN (*stroking* FLOR'S *waistcoat*). I should think your own would hold a good deal.

FLOR. Ah, yes, if it could only digest what it can hold——

GREGERS WALLE. There's a remedy for everything, Mr. Flor. Otherwise why do you suppose an all-seeing Providence created mineral waters?

KASPERSEN. Fie, fie, now you're getting Parisian again.

GREGERS. It sticks to one, unfortunately. But, you see, I've just come from there.

WALLE (*re-entering* [*with* MRS. SÖRBY]). What are you studying so intently, Ekdahl?

HALFDAN. Only an album, Mr. Walle.

WALLE. Ah, photographs! They are quite in your line, of course.

KASPERSEN. Have you brought any with you? Of your own manufacture? What?

HALFDAN. No, I haven't.

WALLE. But you ought to have. Then you might have contributed to the entertainment, you know.

MRS. SÖRBY. In this house every one is expected to do something in return for his dinner, Mr. Ekdahl.

FLOR. Where one dines so well, that duty becomes a pleasure.

MRS. SÖRBY. Chamberlain Flor exerts himself on behalf of the ladies till the perspiration runs off him.

FLOR. On behalf of the *lady*, Mrs. Sörby; the lady of the house——

MRS. SÖRBY. Ah, to-day you have an easy task. And Chamberlain Kaspersen—what does *he* do, I wonder——?

FLOR. He produces witticisms——

MRS. SÖRBY. Did you say, *re*-produces——?

KASPERSEN (*laughing*). Now you're getting too bad!

FLOR. I only said *pro*duces, but——

KASPERSEN. Oh, well, one can only use the gifts one has.

MRS. SÖRBY. That's true; and therefore Chamberlain Sæther is always so ready to turn over music.

SÆTHER. He-he!

GREGERS (*softly*). You must join in, Hialmar.

HIALMAR EKDAHL (*shrugging his shoulders*). What am I to talk about?

WALBERG. Throw away your cigarette end, and take a proper cigar.

KASPERSEN. Yes, but is Mrs. Sörby smoke-dried?

MRS. SÖRBY (*lighting a cigarette*). I take care of that myself.

SÆTHER. Oh, I say!

FLOR. Remarkably delicate Tokay.

VALBERG. Yes, you may well say that. But it cost a pretty penny, too; for it's one of the very finest seasons, you must know.

HIALMAR. Is there any difference between the seasons?

VALBERG. Come! That's good! It really doesn't pay to set good wine before you.

KASPERSEN. Tokay is like photographs, Mr. Ekdahl; they both need sunshine. Am I not right?

HIALMAR. Yes, light is important, no doubt.

MRS. SÖRBY. And it's exactly the same with Chamberlains; they, too, depend very much on sunshine.

KASPERSEN. Oh, fie! That's a very threadbare sarcasm!

FLOR. Mrs. Sörby is reproducing——

MRS. SÖRBY. Possibly; but it's true that the seasons differ greatly.

KASPERSEN. But you reckon me among the fine vintages, don't you, Mrs. Sörby?

MRS. SÖRBY. Oh, I'm sure you all belong to the same vintage, all three.

VALBERG. Ha, ha, ha!—that's one for you! Fill your glasses, gentlemen. In such villainously cold weather. A good glass, a warm, comfortable home—at least I think it is so. Within one's own four walls is the place to look for true comfort.

(*The guests touch their glasses and drink.*)

GRÅBERG (*at the baize door*). Excuse me, sir, but I can't get out.

WALLE. Have you been locked in again?

GRÅBERG. Yes, and Flaksrud has carried off the keys——

WALLE. Well, you can pass out this way.

GRÅBERG. But here's some one else——

WALLE. All right; come through, both of you. Don't be afraid.

(GRÅBERG *and* OLD EKDAHL *come through the baize door.*)

WERLE (*involuntarily*). Ugh!

(*The laughter and talk among the guests cease suddenly.* HIALMAR *starts at the sight of his father, and turns aside.* GRÅBERG *and* EKDAHL *go out through the billiard-room [and out to the right].*)

WERLE (*mutters*). That damned fool Gråberg!

GREGERS. Why surely that wasn't——

SÆTHER.   What's the matter?   Who was it?

GREGERS.   Oh, nobody.

SÆTHER (to HIALMAR).   Did *you* know that man?

HIALMAR.   I don't know—I didn't notice——

SÆTHER.   And getting in like that through closed doors.   I must find out about this.

> (*Goes away to the others.*)

MRS. SÖRBY (*whispers to the Servant*).   Give him something to take with him;—something good, mind.

PETTERSEN.   I'll see to it.   (*Goes out.*)

GREGERS (*softly*).   So that was really he!

HIALMAR.   Yes, it was.

GREGERS.   And you denied him!

HIALMAR.   But how *could* I——

GREGERS.   I'm afraid you've become a coward, Hialmar.

HIALMAR.   Oh, if you were in my place——

> (*The conversation amongst the Guests, which has been carried on in low tones, now swells into forced joviality.*)

KASPERSEN (*approaching* HIALMAR *and* GREGERS *in a friendly manner*).   Aha! here you are reviving old memories.   Won't you have a light to your cigar, Mr. Ekdahl?   (*Handing him a candle.*)   Allow me.

HIALMAR.   No, thank you, I won't smoke now.

FLOR.   Haven't you some verses to read to us, Mr. Ekdahl?   You used to write such charming verses.

HIALMAR.   No, I haven't any.

FLOR.   Are you all well at home?   Your children—. You have children, I think——?

HIALMAR.   I have a daughter.

FLOR.   And what does she do?

HIALMAR.   Hedvig draws.

FLOR. No, really? That's the artistic nature she has inherited.

SÆTHER (*joining them*). No, it wasn't through closed doors. He came on business.

KASPERSEN (*good-humouredly turning him round*). Oh, you're talking nonsense, Chamberlain. (*Draws him away.*)

FLOR. Heaven knows what *he's* jabbering about.
(*Goes away.*)

HIALMAR (*whispers*). I'm going now, Gregers. Say good-bye to your father for me.

GREGERS. Yes, yes. Are you going straight home?

HIALMAR. Yes. Why?

GREGERS. Oh, because I may look you up later.

HIALMAR. No, you mustn't do that. Not at home. We can always arrange to meet somewhere in the town.

MRS. SÖRBY. Are you going, Ekdahl?

HIALMAR. Yes.

MRS. SÖRBY. Remember me to Gina.

HIALMAR. Thanks.
(*He tries to get out, as far as possible unnoticed, to the right.*)

MRS. SÖRBY (*softly, to* PETTERSEN). Well, did you give the old man something?

PETTERSEN. Yes; I sent him off with a bottle of cognac.

MRS. SÖRBY. Oh, you might have thought of something better than that.

PETTERSEN. Oh, no, Mrs. Sörby; cognac is what he likes best in the world.

FLOR (*in the doorway of the billiard-room, with a sheet of music in his hand.*) Shall we play something to you, Mrs. Sörby?

MRS. SÖRBY. Yes, suppose you do.

THE GUESTS. Bravo! Bravo!

(*They all go out to the right through the billiard-room. During what follows, the pianoforte is faintly heard.*)

GREGERS. Father, won't you stay a moment?

WERLE. What is it?

GREGERS. I must have a word with you.

WERLE. Can it not wait till the others are gone?

GREGERS. No, it cannot; for perhaps I shall go before the others.

WERLE. Go? Will you go? What do you mean by that?

GREGERS. How has that family been allowed to go so miserably to the wall?

WERLE. Do you mean the Ekdahls?

GREGERS. Yes, I mean the Ekdahls. Old Ekdahl was once so closely associated with you. And once in his life, at any rate, he was very useful to you.

WERLE. Oho! you're thinking of the old story in the criminal court? Those affairs were settled long ago. You may be sure he was very well paid.

GREGERS. That may be. But afterwards, father; all the other things——

WERLE. I don't know what you mean by "other things." There are no other things! He never once applied to me while there was yet time. He did not know himself what a mess he was in, until everything came to light, and then of course it was too late.

GREGERS. It's not that I'm talking about, either. But afterwards, since that——

WERLE. Ah, since that. When he came out of prison he was a broken-down being.—I can assure you, Gregers, I have done everything in my power to help him. I have

given him copying to do for the office, and I have paid
him far, far more than his work is worth. Do you laugh
at that? Do you think I am not telling you the truth?
Well, I certainly can't refer you to my books, for I never
enter payments of that sort——

GREGERS (*smiles*). No, there are certain payments
it is not worth while to keep an account of.

WERLE (*taken aback*). What do you mean by *that?*

GREGERS. Have you entered what it cost you to
have Hialmar Ekdahl taught photography?

WERLE. I! How "entered" it?

GREGERS WERLE. I have learnt that it was you who
paid for his training. And I have learnt, too, that it was
you who enabled him to set up house so comfortably.

WERLE. Well, and yet you talk as though I had not
done enough for Ekdahl's family. I can assure you
these people have cost me enough.

GREGERS. Have you entered any of these expenses
in your books?

WERLE. Why do you ask?

GREGERS. Oh, I have my reasons. Now tell me;
when you interested yourself so warmly in your old
friend's son—it was just before his marriage, was it not?

WERLE. Why, deuce take it—after all these years,
how can I—it must be eighteen or nineteen years ago——

GREGERS. It is now about seventeen years ago. You
wrote me a letter about that time—a business letter, of
course—and in a postscript you mentoined, quite briefly,
that Hialmar Ekdahl had married a Miss Hansen.

WERLE. Yes, that was quite right. That was her
name.

GREGERS. But you did not mention that this Miss
Hansen was Gina Hansen—our former housekeeper.

WERLE (*with a forced laugh of derision*). No; to tell the truth, it didn't occur to me that you were so particularly interested in our former housekeeper.

GREGERS. No more I was. (*Lowers his voice.*) But there were others in this house who *were* particularly interested in her.

WERLE. What do you mean by that? (*Flaring up.*) You are not alluding to me, I hope?

GREGERS (*softly but firmly*). Yes, I am alluding to you.

WERLE. And you dare—You presume to—How can that ungrateful hound—that photographer fellow—how dare he accuse me——!

GREGERS. Hialmar has not said a word about these things. I don't even know that he has any suspicion of such a thing.

WERLE. Well then, where have you got it from? Who can have given you such notions about me?

GREGERS. My poor unhappy mother once told me this.

WERLE. Your mother! I might have known as much! You and she—you always held together against me. It was she who turned you against me, from the first.

GREGERS. No, it was all she had to suffer and submit to, until she broke down and came to such a pitiful end.

WERLE. Oh, she had nothing to suffer or submit to; —not more than most other people, at all events. But there's no getting on with overstrained creatures. And you could credit such an accusation—a bare suspicion——!

GREGERS. Very well; then I will make it my business to find out the truth——

WERLE. You will never go burrowing into old rumours and stories? I really think that at your age you might find something more useful to do.

GREGERS. You and I have never agreed as to what is useful.

WERLE. Neither about that nor about anything else. Gregers, I believe there is no one in the world you detest as you do me.

GREGERS (*whispering*). I have seen you at much too close quarters.

WERLE. You have seen me with your mother's eyes, that's what it is.

GREGERS. And you have never been able to forgive me for taking after my mother—and for having a kind of feeling for her.

WERLE. Listen, Gregers; there are many things that stand between us; but we are father and son, after all. We ought surely to be able to come to some sort of understanding with each other. Outwardly, at any rate.

GREGERS. You mean, in the eyes of the world, as it is called?

WERLE. Yes, if you like to call it so. Think it over. Wouldn't one think it ought to be possible? Eh?

GREGERS (*looking at him coldly*). Now I see that you want to make use of me in some way.

WERLE. In such a close relationship as ours, the one can always be useful to the other.

GREGERS. Yes, so people say.

WERLE. When I wrote to you about coming home, I won't deny that I had something in my mind.

GREGERS. H'm!

WERLE. You see, our business, the settlement of your mother's inheritance and all the rest, might if necessary have been arranged between us by correspondence.

But now, as it is—unfortunately—no longer necessary for you to live out there——

GREGERS. Well, what then——?

WERLE. I want very much to have you at home with me for a time. I am a lonely man, Gregers; I have always felt lonely, all my life through; but most of all now that I am getting up in years. I feel the need of some one about me——

GREGERS. You have Mrs Sörby.

WERLE. Yes, I have her; and she has become, I may say, almost indispensable to me. She is lively and even-tempered; she brightens up the house; and that is a great thing for me——

GREGERS. Well then, you have everything just as you wish it.

WERLE. Yes, but I'm afraid it can't last. A woman so situated may easily find herself in a false position, in the eyes of the world; for that matter it does a man no good, either.

GREGERS. Oh, when a man gives such dinners as you give, he can risk a great deal.

WERLE. Yes, but how about the woman, Gregers? I fear she won't accept the situation much longer. And even if she did, even if, out of attachment to me, she were to take her chance of gossip and scandal and all that——? Do you think, Gregers, you with your strong sense of justice——

GREGERS (interrupts him). Tell me in one word;—are you thinking of marrying her?

WERLE. Suppose I were thinking of it? What then?

GREGERS. That's what I say: what then?

WERLE. Should you be inflexibly opposed to it?

GREGERS. Not at all. Not by any means.

WERLE.   I thought that perhaps your devotion to your mother's memory——

GREGERS (*stopping him with a gesture*).   No, no, no, don't let us use fine phrases, father.   I am not over-strained.

WERLE.   Well, whatever you may or may not be, at all events you have lifted a weight from my mind.   I am extremely pleased that I may reckon on your concurrence in this matter.

GREGERS.   Now I understand the use you want to put me to.

WERLE.   Use to put you to?   What an expression!

GREGERS.   Oh, don't let us be nice in our choice of words—not when we are alone together, at any rate.— (*With a laugh.*)   So this is what made it absolutely essential that I should come to town in person.   For the sake of Mrs. Sörby, we are to get up a pretence at family life in the house;—that will be something new indeed!

WERLE.   How dare you say such things!

GREGERS.   Was there ever any family life here?   But now your plans demand something of the sort.   Of course; I can see that.   And no doubt it will have an excellent effect when it is reported that the son has hastened home, on the wings of filial piety, to the grey-haired father's wedding-day.   So, after all, the relations between them are perfectly cordial.   Yes, of course. Father and son—how indeed could it be otherwise! Why, it's the order of nature——

WERLE.   Yes, it ought to be the order of nature, Gregers——

GREGERS.   Oh, I haven't a rag of belief either in nature or in its order.

WERLE.   Listen to me; I will tell you that there may be much to blame in my way of life—(*raising his voice*) but there are certain things for which I demand respect in my house!

GREGERS (*bowing slightly*). So I have observed; and therefore I take my hat and go.

WERLE. You are going—! Out of the house?

GREGERS. Yes, for there is only one thing in the world that *I* have respect for.

WERLE. And what is that?

GREGERS. You would only laugh if I told you.

WERLE. A lonely man doesn't laugh so easily, Gregers.

GREGERS (*pointing towards the billiard-room*). Look father; the Chamberlains are playing blind-man's-buff with Mrs. Sörby.—Good-night and good-bye.

(*He goes out to the right.*)

WERLE (*smiling contemptuously after him*). Ha—! And he says he is not overstrained.

SECOND ACT

HIALMAR EKDAHL'S *studio, a good-sized room, but poorly furnished, evidently in the top storey of the building. On the right, a sloping roof of large panes of glass, half-covered by a blue curtain. In the right-hand corner, at the back, the entrance door; two doors on the opposite side. At the back, in the middle, a large double sliding-door. Towards the front, by the right-hand wall, an old, worn sofa with a table and a couple of chairs. On the table a lighted lamp. Photographic apparatus of different kinds about the room, Photographs lying on the table; bottles and boxes of various chemicals on a bookcase at the back.*

(MRS. EKDAHL *sits on a chair by the table, sewing.* HEDVIG *is sitting on the sofa, drawing.*)

Mrs. Ekdahl. How much was it you paid for the butter to-day?

Hedvig. It was forty-five öre.

Mrs. Ekdahl. And then there's the beer. Look there—that makes it over a crown.

Hedvig. Yes, but then father took four crowns fifty for the photographs.

Mrs. Ekdahl. So much as that?

Hedvig. Yes, exactly four crowns fifty.

(*Silence.*)

Mrs. Ekdahl. H'm—I'd just like to know how your father's getting on at the party.

Hedvig. Yes, it would be fun if we could see him.

(*Old* Ekdahl, *with the paper parcel under his arm, comes in by the door on the right.*)

Hedvig. How late you are to-day, grandfather!

Ekdahl. Gråberg kept me so long; he's always so long-winded, that man.

Mrs. Ekdahl. Did you get any more copying to do, father?

Ekdahl. Yes, this whole packet.

Mrs. Ekdahl. That's capital.

Ekdahl (*putting down his umbrella*). This work will keep me going a long time, Gina. (*Opens one of the sliding-doors at the back a little*). Hush! (*Looks into the dark room; pushes the door to again.*) Hee-hee-hee! They're all sitting fast asleep. (*Goes towards the farther door on the left.*) There are matches in here, I suppose?

Mrs. Ekdahl. The matches is on the drawers.

(Ekdahl *goes out.*)

Hedvig. It's nice that grandfather has got all that copying.

MRS. EKDAHL.   Yes, poor old father; it means a bit of money for him.

HEDVIG.   And he won't be able to sit the whole forenoon down at that horrid Madam Eriksen's.

MRS. EKDAHL.   No more he won't.   All the same— well, I don't know—but I think somehow men are more pleasant like when they've had something to drink.

HEDVIG.   Ugh, no!   Well, they may be more pleasant; but it makes it so unsafe——

MRS. EKDAHL.   How unsafe?

HEDVIG.   I mean, it's so unsafe for the rest of us; we never know quite how to treat them.

MRS. EKDAHL (*looks at her*).   When have you noticed that?

HEDVIG.   Oh, you can always notice that.   Moldstad and Riser are both of them tipsy very often——

MRS. EKDAHL.   Then it was them two you were thinking of.

(*Old* EKDAHL *comes in again and is going out by the foremost door to the left.*)

MRS. EKDAHL (*half turning in her chair*).   Do you want something out of the kitchen, father?

EKDAHL.   Yes, I do.   Don't you trouble.

(*Goes out.*)

MRS. EKDAHL.   He's not poking away at the fire, is he?   Hedvig, go and see what he's about.

(EKDAHL *comes in again with a small jug of steaming hot water.*)

HEDVIG.   Have you been getting some hot water, grandfather?

EKDAHL.   Yes, I have.   I want it.   I want to write, and the ink has got as thick as porridge.

MRS. EKDAHL.   But you mustn't sit up so late and hurt your eyes, father.

EKDAHL. My eyes must take care of themselves, Gina. I'm busy, I tell you. No one's to come in to me. (*He goes into his room.*)

MRS. EKDAHL (*softly*). Can you imagine where he's got money from?

HEDVIG. From Gråberg, perhaps.

MRS. EKDAHL. Not a bit of it. Gråberg always pays me.

HEDVIG. Then perhaps he's got a bottle on credit.

MRS. EKDAHL. Poor father, who'd give him credit?

(HIALMAR EKDAHL *comes in from the right.*)

MRS. EKDAHL (*rising*). Why, is that you already?

HIALMAR (*taking off his hat*). Yes, most of the people were coming away.

HEDVIG (*who has risen*). So early, father?

HIALMAR (*taking off his overcoat*). Yes, it was a dinner-party, you know.

MRS. EKDAHL. Let me help you. (*Hangs up his coat.*) Were there many people there?

HIALMAR. Oh no, not many. We were about twelve or fourteen. (*To* HEDVIG.) Hasn't grandfather come home?

HEDVIG. Yes, he's in his room.

HIALMAR. Well, did he say anything?

MRS. EKDAHL. No, nothing particular.

HIALMAR. Didn't he say anything about——? I heard something about his having been with Gråberg. —I'll go in and see him for a moment.

MRS. EKDAHL. No, no, better not.

HIALMAR. Why not? Did he say he didn't want me to go in——?

MRS. EKDAHL. I don't think he wants to see nobody; he has been in to fetch hot water.

HIALMAR. Oho! Then he's—— (*making a sign*).

MRS. EKDAHL. Yes, I expect so.

HIALMAR. Oh, God! my poor old father! Well, well; there let him sit and get all the enjoyment he can.

(OLD EKDAHL, *in an indoor coat and with a lighted pipe, comes from his room.*)

EKDAHL. Ah, there he is. I thought I heard you.

HIALMAR. Yes, I have just come.

EKDAHL. You didn't see me there, did you?

HIALMAR. No, I didn't. I heard you had passed through——

EKDAHL. Who were they, all those fellows?

HIALMAR. Oh, all sorts of people. There was Chamberlain Flor and Chamberlain Kaspersen and Chamberlain——

EKDAHL. Hear that, Gina! Chamberlains, every one of them!

MRS. EKDAHL. Ah, it must have been terrible genteel.

HEDVIG. Did they want you to read something aloud, father?

HIALMAR. Yes, they wanted me to; but I knew better than that.

EKDAHL. You weren't to be persuaded, eh?

MRS. EKDAHL. But you might have done it.

HIALMAR. No; one mustn't be at everybody's beck and call. That's not *my* way, at any rate. And I wasn't at all in the mood for it, either.

EKDAHL. No, no; Hialmar's not to be had for the asking, he isn't.

HIALMAR. I don't see why *I* should bother myself to entertain people on the rare occasions when I go into society. And I let them know it, too. Yes, I even found myself called upon to administer a pretty sharp correction to one or two of those gentlemen.

MRS. EKDAHL. No, did you do that?

EKDAHL. Was it any of the Chamberlains?

HIALMAR. Indeed it was. We had a little discussion about Tokay——

EKDAHL. Ah, yes, there's a fine wine.

HIALMAR. Yes, but of course you know the vintages differ; it all depends on how much of the sun's heat the grapes have had.

MRS. EKDAHL. Why, you know everything, Ekdahl.

EKDAHL. And did they dispute that with you?

HIALMAR. Yes, they tried to; but then I let them know [they were requested to observe] that it was just the same with Chamberlains; that with them, too, different batches were of different qualities,—I said.

MRS. EKDAHL. What things you do think of!

EKDAHL. And you said that to them——

HIALMAR. Right in their teeth.

EKDAHL. Do you hear that, Gina? He said it right in their very teeth.

MRS. EKDAHL. Fancy—! Right in their teeth!

HIALMAR (*taking up a position on the pedestal*). Yes, I stood like this; look here—leaning against the mantle-piece and playing with my right glove while I told them that.

EKDAHL. Right in their teeth.

HEDVIG. How nice it is to see father in a dress-coat! It suits you so well, father.

HIALMAR. Yes, doesn't it? And this one fits as if it had been made for me. A little tight in the arm-holes, perhaps.—(*Takes off the coat.*) But now I'll put on my frock-coat—(*does so*) there's a more homely feeling about it. (*To Gina.*) Don't forget to send the coat back to Molvik first thing to-morrow morning.

MRS. EKDAHL. I'll be sure and see to it.

HIALMAR (*seating himself on the sofa*). Ah, one is never so comfortable as in the corner of one's own sofa— with one's feet under one's own table.——

MRS. EKDAHL. And with a glass of beer and a pipe——

HIALMAR. Have we any beer in the house?

MRS. EKDAHL. Yes, we haven't forgotten that.

(*Goes into the kitchen.*)

HEDVIG. Here's your pipe and tobacco——

HIALMAR. Thanks! I've been regularly longing for my pipe. Werle's cigars may be good enough; but a good pipe is something different in the long run.

MRS. EKDAHL (*comes in from the kitchen with bottles of beer and glasses*). There, now you can quench your thirst.

HIALMAR. That's capital. Come now, father, we'll have a glass together.

EKDAHL. Hum; I think I'll fill my pipe first.

(*Goes into his room.*)

MRS. EKDAHL. (*smiling*). Fill his pipe!

HIALMAR. Oh, well, well, well; leave him alone, poor old father.

(*There is a knock at the door on the right.*)

MRS. EKDAHL. Hush, wasn't that a knock at the door? Who can it be? (*Goes and opens the door.*)

GREGERS (*in the passage*). Excuse me; does not Mr. Ekdahl, the photographer, live here?

MRS. EKDAHL. Yes, he does.

HIALMAR (*rising*). Gregers! You here after all? Well, come in then.

GREGERS (*coming in*). I told you I would come and see you.

HIALMAR. But this evening——? Have you left the party?

GREGERS. I have left both the party and the house. Good evening, Mrs. Ekdahl; can you remember me after all these years? Do you recognise me?

MRS. EKDAHL. Oh, yes, I do indeed.

HIALMAR. Left your father's house, did you say——?

GREGERS. Yes, I'm staying at a hotel to-night, and to-morrow I shall take a lodging. By-the-bye, Hialmar, you have a couple of rooms to let.

HIALMAR. Yes, so we have, but——

MRS. EKDAHL. But I'm sure they're not the sort of rooms for you, Mr. Werle.

GREGERS. You need not be afraid of that; I expect I shall be satisfied; and we can easily agree about the rent.

HIALMAR. Well, that is very fortunate for us.—Now, since you're here, you'll sit down, won't you?

GREGERS. Thanks; these are regular artists' quarters.

HIALMAR. This is the studio, as you see——

MRS. EKDAHL. But it's the largest of our rooms, so we generally sit here.

II

FROM THE SECOND ACT

GREGERS. You were a great sportsman then, Lieutenant Ekdal.

EKDAL. So I was; so I was; went shooting every day. [Uniform——]

GREGERS. And now I suppose you never get any shooting?

EKDAL. No, I never get any shooting now. That is, not in the old way.

HIALMAR. Sit down, father, and have a glass of beer. Sit down, Gregers, and help yourself.

(EKDAL *and* GREGERS *seat themselves on the sofa; the others sit at the table.*)

GREGERS. Can you remember, Lieutenant Ekdal, that Christmas I came up and visited you with Hialmar?

EKDAL. At the works? That must be a long time ago.

GREGERS. I suppose it is now more than twenty years ago. It was the winter there were so many wolves up there.

EKDAL. Ah, was it that winter! Then perhaps you used to be with us at night, when we lay in the stables and watched for them?

GREGERS. Yes, I was there. Hialmar came too the first night; but then he got tired of it. But I kept on. Don't you remember, you put out the carcase of a dead horse in front of the stable-door?

EKDAL. Yes, to be sure: it lay close to a big briar bush.

GREGERS. Quite right.

EKDAL. And then there was a heap of stones alongside, that cast a shadow in the moonlight——

GREGERS. Yes, and there *was* moonlight those nights, as clear as to-night——

EKDAL. But the wolves didn't come in the moonlight. But don't you remember that morning in the early dawn, after the moon had set——?

GREGERS. When thirteen of them came together——?

EKDAL. No, do you remember that! I shot one of them by the carcase and another as they were running away.

GREGERS. Yes, you were indeed a great sportsman, Lieutenant Ekdal.

EKDAL. Oh yes, oh yes; not so bad. I've shot bears too; shot all kinds of things, both beasts and birds. For the woods, you see—the woods, the woods—! What are the woods like up there now?

EKDAL. But we have to thank him for her, all the same. He was out shooting, you see; and he brought her down; but she was only wounded——

GREGERS. Ah! She got a couple of slugs or so in her body——

HIALMAR. Yes, she got a couple from behind.

GREGERS. Oh! from behind?

EKDAL. You always have to shoot wild duck from behind.

GREGERS. Of course; from behind they are easier to hit.

EKDAL. I should think so; if you shoot against the breast, the shot glances off.

EKDAL. Well, your father had such an amazingly good dog, you see; one of these new-fangled, long-haired water-dogs, and he dived in after the duck and fetched her up again.

GREGERS. And then she was sent to you?

HIALMAR. She was not sent to us at once; at first your

father took her home. But she wouldn't thrive there properly.

GREGERS. No, no, that's not a good place for wild-fowl [wild duck].

HIALMAR. No, you can imagine it wasn't, among all the tame ones. They were always setting upon her and taking her food from her, so that she had no chance of recovering. So Pettersen was told to put an end to her.

EKDAL (*half asleep*). H'm—yes—Pettersen—yes——

HIALMAR (*softly*). That was how we got her, you see; for father knows Pettersen a little; and when he heard about the wild duck he got her handed over to us.

GREGERS. And now she thrives [as] well [as possible] in the garret there?

HIALMAR. Splendidly, yes. She has lived in there so long now that she has forgotten her natural wild life; and it all depends on *that*.

GREGERS. You are right there, Hialmar. If one would keep wild duck—and if they are to thrive and grow big and fat—I think the only way is to shut them up in a garret, so that they never get a glimpse of the clouds or the sea.

HIALMAR. Yes, yes, and then they forget, you see. And after all, what they have forgotten, they will never feel the want of.

GREGERS. No, and then in time they can grow fat. —But look here, Hialmar, you said you had rooms to let, spare rooms.

THIRD ACT

HIALMAR EKDAL'S *studio. It is morning; the daylight shines through the window on the right.*

HIALMAR *is sitting at the table, busy with some photographic negatives and prints. Presently* GINA, *wearing her hat and cloak, enters from the right. She has a covered basket on her arm.*

HIALMAR. Back already? Did you look in at Gregers' room?

GINA. Yes. He has arranged everything as he likes it. He'll do everything for himself, he said.

HIALMAR. I looked in upon him too.

EKDAL. Yes, exactly; exactly.

(HIALMAR *and* EKDAL *open the upper half-door of the garret. The morning sun is shining in through the skylights; doves are flying in all directions; some sit cooing, upon the perches; the cocks and hens are heard crowing and clucking now and then.*)

HIALMAR (*opens one of the lower half-doors a little way*). Squeeze through now, father.

EKDAL (*creeps through the opening*). Aren't you coming too?

HIALMAR. Well, I almost think— (*Sees* GINA *at the kitchen door.*) No, I haven't time; I must work. And then there was the net— (*He pulls a cord, a piece of stretched fishing net slips down in front of the opening.*) So! (*Goes to the table.*)

GINA. Is he in there again?

HIALMAR. Would you rather have had him slip down to Madam Eriksen's? Do you want anything? You know you said——

GINA. I only wanted to ask if you think we can lay the table for lunch here?

HIALMAR. Yes; we have no appointment for to-day, I suppose?

GINA. No.

HIALMAR. Well then I hope there won't be any appointment either; and so we can have lunch here.

GINA. All right; but there's no hurry about it; you can have the table yet awhile.

HIALMAR (*sitting down again*). Oh, bless me, I'm sticking at it as hard as I can!

(GINA *goes out into the kitchen again.*)

EKDAL (*appears behind the net*). I'm afraid we shall have to move the water-trough after all, Hialmar.

HIALMAR. What else have I been saying all along?

EKDAL. H'm—h'm—h'm. (*Is no longer seen.*)

(HIALMAR *goes on working a little; glances towards the opening and half rises. Hedvig comes in from the kitchen.*)

HIALMAR (*sits down hurriedly*). What do you want? Perhaps you are told off to watch me?

HEDVIG. No, no. Isn't there anything I could help you with?

HIALMAR. Oh, no; it is right that I should bear the burden alone—so long as my strength holds out.

(HEDVIG *goes over to the doorway and looks for a moment into the garret.*)

HIALMAR. Tell me, what is he doing?

HEDVIG. I think he's making a new path to the water-trough.

HIALMAR. He can never manage that alone. Look, Hedvig—you are so clever; take this brush——

HEDVIG. Oh, yes, father!

HIALMAR. Only for a second, you know. It's this retouching—here is one to copy.

HEDVIG. Yes, I know how to do it; I've done it with the others, you know.

HIALMAR. Only a second; and then I shall have finished this job.

(*He pushes one of the lower half-doors a little to one side, creeps into the garret and draws the door to after him.* HEDVIG *sits at work, retouching;* HIALMAR *and* EKDAL *are heard disputing inside.*)

———

GREGERS. I suppose so; it must be a sort of world by itself.

HEDVIG. Oh, yes, quite. And there are such lots of wonderful things.

GREGERS. Indeed?

HEDVIG. Yes, there are big cupboards full of books; and a great many of the books have pictures in them.

GREGERS. Aha!

HEDVIG. And there's an old bureau with drawers and flaps, and a big clock with figures that come out; but it isn't going now.

GREGERS. So time has come to a standstill in there— in the wild duck's domain.

HEDVIG. Yes. And then there's an old paint-box, and all the books.

GREGERS. And you read the books, I suppose?

HEDVIG. Oh, yes; most of them are English though, and I don't understand English. But then I look at the pictures. There is one great big book called "Harrison's

History of London," [it must be a hundred years old]; and there are such heaps of pictures in it. At the beginning there is Death with an hour-glass, and other figures. I think that is horrid. But then there are other pictures of churches, and castles, and streets, and great ships sailing on the sea.

GREGERS. And when you look at all these pictures, I suppose you want to go over to London?

HEDVIG. Oh, of course I can't go there; but there is no need to, either.

GREGERS. No, no, because you know it, of course. And besides, you couldn't very well tear yourself away from the wild duck.

HEDVIG. I should miss her, I know. For there is so much that is strange about her. Nobody knows her, and nobody knows where she came from——

(GINA *comes in from the kitchen with the table things.*)

GREGERS (*rising*). I have come in upon you too early.

GINA. Oh, no; we're nearly ready now. Clear the table, Hedvig.

(HEDVIG *clears away her things; she and* GINA *lay the cloth during what follows.* GREGERS *sits down and turns over an album.*)

GREGERS. I hear you can retouch, Mrs. Ekdal.

GINA (*with a side glance*). Yes, I can.

GREGERS. That was exceedingly lucky.

GINA. How—lucky?

GREGERS. That Hialmar took to photography, I mean.

GINA. I can take photographs too; I learned that.

GREGERS. So it is really you that carry on the business, I suppose?

GINA. Yes, when Ekdal hasn't time himself——

(*A shot is fired within the garret.*)

GREGERS (*starting up*). What's that?

GINA. Ugh! now they're firing again!

GREGERS (*going towards the doorway*). Have they firearms in there?

HIALMAR (*inside the net*). Are you there? I didn't know.

GREGERS. Do you go shooting in there?

HIALMAR (*showing a revolver*). Only with this thing——

GINA. Yes, you'll do yourself a mischief some day with that there pigstol.

HIALMAR (*snappishly*). I have told you so often that it's called a pistol!

GINA. Oh, one's just as good as the other.

GREGERS. So you go shooting, too, up here?

HIALMAR. Only a little target practice. Mostly to please father, you understand. And then the fortunate thing about it is that no one can hear it on the floor below.

GREGERS. You have a fowling-piece too, I see.

HIALMAR. That is father's. It's of no use; something has gone wrong with the lock. But it's fun to have it all the same; for we can take it to pieces now and then, and clean and grease it, and screw it together again, you see.

HEDVIG (*who has approached*). Now you can see the wild duck properly.

GREGERS. I was just looking at her. One of her wings seems to me to droop a bit.

HIALMAR. Well, no wonder; her wing was broken, you know.

GREGERS. And she trails one foot a little; isn't that so?

HIALMAR.   Perhaps a very little bit.

HEDVIG.   Yes, it was by that foot the dog took hold of her.

HIALMAR.   But she is not a bit the worse for it; and that is simply marvellous for a creature that has had a charge of shot in her body, and has been between a dog's teeth——

GREGERS.   —and that has lain in the depths of the sea—so long.

HEDVIG (*smiling*).   Yes.

GINA (*at the table*).   Hedvig, you must come and help me now.

(GINA *and* HEDVIG *go out into the kitchen.*)

HIALMAR (*crawls through the lower half-door and comes into the studio*).   I won't ask you to go in to father; he doesn't like it.   I may as well shut up before the others come.   (*Draws up the net and shuts the upper half-doors.*)   All these contrivances are necessary, you see, for Gina objects to having rabbits and fowls in the studio.

GREGERS.   Of course; a good housekeeper like your wife——

HIALMAR.   This arrangement of the fishing net is my own invention.   And it's really quite amusing to have things of this sort to potter with, and to put to rights again when now and then they get out of order.

GREGERS.   You and I have got on well in the world, Hialmar.

HIALMAR.   How do you mean?

GREGERS.   I have gone farthest; for I have gone so far that soon I shall be fit for absolutely nothing.

HIALMAR.   You needn't be fit for anything either. You can live very well without that.

GREGERS.   Do you think so?

HIALMAR.   Yes, I certainly think that you are well enough off.

GREGERS.   Well, but what about yourself?

HIALMAR (*in a lower voice*).   Is it my fault that things went as they did—that I was thrown out of my course——?

GREGERS.   That is not what I mean——

HIALMAR.   Then perhaps you mean that I don't work my way to the front;—perhaps you think I don't toil and drudge enough.

GREGERS.   I don't know at all how much you toil and drudge.

HIALMAR.   Yes, of course you think there's too much time wasted over useless things.

GREGERS,   Not time but will.

HIALMAR.   But how can I let my poor old father go so absolutely alone?   Isn't it right that I should give a little thought to the trifles that amuse him?

GREGERS.   Is it altogether for your father's sake——?

HIALMAR.   Oh, no, I dare say it's for my own as well. I need something to take me out of reality.

GREGERS.   Then you are not happy after all?

HIALMAR.   Happy—happy?   Oh, yes, I am, in a way. I am quite comfortable—as far as *that* goes.   But of course you can imagine that a position like that of a photographer—for a man like me, is nothing but a transitional phase.

GREGERS.   Ah!

HIALMAR.   Of course.   And therefore—I tell you plainly, Gregers, I need something to fill up the interval——

GREGERS.   Could not your work do that?

HIALMAR.   No, no, no, not work alone; I must dream the interval away—leap over it.

GREGERS. And when the interval is past—what comes then?

HIALMAR. Ah, then comes the moment, it is to be hoped.

GREGERS. What moment?

HIALMAR. I have a mission, you must know.

GREGERS. Well, what do you mean by that?

HIALMAR. A mission—a life's mission. It is I, you see, who must restore our family name to honour. Who else should do it?

GREGERS. Then that is your mission.

HIALMAR. Yes, of course.

GREGERS. And what course do you propose to follow?

HIALMAR. Oh, my dear fellow, how can I tell you that beforehand? It depends so enormously upon how circumstances shape themselves when the moment arrives.

GREGERS. And you have no doubt at all about the moment?

HIALMAR. That would be doubting my own purpose in life.

GREGERS. Do you know for certain that you *have* any purpose?

HIALMAR. Are you mad?

GREGERS. Look here, Hialmar, there is something of the wild duck in you. You were once wounded, and you dived down and bit yourself fast in the undergrowth.

HIALMAR. That was odd.

GREGERS. But now I'm going to see if I can't get you up again. For *I* too think I have a sort of mission in life, you must know. Not in the way you mean;— not because I feel it as a purpose or as a duty towards others, but because I feel it as a necessity to myself.

HIALMAR. No, my dear Gregers, I don't understand a word of all this.—Ah, now we're going to have lunch.

(GINA *and* HEDVIG *bring bottles of ale, a decanter of brandy, glasses, etc.   At the same time,* RELLING *and* MOLVIK *enter from the right.*)

GINA. Ah, you two have come in the nick of time.

RELLING. Molvik got it into his head that he could smell herring-salad, and then there was no holding him. —Good morning again, Ekdal.

HIALMAR. Gregers, may I introduce you to Doctor Relling—Mr. Molvik.

RELLING. Oh, Mr. Werle! You've just moved in?

GREGERS. I moved in this morning.

RELLING. Molvik and I live right under you; so you haven't far to go for the doctor and the clergyman, if you should need anything in that line.

GREGERS. Thanks, it's not quite unlikely; for yesterday we were thirteen at table.

HIALMAR. Were we thirteen?

RELLING. You may make your mind easy, Ekdal; I'll be hanged if the finger of fate points to you.

HIALMAR. I hope not. But come and sit down.

GREGERS. Shall we not wait for your father?

HIALMAR. No, his lunch will be taken in to him. Come along!

(*The men seat themselves at table.* GINA *and* HEDVIG *go backwards and forwards and wait upon them.*)

RELLING. Molvik was frightfully screwed yesterday, Mrs. Ekdal.

GINA. Really? Is that true, Molvik?

MOLVIK. Oh, that depends on how you take it.

RELLING. Didn't you hear us when we came home?

GINA. No, I can't say I did.

RELLING. Well, Molvik was disgusting yesterday. But it agrees with Molvik, Mr. Werle. I'm his doctor and I prescribe a spree for him now and then.

GREGERS. Is Mr. Molvik an obedient patient——?

RELLING. I can't complain. But he understands that it has got to be, you see; for Molvik is dæmonic.

GREGERS. Dæmonic?

RELLING. Molvik is a dæmonic nature, yes.

GREGERS. H'm.

MOLVIK. Yes, that's what they say about me.

RELLING. And persons of dæmonic character can't walk straight through the world, you see. That kind of people must meander a little now and then. You must have lived a very long time up at the works, Mr. Werle.

GREGERS. I have lived there a good many years.

RELLING. How the devil have you managed to endure it?

GREGERS. Oh, if one has books——

RELLING. Books! They will only make you read yourself mad.

GREGERS. Well, there are people up there too.

RELLING. Yes, the work-people. Look here, my good sir, I dare swear you have a mission in life.

GREGERS. I believe so too.

HIALMAR. And it is a belief that gives one strength, Relling.

RELLING. Yes, I know you can say a word or two about that.

HIALMAR. Oh, yes.

(*A knock at the garret door.*)

GINA. Hedvig, opens the door for grandfather.

(HEDVIG *opens the door a little way;* OLD EKDAL *crawls out.*)

EKDAL (*mumbling*). Good morning, gentlemen! Good appetite to you! H'm—! (*Goes into his room.*)

RELLING. Let us drink a glass to him, Ekdal, and may he soon be in regimentals again.

HIALMAR. Thanks.

GREGERS. Regimentals?

RELLING. His lieutenant's uniform, of course.

GREGERS (*looking at* HIALMAR). Is that all you think about?

HIALMAR. Well, of course the rehabilitation of his honour goes with it. But the uniform is the most important thing to father. An old soldier——

GREGERS. Yes, but you! Yourself, Hialmar: you are not going to be satisfied with that sort of thing.

RELLING. Then what the devil more should he want?

GREGERS. So it is only the brand of punishment you would wash off him!

RELLING. Upon my soul, I think that wouldn't be a bad thing at all.

GREGERS. And I imagined it was the guilt itself you wished to release him from!

RELLING. Now we are going to hear something!

HIALMAR. What is past cannot be altered.

GREGERS. Do you believe he was as guilty as he appeared to be?

HIALMAR. I don't believe he had any idea of what he was doing.

GREGERS (*rising*). And even so you have lived here all these years, gone sluggishly through life and waited and waited—or perhaps not even that——

RELLING. You've been brooding too long up in those woods, Mr. Werle.

GREGERS. If I had had the good fortune to have such a father as you have——

HIALMAR. The good fortune——!

GREGERS. —then I would have been a different sort
of son to him— But it is your surroundings that have
pulled you down into the mire.

RELLING. Look here, I say!

MOLVIK. Are you referring to me?

HIALMAR. What have you to say about my surroundings?

GINA. Hush, hush, Ekdal. Don't say any more
about it.

GREGERS. I have this to say, that a man who lives
his life, his most intimate home life, in a marsh of lies
and deceit and concealment——

HIALMAR. Have you gone mad!

RELLING (*jumps up*). Be quiet, Mr. Werle!

HIALMAR. His most intimate home life——!

(*A knock at the door on the right.*)

GINA. Hush, be quiet; somebody's coming.

(*Goes over to the door.*)

HIALMAR. Have you gone stark mad, Gregers!

GINA (*opens the door and draws back*). Oh—what's
this!

(WERLE, *in a fur coat, advances one step into the
room.*)

WERLE. Excuse me; but I think my son is staying
here.

GINA (*with a gulp*). Yes.

HIALMAR (*who has risen*). Won't you——?

WERLE. Thank you, I wish to speak to my son.

GREGERS. What is it? Here I am.

WERLE. I want a few words with you, in your
room.

GREGERS. And I, for my part, desire witnesses.

WERLE.   What I wish to speak to you about is not of such a nature that——

GREGERS.   I am not disposed, for the present, to speak about anything but the Ekdals' affairs.

WERLE.   The Ekdals' affairs?

GREGERS.   And these two gentlemen belong to the house in a way.

WERLE.   What I have to say to you concerns only you and me.

GREGERS.   Since I lost my mother I think there is only one thing in the world that concerns me, that is the Ekdals' affairs.

HIALMAR.   I don't know what there is especially to talk about in our affairs.

WERLE.   Nor I either.

GREGERS.   But I know it, and I intend to shout it out at every street corner.   Every man in the country shall hear that the culprit was not Lieutenant Ekdal, but one who goes about free and unfettered to this very day.

WERLE.   And you dare to say that, you madman!— For I suppose it's to me that you allude.

GREGERS.   No, I allude more particularly to myself.

WERLE.   What are you thinking of?   You knew nothing——

GREGERS.   I had my doubts at the time it all happened; if I had spoken to Ekdal then, while there was yet time——

WERLE.   Well, why didn't you speak?

GREGERS.   I was afraid of you.

WERLE.   Evasions, inventions, imagination.   You yourself gave evidence in court——

GREGERS.   Yes, I was cowardly enough for that.   I was afraid to take my share of the guilt.

WERLE. Oh, this is that desperately sick conscience of yours.

GREGERS. It is you who have made my conscience sick.

WERLE. You're mistaken; it is a legacy from your mother, Gregers. The only one she left you.

GREGERS. Are you still unable to forget that you [were mistaken when you] thought she would bring you a fortune?

WERLE. We won't speak of these matters. I came to ask whether you will return home with me.

GREGERS. No.

WERLE. And you won't enter the firm either?

GREGERS. No.

WERLE. Very good. But as I am thinking of marrying again, your share of the property will fall to you at once.

GREGERS. I do not want that.

WERLE. You don't want it?

GREGERS. No.

WERLE. Are you going up to the works again?

GREGERS. No; I consider myself released from your service.

WERLE. Then what are you going to live upon?

GREGERS. I have laid by a little out of my salary.

WERLE. How long will *that* last?

GREGERS. I think it will last my time.

WERLE. What do you mean?

GREGERS. I shall answer no more questions.

WERLE. Good-bye then, Gregers.

GREGERS. Good-bye.

(WERLE *goes out to the right.*)

HIALMAR (*looking in through the sitting-room door*). He's gone, isn't he?

GREGERS.   Yes.

(GINA *and* HEDVIG *enter from the kitchen;* RELLING *and* MOLVIK *from the sitting-room.*)

RELLING.   That luncheon-party was a failure.

GREGERS.   Put on your coat, Hialmar; I want you to come for a long walk with me.

HIALMAR.   With pleasure.

GREGERS.   I'm only going to fetch my overcoat.

(*Goes out to the right.*)

GINA.   Don't go with him, Ekdal.

RELLING.   Stay where you are; don't go out now.

HIALMAR (*putting on his overcoat*).   Not for the world. I must find out what all this means——

RELLING.   But devil take it, don't you see that the fellow's mad, cracked, demented!

GINA.   There, what did I tell you, Ekdal. [His mother before him had strange fits like that sometimes.]

RELLING.   You mustn't pay any attention to his nonsense.

GINA.   No, no, don't.

HIALMAR.   Then I'll keep an eye on him at any rate. Good-bye.   (*Goes out to the right.*)

RELLING.   It's a thousand pities the fellow didn't fall on his head down one of those mines!

GINA.   Do you think Gregers Werle is mad?

RELLING.   No, worse luck; he's no madder than most people.

MOLVIK.   Not dæmonic either?

RELLING.   No, it's only you that are that, Molvik. But one disease he has certainly got in his system.

GINA.   What's the matter with him then?

RELLING.   Well, I'll tell you.   He is suffering from an acute attack of integrity.

GINA.   Integrity?

HEDVIG. What kind of disease is that?

RELLING. It's a national disease; but it only appears sporadically.—Come on, Molvik.

(*He nods and goes out to the right with* MOLVIK. GINA *moves restlessly across the room;* HEDVIG *looks searchingly at her.*)

FOURTH ACT

HIALMAR EKDAL'S *studio. Afternoon. It is beginning to grow dusk.*

(HEDVIG *is moving about the studio.* GINA *enters from the kitchen.*)

GINA. Not yet?

HEDVIG. No.

GINA. Are you sure he's not in Werle's room?

HEDVIG. No, it's locked.

GINA. Nor down in Relling's either?

HEDVIG. No, I've been down twice and asked.

GINA. And his dinner's standing and getting cold out there.

HEDVIG. Yes, can you imagine what has become of him, mother? He's always home so punctually to dinner.

GINA. Oh, he'll be here directly, you'll see.

HEDVIG (*after a short silence*). Do you think it's a good thing that Werle has come to live with us?

GINA. Why shouldn't it be a good thing?

HEDVIG. Well, I don't know; but we were so comfortable by ourselves. And I think Relling suits father much better than Werle.—Oh, what can have become of him!

GINA (*calls out*). There he is!

(HIALMAR EKDAL *comes in from the right.*)

HEDVIG (*going to him*). Father! So you've come at last!

GINA. We've been waiting such a long time for you, Ekdal!

HIALMAR. I was out rather long, yes.

GINA. Perhaps you've had dinner with Werle?

HIALMAR. No.

GINA. Then I'll bring some in for you.

HIALMAR. No, let it alone; I want nothing to eat.

HEDVIG. Are you not well, father?

HIALMAR. Oh yes, well enough. We have had a very long walk——

GINA. You didn't ought to have gone so far, Ekdal; you're not used to it.

HIALMAR. One can get used to a good many things. Have any orders come in to-day?

GINA. No, not to-day.

HEDVIG. There will be some to-morrow, father, you'll see.

HIALMAR. I should be glad of it; for to-morrow I am going to set to work properly; I mean to do everything myself; I shall take it into my own hands.

GINA. But why do you want to do that, Ekdal? What is the use of making your life a burden to you?

HIALMAR. That is my business. And then I should like to keep proper accounts too.

GINA. You?

HIALMAR. Yes, don't you keep accounts?

HEDVIG. But mother keeps the accounts so well.

HIALMAR. And she seems to make the money go a very long way, too. It's remarkable that we can live so well on the little money I have made this winter.

HEDVIG. Yes, but remember all the copying for Grå-berg, father.

HIALMAR. Copying, yes!

GINA. Nonsense, that doesn't come to much—

HEDVIG. Yes, indeed it does; it's mostly that we live on.

GINA. How can you say such a thing?

HEDVIG. Dear me, why mayn't father know that?

HIALMAR. So that is what we are living on. Copying for Mr. Werle.

GINA. You know very well that it's Gråberg who pays for it.

HIALMAR. Out of his own pocket?

GINA. Yes, I suppose so.

HEDVIG. But it's all the same to us, father.

HIALMAR. Of course; it's all the same to us where the money comes from.

GINA. That's what I think too. But as we're talking about it—! You haven't been doing anything all day, Hedvig——

HEDVIG. Then I had better go in and——

GINA. Yes, do. (HEDVIG *goes into the sitting-room.*)

GINA. What has happened to you, Ekdal?

HIALMAR. Do you think Gregers is in his senses?

GINA. How should I know? I don't know much about him.

HIALMAR. If I only knew that.

GINA. Well, you heard what Relling said about him.

HIALMAR. Oh, Relling, Relling—. Light the lamp for me, please.

GINA (*lighting the lamp*). Gregers Werle has been —odd—all his life.

HIALMAR. It seems to me your voice is trembling.

GINA. Is it?

HIALMAR. And your hands are shaking, are they not?

GINA. Yes. I don't know what makes them.

HIALMAR. Now I'll tell you what Gregers said about you.

GINA (*uneasy, holding her hands to her ears*). No, no; I won't hear it!

HIALMAR (*pulling her hands away*). You shall hear it!

GINA. There's no need for you to say it.

HIALMAR. Then you know what it is?

GINA. I can guess.

HIALMAR. So it is true. True, true! Oh, this is awful!

GINA. I see very well that I ought to have told you long ago.

HIALMAR. You should have told me at the very first; —while there was yet time.

GINA. What would you have done then?

HIALMAR. Then of course I should have had nothing to say to you.

GINA. Yes, that's what I thought; and that's why I didn't say anything.

HIALMAR. Unsuspecting fool that I was to imagine that you had a great love for me!

GINA. That has come with years, Ekdal; as true as I stand here. Oh yes, I'm fond of you, indeed I am, more than any one else can be.

HIALMAR. I don't want to know anything about that. What are you now in my eyes; you who could yield to a middle-aged married man?

GINA. Yes, I can't think now how I could do it.

HIALMAR. Can't you? Perhaps you have become moral with years. But *then*—how in the world could you enter into such a thing?

GINA. Oh, you must know, Ekdal, it isn't so easy for poor girls. The rich men begin by degrees with presents and so on—

HIALMAR. Yes, ready money, you're very fond of that.

GINA. It was mostly jewellery and clothes and that sort of thing.

HIALMAR. And of course you have sent it all back to him long ago.

GINA. I've worn out the clothes, and I sold the gold things one by one when we were wanting money——

HIALMAR. We've been living on that man's money. Everything we have in the house comes from him!

GINA. Ever since we were married I haven't seen a penny of his; and I don't believe I've seen him once.

HIALMAR. But the copying!

GINA. Bertha got me that, when she went to keep house for him.

HIALMAR. Yes, you and Bertha, you're both of the same sort.

GINA. Tell me, Ekdal—haven't I been a good wife to you?

HIALMAR. And what haven't you to thank me for! Haven't I raised you from an inferior position? Haven't I given you a name to bear?—yes, a name—for it shall come to be respected and honoured again.

GINA. That don't make any difference to me.

HIALMAR. Doesn't it? Oh well, I can quite believe it.

GINA. Yes, because I love you as you are, Ekdal; even if you never do the great things you're so fond of talking about.

HIALMAR. That's your lower nature showing itself. I am misunderstood in my own home; I have always been misunderstood by you.

GINA. But I've been a good wife to you, all the same.

(GREGERS WERLE *comes in from the passage door.*)

GREGERS (*in the doorway*). May I come in?

HIALMAR.   Yes, come in.

GREGERS.   Have you not done it yet?

HIALMAR.   It is done.

GREGERS.   It is?

HIALMAR.   I have passed through the bitterest moments of my life.

GREGERS.   But also, I trust, the most ennobling.

HIALMAR.   Well, at any rate, we have got through it for the present.

GINA.   God forgive you, Mr. Werle.

GREGERS.   But I don't understand this.

HIALMAR.   What don't you understand?

GREGERS.   A crisis so great as this—so exhaustive—a crisis that is to be the starting-point of an entirely new life—a life founded on truth——

HIALMAR.   Yes, yes, I know, I know.

GREGERS.   I was so confident that when I came in after this, I should find the light of a higher transfiguration shining over your home; and now I am met by this dulness, oppression, gloom——

GINA.   Oh, is that it?   (*Turns up the lamp.*)

GREGERS.   Or tell me frankly, Mrs. Ekdal, is it not a joy to you to be rid of this burden of concealment?

GINA.   I must tell you, Mr. Werle, that I've had so little time to remember all these old stories.

GREGERS.   I should have thought that they were never out of your thoughts for a day, for an hour.

GINA.   I'm sure I've had all I could do to look after the house.   And since I've been married no one can say anything but that I've been upright and respectable.

GREGERS.   Your whole view of life is incomprehensible to me—so widely, so immensely different from my own.   But you, Hialmar—surely you feel a new consecration after such a moment?

HIALMAR. Yes, of course I do. That is—in a sort of way——

GREGERS. The joy of forgiving one who has erred, of raising one who has strayed up to yourself in love——

HIALMAR. Do you think a man can so easily throw off the effects of an hour such as I have passed?

GREGERS. No, not a common man—perhaps; but a man like *you*——!

HIALMAR. Good God! I know that well enough. But it takes time, you know.

GREGERS. You have been too long at the bottom of the sea, Hialmar; you have bitten yourself fast there; and so it always hurts at first when one comes up into the clear daylight.

HIALMAR. You are right there; it hurts.

GREGERS. Yes, for there is too much of the wild duck in you. (RELLING *comes in from the passage.*)

RELLING. Oho! is the wild duck on the *tapis* again?

GREGERS. Yes, for it is the evil spirit of the house. Ah, it is not without significance that it came from Mr. Werle.

RELLING. So it's Mr. Werle you are talking about?

HIALMAR. Him and—certain others.

RELLING (*turning to* GREGERS). May the devil fly away with you.

HIALMAR. Then perhaps you know it too!

RELLING. Oh, never mind what I know or don't know. From that quarter one can expect all kinds of things.

GREGERS. Yes, but I who know, am I not to speak! Am I to look on while two dear, good creatures come to grief because they are living their life on a false foundation?

RELLING But it's no business of yours. You must leave off playing the quacksalver with my patients.

HIALMAR. Patients?

RELLING. Oh yes, there's always somebody who's in need of a doctor. But you don't understand that, Mr. Werle.

GREGERS. I know from experience what it is to have a gnawing conscience, such as has poisoned my life; but here I found my life's mission. Now I am so happy. And should I not then open the eyes of two people, who have such a profound need of seeing?

RELLING. What is it that they are to see?

GREGERS. The truth. The recognition that their association has not until tc-day been a true marriage.

RELLING. Do you think it will be truer hereafter?

GREGERS. Yes, I have a cheerful hope of that.

RELLING. Of course; people like you are always uncommonly hopeful. Time after time you're taken in, made fools of—hasn't that happened to you?

GREGERS. Certainly; I have suffered many disappointments.

RELLING. And yet you have a cheerful hope.

GREGERS. But here is something different, something out of the common. An individuality like Hialmar Ekdal's——

RELLING. Ekdal——!

HIALMAR. Yes, that may be true enough, but——

RELLING. Very well, Ekdal, then. But you see, his mission lies elsewhere; he doesn't need any better marriage than that he has lived in hitherto.

GINA. Yes, don't you think so, Relling! We were getting on so well——

HIALMAR. You don't understand the claims of the ideal.

RELLING.   No, you see, Hialmar Ekdal will come out all right; he can't come to grief altogether.   He has his great problem to wrestle with——

HIALMAR.   Yes, my problem—I have that, of course.

RELLING.   And when that is solved, he will once more have cast honour and glory upon the name of Ekdal.

HIALMAR.   I hope so, in any case.

GREGERS.   Well, the problem is all very well; but it is something that lies outside the individuality, something purely scientific, or technical, or whatever you like to call it.   And it is impossible for such a thing to satisfy an individuality such as Hialmar's.   Or do you think it satisfies you?

HIALMAR.   No, not entirely, I think——

GREGERS.   There, you see, Doctor Relling.   And if it does not satisfy his individuality *now*, when that individuality has not developed into perfect freedom—; well, let me put a question to you; do you think any great problem *can* be solved by an imperfect individuality?

RELLING.   Do you mean that photography cannot be raised to an art so long as the photographer's relation to his wife is not a true marriage?

GREGERS.   You put it rather bluntly; but I have such an unfailing belief in the powers of development of true marriage——

RELLING.   Excuse me, Mr. Werle, have you seen many true marriages?

GREGERS.   No, scarcely a single one.

RELLING.   Nor I either.

GREGERS.   But I have seen marriages of the opposite kind; and what ruin they can work in a human soul——

RELLING. And from them you draw your conclusions. Well, well, Ekdal, now you know what is wanted for your great discovery.

GINA. But you shouldn't talk so much about that invention, Relling, for it won't come to anything after all.

HIALMAR. Won't come to anything!

RELLING. Well, that's a fine thing to say!

HIALMAR. My problem won't come to anything, do you say!

GINA. No, I'm pretty sure it won't. You've been waiting all this time to find out something; and you're just where you were——

RELLING. Such things often come about by a sort of revelation, Mrs. Ekdal.

HIALMAR. But she doesn't understand that.

GINA. Well, revelations are all very fine, but you want something else besides. I should think it would be better if you worked with the instruments you've [we've] got, Ekdal; and then other people can find out these new ones.

HIALMAR. Not understood; not understood in one's own home. (*Sees* HEDVIG.) Yes, she understands me. Or do you not believe in me either, Hedvig?

HEDVIG. What am I to believe in, father?

HIALMAR. You are of course to believe in me in a general way, to believe in my mission, and to believe in the problem.

HEDVIG. Yes, I believe you will one day find it out.

HIALMAR. H'm——

GINA. Hush, there's a knock.

> (*Goes toward the passage door.*)
> (MRS. SÖRBY *comes in.*)

GINA. Is it you, Bertha?

MRS. SÖRBY. Yes, of course it is.

HIALMAR. If you have anything to say to Gina, won't you go in— (*Indicating the sitting-room.*)

MRS. SÖRBY. Thanks, I'd rather stay here. I have a message from Mr. Werle.

HIALMAR. What does he want with us!

GREGERS. Perhaps it is something about me.

MRS. SÖRBY. At any rate he wishes you to know it. To begin with, a somewhat important change is impending in Mr. Werle's domestic and other relations.

GREGERS. Aha!

MRS. SÖRBY. Mr. Werle has decided to make over the business here to Gråberg, and will himself move up to the works.

GREGERS. He will!

HIALMAR. Really, will Mr. Werle move up to the works?

RELLING. He won't stand that for long; it will be much too lonely.

MRS. SÖRBY. Well, he won't be altogether alone either.

GREGERS. Ah, then it's coming off after all?

MRS. SÖRBY. Yes.

RELLING. What's coming off?

HIALMAR. I don't understand a word.

GREGERS. I must explain the situation. My father and Mrs. Sörby are going to be married.

HIALMAR. Going to be married!

GINA. Oh! so it's come to that at last!

RELLING. This is surely not true?

MRS. SÖRBY. Yes, it is true; he has got a special license and goes up there this evening. And I think of going to-morrow morning. Well, now I have told you; so it is over.

RELLING. So that was the end of it.

GREGERS.   What do you think this will lead to, Mrs. Sörby?

MRS. SÖRBY.   To good, I think.   Mr. Werle is not nearly so difficult to get on with as some people think.

GREGERS.   No doubt you have no cause to complain.

MRS. SÖRBY.   Oh no; he may be unreasonable now and then; but I have been through worse things, Mr. Werle.   And of course one is glad to be provided for.

RELLING.   And Mr. Werle is the man to provide for you.   He's no beggar.

MRS. SÖRBY.   There are many who need not be beggars, if only they had put their whole hearts into something.

RELLING.   Put their whole hearts—tell me, how much would that help?

MRS. SÖRBY.   Ah, a man can be so far gone that he no longer has a heart for anything.

RELLING.   I shall go out with Molvik this evening.

MRS. SÖRBY.   You mustn't do that, Relling.

RELLING.   There's nothing else for it.

(*Goes out through the passage door.*)

MRS. SÖRBY.   And then there's another thing.   No doubt some people think Mr. Werle ought to have done a little more for an old friend like Lieutenant Ekdal.

HIALMAR.   Mr. Werle does a very great deal for father: he pays so liberally——

MRS. SÖRBY.   Yes, for the copying; but now your father's getting old; his eyesight will not be equal to the work much longer; so here is an order to pay once for all.   You or Gina can draw every month a hundred crowns for your father——

HIALMAR.   Gina?

MRS. SÖRBY. Yes, or you; just as you like. And when your father—well, when he no longer requires anything, it passes on to Hedvig.

HIALMAR (*draws back, as though stabbed*). To Hedvig!

HEDVIG. Fancy! All that money!

HIALMAR. Hedvig! What do you say to that, Gina!

GINA. Mr. Werle must have thought that——

MRS. SÖRBY. It seemed to him the most honourable way——; you see, Hedvig is a child; she can quite well accept it.

HIALMAR. Yes, she has most claim to it, unless Gina herself——

MRS. SÖRBY. Gina herself!——

HIALMAR. But I, I, I, you see!

HEDVIG. I won't take anything. You shall have it all, father.

MRS. SÖRBY. What has happened here?

HIALMAR. Something that ought to have happened long, long ago.

MRS. SÖRBY. Already.

GREGERS. I understand very well why father has arranged this. He wanted to convince me that Hialmar Ekdal was not the man I took him for.

HIALMAR. He will be out in his calculations, then. Look here, Gregers. (*Tears the paper across.*) There, Mrs. Sörby, will you be so good as to give this back to Mr. Werle.

MRS. SÖRBY. I won't take it.

HIALMAR (*throws it on the table*). Then let it be. But tell him at all events that I have torn his deed of gift in pieces.

GREGERS. And then ask your future husband who was right, he or I.

Mrs. Sörby. I will. Good-bye, Gina; good luck to you.

Gina. You too, Bertha. Good-bye.

(Mrs. Sörby *goes.*)

Hialmar (*in a whisper*). Now you're to answer me, as though you were on your oath: does Hedvig belong to me or not?

Gina. I don't know.

Hialmar. You don't know!

Gina. How should I know—; a creature like me.

Hialmar. And you brazen it out, too.—Gregers, to-morrow I leave this house.

Hedvig (*with a scream*). Father! Oh, no, no!

Gina. You'll never do that, Ekdal!

Gregers. Must it be so, Hialmar?

Hialmar. It must. I'm going at once. (*Puts on his overcoat.*) I shan't be home to-night

Hedvig (*throws herself down on the sofa*). He is going away from us! Father, father is going away from us! Oh, mother, mother!

Gina. You mustn't cry, Hedvig; he's sure to come back again.

Hedvig. No, he'll never come back again! Didn't he say so?

Gina. Don't you think he'll come back, Mr. Werle?

Gregers. I feel sure of it. Hialmar will come back to his home; and you will see how exalted he will return.

Hedvig. But what have we done to him? Mother, tell me what it is? Why doesn't he want me any more? Tell me that! Oh, tell me that!

Gina. Hush, hush, you'll know when you're older.

Hedvig. Yes, but I'll never be older if father doesn't want me. (*Bursts into sobs and tears.*)

GINA. You musn't cry, Hedvig; you mustn't indeed. It does you harm; Doctor Relling said so.

HEDVIG. I can't help it. Oh, mother, mother, fetch him home again——

GINA. Yes, I'll go and look for him. Perhaps he's only gone down to Relling's. (*Puts on her shawl.*) But you must be quiet, Hedvig; promise me!

HEDVIG. Yes, yes.

GREGERS. Had you not better leave him to fight out his bitter fight to the end?

GINA. Oh, he can do that afterwards. First of all, we must get the child quieted.

(*She goes out by the passage door.*)

GREGERS. There now; cheer up, Hedvig. All may yet be well.

HEDVIG. Why doesn't father want me any more, Mr. Werle? You must tell me that.

GREGERS. I can only say as your mother says: some day you will know.

HEDVIG. But I can't go on waiting and being as miserable as this.

GREGERS. What right have you, or any human being to be happy? What right, I ask.

HEDVIG. Oh, I don't care about that; it is so lovely to be happy and cheerful.

GREGERS. There is something in life that is higher than that, Hedvig.

HEDVIG. Yes, but that doesn't matter if only everything is right again at home, between father and mother and me. Don't you think everything can come right between us?

GREGERS. I have a sure hope that some day everything will be right again between your father and mother.

HEDVIG. Yes, but me!

GREGERS. You must remember one thing, Hedvig: you are not destined to spend your whole life here at home.

HEDVIG. Oh yes, oh yes! I will always stay at home. I will never, never leave father and mother.—And then —just think—then father doesn't want me any more!

GREGERS. You must wait and hope; your father has first to fight out his battle.

HEDVIG. But I can't wait and be as miserable as this. Why doesn't father want me any more? Am I not really father's and mother's child? Perhaps they only found me?

GREGERS. Found you? Well, it might be that your father believes something like that.

HEDVIG. Yes, but then mother can tell him that it isn't true.

GREGERS. And supposing he doesn't believe her.

HEDVIG. Well, but even if it *was* true, father might be just as fond of me for all that. We don't know where the wild duck came from either, and yet we love it so intensely.

GREGERS. The wild duck. Yes, you love that wild duck so intensely, Hedvig.

HEDVIG. Yes, so intensely.

GREGERS. And the wild duck is your property, isn't she?

HEDVIG. Yes, she belongs to me. But why——?

GREGERS. Have you anything else that you love so well?

HEDVIG. Oh no; nothing in the world.

GREGERS. Then you must sacrifice the dearest treasure you have——

HEDVIG. The wild duck!

GREGERS. Yes, and get back your father's love instead.

HEDVIG. But how can you think——

GREGERS. He said so himself before he went; neither you nor the old man cared to make such a sacrifice for his sake; it is your love for him that he doubts; that is why he doesn't want you any more.

HEDVIG. Oh, if it was only that——

GREGERS. Show him that to win him back means more to you than anything in the world. Give up your dearest treasure, and give it gladly.

HEDVIG. Ah, if that could only make everything come right again——

GREGERS. You must not doubt the power of self-sacrifice; that is just what is ideal in family life, you see——

HEDVIG. Oh, but I don't care about anything of that sort; I don't understand it.

GREGERS. But don't you see that this would be a deed that bore the stamp of the uncommon; and for that very reason your father would recognise the kinship between you and him.

HEDVIG. Do you think so?

GREGERS. Yes, I'm sure of it. And your father would say: Hedvig is my child in spirit and in truth, even if she came from the ends of the earth.

HEDVIG. Or from the depths of the sea.

GREGERS. Yes, yes, from the depths of the sea, if you like.

HEDVIG. And then everything might come right again between me and father? Oh, that would be splendid.

GREGERS. Everything is splendid when one's course of life is raised to a higher plane. So the dearest you have must be sacrificed, Hedvig. Take your grandfather into the secret; get him to do it; look out for a time when he wants to go shooting—you know——

HEDVIG.   Yes, yes, I know——

GREGERS.   But don't tell your mother about it——

HEDVIG.   Why not mother?

GREGERS.   Because she would scarcely understand us.

(GINA *comes in from the passage.*)

HEDVIG.   Mother! Did you find him?

GINA.   No. I only heard as he had called and taken Relling with him.

GREGERS.   Are you sure of that?

GINA.   Yes, the woman in the yard said so. Molvik went with them too.

GREGERS.   This evening, when his mind so sorely needs to wrestle in solitude.

GINA.   Yes, that's what I thought. The Lord only knows where they have gone to. They weren't at Madam Eriksen's.

HEDVIG (*bursting into tears*). Oh, if he never comes home any more!

GREGERS.   He *will* come home again. And then you shall see *how* he comes home!—Good evening. And sleep in peace.   (*He goes out by the passage door.*)

HEDVIG (*throws herself weeping on* GINA'S *neck*). Mother, mother!

GINA.   Ah yes, that's what comes of it when you have crazy creatures in the house.

FROM THE FIFTH ACT

GREGERS. What is your explanation of the **mental** agitation that is going on in Ekdal?

RELLING. Devil a bit of mental agitation do *I* think there is in him.

GREGERS. But can you think that an individuality like his——!

RELLING. Oh, individuality, individuality! I don't know what individuality is. Hialmar Ekdal is a good, kind, well-behaved creature, whose chief wish is to live as comfortably and as free from care as he can manage.

GREGERS. He—who has to restore his name and the honour of his family.

RELLING. Yes, yes, I know all about that; he was drivelling about that last night. But how the devil should he be able to retrieve the past? Can you tell me that?

GREGERS. Have you forgotten the remarkable invention he is working at?

RELLING. So you believe in that invention in sober earnest?

GREGERS. Yes, certainly. And you believe in it yourself, too.

RELLING. No, look here, Mr. Werle—I may be something of a beast, but a fool I am not.

GREGERS. Well, anyhow you spoke highly enough of his endeavours yesterday.

RELLING. Deuce take it, can't you see why? All this about the remarkable invention is just the life-illusion that keeps *him* going.

GREGERS. Life-illusion?

RELLING.   Yes, of course. Most people occupy themselves with an illusion that helps them to live their lives.

GREGERS.   That would be a distressing state of
things.

RELLING.   Who said it was a cheerful state of things?
It is so, and there's an end of it. The remarkable
invention is to Ekdal what the dæmonic nature is to
Molvik.

GREGERS.   Isn't it true ʼwith him either?

RELLING.   An idiot like him—dæmonic?   How the
devil can you believe such a thing?   And there's nothing
of the kind either.   But if I hadn't given him that idea,
he would have come to grief in self-contempt long ago.

GREGERS.   And perhaps it is you who gave him the
idea.

RELLING.   Yes, I'm his doctor, you see; curing him
is out of the question; but a little injection of illusion
now and then—it acts as a palliative.

GREGERS.   That may be; but it is not so with Hialmar Ekdal.

RELLING.   Isn't it?   Rob Hialmar Ekdal of his illusion, and you rob him of his happiness at the same
stroke.

GREGERS.   Ah, his illusion, I dare say.   But what
about his striving after the ideal?

RELLING.   Good Lord, man! they are only two dif-
erent names for the same thing. (To HEDVIG, who
comes in.)   Well, Hedvig, I'm just going down to look
after your father.   (He goes out to the right.)

GREGERS.   Have you enough courage and strength of
will to-day?

HEDVIG.   Well, I don't know; I don't seem quite able
to believe in such a thing.

GREGERS. Then let it be; without true resolution there is nothing in it. (*Goes out to the right.*)

(HEDVIG *is on the point of going into the kitchen when a knock is heard at the door to the garret; she goes over and opens it; old* EKDAL *comes out; she shuts the door again.*)

EKDAL. It's no good being in there alone. What's become of Hialmar?

HEDVIG. Wouldn't you like to shoot the wild duck, grandfather?

EKDAL. Hush, hush, don't talk like that. It's only something that comes over me. Old sportsman, you see.

HEDVIG. Oughtn't they to be shot in the breast?

EKDAL. Under the wing, when you can manage it. And it's best a little from behind.

HEDVIG. Do you often want to shoot her?

EKDAL. Needn't be afraid. I can make a rabbit do. (*Goes into his room.*)

(GINA *comes from the sitting-room and begins to clean up the studio. Presently the passage door is opened slowly;* HIALMAR *is seen; he is without hat or overcoat, unwashed and with unkempt hair.*)

GINA. There now, you've come at last!

HIALMAR (*comes in*). I'm going again at once [this instant].

GINA. Yes, yes, I suppose so.

HEDVIG (*from the kitchen*). Oh, father!

HIALMAR (*turns away and makes a gesture of repulsion*). Away, away, away!

GINA. Go into the sitting-room, Hedvig. (HEDVIG *does so.*)

HIALMAR. I must have my books with me. Where are my books?

GINA. What books?

HIALMAR. My scientific books, of course; the technical magazines I require for my invention.

GINA (*searches in the bookcase*). Is it these here that isn't bound?

HIALMAR. Yes, of course.

GINA (*lays them on the table*). Shan't I get Hedvig to cut them for you?

HIALMAR. There is no need.

GINA. Then you still stick to it that you'll leave us?

HIALMAR. Yes, that is a matter of course, I should think.

GINA. But what about grandfather?

HIALMAR. He'll come with me. I am going out into the town to make arrangements—. H'm— Has any one found my hat on the stairs?

GINA. No. Have you lost your hat?

HIALMAR. Of course I had it on when I came in; I'm quite certain of that; but I couldn't find it this morning.

GINA. If only you haven't caught cold, Ekdal.

(*Goes out into the kitchen.*)

(HIALMAR *rummages among the papers and photographs on the table, finds the torn document of yesterday, takes it up and looks at it; sees* GINA *and puts it down.*)

GINA (*brings a tray with coffee from the kitchen*). Here's a little something hot, if you'd fancy it.

HIALMAR (*glances at it*). Coffee!—Do you suppose I'm in the mood to drink coffee?—My manuscripts, my letters and my important papers. (*Opens the sitting-room door.*) Is she there too? Come out. (HEDVIG *comes.*) In the last moment I spend here, I wish to be spared from interlopers. (*Goes into the room.*)

GINA. Stay out in the kitchen, Hedvig.

(*Goes into the sitting-room.*)

HEDVIG (*stands a moment immovable, biting her lips to suppress the tears; then clenches her hand and says softly:*) The wild duck.

(*She goes over to the garret door, slides it a little to one side, steals in and shuts it after her.*)

HIALMAR (*with some letters [manuscript books], which he lays on the table*). Oh, there are a thousand and one things I must drag with me.

GINA. Yes, you won't have an easy job getting everything in order. And now your coffee's getting cold.

HIALMAR. H'm.

(*Drinks a mouthful or two without thinking of it.*)

GINA (*dusting*). A nice job you'll have to find a room for the rabbits.

HIALMAR. What! Am I to have all those rabbits with me?

GINA. You don't suppose father can get on without his rabbits.

HIALMAR. He must get used to doing without them. The pigeons too must remain here for the present. I must try to dispense with them. Henceforward there are many things I must dispense with.

(*Takes a piece of bread and butter, eats it and drinks some coffee.*)

GINA. If we hadn't let that room, you could have moved in there.

HIALMAR. And remained under the same roof with you and her—her—that——

GINA. Hush, don't talk so loud; father's in the garret.

HIALMAR. What, is he in the garret again?

GINA. But couldn't you move into the sitting-room for a day or two? You could have it all to yourself.

HIALMAR. Never within these walls.

GINA. Well then, down with Relling?

HIALMAR. Don't mention that wretch's name to me. The very thought of him makes me sick. Oh no, I must go out into the snow-drift and seek shelter for father and myself.

———————

HIALMAR. Of course I shall leave this house as soon as possible. I am in the act of packing my things. I cannot go on living in a home that has fallen to pieces.

GINA. Will you give me the key of your chest of drawers, Ekdal?

HIALMAR. What do you want with it?

GINA. I'll put your shirts into the portmanteau.

HIALMAR. Here! And keep it. I have no more use for it.

(GINA *goes into the sitting-room.*)

GREGERS. Do you really feel this a necessity?

HIALMAR. Do you not know me well enough to understand that I cannot live in a ruined home?

GREGERS. But this is just the moment when this home might be built up again on a foundation tenfold more secure than before; upon truth, forgiveness, reconciliation.

HIALMAR. Would you be able to approve of that?

GREGERS. My dear fellow, isn't that just what I was aiming at?

HIALMAR. Yes, but then there is the awful, the desperate side of the situation, that happiness in any case is gone for ever! Just think of Hedvig, whom I have loved so dearly.

GREGERS. And who loves you so dearly, Hialmar.

HIALMAR. But that, you see, is what I cannot believe after this. Whatever she may say, whatever she may do, I shall always doubt her. For I can never know whether she is not acting from a sense of insecurity, from fear and a feeling that she has become, as it were, a stranger in the house.

GREGERS. Hedvig knows nothing of dissimulation. What if she now brought you her best possession as a sacrifice—would you not then believe in her?

HIALMAR. Oh, what sacrifice could she make that——

GREGERS. A small thing, perhaps; but to her the most precious. Let us just suppose that for your sake she gave up the wild duck.

HIALMAR. The wild duck? What would be the use of that?

GREGERS. To give up her most precious possession.

HIALMAR. This is overstrained talk. Even if she gave up the wild duck ten times over, there would still be a kind of concealed gulf between us. Both Hedvig and I would feel it and suffer. No, I tell you; happiness is past for us. Never again can Hedvig and I be on a footing of father and child.

(*A shot is heard from within the garret.*)

HIALMAR. What! Is he shooting again!

GINA (*comes in*). If only he doesn't end by doing himself a mischief.

HIALMAR. I'll look in——

GREGERS. Wait a moment. Do you know what that was?

HIALMAR. How—was?

GREGERS. It was a useless sacrifice that poor Hedvig made. She has got him to shoot the wild duck.

GINA. Are you sure of that?

GREGERS. I know it.

HIALMAR. The wild duck.

GINA. Yes, she's been so tormented and despairing, Ekdal.

GREGERS. And she knew no other way but to sacrifice to you the best she had.

HIALMAR. And I could be so harsh towards her! Where is she, Gina?

GINA (*struggling with her tears*). She's sitting out in the kitchen.

HIALMAR. It must and shall come right again. (*Goes over and opens the kitchen door.*) Hedvig, come in to me! —No, she's not here.

GINA. Isn't she? Then she must have gone out.

HIALMAR. Oh, if she would only come quickly, so that I can tell her— For I really didn't mean anything by it.

GREGERS. You didn't mean anything by it?

GINA. It wasn't like you either, Ekdal.

HIALMAR. No, it was mostly on your account, Gregers. You came here and made such unreasonably heavy claims on me——

GREGERS. Do you think that!

HIALMAR. Yes, you don't know me properly, you see: I am not altogether as you imagine me—I want everything to be pleasant and easy and comfortable——

GINA. Ekdal is not made to be unhappy——

GREGERS. I'm beginning almost to believe that.

HIALMAR. Yes, and so I am going to stay here with Gina and Hedvig, just as before——

GINA. That's right.

GREGERS. But, my dear fellow, that's exactly what I've been striving for.

HIALMAR. Yes, but you wanted it brought about by a lot of hocus pocus, that I don't understand at all.

GREGERS. Ah, there can't be any doubt that it is I whose judgment was at fault.

HIALMAR. Yes, for, you see, we are not that sort, neither Gina nor I. But what has become of Hedvig? Oh, dear, I wish she would come. And then she shall hear that I care for her——

GINA. Just as much as she cares for you, Ekdal.

HIALMAR. And just as much as she cared for the wild duck.

GREGERS. The sacrifice has not been in vain after all.

HIALMAR. No. After this Hedvig shall be our wild duck——

(OLD EKDAL *appears at the door of his room.*)

HIALMAR. Father!

GINA. Has he been firing in there?

EKDAL. So you go shooting alone, do you, Hialmar?

HIALMAR. Wasn't it you that fired that shot?

EKDAL. *Me* that fired?

GREGERS. Then she has shot it herself.

HIALMAR. What can it mean? (*Runs to the garret door, tears it aside, looks in and calls loudly:*) Hedvig!

GINA (*going to the door*). What is it?

HIALMAR. She's lying on the floor!

(*Goes into the garret.*)

GREGERS. Hedvig!

GINA. Hedvig! No, no, no! (*Goes into the garret.*)

EKDAL. What is it? Was it Hedvig——!

HIALMAR (*carries* HEDVIG *into the studio*). She has wounded herself! Call for help!

GINA (*runs into the passage and is heard calling:*) Relling! Relling! Doctor Relling!

HIALMAR (*lays* HEDVIG *down on the sofa*). She's coming to—she'll soon come to now. The pistol has gone off.——

EKDAL. There was a bullet in it. She didn't know that. Didn't know it was loaded.

GINA (*who has come back*). Where has she hurt herself? I can't see anything.

(RELLING, *and immediately after him* MOLVIK, *from the passage; the latter without his waistcoat and necktie, and with his coat open.*)

RELLING. What's the matter here?

GINA. Hedvig has shot herself.

HIALMAR. Come and help us!

RELLING. Shot herself!

(*Goes over to the sofa and examines her.*)

HIALMAR. It can't be dangerous; she is scarcely bleeding at all; it can't be——

RELLING. How did it happen?

HIALMAR. Oh, we don't know——!

GINA. She wanted to shoot the wild duck——

RELLING. The wild duck?

HIALMAR. The pistol must have gone off.

RELLING. H'm!

EKDAL. Shoot the wild duck. Don't understand a word of it. Won't hear any more.

(*Goes into the garret.*)

RELLING. The ball has entered the breast——

HIALMAR. Yes, but she's alive!

GINA. Surely you see that Hedvig is dead.

HIALMAR. No, no, she *must* live. Only a moment. Only just till I can tell her——

RELLING. The bullet has gone through her heart;— internal hemorrhage. Death must have been instantaneous.

HIALMAR. Oh Gina, Gina, and I have done this to you!

GINA. Perhaps I had no right to keep her though.

HIALMAR. Had I then a right to take her from you? From *you*, after all you have been to us for so many years.

GINA. She shall be laid on her own bed. Take and help me, Ekdal.

(*She and* HIALMAR *take* HEDVIG *between them.*)

HIALMAR (*as they are carrying her*). Oh Gina, Gina, can you survive this.

GINA. We must help each other to bear it. I brought her into the world, and you took her out of the world;— so *now* at least she belongs to both of us.

(*They carry her into the sitting-room.*)

MOLVIK (*stretches out his arms and mumbles*). Blessed be the Lord! to earth thou shalt return, to earth thou shalt return.

RELLING (*softly*). Hold your tongue, Molvik; you're drunk. Go downstairs.

(HIALMAR *and* GINA *carry the body into the sitting-room.*)

RELLING (*shuts the door after them, goes over to* GRE-GERS *and says:*) That pistol never went off by accident.

GREGERS. Are you quite sure of that?

RELLING. There's no doubt about it; from the way the powder has burnt the body of her dress—. She pressed the pistol right against her breast and fired.

GREGERS. I almost think that is how it happened.

RELLING. And can you say that you are free from guilt?

GREGERS. I intended it for the best.

RELLING. Yes, you wanted to bring about something you call a true marriage here; and then you made your calculations for only the husband and wife, but you forgot [left out] the child.

GREGERS. She could not bear the light of truth; it dazzled her eyes.

RELLING. Truth is not particularly wholesome for most people. Take away the illusion from a relationship, and you take away happiness at the same stroke.

GREGERS. If that held good, it would not be worth while to live one's life.

RELLING. Then do *you* think it's such an important thing to live your life?

GREGERS. Not I; on the contrary; but it isn't my destiny either to live my life; I have another mission.

RELLING. What mission is that?

GREGERS. To be the thirteenth at table.   (*Goes.*)

RELLING. The devil it is.

ROSMERSHOLM

"WHITE HORSES"

He, the noble, refined nature, who has come round to a liberal point of view and from whom all his former friends and acquaintances have withdrawn. A widower; was unhappily married to a melancholy, half-mad wife, who ended by drowning herself.

She, his two daughters' governess, emancipated, warm-blooded, somewhat remorseless in a refined way. Is regarded by their acquaintance as the evil spirit of the house; is the object of misinterpretation and scandal.

Elder daughter; is in danger of succumbing to inactivity and loneliness; highly gifted, without any application for her talents.

Younger daughter; observant; dawning passions.

The journalist; genius, vagabond.

DRAFT

In the drawing-room of the parsonage. Dialogue between S. and Miss B. The student comes in from a walk. The old retired apothecary calls on business; goes away. The family assembled. The cavalry captain. The magistrate and his daughter come to call and bring an invitation; it is accepted; then the change of views is to be disclosed. The family alone; conversation turns on the white horses.

DRAFT

1st Act

In the drawing-room of the country house. The clergyman and the young lady;

She is an intriguer and she loves him. She wishes to be his wife and she pursues this end with determination. Then he finds this out and she frankly admits it. There is now no more happiness in life for him. The dæmonic in his nature is awakened by pain and bitterness. He desires to die, and she is to die with him. She does so.

I

FIRST ACT

Sitting-room at Boldt-Römer's. The room is old-fashioned but comfortable. On the right a large stove; farther back a door. In the back wall, a double door opening into the hall. To the left, two windows, with flowers in pots on the window-frames. By the farther window, a table with a sewing-machine; in the corner, on the right, a sofa with a table and easy chairs. On the walls, old family portraits, representing officers and clergymen. It is afternoon. The sun is shining into the room.

(BOLDT-RÖMER *is sitting in a rocking-chair in front of the stove, reading a magazine.* MISS RADECK *sits over by the window, working at the sewing-machine.*)

BOLDT-RÖMER (*letting his book drop*). H'm, it is strange for all that.

MISS RADECK (*looking at him*). What is it you mean?

BOLDT-RÖMER. It is strange for me to be sitting here —in Easter week—without anything to attend to; without anything to be responsible for.

MISS RADECK. But don't you feel that is a relief?

BOLDT-RÖMER. Yes, you may be sure I do. It's only at first—. Where are the girls to-day?

MISS RADECK. I expect they're down at the mill-pond skating.

BOLDT-RÖMER (*rising*). I didn't like to say so before. For they must have some amusement. But I so greatly dislike their skating down on the pond.

MISS RADECK. Oh, there's no danger at all. It's not so deep; and besides, the ice is perfectly safe.

BOLDT-RÖMER. I know that; it isn't *that* I was thinking of.

MISS RADECK (*looking at him*). I see, it's on account of—the other thing?

BOLDT-RÖMER. Yes. I think there is something un-canny in the children skating and playing and making a noise just over the spot that was their mother's death-bed.

MISS RADECK. But the girls know nothing about that.

BOLDT-RÖMER. No; but we know about it unfortunately; and therefore I cannot get rid of—. Well, well, I know of course it's meaningless; nothing but a sort of prejudice, or whatever we may call it; but nevertheless——

MISS RADECK. Then you haven't got over that kind of thing yet?

BOLDT-RÖMER. I doubt if I shall ever get over it entirely.

MISS RADECK. Then you ought to try whether you cannot recover your former standpoint.

BOLDT-RÖMER. That? Never while I'm alive! That I neither can nor will do.

MISS RADECK. At all events it would have been better for you if you had never left it.

BOLDT-RÖMER. And *you* can say that? To *me?* To me, who never knew what it was to be happy until I had achieved spiritual emancipation.

MISS RADECK. Oh, you have a long way to go yet before you achieve complete emancipation. I believe it would have been better for you if I had never entered your door.

BOLDT-RÖMER. Then what should I have been now?

MISS RADECK. What you were before.

BOLDT-RÖMER. Yes, that is true. A creature without breadth of vision; without the least understanding of the life of reality that is struggling and working around us.

MISS RADECK. Ah, but for all that; with a nature so gentle as yours; and then all that you have inherited and that has left its mark on you. Oh no, it's not so easy—. (*Looks out.*) Look; here comes the Rector.

BOLDT-RÖMER. Who is it?

MISS RADECK. Your brother-in-law.

(RECTOR HEKMANN *enters from the hall.*)

HEKMANN. But what is this I see in the papers?

ROSENHJELM. Have the papers come?

HEKMANN. Yes, and they say you have resigned your living.

ROSENHJELM. I've been thinking of it for a long time. I cannot continue. It is impossible.

HEKMANN. One can understand very well that you cannot associate yourself with all these gloomy pietistic tendencies that have gained the upper hand in so many circles. But isn't it then your duty to counteract——

ROSENHJELM. Not as a clergyman. I cannot continue in that position.

H. That I don't understand.

R. I ought never to have taken orders. Nor was it of my own free will that I did so. But, you see, it was a family tradition. The Church and the Army by turns—from father to son. And as my father was a soldier, it was perfectly natural that I should take up theology. At that time I thought myself that it was as it should be.

H. And now you had become so firmly fixed in it. What will you turn to now—in the prime of life?

R. Well, I have all the affairs of the estate——

H. That won't fill up your time; and you have a steward and tenants too. No, it's no use making any more excuses. You must and shall take part in public life.

R. I had been thinking of that too—in my own way.

H. Not in any private way of your own. You must enter the ranks of the party. You can see well enough how great a need there is. Choose a special line. Oppose this Mortensgård who's stirring up all the ignorant mob. And now I hear he is thinking of starting a paper.

R. Is he? Well, the man has gifts. He knows how to write and speak.

H. Oh, my dear fellow, that's an easy matter when a man is not too particular as to the truth or the facts.

R. Well, I know so little of the facts in such matters.

H. But I know them. And I have had occasion to verify this Mortensgård. He is one of the most unprincipled pettifoggers we have in these parts. And that's saying a good deal, I can tell you.

R.   But is it not the fact that these Radicals have accomplished much good in the last few years?

H.   That I will never admit as long as I live.   They? What good should they accomplish?   Can any good come from such an impure source?

R.   But have we the right to be so positive in our judgment of the source?

H.   Don't carry your humanity to extremes, my dear Rosenhjelm.   And what is the good you have discovered? Perhaps you allude to the demagogues' *coup d' État?*

R.   I don't understand such matters.   But it seems to me that there is rather more independence in the ideas of individuals.

H.   And you reckon that a good thing among people who are so unstable and immature?   I think you are considerably mistaken.   And I must say I am greatly surprised to hear such words from you.   You who, after all, have inherited all your family's respect for authority and good order.

R.   Who knows?—perhaps one cannot altogether avoid being infected by the time one lives in.

H.   Still I hope that will never be the case with either you or me.   We will keep ourselves unstained.   Will we not, Rosenhjelm?

R.   To keep one's self unstained, so far as possible, is undoubtedly the task of everyone.

H.   Yes, and to spread purity around one, or in any case to keep contamination at a distance.

R.   There I certainly agree with you.

H.   Well, then you must also join us in acting, taking part in public life, combating all these fatal tendencies——

R.   But, my dear fellow, if one is not made for any of this?

H. In a cultured society everyone is made to be a citizen.

R. Everyone?

H. I mean, of course, everyone who has the necessary qualifications, everyone who possesses a certain modicum of education and intelligence, I don't ask for actual scholarship. But ordinary education and knowledge one ought really to be able to demand. Now *that* is what it would be so extremely beneficial to bring home to the masses.

II

WHITE HORSES

A PLAY IN FIVE ACTS

BY

HENRIK IBSEN

1886

FIRST ACT

An old-fashioned, but large and comfortable sitting-room at ROSMER'S. *On the right, a stove; farther back, on the same side, a door. In the back wall, folding-doors opening into the hall. To the left, two windows, with flowers in pots on a stand. Beside the stove a sofa with table and easy chairs. On the walls, old family portraits representing officers and clergymen. It is late afternoon. The winter sun shines into the room.*

(MRS. ROSMER *is standing by the farthest window, arranging the flowers.* MADAM HELSET *enters from the right with a basket of table linen.*)

MADAM HELSET. I suppose I had better begin to lay the tea-table, ma'am?

MRS. ROSMER. Yes, please do. He must soon be in now.

MADAM HELSET (*laying the cloth*). No, he won't come just yet; for I saw him from the kitchen——

MRS. ROSMER. Yes, yes——

MADAM HELSET. —on the other side of the mill-pond. At first he was going straight across the footbridge; but then he turned back——

MRS. ROSMER. Did he?

MADAM HELSET. Yes, and then he went all the way round. Ah, it's strange about such places. A place where a thing like that has happened—there—. It stays there; it isn't forgotten so soon.

MRS. ROSMER. No, it is not forgotten.

MADAM HELSET. No, indeed it isn't.

(*Goes out to the right.*)

MRS. ROSMER (*at the window, looking out*). Forget. Forget, ah!

MADAM HELSET (*in the doorway*). I've just seen the Rector, ma'am. He's coming here.

MRS. ROSMER. Are you sure of that?

MADAM HELSET. Yes, he went across the mill-pond.

MRS. ROSMER. And my husband is not at home.

MADAM HELSET. The tea is ready as soon as you want it.

MRS. ROSMER. But wait; we can't tell whether he'll stay.

MADAM HELSET. Yes, yes. (*Goes out to the right.*)

MRS. ROSMER (*goes over and opens the door to the hall*). Good afternoon; how glad I am to see you, my dear Rector!

RECTOR GYLLING (*taking off his overcoat*). Thanks. Then I am not disturbing you?

MRS. ROSMER. Oh no, how can you think so? On the contrary.

RECTOR GYLLING (*coming in*). Well, that's all right. But where's your husband?

MRS. ROSMER. He has only gone for a little walk. I think he'll be in directly. Won't you sit down till he comes?

GYLLING (*sits down by the stove*). Many thanks. There is something I should like to speak to him about.

MRS. ROSMER (*sits down at the table*). That is fortunate, for it has given us a chance of seeing you at last. How is it you haven't been near us before?

GYLLING. Oh, it doesn't do to make oneself a nuisance to young married people.

MRS. ROSMER (*smiling*). H'm—we are not so very young, you know.

GYLLING. Well, newly-married anyhow. But I have been away too, as you know, for a couple of weeks.

MRS. ROSMER. Yes, we have heard of you at political meetings.

GYLLING. I've turned political agitator, as the radical papers call it—in speaking of *us*. Or perhaps you never see those papers?

MRS. ROSMER (*quickly*). Oh yes, we see them now and then——

GYLLING. Well, then you have seen, I suppose, how I have been abused and slandered? What rough treatment I have had to put up with?

MRS. ROSMER. Yes, but it seems to me you gave as good as you got.

GYLLING. So I did, though I say it that shouldn't. If I have to appear in public, I am certainly not the man to turn the other cheek.—But don't let us get upon the subject of that painful and irritating wrangle. Tell me now—how do you like being mistress of the house?

MRS. ROSMER (*in a lower tone*). I feel in every way so unspeakably happy.

GYLLING. Well, I'm heartily glad of it. Nor could it be otherwise. A husband like Eilert Rosmer! And then the fact that you do not find yourself amid strange surroundings which you have to accustom yourself to. For this house and everything belonging to it has been like a home to you for a long time. The only difference is that now it is all your own.

MRS. ROSMER (*moving a little nearer*). My dear Rector, you say that so sincerely that I cannot think there is any ill-feeling lurking in the background.

GYLLING. Ill-feeling? Why, what do you mean?

MRS. ROSMER. It would be only natural if you felt a little hurt at seeing another in possession, where you were accustomed to see your own sister until a year or two ago. But you don't feel that? (*Giving him her hand.*) Thanks, my dear Rector! Thanks, thanks for that!

GYLLING. But tell me, how on earth did you get such an idea into your head? That I should object—now that my poor sister is gone—that I should now object to your taking her empty place—to your making Rosmer happy—after all his melancholy experience—and to your being yourself happy after all your untiring care for her —for her, that poor irresponsible creature, who chose to —who ended by—leaving it all.

MRS. ROSMER. Oh, don't let us speak of these gloomy things. Don't let us think of them.

GYLLING. No, let us not. Let us keep to what is bright. Tell me now, Mrs. Rosmer—. But first one thing—; may I be allowed to call you Agatha, as she did?

MRS. ROSMER (*joyfully*). Oh yes, please do (*Shaking his hands.*) Thanks, thanks for wanting to!

(EILERT ROSMER *comes in from the right.*)

MRS. ROSMER. Rosmer, do you see who is here?

ROSMER. Madam Helset told me. (*Pressing the* RECTOR'S *hands.*) Welcome back to this house, old friend. I knew that sooner or later things would come all right between us.

GYLLING. Why, man, do you mean to say you too have been so foolish as to fancy that I was on a strained footing with you?

MRS. ROSMER. Yes, only think, it was nothing but fancy after all.

ROSMER. Is that really the case, Gylling? Then why did you desert us so entirely?

GYLLING. Because my presence would always have been reminding you of the years of your unhappiness, and and of—the life that ended in the mill-pond.

ROSMER. Well, it was a kind and considerate thought of yours, Gylling. But I must tell you that it was altogether unnecessary. Neither Agnete nor little Alfred is a memory that it pains us to dwell upon. On the contrary. We often speak of them. We feel almost as if they still belonged to the household.

GYLLING. Do you really? Can you do that?

MRS. ROSMER. Yes, why not——?

ROSMER. It is quite natural. Both Agatha and I were so deeply attached to those who are gone. Oh, it is a great happiness to have nothing to reproach oneself with——

GYLLING. Henceforward, I declare I shall come out and see you every day.

Mrs. Rosmer.   Oh, if you would do that!

Rosmer.   I wish very much that our intercourse had never been interrupted.   There are many things that I would give a great deal to talk over with you, quite frankly,—straight from the heart.

Mrs. Rosmer.   Ah yes, Rosmer!   Do so now.

Gylling.   Oh I can tell you I have no less to talk to you about.   I suppose you know I have turned agitator?

Rosmer.   Yes, so you have.

Gylling.   It's quite impossible now for any thoughtful and right-minded man to stand idly looking on any longer.   Now that the Radicals have really come into power, it is time for all well-disposed citizens to unite— it is high time, I say——

Mrs. Rosmer (*with a suppressed smile*).   Don't you think it may even be a little late?

Gylling.   Unquestionably it would have been better if we had checked the stream at an earlier point in its course.   But who could foresee what was going to happen?   Certainly not I.   But now I have had my eyes opened once for all; for, would you believe it? now the spirit of revolt has crept into the school itself.

Rosmer.   Into the school?   Into your school?

Gylling.   I tell you it has.   Into my own school. What do you think?   It has come to my knowledge that the sixth-form boys—a number of them at any rate, have formed a society, and they take in Mortensgård's paper.

Rosmer.   H'm——.

Mrs. Rosmer.   I have generally noticed that young men are not inclined to be Radicals.

Gylling.   Most of them are not.   That is perfectly true.   Most of us, thank God, are still at that age so far subject to respect for authority, both at home and in school, that we do not lend an ear to immature criticism of recognised institutions. But unfortunately there are exceptions to the rule. And to us schoolmasters it is a melancholy fact that the very boys who are best equipped with mental ability form the exceptions.

MRS. ROSMER. Yes, I have noticed that too.

GYLLING. But that makes them all the more dangerous, these few black sheep. They are capable of infecting my whole flock. The whole form. The whole school. You see, that is why I have not hesitated to take an active part in these political meetings and to warn people against the corrupt spirit that has appeared among us for the moment.

ROSMER. But have you any hope that the tide can be stemmed in that way?

GYLLING. At any rate I shall have done my duty as a citizen in defence of the State. And I hold it the duty of every right-minded man with an atom of patriotism to do likewise. In fact, that was my principal reason for coming out here to-day——

ROSMER. What? Do you mean that I should——?

MRS. ROSMER. But, my dear Rector, you know his distaste——

GYLLING. He must get over it. (*To* ROSMER.) You don't keep abreast of things. You cannot imagine the state things are in, all over the country. There isn't a single accepted idea that hasn't been turned topsy-turvy. It will be a gigantic task to get all the errors rooted out again.

ROSMER. I have no doubt of it. But I am the last man to undertake such a task.

MRS. ROSMER. Rosmer, I think it is time you spoke out frankly.

GYLLING. You are too shy, Rosmer. You hold your-self too much aloof from life. You gave up your liv-ing——

ROSMER. Well, now I will speak. Why do you think I gave up my living?

GYLLING. Oh, I know that well enough. I don't think there was anything surprising in your feeling the unpleasantness of not being able to join in the pietistic tendencies which then found favour in so many circles here.

ROSMER. I ought never to have taken orders, never to have entered upon that class of studies; that is the main point.

GYLLING. But, my dear fellow, then you would have broken with one of the best and most unalterable tra-ditions of your family. Eilert Hannibal Rosmer was a soldier. Consequently his son, Eilert Alfred Rosmer, had to be a clergyman. Thus it has alternated for over two hundred years. I am well acquainted with these things, from my work on the family pedigree.

ROSMER. Yes, and no doubt it was that which deter-mined me in those days. Or rather, there was no ques-tion of a determination on my part. Father—h'm, you know he was a martinet in his family circle as well as in his regiment—father would have it so, and there was an end of it.

GYLLING (*with a sigh*). Ah, that was in the days of decent social conditions!

ROSMER. And I, unfortunately, must have belonged to the class of young men you were talking of just now—those with a poor mental equipment.

GYLLING. You! How on earth do you make that out?

ROSMER. Why, there wasn't a spark of rebellious spirit in me then.

GYLLING. No, with God's help *that* spirit will never possess *you.*

ROSMER. Yet I have come to take a wider view of life than I used to.

GYLLING. Look here, Rosmer—surely you are not so weak as to be influenced by the accident that the leaders of the mob have won a temporary advantage?

ROSMER. I am little acquainted with these questions; but I confess it seems to me that within the last few years people are beginning to show greater independence of thought.

GYLLING. And what if they are? Would you really take that to be an improvement among unstable and immature people? But in any case you are quite mistaken. Or what kind of ideas and opinions are they that are rife among the malcontents in your rural district? Are they not the same ideas and opinions that excite the ill-disposed in the town? Yes, precisely. And do you suppose the mob sucks these ideas and opinions from its own breast? No, of course not—they find them in Peder Mortensgård's paper. And that's an appetising source to draw from!

MRS. ROSMER. It can't be denied that Mortensgård knows how to write.

GYLLING. Yes, but, good heavens—a man of his foul antecedents! Well, the Radicals are not very particular as regards moral character. That is why he is a dangerous man, this Mortensgård. He is one of the most dangerous we have here. And he may give us even more trouble in the future. For now he is thinking of enlarging his paper; it is to appear daily; I know on good authority that he is looking for a capable assistant.

ROSMER. But why don't you and the others think of starting a paper in opposition to him? Your friends in the town could provide the capital. I'm sure it would not be difficult——

GYLLING. Ah, now you've brought me to my real errand. That is the very thing we have thought of. As far as the money question is concerned, the undertaking is assured. But the conduct of the paper—the editing, Rosmer. Tell me—don't you feel it your duty to undertake it, for the sake of the good cause?

ROSMER. I!

MRS. ROSMER. Oh, how can you ask——!

GYLLING. I should be quite willing to try my hand at that style of work too; but it is altogether impossible. I have such a multitude of irons in the fire already. But for you, with no profession to tie you down——

ROSMER. In any case I have the management of the estate.

GYLLING. Nonsense; the management of your estate doesn't take up much of your time.

ROSMER. But nevertheless, it is quite impossible. I feel so altogether unsuitable—; I am not fitted——

GYLLING. You can never know that until you have tried. Besides, the rest of us would give you as much help as we could. And then, too, you start with an immense advantage in the unbounded prestige you enjoy in the whole county. No other man can compare with you in that respect. The name of Rosmer—good heavens—the family of Rosmer, that from time immemorial has stood as the symbol of all that is old and good and just and upright. That, you see, is just what will enable you to act with tenfold weight.—What do you say, Mrs. Rosmer?

MRS. ROSMER (laughing). My dear Rector, I can't tell you how ludicrous all this seems to me.

GYLLING. What do you say? Ludicrous?

Mrs. Rosmer. Yes, ludicrous,. For you must let me tell you frankly——

Rosmer. No, let me say it myself——

(Madam Helset *appears in the doorway on the right*).

Madam Helset. There's a man out in the kitchen passage says he wants to see Pastor Rosmer.

Rosmer. Oh? Ask him to come in.

Madam Helset. Into the sitting-room?

Rosmer. Yes, of course.

Madam Helset. But he looks scarcely the sort of man to bring into the sitting-room.

Mrs. Rosmer. Why, what does he look like, Madam Helset?

Madam Helset. Well, he's not much to look at, ma'am.

Rosmer. Did he not give his name?

Madam Helset. Yes, he said his name was Uldric.

Rosmer. Ulric?

Madam Helset. Yes, and then he gave another name. I think it sounded like Rosen—holm, or something like that.

Rosmer. Ulric Rosen—? Surely it can't be Ulric Rosenhjelm?

Madam Helset. Yes, that's what he said.

Mrs. Rosmer. That unfortunate Ulric Rosenhjelm.

Gylling. That black sheep Rosenhjelm. So he's in these parts.

Rosmer. Ask him to come in, Madam Helset.

Madam Helset. Oh, very well.   (*Goes out.*)

Gylling. Are you really going to have an individual like that in your house?

Rosmer. I knew him a little in the days of his prosperity.

MRS. ROSMER.   Didn't you know him too, Rector?

GYLLING.   Never personally.   H'm——.

(MADAM HELSET *opens the door on the right for* ULRIC ROSENHJELM, *and then withdraws, shutting the door behind him.   He has unkempt hair and beard, and is dressed like a common tramp.   No overcoat; worn-out shoes; no shirt visible.   He wears an old pair of black gloves; a bowler hat under his arm and a stick in his hand.*)

ROSENHJELM (*hesitates at first, then goes quickly up to the* RECTOR, *and holds out his hand*).   How are you, Rosmer!

GYLLING.   Excuse me; (*points*) there——

ROSENHJELM (*turns*).   Right, yes; there he is.   How are you, Rosmer.   I could not pass by the house without paying you a visit.

ROSMER.   Travellers are always welcome here.

ROSENHJELM.   I had no card on me; but I hope the elderly lady I met outside has announced me?   Well, that's all right.   (*Bows.*)   Ah, Mrs. Rosmer, of course.   And *there*?   A brother of the cloth, I see.

ROSMER.   The Rector.   Rector Gylling.

ROSENHJELM.   Gylling?   Gylling?   Wait a bit; weren't you a student of philology?

GYLLING.   Of course I was.

ROSENHJELM.   Why, devil take it, then I knew you——

GYLLING.   Pardon me——

ROSENHJELM.   Weren't you——

GYLLING.   Pardon me——

ROSENHJELM.   —one of those who got me expelled from the Students' Club?

GYLLING.   Certainly; but I disclaim any closer acquaintanceship.

ROSENHJELM. Well, well; *nach Belieben, Herr Rector.*
It's all one to me. I remain the man I am for all that.

MRS. ROSMER. You are on your way into town, Mr.
Rosenhjelm?

ROSENHJELM. Yes, gracious lady, I am. I feel almost ashamed of not knowing this part of the country.
What is the state of feeling in this town? You see, I'm
thinking of getting up an evening entertainment.

MRS. ROSMER. What is it to consist of?

ROSENHJELM. Whatever may be to the taste of the
public. Could you not give me some good advice, Rector? I will take the liberty of paying you a visit.

GYLLING. Thanks; but you'd better apply direct to
Peder Mortensgård.

ROSENHJELM. Mortensgård? Don't know any Mortensgård. What sort of an idiot is he?

GYLLING. Why do you call the man an idiot, if you
don't know him?

ROSENHJELM. Can't I tell at once by the name that
it belongs to a plebeian?

GYLLING. Oh? I didn't expect that answer.

ROSENHJELM. Perhaps you think that Ulric Rosenhjelm hob-nobs with Tom, Dick and Harry?

GYLLING. So far as I know, you used to be specially
interested in the lower orders of society.

ROSENHJELM. Yes, I was; and I had to suffer for it.
Persecution from those in authority; ridicule, scorn and
mockery from the thousands of indifferent people who
will not understand anything—and ingratitude from the
oppressed, whom I tried to help. Look at me. Here
you see Ulric Rosenhjelm, who belonged to good society,
to the best society—and who was the first in good society.
They turned me out because I had the ability and the
courage to say and write things that the polite world

would rather have hidden. Now I never go into good society—except when I am alone.

GYLLING. It may not be merely ability or opposition that determine one's destiny. It may also be one's mode of life.——

ROSENHJELM. I understand. We have an official code of morality, and I have not lived in harmony with it. However, I am tired of *that* too. I will put on the new man, as it is written somewhere. Is there such a thing as a Temperance Society in the town? A Total Abstinence Society? I need scarcely ask.

GYLLING. Yes; I am the president.

ROSENHJELM. I saw that in your face! Well, it is by no means impossible that I may come to you and enroll myself as a member.

GYLLING. Yes; I must tell you that we don't receive everybody without further ceremony.

ROSENHJELM. *À la bonne heure!* Ulric Rosenhjelm has never forced himself into that sort of Society. But I must not prolong my visit. I must be on my way to the town and look out for a lodging. I presume there is a decent hotel in the place.

MRS. ROSMER. Mayn't I offer you anything before you go?

ROSENHJELM. Of what sort?

MRS. ROSMER. A cup of tea, or——

ROSENHJELM. No, no, thanks. I am always loath to trespass on private hospitality. Good-bye. Oh, by the way, Rosmer; for the sake of our old friendship, will you do me a service?

ROSMER. Yes, gladly. What is it?

ROSENHJELM. You see, I am travelling on foot. My things won't arrive till later. Will you lend me a shirt for a day or two?

ROSMER. With all my heart. Is there nothing else?

ROSENHJELM. Could you spare an overcoat?

ROSMER. Yes, yes; certainly I can.

ROSENHJELM. And perhaps a pair of winter boots—I have nothing but spring shoes with me.

ROSMER. That I can manage too. As soon as you let me know your address, I will send the things in.

ROSENHJELM. Not on any account. So much trouble. I will take the trifles with me.

ROSMER. As you please. Come here with me then.

MRS. ROSMER. Let *me* go. Madam Helset and I will see to it. (*Goes out to the right.*)

ROSMER. Is there nothing else I can do for you?

ROSENHJELM. No, thanks. Well, yes, damn it, I'd forgotten—do you happen to have ten crowns in your pocket?

ROSMER. I expect so. (*Opens his purse.*) Here are fifteen.

ROSENHJELM. Well well, thanks, never mind. Thanks in the meantime. Remember you lent me fifteen. Good-bye, gentlemen.

(*Goes out to the right.* ROSMER *takes leave of him, and shuts the door behind him.*)

GYLLING. What do you think of that! This is what has become of the brilliant Ulric Rosenhjelm!

ROSMER. Unfortunately; I have known it a long time.

GYLLING. Yes, it was pretty well known. But to see it with one's own eyes! Such talent rendered useless by moral foulness—

ROSMER. Do you think he is past saving? Would it not be possible to raise him again?

GYLLING. Oh, my dear fellow, how could that be managed?

ROSMER. I mean by going to work in a forebearing—kindly way with him, showing confidence in him, relying on his good intentions—[a kind of self-knowledge——]

GYLLING. Then you do rely on those intentions?

ROSMER. I would gladly do so.

GYLLING. In that case he might perhaps be useful to us. The brilliant style he was once master of—; his pitiless, slashing pen—; and it did not look as if he had any very friendly disposition towards the Radicals——

ROSMER. Do you mean that he might be placed in charge of the new paper?

GYLLING. In charge! Heaven preserve us, how can you think of such a thing! No, on the contrary, he would of course have to be kept in the background until he had rehabilitated himself. He would have to apply himself to leading a decent life,—in any case to be careful and to avoid public scandal. And if he could so far conquer himself, and if he could be induced for a certain time to lend the good cause his *bona officia*—; observing the strictest anonymity, of course——

(MRS. ROSMER *has re-entered in the meantime.*)

ROSMER. Has he gone?

MRS. ROSMER. Yes.

GYLLING. And now I must think about leaving too. It is beginning to get dark.

MRS. ROSMER. Won't you take tea with us?

GYLLING. No, no, thanks; I cannot.—Well, my dear friend, I won't press you further to-day. You must turn it over in your own mind——

ROSMER. Will you be at home to-morrow morning——?

GYLLING. To-morrow? I'm sorry I can't say for certain—for——

ROSMER. Never mind, I'll enquire for you in any case. I want to talk to you, I want to have a long talk with you, my dear Gylling——

GYLLING. You mean about the affair of the *County News* ?

ROSMER. About that and other things.

GYLLING (*shaking his hand*). You will be welcome, my dear friend. And I am sure you and I will soon agree as to what is the duty of a good and well-disposed citizen in these troublous times. Good-bye, Mrs. Rosmer! Good-bye, dear friends.

(ROSMER *and* MRS. ROSMER *accompany him into the hall. As he puts on his overcoat, loud conversation is heard, the words of which do not however reach the audience. Finally,* "Good-bye, good-bye, good-bye," *as the* RECTOR *goes.* ROSMER *and his wife re-enter the room.*)

MRS. ROSMER. What was that he was saying as I came in ? I understood that he wanted to try Rosenhjelm on the new paper.

ROSMER. He threw it out casually as a possibility. But nothing is likely to come of it.

MRS. ROSMER. No, I should hope not. At all events I have done my best that nothing shall come of it.

ROSMER. You, my dear ? What have you done ?

MRS. ROSMER. Now you won't be vexed with me for acting on my own responsibility, will you ? Such good friends as we are ?

ROSMER. Of course not; you may do everything you wish. But what was it ?

MRS. ROSMER. I gave Rosenhjelm à card of introduction to Mortensgård.

ROSMER. You did ? To Mortensgård!

MRS. ROSMER. Yes, I scribbled a few hurried words——

ROSMER. But you heard him call Mortensgård an idiot and a plebeian.

MRS. ROSMER. We needn't pay any attention to that. When a man has fallen so low as Rosenhjelm, he plays the gentleman. He thanked me too, and promised to deliver the card.

ROSMER. Oh, he did that? But perhaps Gylling will get hold of him to-morrow.

MRS. ROSMER. If he has already compromised himself with Mortensgård's paper, the *County News* won't be able to make use of him.

ROSMER. And then it will come out that it was we who recommended him.

MRS. ROSMER. What harm can that do? Haven't you made up your mind to have it out to-morrow?

ROSMER. Yes, that's settled. To-morrow it must and shall be done. But, dear me, how hard it is nevertheless to have to grieve one's faithful friends—to cause them real heartfelt sorrow.

MRS. ROSMER. Is that all, Rosmer? Is it not something that survives in you, without your knowing it?

ROSMER. My dear, what should it be? Do you mean uncertainty or doubt?

MRS. ROSMER. Not exactly that.

ROSMER. No, you may depend upon that. I feel so free, so sure of myself. (*Sits down beside her.*) You have faithfully helped me. My former self is dead. I look upon it as one looks upon a corpse.

MRS. ROSMER. Yes, but that is just when these white horses appear.

ROSMER. White horses? What white horses?

(MADAM HELSET *brings in the tea-urn and puts it on the table.*)

MRS. ROSMER. What was it you told me once, Madam Helset? You said that from time immemorial a strange thing happened here whenever one of the family died.

MADAM HELSET. Yes, it's as true as I'm alive. Then the white horse comes.

ROSMER. Oh, that old family legend——

MRS. ROSMER. In it comes when the night is far gone. Into the courtyard. Through closed gates. Neighs loudly. Launches out with its hind legs, gallops once round and then out again and away at full speed.

MADAM HELSET. Yes, that's how it is. Both my mother and my grandmother have seen it.

MRS. ROSMER. And you too?

MADAM HELSET. Oh, I'm not so sure whether I've seen anything myself. I don't generally believe in such things. But this about the white horse—I do believe in that. And I shall believe in it till the day of my death. Well, now I'll go and—— (*Goes out to the right.*)

ROSMER (*after a short silence*). Do you mean that this can be applied to me?

MRS. ROSMER. All the emancipated people I have known—all those who believe themselves to be emancipated—every one of them has had somewhere or other a white horse like this, which they never give up believing in.

ROSMER. And complete emancipation, you think, means——

MRS. ROSMER. It means getting rid of one's white horses. [We must have light, Rosmer.]

MADAM HELSET [(in the doorway to the right)]. Here is the lamp, ma'am.

SECOND ACT

The sitting-room at Johannes Rosmer's. It is forenoon.
(ROSMER *is walking about the room and putting on his
    overcoat.* MRS. ROSMER *is brushing his hat, which
    she then hands to him.*)

ROSMER. To think that I could have been so cowardly, so shy, so afraid of telling them everything frankly.

MRS. ROSMER. Yes, was it not strange?

ROSMER. I don't understand it myself.

MRS. ROSMER. But now it is over. There now. Go
straight in to the Rector.

ROSMER. I'm going straight in——

MRS. ROSMER. And then come back as soon as you
can. I'm excited to hear what he will say.

ROSMER. Don't be too impatient. Good-bye for the
present. Good-bye!

MRS. ROSMER. Good-bye, dear Rosmer!
    (*He opens the door to the hall.* MRS. ROSMER *goes
        out with him. At the same moment* RECTOR
        GYLLING, *in outdoor clothes, comes into the hall.*)

ROSMER. What! Have you come here?

GYLLING. Yes, I have.

ROSMER. And I was just on my way to you.

GYLLING. I did not want to wait; and I was not so
sure that you would come——

ROSMER. Well, take off your coat.

GYLLING. If you will permit me.
    (*He takes off his overcoat and lays it on a chair.*
        ROSMER *does the same.*)

ROSMER. Is there anything wrong with you? You
look so serious.

GYLLING. I should be glad to speak to you in private. Could we go into your study?

MRS. ROSMER. It is not tidy yet. Stay here; I have to go out. . (*Goes out to the right.*)

ROSMER. What is it then? Has Ulric Sejerhjelm been to see you?

GYLLING. No; and he's not likely to come either. But he is already being talked about. He introduced himself in a fine fashion.

ROSMER. Well?

GYLLING. He took up his quarters in a low house, spent the evening in a low tavern—in the lowest company of course—and drank and stood treat as long as he had any money; then he began abusing the whole company as a set of disreputable blackguards—and so far he was quite right;—whereupon they thrashed him and pitched him out of doors.

ROSMER. So he is incorrigible.

GYLLING. He had pawned the overcoat too; but I am told that has been redeemed for him. And can you guess by whom?

ROSMER. By whom then?

GYLLING. By Mr. Mortensgård. Sejerhjelm's first visit was to the "idiot" and "plebeian."

ROSMER. Rebecca prophesied that yesterday.

GYLLING. Indeed. And that brings me to a matter it is my duty to warn you about, for our old, faithful friendship's sake.

ROSMER. But, my dear Gylling, what can that be?

GYLLING. It is this: that there are things being done in this house independently of you and behind your back.

ROSMER. Who is doing this?

GYLLING. Your wife. I can quite understand it. Ever since the last sad years of Beata's life she has

been accustomed to manage things here; but nevertheless——

ROSMER.   My dear Gylling, you are utterly mistaken.
Rebecca hides nothing from me.   She tells me everything.

GYLLING.   Then has she told you that yesterday she
gave Sejerhjelm a card of introduction to Mortensgård?

ROSMER.   Yes, of course.

GYLLING.   She has——!   And what do you say to that?

ROSMER.   I altogether approve of what Rebecca has
done.

GYLLING.   Are you mad?   You approve of her corre-
sponding with the lowest and most dangerous opponent
we have here?

ROSMER.   I will tell you candidly.   Mortensgård's
conduct on many occasions has been repulsive to you.
But I can no longer side with you and our friends on
public questions.   In those matters and in many others
I must entirely dissociate myself from you.

GYLLING (*starting back*).   What do you say!   You,
you will dissociate yourself from your friends!   Go over
to the enemy's camp!   But that's impossible!

ROSMER.   I am not thinking of taking any part in the
conflicts of the day.   I have a horror of interfering in
all this hubbub, of which I do not know the ins and outs.

GYLLING.   But what are you going to do then?

ROSMER.   I will try to ennoble the work of emancipation.   Do you think I don't see all the foulness that development brings with it and gives rise to in its course?
That is what I want to oppose, to warn people against, to
dam up, to confine, so that the stream may flow pure and
clear——

GYLLING.   Oh, Rosmer, what a confiding man you
are!   You don't know what elements you will have to

deal with. But when was it that you entered on these paths of aberration?

ROSMER. I call it comprehension.

GYLLING. Call it what you will. But when, I ask?

ROSMER. It goes back a long time. I believe the foundation was laid when I was engaged on my theological studies.

GYLLING. And yet you entered the Church?

ROSMER. Our family has always had great respect for the conventional.

GYLLING. That quality appears to be dying out in the family.

ROSMER. I think such things always die out—sooner or later—and then there is a reaction to the opposite.

GYLLING. But that this should come about through you! And that with such a turn of mind you could accept the position of a clergyman——

ROSMER. But as soon as I was perfectly clear I resigned.

GYLLING. Perfectly clear. About what?

ROSMER. I can no longer accept this mysticism. I must reject the whole of the old doctrine.

GYLLING. An apostate then! A free-thinker! An apostate from the faith of your fathers!

ROSMER. I have reasons for supposing that the faith of my fathers did not go very deep.

GYLLING. So you are an apostate. What have you now to fill up your life?

ROSMER. I will continue untiringly to investigate and think. I will try, as far as possible, to get to the bottom of things. And then I will live. Be happy.

GYLLING. Do you know that this opens an abyss of thoughts in my mind?

ROSMER. I don't understand you.

GYLLING. Now I will go to the root of the whole matter. Will you be frank? Will you answer my questions candidly?

ROSMER. Speak, my dear Gylling, ask what you will. I have nothing to conceal.

GYLLING. What was the ultimate reason why Beata put an end to her life?

ROSMER. I don't understand you. Can you have any uncertainty on the subject? And can one ever ask for reasons for what an unhappy, irresponsible invalid may do?

GYLLING. Are you certain that Beata was completely irresponsible for her actions? The doctors, at any rate, were by no means convinced of it.

ROSMER. If the doctors had ever seen her as I have so often seen her, they would have had no doubts.

GYLLING. I had no doubts either—then.

ROSMER. Unhappily there wasn't the smallest room for doubt. I have told you of her unfortunate frenzies of passion, which she expected me to return. Oh, how they terrified me! And then her sudden changes of mood; her dumb, consuming hatred——

GYLLING. Hatred? Of whom?

ROSMER. Of us, who were about her. Of me, first and foremost——

GYLLING. And I have to tell you that poor unhappy Beata died of her love for you.

ROSMER. What do you mean by that?

GYLLING. In her last year—when it seemed to her that she could not bear her life any longer, she had recourse to me, to pour forth all her anguish—first, because she declared that you were on the road to perversion——

ROSMER. But I don't think I was at that time. In any case I never confided to her my doubts and my inward conflicts.

GYLLING. That proves all the more clearly what a wonderfully true intuition a deranged person may have.

ROSMER. But why did you hide this from me?

GYLLING. I did not want to torture and harass you still further by disclosing these accusations, which I myself did not believe in at the time.

ROSMER. But now——?

GYLLING. Ah, now my eyes are opened to the incredible—to your great crime——

ROSMER. Crime!

GYLLING. Yes, to the criminal life that has been and is being led in your house.

ROSMER. I don't understand a word of this.

GYLLING. Sometimes Beata came to me, weeping and lamenting. "Rosmer no longer loves me," she said. "He loves Rebecca; and she loves him."

ROSMER. She said that!

GYLLING. She said that. And that of course made me think her mad.

ROSMER. Yes, you must have thought so.

GYLLING. The last time she came to see me, she said: "Now no one must stand in the way of Johannes and his happiness. The White Horse must soon come now." I did not understand her.

ROSMER. Never did it occur to me that her diseased fancies had led her astray in that direction. My poor unhappy Beata.

GYLLING, Hypocrite!

ROSMER (*with a start*). What do you say!

GYLLING. Can I doubt any longer, after all these revelations, that a criminal life was being led here— even then?

ROSMER. Let me tell you that if any other man but you dared——

GYLLING. If it had been any other man but you, it would not have cut me to the heart like this. But you, Johannes Rosmer—to have to tear you out of my mind with a single wrench.

ROSMER. Tell me now: you did not at the time believe a word of these accusations of Beata's?

GYLLING., How could I believe such things of a man like you—a man of honour, for you were once that.

ROSMER. But now——?

GYLLING. Have you not confessed that you have long been secretly an apostate from the faith of your fathers?

ROSMER. I have long been in doubt and conflict. Now I see clearly where I stand; that is the truth. But what then?

GYLLING. The rest I can surely leave you to say to yourself.

ROSMER. No, I tell you; no; I cannot. You are bound to speak out what you mean without reserve.

GYLLING. I mean that there cannot be any vast gulf, any impassable abyss between free thought and——

ROSMER. And what——?

GYLLING. —and free love.

ROSMER. And you dare say this to me! You are not ashamed of thinking and believing this!

GYLLING. I don't know what there is to hinder a man when he has once disavowed the moral commandments.

ROSMER. Have *I* done *that?*

GYLLING. To my mind faith and morality cannot be separated. And I know no other morality than our Christian one.

ROSMER. And I know no Christian morality: I know no other morality than that I have within me.

GYLLING. Private, human morality is but a feeble protection.

ROSMER. Oh, this boundless fanaticism that has possessed you.

GYLLING. Yes, you may call me a fanatic in that respect. To my last hour I shall hate and fight against these fatal tendencies of the age. They have brought strife and disruption into my home—and into hundreds of others as well. They have embittered my life's work——

ROSMER. Political controversies, yes. But I do not mix myself up with those.

GYLLING. One thing cannot be separated from the other. And that apostacy should seize you too. Should separate us so irrevocably from each other. But I see it, I see it;—this case of yours—it is the work of a cunning and remorseless woman.

ROSMER. Not another word about her.

GYLLING. Was it not she who from the very first brought you into the path you are now following?

ROSMER. Yes; to her praise be it said. And since then we have faithfully worked together like two comrades.

GYLLING. You are like a child in her hands; and you don't see it.

ROSMER. I am happy and free; I can live my own life.

GYLLING (*putting on his coat*). Then see what that life will be like when you are cut off from all those who have hitherto been near to you.

ROSMER. They cannot all be such fanatics as you.

GYLLING. You will soon find out about that.

(*He gives a curt nod and goes out through the hall.*)

(*Miss DANKERT enters shortly afterwards from the right.*)

Miss Dankert.   I saw him go out.

Rosmer.   He will never come back.

Miss Dankert.   You have told him everything.

Rosmer.   Yes.

Miss Dankert.   And then?

Rosmer.   Complete rupture.   Irremediable——

Miss Dankert.   Not irremediable, Rosmer.   Just wait.   You shall see.

Rosmer.   Our old relations can never be restored.

Miss Dankert.   Well, believe me; that is best for you.

Rosmer.   Yes, I know you think so.   But such old habits are deeply rooted in me.

Miss Dankert.   Much too deeply.   You would never have been free if that circle had been allowed to go on exercising its influence on you.

Rosmer.   I am bound to tell you this.   Now that I have openly withdrawn from them, they will cease to regard our relationship as what it is.

Miss Dankert.   Our relationship——!

Rosmer.   Purity of life is not to be looked for in apostates, he said.

Miss Dankert.   Oh, these madmen!

Rosmer.   What is to be done?

Miss Dankert.   Do you wish me to leave here?

Rosmer.   Do I wish that!

Miss Dankert.   Well, it is not necessary on my account.

Rosmer.   No, it's not, is it, Rebecca?   Your spirit is so proud and free.   Your own consciousness is sufficient to you.

Miss Dankert.   Yes, it is.   Why should we flinch before the low and vile thoughts of some people?   Why should we make ourselves unhappy? For we should be so——

ROSMER. Yes, yes.

MISS DANKERT. No, we shall keep together in good comradeship and help and support one another as well as we can. But look there——!

ROSMER (*with a cry*).

(RECTOR GYLLING *has opened the door at the back.*)

GYLLING. Well, I don't know whether I may come in again.

ROSMER. Pray come in.

(*The* RECTOR *comes in, keeping his overcoat on.*)

GYLLING. What is past cannot be altered; but now listen, Rosmer——

ROSMER. I'm listening, I'm listening——

GYLLING. Is there any necessity for your sad apostacy to be proclaimed over the whole country?

ROSMER. I must and will get out of the false position I have been in so long. My book is ready.

GYLLING. And you don't consider what consequences this will have for you? The whole conservative press will attack you and your book——

MISS DANKERT. But how can you tell that, Rector? You don't know the book, do you?

GYLLING. H'm, I suppose you will accuse us of fanaticism and persecution of those who differ from us. But this cannot be avoided in a period of agitation like ours. It is an absolute duty for every good citizen who has the power to do it, to root up all the dangerous weeds, whenever and wherever they may show themselves.

ROSMER. Well, well; then I know what to be prepared for.

GYLLING. No, you don't know. It will be something far more violent than you think. Therefore I beg you, Rosmer—hold your hand; do so—you, the quiet, retiring enquirer;—this is not suited to you.

ROSMER.   But can you ask me to be so cowardly!

GYLLING.   It is your duty to your environment. Remember the prominent position your family has occupied for so long.   The respect you yourself enjoy. You will make many unstable people irresolute, vacillating, unhappy.

ROSMER.   Do you think so?

GYLLING.   You surely can't have a doubt of it yourself?

ROSMER.   But I cannot stand looking on for ever. All around, in every department of life, a luxuriant germination is going on.   And it is time that I too began to live.   I must and will be happy in this world.

GYLLING.   I can guess where this hunt for happiness is derived from.   Don't you seek it too, Miss Dankert?

MISS DANKERT.   It is in the air.   It is one of the greatest things about the new age that we dare openly proclaim happiness as our end in life.

GYLLING.   You do so?

MISS DANKERT.   Certainly I do.

GYLLING.   Is it principles of this kind that are preached in your new book?

ROSMER.   Yes, if it is rightly understood.

GYLLING.   Poor man—you, with your conscience burdened with guilt—you think you can find happiness by those paths.

MISS DANKERT.   Burdened with guilt!   What does that mean?

ROSMER.   I feel that I am free and pure.

GYLLING.   You believe that perhaps.   But you are mistaken.   You have betrayed yourself.   And unhappy

Beata gave you her life as a sacrifice. You are founding
your happiness on water. Remember the mill-pond.

(He goes.)

ROSMER. But this is not true, Rebecca.

MISS DANKERT. I know that, of course.

ROSMER. But nevertheless—well, it must be said
some time or other. Did I really love you even then?

MISS DANKERT. Love! You, Rosmer!

ROSMER. Will you go away now?

MISS DANKERT *(giving him her hand)*. No, my
friend, *now* I stay with you.

ROSMER. Thanks, Rebecca!

THIRD ACT

JOHANNES ROSMER'S *study. A door at the back; also
on the left. Bookcases and shelves on the walls. A
window on the right, and before it a writing-table,
covered with books and papers.—Old-fashioned furniture; a table, with table-cloth, in the middle of the
room.*

(JOHANNES ROSMER *is sitting in a high-backed chair at
the writing-table, reading a pamphlet, the pages of
which he cuts as he reads. There is a knock at the
door on the left.*)

ROSMER *(without turning.)* Pray come in.

(MISS WEST *enters in a morning gown, with a newspaper in her hand.*)

MISS WEST. Good morning.

ROSMER *(reading)*. Good morning, dear. Is there
anything you want?

MISS WEST. Here is to-day's *County News.*

ROSMER *(turning)*. Is there anything in it?

Miss West. Yes, there is. (*Gives him the paper.*)

Rosmer. Already. (*Reads.*) Now let us see.

Miss West (*behind him, leaning over the back of the chair, also reads*). They wanted to be the first——

Rosmer. —to weaken the effect, yes.—"We cannot sufficiently express our contempt"—Contempt?—"for renegades who have lain in hiding while the situation remained uncertain"—Gylling never wrote that——

Miss West. Who knows?

Rosmer. No, no. "Renegades . . . but who march over with colours flying as soon as victory seems assured." And they can write such things, that they themselves don't believe. "When confused visionaries with no will of their own fall into the hands of calculating intriguers"—I won't read any more. (*Rises.*) At any rate not now.

Miss West. Will you answer it?

Rosmer. Oh, what is the use? And my name is not actually mentioned either.

Miss West. But it will soon get about that it is aimed at you. The calculating intriguer is of course myself.

Rosmer (*walking nervously about*). These days of denunciation—ah, it is indeed a great mission to make an end of them.

(Madam Helset *opens the door on the left.*)

Miss West. What is it, Madam Helset?

Madam Helset. It's that Mortensgård, who'd like to speak to Mr. Rosmer.

Rosmer. Mortensgård? What can he want?

Miss West. You'll let him come in, won't you?

Rosmer (*to* Madam Helset). Yes, let him come in.

(Madam Helset *opens the door to* Mortensgård, *closes it behind him and goes.*)

MORTENSGÅRD. It is a long time since I stood before you, Pastor.

ROSMER. Yes, it is years ago. I have often asked myself whether I did not act too harshly at that time.

MORTENSGÅRD. Do you say that, Pastor?

ROSMER. Well, you have found another position, with which I am sure you feel more satisfied.

MORTENSGÅRD. Oh yes, in a way.

ROSMER. Have you anything in particular to say to me?

MORTENSGÅRD. First I think I ought to thank you for the card Mr. Hekfeldt brought me.

ROSMER. You may thank Miss West for that.

MORTENSGÅRD. Of course. Miss West also.

MISS WEST. Can you make use of him?

MORTENSGÅRD. Unhappily, I think it is too late.

ROSMER. Do you think so?

MORTENSGÅRD. He is not abreast of the times; stands so strangely outside what is going on. Looks upon things with eyes that may have been radical enough twenty years ago——

ROSMER. Yes, they were.—Tell me, have you read to-day's *County News*?

MORTENSGÅRD. No, not yet.

ROSMER. Don't say that, Mr. Mortensgård. I am sure you have read it.

MORTENSGÅRD. Well yes, I've glanced at it—here and there.

ROSMER. Then you must have seen the leading article?

MORTENSGÅRD. Yes, it struck me as rather strange.

ROSMER. Did you understand whom it was meant for?

MORTENSGÅRD. I don't think I could believe it myself.

ROSMER. No, no.

MORTENSGÅRD. So there is something wrong between you and the other gentlemen?

ROSMER. I have left that circle. I am going to take up a position of my own.

MORTENSGÅRD. So you have left them, Pastor? Really? I didn't expect that.

MISS WEST. It is a step that has been long prepared, Mr. Mortensgård.

MORTENSGÅRD. Is it so? Must say, I didn't expect it. Are you going to reply to this attack, Pastor?

ROSMER. I hardly think so. I so cordially dislike these squabbles between man and man.

MORTENSGÅRD. But if it should be necessary—for perhaps there may be more to come——

ROSMER. Do you think so?

MORTENSGÅRD. It is their usual way. And if you should find it difficult to get anything into the *County News*, my paper is open to you. It would be a great honour to us.

ROSMER. Thanks. I may perhaps avail myself of your offer. Not in this connection. But there are other subjects that I wish to deal with.

MORTENSGÅRD. Whatever you like, Pastor. The more the better. It will be an incalculable gain to the cause of progress throughout the country, if a man like you, a Churchman, takes our side.

ROSMER. But look here; I must first tell you that I am no longer a Churchman.

MORTENSGÅRD. Of course, I know that; but your having resigned your living makes no difference.

ROSMER. I don't mean that either. But the fact is that I no longer hold the faith of the Church.

MORTENSGÅRD. You don't hold—? You?

ROSMER. No. I have entirely broken with everything of that sort.

MORTENSGÅRD. I should advise you to keep that to yourself, Mr. Rosmer.

ROSMER. You give me that advice?

MISS WEST. You are at no pains to conceal your own opinions.

MORTENSGÅRD. It would be of little use. A man who has once been so incautious—so unfortunate, as I——

ROSMER. Then do you not put the truth before everything?

MORTENSGÅRD. I put my ends before everything. I have continued to be a teacher of the people; only in another way. What brought me to my fall was want and lack of knowledge. Now I wish to help as many as possible on the way to enlightenment and better circumstances. And this can only be done on the path of freedom.

ROSMER. Yes, there we are quite agreed.

MORTENSGÅRD. In this way I am redeeming my offence against society. For myself I have no hope of any gain. For I am civilly dead, as you know.

III

FROM THE FIRST ACT

MADAM HELSET. Yes, he said his name was Uldric.

ROSMER. Ulric?

MADAM HELSET. Yes, and then there was something more. I thought it sounded like Hetmand or something of the sort.

ROSMER (*to* GYLLING). That unfortunate Ulric Hetman!

GYLLING. That black sheep Ulric Hetman? Then he is still alive.

ROSMER. Ask him to come in, Madam Helset.

MADAM HELSET. Oh, very well.   (*She goes out.*)

GYLLING. Are you really going to let such a man into your house?

ROSMER. I knew him a little in the days of his prosperity.

GYLLING. When last *I* heard of him, he was in the House of Correction.

(MADAM HELSET *opens the door on the right for* ULRIC HETMAN, *and then withdraws, shutting the door behind him. He is a handsome man, with hair and beard streaked with grey. He is dressed like a common tramp; no overcoat; worn-out shoes; no shirt visible. He wears an old pair of black gloves, and carries a soft, greasy bowler hat under his arm and a walking-stick in his hand.*)

ULRIC HETMAN (*hesitates at first, then goes quickly up to the* RECTOR, *and holds out his hand*). How are you, Rosmer!

GYLLING. Excuse me——

HETMAN. Didn't expect to see me again in these parts, did you?

GYLLING. Excuse me— (*Pointing.*) There——

HETMAN (*turns*). Right. There he is. How are you, Rosmer? I could not pass by Rosmersholm without paying you a visit.

ROSMER. Travellers are always welcome with us.

HETMAN. I had no card on me. But I hope the elderly lady I met outside has duly announced me.

Well, that's all right. (*Bows to Rebecca.*) Ah, Mrs. Rosmer, of course.

ROSMER. Miss West.

HETMAN. A near relation, no doubt. And there— (*Pointing to the* RECTOR.) A brother of the cloth, I see.

ROSMER. Rector Gylling.

HETMAN. Gylling. Gylling? Wait a bit; weren't you a student of philology?

GYLLING. Of course I was.

HETMAN. Why *Donnerwetter*, then I knew you!

GYLLING. Pardon me——

HETMAN. Weren't you——

GYLLING. Pardon me——

HETMAN. —one of those champions of morality that got me expelled from the Students' Club?

GYLLING. Very likely. But I disclaim any closer acquaintanceship.

HETMAN. Well, well; *nach Belieben, Herr Rector.* It's all one to me. Ulric Hetman remains the man he is for all that.

REBECCA. You are on your way into town, Mr. Hetman?

HETMAN. Yes, gracious lady, I am. I should be so unspeakably reluctant to lose anything of the respect of a young, pretty, amiable and charming lady. But unhappily—I am forced to confess it—as yet I do not know this part of the country.

GYLLING. Indeed. But you have roamed a good deal about other parts of the country, from what I have heard.

HETMAN (*gruffly*). That is so, Herr Professor. I have undertaken fairly extensive journeys. (*To* ROSMER.) But now you shall hear my plan. I have decided to give a series of lectures throughout the country. And I am

thinking of making this my starting-point, although—I
suppose my name is not very familiar in these parts?

ROSMER. No, I don't think so.

HETMAN. Oh no, it wasn't to be expected of the inhabitants of such a hole-and-corner place. (*To* GYL-
LING.) But tell me, Herr Inspector—*unter uns*—have
you a tolerably decent, reputable, and commodious Public Hall in your honoured city?

GYLLING. The hall of the Workmen's Society is the
largest.

HETMAN. And has the Herr Docent any official influence in this doubtless most beneficent Society?

GYLLING. I have nothing to do with it.

REBECCA (*to* HETMAN). You should apply to Peter
Mortensgård.

HETMAN. *Pardon, madame*—what sort of an idiot is
he?

ROSMER. What makes you take him for an idiot?

HETMAN. Can't one tell at once by the name that he
is a plebeian?

GYLLING. I didn't expect that answer.

HETMAN. Perhaps the Herr Professor thought that
Ulric Hetman was ready to demean himself with anyone
you please? But one has to conquer one's antipathy
when one stands at a turning-point in one's career. I
will approach this individual, will open negotiations——

ROSMER. Are you really and seriously standing at a
turning-point?

HETMAN. Seriously, Herr Pastor? Stand he where
he may, Ulric Hetman always stands seriously. Now it
is decided. One of these days I shall emerge from my
somewhat unnoticed and unappreciated existence. The
series of lectures that I am about to give—that is to un-
ravel my life's greatest and newest idea.

REBECCA. What idea is that, Mr. Hetman? Oh, tell us that.

HETMAN. Well, here, in a confidential circle of more or less close acquaintances, there is nothing to conceal. I will open my long-contemplated war against all the landowners in the country.

GYLLING. Against the landowners? Against the peasantry then?

HETMAN. Certainly, Herr Professor. Are you with me?

GYLLING. I am with you in so far as I am already at enmity with the Radical majority——

HETMAN. Bosh about majorities and such things! It's the peasants in general that I'm at war with. Both the great and the small. Both the Radicals and the idiots——

GYLLING. But allow me, Mr. ——; you can't do things without any party point of view whatever——

HETMAN. Now listen to me. And follow me carefully; then perhaps you will be able to understand. Suppose now I associate myself with three or four capitalists in town. We establish a large factory for the preparation of some product or other, which has not yet been discovered.

GYLLING. But where does this take us?

HETMAN. Patience, Herr Professor. In the preparation of this product we require all the oxygen that is contained in or brought to the atmosphere of the county —or we require all the carbon in the air. We—I and the other two or three capitalists might be using it to make diamonds of. But in both cases the air of the whole county would be unserviceable for men and other animals and for everything organic. Everyone of them would have to buy his portion of vital air from us—perhaps at an exorbitant price. If not—*heraus!* What do you say to that?

GYLLING. I don't think the authorities here would permit such an industry.

HETMAN. I don't think so either, honoured Sir. Nor do I think they would permit it if our little syndicate proposed to use the river or the fiord in such a way that no fish could swim there and no craft float. (*Coming nearer.*) Or perhaps you don't agree with me there?

GYLLING (*drawing back a step*). Well, well, well! Of course I agree.

HETMAN. I have a faint suspicion that you think I'm suffering from some form of mental disease or other. But that is an error for the moment. I have only been trying to emphasise the fact that we all agree that the air and water of our planet are common property to everybody. But when the solid earth is in question—the ground under our feet, that no one can do without, well, *das ist was Anderes!* Nobody breathes a word against the solid earth of the globe being in the hands of a comparatively small band of robbers, who have made use of it for centuries, who are making use of it to-day, and who propose to make use of it for all futurity. You see, honoured Sirs—and you, fair lady, that is the obscure matter of vital importance that I wish to throw light upon.

GYLLING. Doubt if it will be a profitable undertaking.

HETMAN. What do I care for profit? It is the idea —my greatest and my newest idea, that matters to me. It struck me in a flash that mankind's sense of justice is suffering from partial insanity. That is the heart of the matter. This idea has come to me from above—or from below—or from the obscure inscrutable powers. It has

come to me through an inspiration, I say. Therefore it
is mine alone. And now I am going into the town to
present it to mankind.

REBECCA. But excuse me, Mr. Hetman—that idea is
not altogether new.

HETMAN (*with a start*). What do you say—fair lady?
My idea is not new!

REBECCA. I am afraid, not altogether. We were just
reading a book this winter that deals with something
similar.

HETMAN (*to* ROSMER). Does this lady speak the truth?

ROSMER. Yes, of course.

HETMAN. And in this book there is that about the
land and——?

ROSMER. That is what the book turns upon.

HETMAN (*pale and tottering*). The meeting will—
kindly—allow me to—to sit down.

(*He sinks into an easy chair and sits leaning forward, with his hands on his knees.*)

REBECCA. Can't I fetch you something? What can
I——?

HETMAN (*gazing before him*). Too late. I came too
late. This time again. Always too late.

GYLLING. That doesn't really make any difference.
I'm sure it will be quite new to most of the people about
here.

HETMAN (*with a look of misery*). How can it help me
or cheer me if the whole world thought it was new, now
that I know myself that it is not?

REBECCA. Oh, how I wish I had said nothing.

HETMAN (*rising*). Fair lady—it was a hard blow
that your love of truth dealt me. I had treasured that
idea, brooded over it with jealous affection, felt it grow,
thought that I should never have the heart to let it go

from me. And now, when I let it go, I am too late.
This time again. Well, well, well! No tears of sympathy, ladies and gentlemen. I submit to no pity. Deserve none either. Perhaps there is a just Nemesis in
this. Perhaps there has been something or other in my
way of living——

ROSMER. Yes, don't you think so yourself?

HETMAN. I will put on a new man. And then I will
get up one or two evening entertainments. A little dec-
lamation and singing and so on. (*To* GYLLING.) Is
there such a thing as a Temperance Society in the town?
A Total Abstinence Society? I need scarcely ask.

GYLLING. Yes. I am the president.

HETMAN. No, really? I shouldn't have thought it.
Well, it is by no means impossible that I may come to
you and enrol myself as a member for a week.

GYLLING. Excuse me, but we don't receive members
by the week.

HETMAN. *À la bonne heure.* Ulric Hetman has never
forced himself into that sort of Society. (*Turns.*) But
I must not prolong my visit in this pleasant house. I
must be on my way to the town and select a suitable
lodging. I presume there is a decent hotel in the place.

REBECCA. Mayn't I offer you anything before you
go?

HETMAN. Of what sort, gracious lady?

REBECCA. A cup of tea, or——

HETMAN. I thank my bountiful hostess many times—
but I am always loath to trespass on private hospitality.
(*Bows.*) Good-bye, gentlefolks all! (*Goes toward the
door, but turns again.*) Oh, by the way—. Pastor Rosmer, for the sake of our ancient friendship, will you do
your old friend a small service?

ROSMER. Yes, gladly. What is it?

HETMAN. You see, I am travelling on foot at present. My wardrobe is being sent after me. Could you lend me a starched shirt—with cuffs—for a day or two?

ROSMER. Certainly. Is there nothing else?

HETMAN. Well, do you know—perhaps you could spare me an oldish, well-worn overcoat.

ROSMER. Oh yes; certainly I can.

HETMAN. And perhaps a pair of winter boots. I have been so imprudent as only to bring these light spring shoes with me.

ROSMER. That we can manage too. As soon as you let us know your address, we will send the things in.

HETMAN. Not on any account. So much trouble. I will take the bagatelles with me.

ROSMER. As you please. Come here with me then.

REBECCA. Let *me* go. Madam Helset and I will see to it.   (*Goes out to the right.*)

ROSMER. Is there nothing else I can do for you?

HETMAN. Upon my word, I know of nothing more. Well, yes, damn it—now that I think of it—do you happen to have eight crowns in your pocket?

ROSMER. Let me see. (*Opens his purse.*) Here is a ten-crown note.

HETMAN. Well, well, never mind! I can take it. I can always get it changed in the town. Thanks in the meantime. Remember it was ten crowns you lent me. Farewell, respected Sirs.

> (*Goes out to the right.* ROSMER *takes leave of him, and shuts the door behind him.*)

GYLLING. Merciful Heaven—so that is the once brilliant Ulric Hetman!

ROSMER. Step by step he must have gone down.

GYLLING. How much people thought of him! The lion of the capital,—in spite of all the excesses he was guilty of. But then came his notorious book. And that broke him.

ROSMER. Do you think he is past saving?

GYLLING. He?

ROSMER. Would it not be possible to raise him again?

GYLLING. Oh, my dear fellow, how could that be managed?

ROSMER. I mean by going to work in a forbearing —kindly way; showing confidence in him; relying on his good intentions. You could see that he showed a kind of self-knowledge.

GYLLING. Do you rely on the moods of such a man?

ROSMER. I would gladly do so.

GYLLING. Ah, Rosmer, you always had hope, when nobody else had.

MADAM HELSET. I suppose I can take away the supper things, Miss?

REBECCA. Yes, please.

MADAM HELSET. (clearing away). It was very early for the Rector to go this evening.

REBECCA. I think we shall see him again to-morrow.

MADAM HELSET. That you won't. There's bad weather brewing.

REBECCA (putting her sewing in its basket). That's good. Then perhaps I too shall have a chance of seeing white horses at Rosmersholm.

FROM THE SECOND ACT

MORTENSGÅRD. That I don't doubt. But it is too late now. I am branded once for all—branded for life.

ROSMER. I did not think you still took that affair so much to heart.

Mortensgård. Because I am now fairly well off, do you mean? Much better off than if I had kept my position at the school? Yes, that is true. I am. But then think of my peculiar situation. A new age has come over the country. I too might have risen to anything —like most of the others. But—all doors were closed to me. The men I have fought for, and who owe it to *me* that they have risen to power and honour—they will have nothing to do with me. They dare not for their own sake.

Rosmer. Do you think then that cowardice extends even to the most powerful?

Mortensgård. It is not cowardice, Pastor Rosmer. These people can't set aside hypocrisy. If they break with hypocrisy, their fall is at hand. Oh yes, you may perhaps come to feel the smart of it yourself now, Pastor.

Mortensgård. Madam Helset brought it to me late one evening.

Rosmer. If you had inquired of Madam Helset, you would have learnt that my poor unhappy wife was not fully accountable for her actions.

Mortensgård. I did make inquiries, Pastor Rosmer. But I must say that was not the impression I received.

Rosmer. Was it not? Then what did Madam Helset think?

Mortensgård. Well, she too was strange. I could not exactly get at what she thought.

Rosmer. Oh? But what is your precise reason for telling me now about this incomprehensible old letter?

Mortensgård. To impress on you the necessity for extreme prudence, Pastor Rosmer.

ROSMER.   In my life, do you mean?

MORTENSGÅRD.   Yes.

ROSMER.   Then you think that I must have something
to conceal?

MORTENSGÅRD.   Putting everything together, I don't
see what other conclusion I can come to.

ROSMER.   Then you believe me capable of leading an
immoral life.

MORTENSGÅRD.   It seems to me that such an expression sounds strange from you now, Pastor.   I should
have thought an emancipated man would have left behind him all these old morbid considerations and scru-
ples.

ROSMER.   Have you done so yourself?

MORTENSGÅRD.   Yes, of course.   I take it that, since
I am in this world, I have the right to live my life after
my own mind and inclination.   But of course, for one's
own sake one must avoid falling out with the hypocrites
and with all the victims of stupefaction one mixes with.

ROSMER.   You and I will never agree on that point,
Mr. Mortensgård.

MORTENSGÅRD.   H'm.   But in any case be cautious,
Pastor.   If anything should come out that conflicts with
current prejudices, you may be sure the whole liberal
movement will get the blame for it.   Good-bye, Pastor
Rosmer.

_____

FROM THE THIRD ACT

REBECCA.   When I came down here from Finmark
with Dr. West—I was then a year or two over twenty——

ROSMER.   Oh yes.   I know that.

REBECCA.   Rosmer—I was no longer what people call
an—an innocent woman.

ROSMER. What do you say! Impossible! You are out of your senses.

GYLLING. Perhaps I had better go.

REBECCA. No, please stay where you are, my dear Rector. Yes, Rosmer—that is the truth about me from the beginning.

ROSMER. Oh, you, you! How could you—! Who was he?

REBECCA. One who had complete power over me. He had taught me everything. All the desultory information I had about life at that time.

ROSMER. But for all that! You—oh, that you could surrender yourself——!

REBECCA. I thought then that it was something that concerned no one but myself. If it were only hidden.— And hidden it was.

GYLLING. So that is the state of the case.

REBECCA (*looking at him*). After such an experience it is not to be wondered at that a woman should hold out. Hold out in spite of pretty harsh usage. Hold out to the last.

GYLLING. Now I understand it—perhaps.

ROSMER. And that is what you were when you came to Rosmersholm. What did you want here!

REBECCA. I wanted to take my share in the life of the new era that was dawning, with its new ideas. You had told me about Ulric Hetman and the revolution he had nearly—. I wanted you to be to me what he had once been to you. And then, I thought, we should march onward in freedom, side by side. Ever onward. Ever farther to the front.—But between you and perfect emancipation there rose the great, insurmountable barrier.

ROSMER. What barrier do you mean?

REBECCA. I mean this: you could grow only in the

sunshine—and here you were sickening in the gloom of such a marriage.

ROSMER. But we never said a word about my marriage. Never a word. I am certain of that.

REBECCA. We did not. Nor was it necessary. For I could see to the bottom of your heart. And then I went to work.

ROSMER. Went to work? In what way?

GYLLING. Do you mean that——

REBECCA. Yes, Rosmer— (*Rises.*) Sit still. You too, Rector Gylling. But now it must out. It was not you, Rosmer. You are innocent. It was *I*—that lured Beata out into the paths of delusion——

ROSMER (*springs up*). Rebecca!

GYLLING (*rises from the sofa*). The paths of delusion!

REBECCA. The paths that led to the mill-pond. Now you know it, both of you.

ROSMER. But I don't understand—. I only hear—and don't understand a word.

GYLLJNG. Oh yes. I am beginning to understand.

ROSMER. But what can you possibly have said? There was nothing—absolutely nothing to tell.

REBECCA. There was this: we were talking together, reading together, working our way to emancipation together.

ROSMER. So she knew that.

REBECCA. She came to know that *you* were working yourself free from all the old, obsolete prejudices.

ROSMER. And then? What more? I must know all now.

REBECCA. Sometime after, I begged and implored her to let me go away from Rosmersholm.

ROSMER. Why did you want to go?

REBECCA. I did not want to go; I wanted to stay where I was. But I told her that it would be best for

us all that I should go away in time. I gave her to understand that if I stayed any longer, I could not—I could
not tell—what might happen.

ROSMER. Then this is what you did.

REBECCA. Yes, Rosmer.

ROSMER. *This* is what you call "going to work."

REBECCA. I called it so, yes.

ROSMER. Have you confessed all now?

REBECCA. Yes.

GYLLING. Not all.

REBECCA. What more should there be?

GYLLING. Did you not at last give Beata to understand that it was necessary—not only that it would be
wisest, but that it was necessary—both for your own
sake and Rosmer's, that you should go away as soon as
possible?

REBECCA. Perhaps I did say something of the sort.

ROSMER (*sinks into a chair and covers his face with his
hands*). And this tissue of lies and deceit she believed
in! Believed in it as firmly, as immovably, as in a gos-
pel. (*Looks up at Rebecca.*) And she never turned to me.
Never said one word to me. Why did she not do so?

REBECCA. I dissuaded her so earnestly from it.

ROSMER. Yes, yes, in everything she bowed before
your will. And then she quietly went out of life. Effaced
herself. Went into—the mill-pond. (*Springs up.*) How
could you—how could you play this ghastly game?

REBECCA. I had to choose between your life and hers,
Rosmer. Either you would have been ruined or——

ROSMER. —or Beata, yes.

GYLLING. This is frightful! Frightful.

REBECCA. You think then that I acted in full, cool
self-possession! Just as I stand here telling it all! There
are two sorts of will in us, I believe. I wanted Beata

away. But I never really believed that it would come to pass. As I advanced, at each step I seemed to hear something within me cry out: No farther! Not a step farther!—And yet I could not stop. I had to venture the least little bit farther. Only one hair's breadth more. And then one more—and always one more. Have you never felt what it is like to be giddy? One dare not take another step. Nor look down. And yet one does it. One can't help it. One almost thinks it's a delightful sensation—. That is the way such things come about.

ROSMER. Now I know how it all happened. But there is one thing I do not understand. How were you able to bring yourself to disclose your whole heartless conduct?

REBECCA. It had to be done for your sake. I did not wish you to feel oppressed and burdened by self-reproach.

FROM THE FOURTH ACT

MADAM HELSET. But the Pastor, he's not home yet?

REBECCA. If I don't see him, you can tell him that I will write to him—a long letter. Tell him that.

MADAM HELSET. But dear Miss West—that'll never do at all——

REBECCA. What, Madam Helset?

MADAM HELSET. That you should go away from Rosmersholm without saying good-bye to the Pastor.

REBECCA. Well, as it happens, perhaps it is best so.

REBECCA. Could you have believed such a thing of Pastor Rosmer and me?

MADAM HELSET. Believed——?

REBECCA. Yes, don't you think it came like a thunder-clap?

MADAM HELSET. Oh, I won't quite say that either. We're all of us human, Miss West.

REBECCA. That's very true, Madam Helset. We are all of us human.

MADAM HELSET (*looking towards the hall*). Oh Lord—if that's not him coming!

REBECCA. After all. (*Resolutely.*) Well, well; so be it.

REBECCA (*pointing out through the hall*). Hush. Do you see who is coming?

ROSMER (*looks out*). It is Ulric Hetman.

(ULRIC HETMAN *comes in through the hall.*)

ULRIC HETMAN (*stops in the doorway*). Rosmer—my boy, my boy—what is this I hear about you?

ROSMER. Have you come to stay with us?

HETMAN. No. I have come to say my last farewell.

REBECCA. Are you leaving the town again already?

HETMAN. Yes. I'm shaking the dust off my feet. A man can't live up in these parts. It's even worse than down below.

ROSMER. I had thought that more light and freedom was coming.

HETMAN. So I hear.

ROSMER (*with a melancholy smile*). Your old pupil has not been false to you, you see.

HETMAN. Beware of what you do. Don't follow my example. All my doctrine is false. Has been false from its very beginning. That I have now found out.

ROSMER. Do you no longer adhere to all the great ideals?

HETMAN. It's all rubbish, my boy. Empty dreams. Nothing but mocking shadows that drag us down to destruction. Humanity is past help.

ROSMER. Do you believe that!

HETMAN. Past help for all eternity.

ROSMER. But why? Why should we believe that?

HETMAN. Because a mistake was made at the very Creation.

ROSMER. And that mistake was——?

HETMAN (*shrugs his shoulders*). Who can say!

ROSMER. Well, but how can you tell that the mistake was there?

HETMAN (*with a mysterious smile*). The Master deceived himself, my boy.

ROSMER. Deceived himself? The Master? How?

HETMAN. Are you a judge of character?

ROSMER. I think myself I am, but——

HETMAN. Well, in any case you used once to mix with artists—with various poets, I remember.

ROSMER. Yes.

HETMAN. Didn't you notice a peculiar trait about those fellows?

ROSMER. What trait do you mean?

HETMAN. When one of these creative gentlemen had finished a work, which had turned out absolutely as it should be, he examined it and let it go. Quite calmly. There was nothing to be said about the work. It was as it should be. Didn't you notice that, my boy?

ROSMER. Yes. And it seems to me perfectly reasonable.

HETMAN. I think so too. But once in a while the master might chance upon a failure. Either he was not in the right mood, or in too much of a hurry, or whatever it might be. What does my gentleman do then? Why, he puts his head on one side. Looks at his work with the air of a connoisseur. Examines it from every side. And then says he: Upon my soul—this is good. Damned good.

ROSMER. Insecurity, you mean?

HETMAN (*nods slowly*). The master feels that there is a flaw in the work. And so he takes a firm stand. Insecurity of conscience, my boy. And that is what we have all inherited. That is why humanity is incurable. Past help.

REBECCA. Then is life worth living?

HETMAN. Oh yes. Only avoid doing silly things. No quackery. Let life swing right or left—just as it chances.

REBECCA. But one's self? Each individual?

HETMAN. Eat, drink and be merry, my fair young lady. And you must take existence in the same way, Rosmer. The Master forgot to give us wings. Both inner and outer ones. So let us crawl on the earth as long as we can. There is nothing else to be done.

ROSMER. Well, in any case there is the alternative of making an end of it all.

REBECCA (*involuntarily*). Yes, happily.

HETMAN. But surely you two can get along——

ROSMER. Do you think so? Then you still believe in love?

HETMAN. My son, I believe in happiness—the happiness of living under the same roof with so attractive a companion.

ROSMER. Unhappily the attractive companion is leaving me.

HETMAN. Leaving you?

ROSMER. To-night.

REBECCA. In half an hour.

HETMAN. You don't seem to understand how to keep your women. Your first one left you too.

ROSMER. Yes, she did.

HETMAN. Brave woman. She went of her own accord —to smooth your path.

ROSMER. Who told you that?

HETMAN. That blackguard Mortensgård let out something about it in a letter.

ROSMER. I see.

HETMAN. Respect and honour her. For that woman must have had a kind of wings, it seems to me.

REBECCA. Wings? Why wings?

HETMAN. Did she not raise herself so high that she could die for her love?

ROSMER. Ah yes—to be able to die for something.

HETMAN. I would have taken my oath there wasn't a single living soul that could do it.

ROSMER. To seek death—and so bear witness of one's love.

REBECCA. I shall not go to-night.

ROSMER (*uneasily*). Yes, go! Go!

HETMAN. Stay, fair lady. To you there is no danger abroad. He will not let *you* be lured beneath the waters. Farewell.

ROSMER. Are you going now? In the dark night?

HETMAN. The dark night is best. Peace be with you.

(*He goes out through the hall. There is a short silence in the room.* REBECCA *is standing by the window.* ROSMER *walks up and down. Then he sits down in a chair by the table.*)

MADAM HELSET. Miss West, the carriage is— (*Looks round.*) Not here? Out at this time of night? Well— I must say—. H'm— (*Goes out into the hall, looks round, and comes in again.*) Not on the garden seat. Ah, well,

well. (*Goes to the window and looks out.*) Good God!—
what's that? The White Horse! Oh no, oh no!—There
it is. On the bridge. To-night he dares— (*Shrieks
aloud.*) In the mill-race! Both of them in the mill-race!
(*Runs to the door on the right and cries:*) Help—help!
(*Stops, glances towards the window, and says in a lower
tone.*) Oh no. This is past all help or remedy. It was
the dead wife that took them.

"THE LADY FROM THE SEA"
A PLAY IN FIVE ACTS
BY
HENRIK IBSEN
1888

DRAFT

Cut

1st act.—The little calling-place for tourist steamers
They only call when there are passengers to be landed or
taken on board. Shut in by high, steep mountains. The
free, open sea is not visible. Only the winding fiord.
Bathing hotel. Sanatorium higher up. When the play
opens the last steamer of the year is going north. The
boats always pass at midnight. Slowly, noiselessly they
glide into the bay and out again.

The persons of the play fall into three groups. First,
there are peculiar figures among the inhabitants of the
place. The lawyer, married for the second time to the
woman from the free, open sea. Has two young grown-
up daughters of his first marriage. Refined, well-bred,
bitter. Past stained by a rash affair. Therefore future
career barred. The starving sign-painter with his artist's
dreams, made happy by imagination. The old married
clerk. In his youth he wrote a play, which was performed
once. Is constantly polishing it, and lives in the illusion
of getting it published and making a success. Takes,
however, no step in this direction. Reckons himself nevertheless among literary men. Wife and children believe
blindly in "the piece." (Perhaps he is a private teacher,
not a clerk ?)—Fresvik the tailor, the radical man-midwife,
who shows his "emancipation" in ridiculous escapades—
intrigues with other men's wives; talks about divorce and
the like.

The second group is formed by the summer visitors
and the invalids at the Sanatorium. Among these is the

young invalid sculptor, who has to recruit his strength to get through the coming winter. For next summer he is promised a grant of money and a commission and other support, and then he will be able to go to Italy. Dreads the possibility of having to die without having seen the south and without having achieved anything good in his art.—His "patron" is staying at the bathing hotel. Assumes guardianship over the invalid. Is a man of principle. No aid, no support this year. The grant to be down in black and white, "then we will see what we can do next year." His wife, stupid, arrogant and tactless, Hurts the invalid, sometimes by design, sometimes unwittingly.—Many secondary persons.

The third group consists of passing tourists, who enter episodically into the action.

Life is apparently bright, easy and lively up there beneath the shadow of the mountains and in the monotony of seclusion. Then the idea is thrown out that this kind of life is a life of shadows. No energy; no struggle for liberation. Only longings and desires. Thus they live through the short, light summer. And afterwards—into the darkness. Then awakes the longing for the life of the great world outside. But what is to be gained by that? With surroundings, with spiritual development, demands and longings and desires increase. He or she, who stands on the height, yearns for the secrets of the future and a share in the life of the future and communication with distant worlds. Everywhere there is limitation. The result is melancholy like a hushed, wailing song over the whole of human existence and over the deeds of men. A light summer day with the great darkness to follow—that is all.——

Has the line of human development gone astray? Why have we come to belong to the dry land? Why not to the

air? Why not to the sea? The longing to possess wings.
The strange dreams that one can fly and that one does
fly without being surprised at it—how is all this to be interpreted?——

We ought to possess ourselves of the sea. Build our
cities floating upon the sea. Move them southward or
northward according to the season. Learn to harness the
storms and the weather. Some such felicity will come.
And *we*—shall not be in it! Shall not live to see
it!——

The sea's power of attraction. Longing for the sea.
Human beings akin to the sea. Bound by the sea. De-
pendent on the sea. Compelled to return to it. A fish
species forms a primitive link in the chain of evolution.
Are rudiments thereof still present in the human mind?
In the minds of certain individuals?

Pictures of the teeming life of the sea and of that which
is "lost for ever."

The sea possesses a power over one's moods that has
the effect of a will. The sea can hypnotise. Nature in
general can do so. The great mystery is the dependence
of the human will on that which is "will-less."

She came from out by the sea, where her father's parsonage lay. Grew up out there—by the free, open sea.
Became engaged to the wayward young mate—a dismissed
naval cadet—whose ship was laid up for repairs for the
winter in an outlying harbour. Had to break off the engagement by her father's wish. Partly also of her own
accord. Could not forgive what came to light about his
past. So prejudiced was she at that time through her
education in her father's home. Nor has she ever since
quite left her prejudices behind, though she knows better.
Stands on the border-line, hesitating and doubting.——

The mystery in her marriage—which she scarcely dares

acknowledge to herself; scarcely dares to think of: Imagination's power of attraction towards the former one.
Towards him who is gone.

In effect—in her unconscious view—it is *he* that she is
living her married life with.

But—on the other hand—are her husband and step-
children living wholly with her? Have not these three,
as it were, a whole world of memories among themselves?
They keep festivals, whose meaning she can only guess.
Conversations come to a standstill—are broken off, when
she comes in. She did not know her predecessor, and
from delicacy the subject is not mentioned when *she* is
present. There is a freemasonry between all the others in
the house. The housekeeper and servants included. She
is never admitted to it. The others have their own affairs.
She stands outside.

She meets "the strange passenger." This is the name
given him by the other visitors. He once felt a deep attachment to her. That was when she was engaged to the
young sailor. Now he is overworked and has been ordered
sea-bathing. Life has not brought him what he looked
for. He is bitter. Cutting in a jocular way.

The sculptor tells his story. Was sent to sea at twelve.
Shipwrecked five years ago. Was then seventeen. On
that occasion he got his "lesion." Lay for a long time in
the cold sea. Inflammation of the lungs followed. Has
never really got over it. But it was a great piece of luck
nevertheless. For it enabled him to become an artist.
Think of being able to model in the delightful clay, which
shapes itself so delicately between one's fingers!

What then does he think of modelling? Figures of
gods? Or perhaps old vikings?

No. Nothing of that sort. As soon as he can manage
it, he will have a try at a big group.

And what is it to represent?

Oh, it is to represent something out of his own experience.

And what was that? He really must tell it.

Well, it is to be a young woman, a sailor's wife, lying asleep. And she is dreaming too. One will be able to see that.

Nothing more?

Oh yes. Her husband is drowned. But he has come home nevertheless. In the night-time; and there he stands by her bedside and looks at her.

But in heaven's name—he said it was to be something out of his own experience!

Yes. This is out of his own experience. In a sense.

He has seen——?!

Well—he doesn't mean to say he has actually seen it, of course. But all the same——

And then comes the tale—fragmentary and abrupt—suggesting to her terrible misgivings and apprehensions.

FIRST ACT

The lawyer's house, with a large, shady veranda on the left. Garden in front and around. At the back, a hedge, with a small gate. Beyond the hedge, a footpath along the shore, shaded by trees on either side. Between the trees there is a view of the fiord, with high mountain peaks in the distance. Brilliantly clear and warm summer morning.

The *Painter* stands with a large palette, painting some new posts on the veranda. The *Private Teacher* enters from the lawyer's office at the back of the house. Has got another execution delayed. Thoroughly good-hearted man, that lawyer. Now if only the play is brought out, we

are over the worst. *Teacher.* Is there company expected
to-day? *Painter.* Looks like it. The daughters are putting flowers in vases on the veranda. *T.* Yes, it is a gay
time in the tourist season. *P.* To-night another of the
big boats is coming. A few words are exchanged with the
girls, who go backwards and forwards.—The Sculptor comes
along the path, stops at the gate and enters into conversation with those within. The painter embarrassed at being
seen at such common work. Good-nature of course. Bitterness against "fashionable artists," whose own country
is not good enough for them. The *Sculptor* comes inside.
Wants to borrow the palette. The girls with more flowers.
S. Is it some anniversary? The younger: Yes, mother's
birthday. *S.* Indeed! The elder (to her sister): Do be
quiet! *S.* says good-bye and goes. *T.* goes also. The
lawyer comes out on to the veranda. Some words are exchanged with *P.*, who has now finished his work and goes.—
Lawyer and daughters. He is not quite satisfied with
the arrangements. The elder: Oh father, "the s. p."
("strange passenger") is coming this morning, you know.
Lawyer smiles: Yes, yes, you're right. Observations about
him. Is still good-looking. An old lion of the capital.
The s. p. comes. Had so little opportunity of talking to
him last night. After a while the girls go. Then a
long conversation between the friends. Details about the
intervening years.—The wife returns from bathing. Lawyer says she disports herself in the water like a mermaid.
Yes, yes, she says, the sea is pleasanter than the dry land.
Lawyer has to go and attend to his business.—Frank and
confidential dialogue between the two others. She has
not been really happy for the last three years. Why?
Cannot tell him. It is so strange.—The sculptor comes
with a large bouquet. Bows and offers his congratula-
tions.—Why? On the occasion of the anniversary.—Is

there any anniversary to-day?—Yes, it is your birthday, isn't it? Mine!—The s. p. No, I'm sure it isn't. *Lady.* What makes you think that? *S.* Miss B. let out the secret. She said, it is mother's birthday to-day. *L.* I see! The s. p. But— Oh, just so. *L.* takes the flowers and thanks him. Then she enters into conversation with *S.* on his affairs.—Here follows the dialogue already sketched (in the 2nd sheet). *S.* is sent down into the garden to the girls. The s. p. finds him too green. Lawyer enters from his office. The girls from the garden room. Outburst over the beautiful flowers. Oh look! Where did they come from? Mr. P. brought them.—The s. p. For a birthday greeting. The younger: Oh—. The elder: There, you see! Lawyer (embarrassed): My dear, etc. Don't be hurt about it—. The girls, you see—etc. Soda-water and fruit-syrup in the garden room. It is cooler. I'll go and open the bottles. (He and the daughters go in.) The s. p. You are being wronged. You have no share in the life that is led here. *L.* I must not complain. For I too live my own life—in a way.—You? How?—That I cannot tell to anybody on earth.—Won't you go in? (They go into the garden room.)

Second Act

(Up at "the Prospect," a wooded height behind the trading station. Far below the outer fiord is seen, with islands and jutting promontories. The open sea is not visible. Up on the height, a flag-staff and one or two seats. A summer night. There is a tinge of orange in the upper air and over the mountain peaks in the far distance.)

CHARACTERS

LAWYER [DOCTOR] WANGEL. [, district physician].
MRS. WANGEL, his second wife.
THEA [ANNETTE] ⎱ his daughters by his former mar-
FRIDA, a young girl ⎰   riage.
HESLER, a Civil servant [, a schoolmaster].
HANS LÖVSTAD [LYNGSTRAND], a young sculptor.
STRÖMME, a merchant.
MRS. STRÖMME, his wife.
SOLFELDT [BALLESEN], a painter.
BALLESEN, a private tutor.
    TOWNSPEOPLE, VISITORS, STEAMBOAT PASSENGERS,
    AND TOURISTS.

(The action takes place at a trading station in Northern
Norway.)

———————

END OF 1. ACT

Those lovely flowers——?
A birthday greeting (*puts them in the vase*). There,
now they are a decoration for mother's birthday.
(*The girls fall on her neck.*)

———————

1ST ACT

A feeling of summer, life and gladness everywhere.
The days pass like a holiday. Thora takes her husband
into her confidence after the conversation with Hesler.
Wangel disturbed at hearing of her former secret engagement. Forgiveness and forgetting. Now at any rate
she belongs to him alone. Hereafter there will be per-

fect confidence between him and her and the children.
They will mutually share each other's memories. Henceforth they will live together as husband and wife. She
(agitated). As husband and wife! Yes, yes! He starts.
Does not understand. She gives no further explanation.

2ND ACT

Wangel tries to find the explanation of her strange
nature by means of hints and indirect enquiries in a conversation with Hesler. It is the sea that attracts her with
mysterious power. Wangel speaks to her about this.
Does she wish to go to the sea? Yes, yes, she wishes to
go to the sea! Then he is willing to move out there!
No, no, no sacrifices like that! No wrenching away
from here, where is his natural home. He holds to his
purpose. She: Set me free! let me go alone! For how
long? For ever! I cannot live with you any longer.
Then follows the explanation. It is really with him she
is living in marriage!

3RD ACT

This act takes place in the secluded part of the garden,
with bridge and bathing-house. Thora is staying there.
Wangel comes to her. Then Hesler. Then at last
Lyngstrand. Great news! The American is here! He
has seen him!—Scene between Thora and Johnson. What
the sea has joined, man cannot put asunder. Wangel
comes. Recognises the American as the mate who killed
the captain. Calls Thora to witness. She: No, no.
Denies all. Johnson goes: Well, now you must get ready
to go, Thora.

4TH ACT

Same place. Now comes the settlement between Wangel and Thora. Hesler appears. Wangel consents to Thora's going. Renounces his claim upon her.

———————

How did you see him?
Just as he was in reality.

She will leave him.
Divorce.
He has bought her.

But yesterday you said that you saw him as he was when you parted.

She has sold herself.
Feeling of shame over it.
This is not pure marriage.

Did I say that—You are mistaken.

No. You said yesterday that at the first moment you did not recognise him.

The first one was so.   His eyes.
It was founded in freedom.   In free will on both sides.
This stands in the way.   Oh, if she could come to love
him as he deserves.

The dæmonic attraction of
the entirely unknown.
But she does not know him!
For that very reason.
She did not know W.
either.
And then to-night the de-
cision!
For a whole lifetime.
Perhaps the true future for-
feited!

Arenholdt.

Life in freedom forfeited.
Tora, you love him!
I feel as though my place
    were with him.
You shall see him. Speak
    to him.

                    Conclusion:
                    Tora: Now I come to you
                        of my own will.

5TH ACT

Arenholdt, Annette, Lyngstrand and Frida in a boat
from left to right.

Jump ashore here. No, make fast there at the bath-
ing-steps.

A little while after, Arenholdt and Annette come in
from r.

Annette. I began to be so afraid that life would go
from me.

Now he is dead to her——

FIRST ACT

*The house of Wangel, the lawyer, with a large, shady
veranda, on the left. Garden in front and around.
[Near the veranda, a flag-staff. To the right, in the
garden, an arbour, with table and chairs.] At the
back, a hedge, with a small gate. Beyond the hedge,
a footpath along the shore, shaded by trees on either
side. Between the trees there is a view of the fiord,
with high mountain peaks in the distance. It is a
warm and brilliantly clear summer morning.*

(BALLESEN, *a middle-aged painter, dressed in an old velvet jacket and broad-brimmed hat, with the look of an artist in his costume, stands with brush and paint-pot below the veranda, painting some new wooden posts in the railing. A little way off stands an easel with a stretched canvas. Beside it, on a camp-stool, are brushes, palette, and a paint-box. He is humming as he works.*)

(THEA WANGEL *comes out upon the veranda through the open garden-room door. She is carrying a large vase of flowers, which she places upon the table.*)

THEA WANGEL (*looking at the freshly-painted posts*). Well, Ballesen—I hope you put plenty of drying-oil into the colour?

BALLESEN. Within an hour it will be as dry as a bone, Miss Wangel. I give you my word as an artist.

(THEA WANGEL *goes into the garden-room again.*)

(*Shortly afterwards,* HANS LYNGSTAD *comes along the path from the right.* [*He is a slightly-built young man, of delicate appearance, poorly but neatly dressed.*] *He stops, interested by the sight of the easel and painter's materials.*)

HANS LYNGSTAD (*outside the hedge*). Good morning.

BALLESEN (*turning quickly*). Ah—! (*Puts down the paint-pot in embarrassment, and begins to busy himself at the easel.*) Good morning. I take my hat off to you, sir—though I don't think I have the pleasure——

LYNGSTAD. You are a painter, are you not?

BALLESEN. Yes, certainly. Why should I not be a painter?

LYNGSTAD. Ah, I can see you are.—Should you mind my coming in for a moment?

BALLESEN. Do you want to have a look at it?

LYNGSTAD. Yes, I should like to extremely.

BALLESEN. Oh there's nothing much to see as yet. But pray come in—you're quite welcome.

LYNGSTAD. Many thanks. (*He comes in through the garden gate.*)

BALLESEN (*painting*). I'm only sketching it in at present,—just the main outlines, you know.

LYNGSTAD. Yes, I see.

BALLESEN. An artist yourself, perhaps?

LYNGSTAD. A painter, you mean?

BALLESEN. Yes.

LYNGSTAD. No, I am not. But I am going to be a sculptor.

BALLESEN. Oh indeed—are you? Well, well, sculpture, too, is a fine, gentleman-like art. (*Goes back a step and looks at his picture through the hollow of his hand, with his head on one side.*) I fancy I've seen you in the street once or twice. Have you been staying here long?

LYNGSTAD. No, I have only been here a fortnight. But I hope I may be able to stay the whole summer.

BALLESEN. To enjoy the gaieties of the season, eh?

LYNGSTAD. Well, rather to get up my strength a bit.

BALLESEN. Not an invalid, I hope?

LYNGSTAD. Well, I'm what you might call a little bit weak. Nothing to speak of, you know. It's only a sort of short-windedness in my chest.

BALLESEN. Pooh—a mere trifle. (*Puts down his palette.*) But, by Jove, I was forgetting that I've promised Miss Wangel to do a bit of decorating here. (*Takes the paint-pot and finishes the woodwork.*) Perhaps you think it strange to see me doing this kind of thing. But I don't see anything to be ashamed of in art lending its aid to handicraft occasionally. Eh? Is there really anything to be said against it?

LYNGSTAD. No, I'm sure there can't be.

(*A steamer's whistle is heard again outside.*)

BALLESEN. Hullo! There's another monster howling. Now I suppose we shall be saddled with a new lot of disturbers of the peace.

LÖVSTAD. There seems to be a continual coming and going of tourists here. All these steamboats calling every single day.

BALLESEN. You might add, at night as well. To-night the big boat for the North Cape will be here. And then we shall get them—all those who stop here to make excursions into the fiords. Ugh!

LÖVSTAD. Don't you care for all the life there is here in the summer?

BALLESEN. No, indeed I don't. For it's quite foreign to the character of the town.

LÖVSTAD. Are you a native of the place?

BALLESEN. No, I am not. But I have become attached to the place by the bonds of time and habit.

LÖVSTAD. You have lived here a long time, then?

BALLESEN. Well, seventeen or eighteen years. I came here with Varde's dramatic company. But we got into financial difficulties; so the company broke up and was scattered to the winds.

LÖVSTAD. But you remained here?

BALLESEN. Yes, I did. For the town needed me, I must tell you. You see, at that time I was working mostly in the decorating line.——

(THEA *comes out with a rocking-chair, which she places in the veranda.*)

THEA (*speaking into the garden-room.*) Frida—see if you can find the embroidered footstool for father.

LÖVSTAD (*approaches the veranda and bows*). Good morning, Miss Wangel.

THEA (*by the balustrade*). Ah, is that you, Mr. Löv-stad? Good morning. Excuse me one moment——
(*Goes into the house.*)

BALLESEN. Do you know the family here?

LÖVSTAD. Very slightly. I have met the young ladies once or twice at other houses. And I had a little talk with Mrs. Wangel the last time the band played up at the Prospect. She said I might come and see them.

BALLESEN. I'll tell you what—you ought to cultivate their acquaintance.

LÖVSTAD. Yes, I've been thinking of paying them a visit—calling on them, you know. If I could only find some pretext for it.

B. Oh nonsense—a pretext——

(FRIDA *comes out with the stool.* THEA *brings more flowers.* LÖVSTAD *bows to* FRIDA *from the garden.* BALLESEN *collects his things and goes.*)

FRIDA (*by the balustrade*). Thea said you were in the garden.

———————

(WANGEL *comes in from the left, behind the house.*)

WANGEL. Well, here I am, little girls!

THEA. Oh, I'm so glad you have come.
(*He goes up into the veranda.*)

FRIDA. Have you finished at the office now, father?

WANGEL. Oh no, I must go down there again presently. I only wanted to see if Hesler had come. He hasn't, then?

THEA. No, we have seen nothing of him yet.

———————

THEA (*nodding confidentially to him*). Of course you understand that it's all in honour of Mr. Hesler. When an old friend comes to pay his first visit to you——

FRIDA. We had the flag up for him yesterday too. When he came by the boat.

WANGEL (*half smiling*). You are a pair of young rogues—Well, well,—after all it's only natural that we should remember—. But all the same—I don't like all this,—the manner of it. Well—what can one say? I suppose there is no other way of doing it.

FRIDA. Look, there he is, father.

(HESLER *appears on the path, coming from the left, and goes in through the garden gate.*)

WANGEL (*going to meet him*). Welcome! A hearty welcome to you!

(*They shake hands and go into the veranda together.* HESLER *bows to the daughters.*)

WANGEL (*forces him into the rocking-chair*). Sit down. Sit down, old friend!

HESLER. Thanks. (*Looking about him.*) So here I am in my old haunts again. It is many years since I last sat here.

WANGEL. Yes, it's eight whole years ago. But I suppose you recognize——?

HESLER. Perfectly. I don't think there are many changes here. Except that the trees have grown a bit, and you have planted a new arbour there——

WANGEL. Oh no, outwardly, I dare say——

HESLER. And now, of course, you have two grown-up daughters in the house.

WANGEL. Oh, only one grown-up, surely.

FRIDA (*half aloud*). Just listen to father!

WANGEL. But now you shall just sit quiet and have a good rest. You are looking rather tired after your journey.

THEA. Shall we bring a little soda-water and syrup into the garden-room? It will soon be too warm out here.

WANGEL. Yes, do, little girls. Soda-water and syrup. And perhaps a little cognac.

THEA. Cognac too?

WANGEL. Just a little. In case any one should care for it.

THEA. Very well.

(*She and* FRIDA *go into the garden-room and close the door behind them.*)

WANGEL (*seats himself*). Are you thinking of taking a regular course of baths here?

HESLER. Not at all. I have no need of that. I am just going to be idle for a month. And not think about anything at all.

WANGEL. And not overwork yourself again when you get back.

HESLER. Well, what the deuce is one to do? When there isn't a blessed thing on earth that's worth devoting one's self to and living for, it makes one glad that there is such a thing as work. And so one works until one drops.

WANGEL. I don't think I could ever bring myself to do that.

HESLER. You don't care for it?

WANGEL. Not for working more than is absolutely necessary.

HESLER. No, no—of course you have other things— and others—to live for.—Do you intend to remain here for the rest of your days?

WANGEL. Oh yes, that's what it will come to, I suppose. Here I have lived very very happily with her who was taken from us. And now I live very very happily with one who has come to me in her stead.—I must say that, take it all in all, the fates have been kind to me.

HESLER. Is your wife not at home to-day?

WANGEL. Oh yes, she'll be here very soon. She has

gone to bathe. She never misses a day at this season, no matter what the weather may be.

HESLER. Is she out of health?

WANGEL. No, not exactly; but she has been curiously nervous the last couple of years or so. But to get into the sea is life and happiness to her.

HESLER. I remember that of old.

WANGEL. Yes, to be sure, you knew her when you held an appointment out there.

HESLER. Of course. I used often to be at the parsonage while her father was alive.

(MRS. WANGEL, *with a large light cloak over her head and shoulders, comes along the path from the right and through the garden gate.*)

WANGEL (*rising*). Ah, here comes the mermaid!

(MRS. WANGEL *goes quickly up into the veranda.* HESLER *rises and bows.*)

HESLER. H'm—. Have you ever told your husband anything about me—about you and me?

MRS. WANGEL. No, I have not. I don't see that it was my duty. For it never came to anything between us.

HESLER. There you are certainly right. But I mean, have you told him that I once took an unsuccessful step——?

MRS. WANGEL. Not a word of it. I have only told him what is true—that I liked you very much, and that you were the truest and best friend I had out there.

MRS. WANGEL. But you do not know that I was engaged at that time.

HESLER. At that time—engaged!

Mrs. Wangel. Yes, engaged, as it is called.

Hesler. But that is impossible! You are mistaking the time. I don't believe you knew Wangel then. And anyhow he was not yet a widower.

Mrs. Wangel. I know that, my dear Hesler. But it is not Wangel that I am speaking of.

Hesler. Not Wangel! Another then! But at that time—! Out there in the solitude by the open sea—. I don't remember another creature that I could conceive your——

Mrs. Wangel. Oh, you couldn't conceive the possibility, even if I told you—. No, no—for the whole thing was such utter madness on my part.

Hesler. Do tell me more about this——

Mrs. Wangel. No, no, my dear Hesler—what would be the use? It is enough for you to know that I was not free at that time. And now you do know it.

Hesler. And if you *had* been free at that time——?

Mrs. Wangel. What then?

Hesler. Would your answer have been different?

Mrs. Wangel. To be perfectly frank with you, I don't think it would.

Hesler. Nor I either. But then, what is the use of telling me this?

Mrs. Wangel (*rises nervously*). Because I must have some one I can speak to about it. No, no, don't rise.

Hesler. Wangel, then, knows nothing of the matter?

Mrs. Wangel. No. No one has ever known anything. I did not think there was anything to tell him. After all, it was nothing but the maddest of madness; and then it all came to an end so quickly. Was done with. —At least—in a way.

Hesler (*rising*). Only in a way? Not entirely!

Mrs. Wangel. Oh yes, of course! My dear good Hesler, it is not at all as you suppose. It's something quite incomprehensible. I don't think I could find words to tell you of it. And even if I could, you would never be able to understand it. You would think I was ill—or else that I was stark mad.

Hesler. My dear Mrs. Wangel—now you must and shall tell me the whole story.

Mrs. Wangel. Well then—how should you, with your common sense, ever be able to understand that— (*Breaks off.*) Wait—another time—here is some one coming.

_____

Lyngstrand. Well, you see, when we were lying in the brig over in Montreal, we had to leave our boatswain in the hospital; so we shipped an American in his place. And then we put to sea. We were bound for Spain. This new boatswain——

Mrs. Wangel. The American?

Lyngstrand. Yes;—one day he borrowed from the captain a bundle of old newspapers that he had come across somewhere. There were many Norwegian papers among them. And it was mostly those he read.

Mrs. Wangel. The American?

Hesler. Did he know Norwegian?

Lyngstrand. Yes, he knew some. He had sailed to Norway, he said.

Mrs. Wangel. Well; and then?

Lyngstrand. Well, one evening it was blowing great guns. All hands were on deck—all except the boatswain and me. For he had sprained his ankle and couldn't walk; and I wasn't very well and was lying in my bunk. Well, there he sat in the fo'c'sle, reading away as usual at one of the old papers—

MRS. WANGEL. Was it a Norwegian paper?

LYNGSTRAND. Yes, it was [I don't know]. And [But] all of a sudden, I heard him give a kind of a roar. And when I turned and looked at him, I saw that his face was as white as chalk. Then he sat crumpling and crushing the paper up, and tearing it into a thousand little pieces. But that he did quite quietly.

MRS. WANGEL. Did he not speak at all?

LYNGSTRAND. Not at first. But presently he looked at me and said, as if to himself: "She has gone and married another man while I was away."

MRS. WANGEL (half to herself). Did he say that?

LYNGSTRAND. Yes, and he said it in perfectly good Norwegian. He must have been a Norwegian after all— [must have sailed in Norwegian ships, I should think].

MRS. WANGEL. Well, Mr. Lyngstrand, I am sure you can make a work of art out of this.

LYNGSTRAND. Yes, don't you think so? I think I must be able to.

MRS. WANGEL. Is the dead man to represent what she is dreaming of?

LYNGSTRAND. Oh yes, he is. But then he is to be a real man at the same time.

HESLER. Who is drowned and has come home afterwards?

LYNGSTRAND. Yes, I had thought of something of the sort. But I find it so difficult to explain what I mean. You will be able to understand it when I have finished the work.

MRS. WANGEL (with slight hesitation). How long may it be since you made that voyage with the American?

LYNGSTRAND. Oh, it's a long while ago now, Mrs. Wangel. It's more than two years ago. We left America in February and were wrecked in March. It was the equinoctial gales that we got into.

MRS. WANGEL. Two years, do you say? Yes, that agrees.

HESLER. What, do you mean?

MRS. WANGEL. Oh no, it was only— (*Rises.*) It seems to me so hot here. Come, let us go in.

THEA and FRIDA. Ah!

WANGEL. H'm—. Well, you see, my dear Thora——

MRS. WANGEL. Come along, girls! Let us put these up among the others.

THEA and FRIDA (*throwing their arms around her*). Oh you dear—! How sweet of you!

WANGEL (*puts his arm round her*). Thank you, thank you! I thank you from my heart for this, Thora!

MRS. WANGEL. Oh, nonsense—why should I not join with you in keeping mother's birthday?

(*They go up into the veranda, in joyful excitement.* HESLER *follows them.*)

FROM THE SECOND ACT

FRIDA. Pooh—supposing it is true, what—(*Looks down*). Hullo—here he comes with them in tow! Look there! There she is, walking with Hesler—not with father —and jabbering away to him! I wonder whether she isn't a bit sweet on that Hesler.

WANGEL (*smiling*). Well, in this case it was not necessary to ask any question. I scarcely needed to be told who it was——

MRS. WANGEL. Could you——!

WANGEL. —so that I was not at all surprised when at last he came here again.

MRS. WANGEL. Who, who?

WANGEL. To be sure, he wrote that it was because of the girls. That he wanted so much to see them again——

MRS. WANGEL (*jestingly*). Oh, then he was careful of what he said.

WANGEL. You too were a girl when he last saw you. And so you must have remained in his recollection.

MRS. WANGEL. But, my dear Wangel, I assure you.——. I beg you——!

WANGEL. Be quite easy about it. I shall not let him see anything. Hesler is a good and faithful friend of mine. I rely on him with as much confidence as I do on yourself.

MRS. WANGEL. That you may certainly do. But I tell you—it was not Hesler.

WANGEL. H'm, how obstinate you can be at times. Wasn't Hesler tutor out there on the island the winter before he came to us?

MRS. WANGEL. Yes, he was.

WANGEL. Well. And wasn't it just that winter that this took place, this affair of the engagement?

MRS. WANGEL. Yes, you're right there again.

WANGEL. Very well. Then will you tell me, my dear good Thora, whether at that time there was any other decent, respectable unmarried man out there, to whom this might refer?

MRS. WANGEL. No. There was certainly no such person.—But——

WANGEL. But——?

Mrs. Wangel. Well, now I must and will tell you. It was not any decent, respectable man——

Wangel (*starts up*). Not any decent, respectable——!

Mrs. Wangel. Not one that *you* would call so.

Wangel. What is there behind all this? Let me hear the whole story.

Mrs. Wangel. Do you remember that, in the late autumn one year, a large American ship came into Skioldvik for repairs?

Wangel. Yes, I remember it well. It was on board her that the captain was found murdered in his cabin one morning. I remember going to make the post-mortem.

Mrs. Wangel. Yes, I know you did.

Wangel. It was an ordinary seaman who had killed him.

Mrs. Wangel. No one can tell that! It was never proved.

Wangel. There is no doubt about it. Why, he ran away immediately afterwards. Though, to be sure, some people thought he had gone and drowned himself.

Mrs. Wangel. He did not. He escaped in a vessel bound for the north.

Wangel (*starts*). How do you know that?

Mrs. Wangel. Because, Wangel—because it was that ordinary seaman to whom I was betrothed.

Wangel. What do you say? Can this be possible?

Mrs. Wangel. Yes, he was the man.

Wangel. But how in the world, Thora—! And as far as I remember he was nothing but a lad at the time.

Mrs. Wangel. Oh no, he was at any rate a year or two older than I. But we were both young, of course.

Wangel. And you went and engaged yourself to him! What was his name?

MRS. WANGEL. He called himself Johnson.

WANGEL. Where did he come from?

MRS. WANGEL. I don't know.

WANGEL. But you can tell whether he was a Norwegian or a foreigner?

MRS. WANGEL. I don't know for certain. He spoke good Norwegian. But there was something foreign about it.

WANGEL. Then did you never ask him?

MRS. WANGEL. No, not very often. Not so much as five times altogether, I think. For then came this affair about the captain; and he had to go away.

WANGEL. Oh yes, let me hear about that.

MRS. WANGEL. Early one morning, in the dusk, I got a line from him, and it said that I must come out to him at Bakkehammer—you know, the headland between the parsonage and Skioldvik——

WANGEL. Yes, yes—I know.

MRS. WANGEL. —I must come there immediately, for he wanted to speak to me.

WANGEL. And you went?

MRS. WANGEL. Yes, you may be sure I did—then. Well, he said that he had stabbed the captain in the night——

WANGEL. He told you himself! Straight out!

MRS. WANGEL. Yes. But he had only done what was right and just, he said.

WANGEL. Right and just? What reason did he give, then, for stabbing him?

MRS. WANGEL. He would not tell me the reason. He said it was not a thing for me to hear about.

WANGEL. And you believed him?

MRS. WANGEL. Yes, you may be sure I did—then.
Well, he had to go away. But when he was on the point
of saying good-bye to me, he did a strange thing. He
did it quite calmly and quietly. For that was his way.
Always calm and quiet.

WANGEL. What was it he did?

MRS. WANGEL. He took a key-ring out of his pocket,
and drew off his finger a ring he used to wear. Then he
took from me a little ring that I had, and these two he
fastened together on the key-ring. Then he said that
now we two should together be wedded to the sea.

WANGEL. Wedded——?

MRS. WANGEL. Yes, so he said. And then he
flung the large ring and the two small ones far, far out
into the sea. Don't you think that was strange?

WANGEL. And you—? Did you agree to that?

MRS. WANGEL. Yes, would you believe it, at the time
I only thought that it was something—that it was all as
it should be. But then he went away.

WANGEL. And when once he was away?

MRS. WANGEL. Oh, good heavens, you can understand,
my dear, that I soon saw how utterly foolish and stupid
and meaningless the whole thing had been.

WANGEL. Yes, yes. But was that the end of it?
Did you never hear from him afterwards?

MRS. WANGEL. Yes, I heard from him.

WANGEL. He wrote——?

MRS. WANGEL. Yes. As soon as he reached England
I got a line or two from him. He said he was going on
to America, and told me where to address a letter.

WANGEL. Did you write?

MRS. WANGEL. Immediately. I said, of course, that
all must be over between us—that he must never think

of me again, as I meant never to think any more of him.

WANGEL.   Did he stop then?

MRS. WANGEL.   No.

WANGEL.   He wrote again.

MRS. WANGEL.   Yes, he wrote again.

WANGEL.   And what was his answer to what you had said?

MRS. WANGEL.   Not a word.   He wrote just as if I had never broken with him.   He told me quite calmly that I must wait for him.   When he was ready for me he would let me know, and then I was to come to him at once.

WANGEL.   He would not release you?

MRS. WANGEL.   No.   So I wrote again, almost word for word the same as before: only more strongly.

WANGEL.   And did he give way?

MRS. WANGEL.   Oh, no, far from it.   He wrote as calmly as before.   Never a word about my having broken with him.   Then I saw it was useless, so I wrote to him no more.

WANGEL.   But he——?

MRS. WANGEL.   I have had three letters from him since.   Once he wrote from California and once from China.   The last letter I got from him was from Australia.   He said he was going to the gold-mines; since then I have heard nothing more from him.

WANGEL.   That man must have had an extraordinary power over you, Thora.

MRS. WANGEL.   Oh yes, yes.   That dreadful man! Oh, how happy and secure I felt when you and I came together.   It seemed to me as if you had saved me from myself—and from something terrible both within me and without.

WANGEL. (*in a low voice*).   Yes, we were happy indeed—the first three years.

MRS. WANGEL.   Yes, yes, we were.   And then—to think of it—then this—this other thing was to come over me.

WANGEL.   This mental ailing, you mean?   Yes, it is hard.   Hard for us both.   But do try now to calm yourself, my dear, my precious Thora.   We will try another cure for you now.   A fresher air than in here.   The saltladen, sweeping sea-breezes, dear!   What do you say to that?

MRS. WANGEL.   Oh, don't speak of it!   Don't think of such a thing!   There is no help for me in that.   I know, I feel, that I should not be able to throw it off out there either.

WANGEL.   To throw off what, dear?   What do you mean?

MRS. WANGEL (*as though brooding over something*).   I mean the terror of him.

WANGEL.   Yes, but what is it after all that is so terrible to you?

MRS. WANGEL (*looking at him despondingly*).   What I have just told you.

WANGEL.   Well—terrible?   But would you really call it so?   No doubt that man once exercised a tremendous power over you.   That one can easily understand.   But such a thing is not nearly so rare as you seem to think. I have had opportunities of observing several similar cases.   And besides—you had the strength to break it all off.   To put an end to it as soon as you were able to reflect a little.   What is there left to brood over?   It is all over, long ago.

MRS. WANGEL (*springs up*).   No, that is just what it is not!   And that is the terror of it!

WANGEL. Not over!

MRS. WANGEL. No, it is not over! And I am afraid it never will be over. Never in this life. That is what is so terrible to think of.

WANGEL (*in a low, agitated voice*). Do you mean to say that you have never in your heart of hearts been able to forget him?

MRS. WANGEL. No, there was a time when he came to mean nothing to me. It was just as though he had never existed. Oh, I felt so free and relieved for those three years. They were the first three years I lived here with you, Wangel.

WANGEL (*in suspense*). And now—! Do you mean then that now it has come over you again?

MRS. WANGEL. Yes, now it has come again. With frightful force. It came like this two years ago.

WANGEL (*painfully moved*). Ah! Two years ago? That was it! In that case, Thora, I begin to understand much more clearly.

MRS. WANGEL. You are wrong, dear—this thing that has come over me—oh, I don't think it can ever be understood!

WANGEL (*half to himself*). To think that for two years her heart has been given to a strange man. To another! Not to me—but to another!

MRS. WANGEL. Yes, yes, to you! To you alone! To no one in the whole world.

WANGEL. Oh, Thora! Oh yes, yes, I knew that. But what is it then—. What is it between you and the strange man——?

MRS. WANGEL. It is the dread he casts over me——

WANGEL. Dread?

MRS. WANGEL. Yes, a dread. Such a dread, such a

terror, as arises only from the sea. For now I must tell
you, Wangel——

> (*Young people, men and girls, come in from the left,
> some in couples, some in groups. A few tourists
> among them. Finally* HESLER, LYNGSTRAND,
> THEA *and* FRIDA *come. They are no longer walk-
> ing arm in arm.*)

WANGEL. Dear Thora—why did you cross-question
him about that voyage?

MRS. WANGEL. Because I believe—. (*Breaking out.*)
Now I have learnt something about Johnson.

WANGEL. What have you learnt?

MRS. WANGEL. Johnson was on board the ship in
which Lyngstrand was wrecked. Of that I am perfectly
certain.

WANGEL. My dear, what makes you think so?

MRS. WANGEL. Something Lyngstrand mentioned
this morning. Johnson came to know, during the voyage—in some way or other—I don't know how. He
came to know that I had married. Had married while he
was away. And then this came!

WANGEL. What came?

MRS. WANGEL. That Johnson all at once became so
fearfully present to me. I seemed to see him before me
wherever I went.

WANGEL. Did he appear to you as you had seen him
in reality?

MRS. WANGEL. No, I don't see him like that. Not
so young as he was then. I see him older. And I see
him with a beard. A reddish beard. He did not have
a beard then. There is one thing especially that I see
with such fearful clearness.

WANGEL. Now——!

MRS. WANGEL. He always wears a red neck-cloth and it is fastened with a large, bluish-white pearl—a scarf-pin, you know——

WANGEL. Yes, yes.

MRS. WANGEL. And when I think of that pin, it seems to turn into a dead fish's eye, that looks at me. Looks fixedly at me.

WANGEL. Good God—. You are more ill than I thought; more ill than you know yourself, Thora. And you have been in this state for over two years. You have suffered this secret anguish without confiding in me.

MRS. WANGEL. Oh, how could I have the heart to do that. In you! In you, whom I love so dearly. But now I must tell you all. For I feel it closing round me more and more. Therefore I must now tell you the most fearful thing of all.

WANGEL. Yes, tell me that—do tell me that!

MRS. WANGEL. The most fearful thing is that when the strange man became so living to me, then—Oh——

WANGEL. Then?

MRS. WANGEL. Then I seemed to lose you, Wangel!

WANGEL. Lose? How——?

MRS. WANGEL. When you were [are] not present, I could [can] no longer recall [retain] your appearance. It was [is] the strange man that I saw [see] instead of you.

WANGEL. Explain yourself more clearly, Thora.

MRS. WANGEL. I mean that when you are out in a boat and a storm comes on and I am waiting here in mortal fear for you, it is not you that I picture to myself in the boat—. Or rather, it *is* you, but I see you in the likeness of the strange man.—And then the unspeakable.

WANGEL. The unspeakable——?

Mrs. Wangel. No, no, no!— Only one thing more, and I have done. Wangel—how shall we fathom—that about the child's eyes——

FROM THE THIRD ACT

Thora (*softly and trembling*). Oh, do you hear that, Wangel? He is coming back!

Wangel. Do not be alarmed. We shall find means to prevent it.

The Stranger. Good-bye for the present, Thora. To-morrow evening then.

Thora (*with a shriek*). Don't look at me like that! Oh, the eyes, the eyes!

Wangel. The eyes! What do you mean by that——

The Stranger. And if by that time you should be of a mind to come with me——

Thora. Never! Never to the end of time! Never!

The Stranger. I only mean that in that case you must be ready to start. To-morrow evening then, you understand.

Thora. Never, I say! Go, go!

Wangel. Go into the house, Thora!

Thora. I cannot. Oh, help me! Save me, Wangel!

The Stranger. For you must remember this, that if you do not come with me this time, it will be too late.

Thora. Too late——?

The Stranger. Beyond recall, Thora. I shall never return to these parts. You will never see me any more nor hear from me either. I shall be as though dead and gone from you, for evermore.

Thora (*breathing as though relieved*). Ah——!

THE STRANGER. So think carefully what you do. Good-bye. (*He climbs over the fence, stops, and says:*) Well, Thora—be ready to start to-morrow evening; for then I will come and take you away.

(*He goes slowly and calmly along the footpath and out to the right.*)

THORA (*looks after him a while*). Oh, that terrible creature!

WANGEL. Be calm, be calm. He is gone now, and you shall never see him again.

THORA. Oh, how can you say that? He is coming again to-morrow [night].

WANGEL. Let him come: I will see that he does not meet you.

THORA. Do you think you can prevent that? Oh, I don't know any place on earth where I can be safe from him.

WANGEL. Before all else you must try to get him out of your ailing mind.

THORA. Yes, yes, if I only could. (*Looking away.*) So sure he was that I would go with him.— Have you ever heard or seen a man so sure as he is, Wangel!

WANGEL. You must put him out of your thoughts, I say.

THORA. Yes, if one only could.

WANGEL. You must! You must! You don't know what it may lead to otherwise.

THORA (*musing*). When he has been here—to-morrow evening—. And [when] he has gone away in the steamer——.

WANGEL. Well, what then?

THORA. Do you think he will never come again?

WANGEL. No, dear Thora, you may feel absolutely secure on that point.

THORA. Never again? Never as long as life lasts. Do you think that?

WANGEL. That I am certain of. You will never see him again.

THORA (*involuntarily*). Never——

WANGEL. How can you be afraid of that? What could he do here after this? Do look at it reasonably, dear. He has heard now, from your own lips, that you will have nothing to do with him.

THORA. No. That is certain. To-morrow evening—. And then never again.

FROM THE FOURTH ACT

WANGEL. Tell me, Mr. Lyngstrand—that American you were speaking of yesterday—do you know much about him?

LYNGSTRAND. No, not much. Only that we were shipmates one voyage.

WANGEL. Do you remember his name?

LYNGSTRAND. Yes, it was Frimann, or something like that.

WANGEL. And then he shipped as nothing more than boatswain.

LYNGSTRAND. Yes, it was a boatswain we happened to want. And he wanted to get across. So he took the berth.

WANGEL. Now he is travelling as a tourist, it seems.

LYNGSTRAND. Did you see him too, Doctor?

WANGEL. I saw a stranger pass below there. It must have been he.— Tell me, what sort of a man did you think he was? I mean, when you were shipmates with him.

LYNGSTRAND. He seemed to me to be a quiet, calm man. But very determined.

WANGEL. Very determined?

LYNGSTRAND. Yes, he was. But that was in a quiet way, too. I only remember one time when he became quite ungovernable.

WANGEL. Oh yes. That time you were speaking of yesterday——.

LYNGSTRAND. —that I am going to put into sculpture, yes. I am so glad both you and Mrs. Wangel think so well of that idea.

WANGEL. How—? Oh yes, yes.

(He goes over to HESLER, *who is standing by the piano.)*

ANNETTE *(softly to* LYNGSTRAND*).* I'll wager my life it was the strange man who came and enquired.

LYNGSTRAND. For Mrs. Wangel!

ANNETTE. I don't know whom he enquired for.

LYNGSTRAND. Yes, it was Mrs. Wangel. But what on earth——!

ANNETTE. Well, come along. Come along.

(She and LYNGSTRAND *go with* FRIDA *down through the garden.)*

WANGEL *(to* HESLER*).* Have you given any more thought to it?

HESLER. I have thought of nothing else, ever since we parted.

WANGEL. And what do you think I ought to do in the matter?

HESLER. My dear Doctor, I think that you, as a physician, ought to know better than I.

WANGEL. H'm. This is no common disorder. And no case for an ordinary physician—or for ordinary remedies.

HESLER. How is she to-day?

WANGEL. I have just been up to see her, and she appeared to me quite calm. But behind all her moods something seems to be hidden that eludes me entirely. And then she is so variable, so incalculable, so subject to sudden changes.

HESLER. No doubt that is due to her morbid state of mind.

WANGEL. Not entirely. The germ of it all is innate in her. Thora belongs to the sea-folk: that is the trouble.

HESLER. What do you mean precisely, my dear Doctor?

WANGEL. The people who live out by the open sea are like a race apart. Widely different from the people of the fiords. Out there they live the life of the sea. And they never bear transplantation. I should have thought of that before. It was a sin against her to take her away from the sea and bring her in here.

HESLER. Have you come to look at it in that light?

WANGEL. Yes, more and more. Especially in the last year or two.—But I ought to have known it from the first. I ought to have known that she would inevitably pine and languish in here. Oh, I did know it too, but I would not acknowledge it. I loved her so much. And consequently I thought first of myself. In fact, I was utterly and unpardonably selfish.

HESLER. I am afraid every one is selfish under those circumstances. But I can't say that I have noticed that vice in you.

WANGEL. Oh yes. But I try to fight against it.

HESLER. Let us speak frankly. Was it mutual affection that brought you and her together?

WANGEL. No, I can't say it was. Not that kind of

feeling on her side. When her father was drowned—her
mother was subject to melancholy, you know—the new
lighthouse-keeper was expected. They had to leave
the house. Oh, I ought never to have availed myself of
her helpless situation. But I did so nevertheless.

HESLER. And it was only gradually that you won her?

WANGEL. I thought at any rate that I had won her.
There seemed to be signs of that. But then this melancholy came upon her. Oh, what remorse I felt. For I
was to blame. I had taken her by surprise. Almost
by force, I may say. For, you see, she had no choice.
And I was at my wits' end to know what to do.— That
is why I turned to you in my perplexity, and asked you
to come to us.

HESLER. Yes, my dear Doctor, but what good did
you suppose *I* could do? I don't understand.

WANGEL. No. For I had got upon a wrong scent.
I fancied that she had once cared for you, and that she
still secretly cared for you. So I thought it might perhaps do her good to see you again.

HESLER. Then it was your wife you meant when you
wrote that some one here was waiting for me!

WANGEL. Yes; who else?

HESLER. Of course. But I did not understand you.

WANGEL. Naturally not. I was on a wrong scent.

HESLER. Then, although you thought your wife had
an inclination for me—cared for me—you nevertheless
wrote for me. Asked me to come here——

WANGEL. I was bent upon seeing her cheerful again.
Rejecting no expedient. Come of it what might.

HESLER. And you think you are selfish——

WANGEL. Oh, I had such a great error to atone for.
But don't tell her I wrote for you. She believes you
came here of your own accord. Tell her nothing.

HESLER. Not a word, since you wish it. Well, after all, it was a good thing I came here. That the misunderstanding was cleared up. For now you know that her heart is not with any other man.

WANGEL. No, it is wholly and solely the dread of this stranger that haunts her thus.

HESLER. How do you explain the power he exercises over her?

WANGEL. H'm, my dear friend, there are sides to that question that don't admit of explanation.

HESLER. Something inexplicable, do you mean? Entirely inexplicable?

WANGEL. Inexplicable to the understanding of our time, at any rate. To the science of our time.

HESLER. Do you believe in such things?

WANGEL. I neither believe nor disbelieve. I simply do not know. So I suspend my judgment. [For I am not really a man of science, I must tell you. I have——]

HESLER. But tell me—. That strange, uncanny idea of hers about the child's eyes——?

WANGEL (eagerly). I don't in the least believe that about the eyes. That is pure imagination on her part. I take that to be nothing but an outcome of her morbid nervous condition. Nothing else!

HESLER. But then the other point: that this haunting fear, this dread and unrest came upon her just at the very time when this stranger would seem to have been on his way home?

WANGEL. Well, that again is a belief she has imagined and dreamt herself into, since the day before yesterday. It did not come upon her at all so suddenly, so instantaneously, as she now maintains. But since she heard from this young Lyngstrand that Johnson, or whatever he is called, was on his way home three years ago in

March, she believes that her mental suffering came over her in the very same month.

HESLER. And did it [not]?

WANGEL. Not at all. It had been noticeable long before that. It is true she had a sharp attack precisely in the month of March, three years ago——

HESLER. Well then——!

WANGEL. Oh, but that is quite easily accounted for by the circumstances—the condition—she happened to be in at that time.

HESLER. The indications may be read in either way, then.

WANGEL. And to be powerless to help her! To have neither resource nor remedy!

HESLER. What if you made up your mind to a change of residence—to move to some other place, where you would live under wider, less restricted conditions?

WANGEL. I have suggested that to her. But she will not.

HESLER. Not that either.

(*Goes up towards the window on the left.*)

WANGEL. Oh, I should be so glad to make any possible sacrifice.

(TORA *enters by the door on the left.*)

TORA (*rapidly to* WANGEL). Be sure you do not go out this morning!

WANGEL. No, no, certainly not; I will stay at home with you. (*Points to* HESLER.) But you haven't said good morning——?

TORA (*turns*). Oh, are you there, Mr. Hesler! (*Holds out her hand.*) Good morning.

HESLER. Good morning, Mrs. Wangel. So you're not bathing to-day?

Tora. No, no. Don't speak to me of bathing. The water is sickly here in the fiord. Won't you sit down?

Hesler. No, thank you. Not now. (*Looks at* Wangel.) I promised the girls I would join them in the garden.

Wangel. Well, my dear friend—I won't keep you.

Tora. You will probably find them by the pond.

Hesler. I shall find them, I'm sure.

(*He nods and passes across the veranda and out to the right.*)

Wangel (*rising*). Then have the years we have lived together been utterly wasted for you?

Tora. Oh, don't think that. I have had all from you that any one could possibly desire. But the years have given me a clearer insight. The sense of shame has awakened in me. I see it now—the life we lead is no real and true marriage.

Wangel. I can strengthen you in fighting against it.

Tora. Yes, if I had the *will* to fight against it.

Wangel. Have you not the will?

Tora. Oh, that is just what I don't know.

Wangel. You must try to make sure of yourself. The decision is to-night.

Tora. Yes, think of it—! The decision so near. The decision for all time.

Wangel. To-morrow he will be gone. Then you will be free [of him]. [And then you will be free of all your doubts——]

Tora. Perhaps I shall have forfeited my true future.

Wangel. Your true——?

TORA. A life of freedom forfeited!

WANGEL. Tora—do you love this man [stranger]?

TORA. Do I—? Oh how can I tell.

WANGEL. That you must try to find out.

TORA. It is no use. I only know that to me he is mysterious, and that——oh!

WANGEL. —and that——?

TORA. —and that I feel as though my place were with him.

WANGEL. I begin to understand.

TORA. And what help have you for me? What remedy do you know of?

WANGEL. To-morrow. He will be gone. Then you will be safe from disaster; then I promise to set you free. We will cancel the bargain, Tora!

TORA. Oh Wangel——!

WANGEL (*looks out into the garden*). More another time.

> (ARENHOLDT, ANNETTE, LYNGSTRAND, FRIDA, *and*
> BALLESTED *appear behind the arbour.* BALLESTED
> *is carrying his painting materials.*)

ARENHOLDT (*coming up on to the veranda*). Ah, I can tell you we have been laying great plans.

FRIDA. We want to go out in a boat this evening, and——

LYNGSTRAND. [B.] No, no, don't tell!

WANGEL. We two have also been laying plans.

ARENHOLDT. No, really?

WANGEL. My wife is going to Skioldvik for a time.

ANNETTE. Going away?

ARENHOLDT. That is very wise.

WANGEL. Tora wants to go home again; home to the sea.

LYNGSTRAND. "The Lady from the Sea." Yes, one can understand that.

BALLESTED. Understand it perfectly. The dying mermaid on the dry land——

TORA. Why do you call me that!

BALLESTED. Oh no. I was only thinking of my picture. Good-bye, good-bye.

(*Goes out by the garden gate.*)

FRIDA (*softly to* ANNETTE). Now they've been having another conference.

(*A maid-servant opens the door on the right.*)

WANGEL. To table. Come along, Arenholdt! We will drink a parting cup with "the lady from the sea."

(*They all go towards the door on the right.*)

FROM THE FIFTH ACT

ELLIDA. I *must* speak with him myself. If you will not set me free, then he must do so. One of the marriages must be dissolved.

WANGEL. You yourself have dissolved the relationship that in your morbid excitability you call a marriage. You have dissolved it and that is enough.

ELLIDA. No, no, that is not enough. What is the use of your putting forward a thousand rational arguments. It does not help me in the least, if my own feelings are different.

WANGEL. And they are so still.

ELLIDA. They will always be so. I shall always feel as I do now. I am not made like you. You can lead your life of reality here with me, and feel secure and happy in it—and at the same time continue to live with your memories.

WANGEL. Oh, if I could only make you understand how immensely different the two things are!

ELLIDA. Not to me. I cannot lead such a dual existence. I cannot continue in it any longer. Impossible! Perfectly impossible. Either wholly with you or wholly with him!

WANGEL. All these are confused feminine ideas, Ellida! Confused feminine fancies. What do you gain by his releasing you from your promise, as you call it. Does that make you free? Do you suppose it will break the power he exercises over you?

ELLIDA. Ah, I don't know! I don't know.

WANGEL. Oh yes, you may be sure that it will not be so. It is not from without that your liberation will come. Not from any one else. It is from within—from yourself that liberation must come.

ELLIDA. Oh yes, yes. Do you think I don't feel that. But you see, Wangel—that is just the terrible part of it, that——

WANGEL. That——?

ELLIDA. —that I often feel as though I did not wish for liberation either.

WANGEL. Then I know no help for you.

ELLIDA. Oh, don't say that so confidently. There must surely be something in the world—something between heaven and earth, that could force my will to extricate me from all this.

WANGEL. I know of nothing.

ELLIDA. And yet it is you I count upon, Wangel. You I expect help from. You alone.

WANGEL. From me, with whom you will not live any longer.

ELLIDA. Will?

WANGEL. Yes, will.

ELLIDA. Say rather, *can.*

WANGEL (*looks searchingly at her*). In that there is hope.

ELLIDA. Yes, do you not think so.

ANNETTE. How could father say such a thing!

ASKEHOLM. It appears that was not what he meant. But I came here in that belief. And I think it is quite excusable, Annette. So many a young girl comes to regard her tutor with more than ordinary attachment——

ANNETTE. Yes, yes, I know that [—in her school-days].

ASKEHOLM. I have myself more than once had occasion to observe something of the sort. But then the young girls leave school and enter life. Other connections are formed, and nothing is left of their relation to the tutor than a warm friendship—a little bashful, perhaps——

ANNETTE. Yes, that is just how it is——!

ASKEHOLM. —a little inclined to avoid dwelling on school-days [the last year at school]. Well then, I got your father's letter——

ANNETTE. Yes, but that letter——

ASKEHOLM. Now you mustn't interrupt me, dear Annette. I thought at any rate that I had come upon an exception. I accustomed myself to the thought that here was a young girl waiting and longing for me to come again. When a man, like myself, is no longer in the first flush of youth, such a belief or illusion makes an exceedingly strong impression. A vivid affection for you grew up in me, Annette. I felt I must come to you;

see you again; tell you that I shared the feelings which
I imagined you entertained for me.

ANNETTE. But now, when you know that it was not
so——?

_____

THE STRANGER. I was not thinking of travelling-
clothes and trunks and that sort of thing. I have on
board with me everything she requires for the voyage; and
I have taken a cabin. (*To* ELLIDA.) I ask, if you
will go with me.

ELLIDA. If I will——!

THE STRANGER. Yes, you must choose now. In
half an hour it will be too late.

ELLIDA. What makes you hold to me so persistently?

THE STRANGER. Do you not feel, as I do, that we two
belong to each other?

ELLIDA. Do you mean because of that promise,
which——?

THE STRANGER. Promises bind no one: neither man
nor woman. If I hold to you persistently, it is because
I cannot do otherwise.

ELLIDA. Why did you not come sooner?

WANGEL. Ellida——!

(THE STRANGER *climbs slowly over the garden
fence and comes nearer.*)

ELLIDA (*shrinks behind* WANGEL). What is it? What
do you want?

THE STRANGER. You ask why I did not come sooner.

ELLIDA. Yes, I asked that.

THE STRANGER. Three years ago I was on my way
to you. At last I had been so far successful that I could
come for you. Take you home with me, Ellida.

WANGEL. Where is your home?

THE STRANGER. A little everywhere. Spread over the whole earth. And over the whole sea too, I think.

ELLIDA. And to that vast home you would have brought me then!

THE STRANGER. I would have, yes. But then came the shipwreck in the Channel. All gone, lock, stock and barrel, all that I had scraped together. Then to work again. For you, Ellida. Now I am back here. For the last time. Will you come with me? Or will you stay here with him!

WANGEL (*looking at her*). Choose!

ELLIDA. Oh, I cannot—! I don't know——!

(*A bell is heard in the distance.*)

THE STRANGER. There goes the warning bell. Now you must say yes or no.

ELLIDA. To have to decide! To decide for all time! To do what can never be undone!

THE STRANGER. Never.

ELLIDA. If I went with you——?

WANGEL. If you went——!

ELLIDA. —should I be going to my happiness!

THE STRANGER. You must find that out. I cannot tell you anything certain.

ELLIDA. Oh, what is it that tempts and allures and seems to drag me into the unknown! The whole might of the sea is centred in this one thing.

WANGEL. I see it. I see it. Step by step you are gliding away from me.

ELLIDA. If I let him go away alone—. If I stay behind with you—Wangel—can you assure me that I shall never come to regret it?

WANGEL. Never regret——?

ELLIDA. Yes, yes, for it can never be undone! Can you assure me that I shall never come to regret it?

WANGEL. No, Ellida—I cannot.

(*The bell is heard again.*)

THE STRANGER (*to* ELLIDA). There is the second bell.

ELLIDA (*goes up to him and lays her hand on his arm.*) Then I am going with you.

WANGEL (*to himself*). I knew it.

THE STRANGER. At last you have made your choice, Ellida.

ELLIDA. There is no choice in this. I am going with you because I must. Cannot do otherwise.

THE STRANGER. No, for I am the strongest. But now you shall hear what I have to offer you. I would not tell you anything before. For I did not wish to entice you. Of your own will you were to go where I go. But now you shall hear——

ELLIDA. I will hear nothing! It is the unknown that draws me. Into that I will go.

WANGEL. Let me give you a little assistance on the way, Ellida.

ELLIDA. What do you mean?

WANGEL. I do not wish your happiness to be clouded by remorse or regret at the thought of me. You are not leaving me against your will. I set you free. I cancel our bargain.

ELLIDA. Is this true, Wangel. Do you mean it from your inmost heart?

WANGEL. Yes, from the inmost depths of my heart I mean it.

ELLIDA. And can you do it!

WANGEL. I can, because I love you.

ELLIDA. And you have come to love me so truly and so dearly.

WANGEL.   The years of our marriage have brought this about.

ELLIDA.   And I have been blind to it.

WANGEL.   Your thoughts went in other directions. Listen to me, Ellida.   It would have been easy for me to prevent your going away with this stranger.   I do not prevent you.   You are now a free woman, with full right to go where you will.

ELLIDA.   This transforms everything.

(*The steamer bell rings for the third time.*)

THE STRANGER.   Do you hear!   Come away!

ELLIDA.   I can never go with you after this.

THE STRANGER.   You will not go!

ELLIDA (*to* WANGEL).   After this I can never leave you.

WANGEL.   Ellida——!

THE STRANGER.   It is all over then.

ELLIDA.   Yes, irrevocably.

THE STRANGER.   I see there is something that is stronger than my will.

ELLIDA.   Your will has no longer a feather's weight with me.   For me you are a dead man, who has come back from the sea.   But I am no longer in terror.   And you fascinate me no more.

THE STRANGER.   Good-bye, Ellida!   (*He vaults over the fence.*)   Henceforth you are nothing but a half-forgotten dream in my life.

(*He goes out to the left.*)

WANGEL.   How came this transformation?

ELLIDA.   Oh, do you not understand that it came through liberation.

WANGEL.   And the unknown fascinates you no longer.

ELLIDA.   No longer.   I was free to choose it; and therefore I was able to reject it.

WANGEL. And now you will come to me again, will you not, Ellida?

ELLIDA (*throwing herself on his neck*). Yes, Wangel —now I will come to you again. I can now, for now I come to you in freedom.

WANGEL. Ellida! Ellida! Oh, to think that we two can now live for each other——

ELLIDA. —and for our memories. Yours as well as mine——

WANGEL. Yes, can we not, dearest!

ELLIDA. —and for our two children, Wangel!

WANGEL. Ours—! (*Kisses her hands joyfully and quickly.*) Oh, I thank you for that word more than I can tell!

> (ARNHOLM, ANNETTE, LYNGSTRAND, FRIDA, BAL-
> LESTED, *and a number of townspeople and summer
> visitors come along the footpath.*)

FRIDA. Just look, isn't father gallant.

BALLESTED. It is summer time, miss.

ARNHOLM. The English steamer is under way.

LYNGSTRAND. The last trip of the season.

BALLESTED. "Soon will all the straits be ice-bound," as the poet says. It is sad, Mrs. Wangel. But I stick to what I've said. Human beings really *can* acclam— acclimatise themselves.

ELLIDA. Yes, in freedom they can, Mr. Ballested.

> (*The great steamer glides noiselessly down the fiord.
> The music is heard closer inshore.*)

HEDDA GABLER
A PLAY IN FOUR ACTS
BY
HENRIK IBSEN
1890

THE pale, apparently cold beauty. Expects great things of life and the joy of life.

The man who has now finally won her, homely in appearance, but honourable, and a gifted, liberal-minded man of science.

———————

Hedda: I have no gift for anything but being bored. That life should have nothing in the world to offer one. Supposing he were to go in for politics.

Brack. That is not in his line.

H. But perhaps I could get him into it. Do you think he would ever get into the ministry.

Brack. For that he would have to be a very rich man.

H. Yes and then—I doubt if it would bring me any satisfaction in the long run.

*

Lövborg: I have led a rather wild life, they say. Now I have to make amends.

But I cannot renounce.

———————

NB!

Brack had always thought that Hedda's short engagement to Tesman would come to nothing.

Hedda speaks of how she felt herself set aside, step by step, when her father was no longer in favour, when he retired and died without leaving anything.—It then came upon her, in her bitterness, that it was for his sake she had

been made much of.—And then she was already between
25 and 26. In danger of becoming an old maid.

She thinks that in reality Tesman only feels a vain
pride in having won her. His solicitude for her is the
same as is shown for a thoroughbred horse or a valuable
sporting dog.—This, however, does not offend her. She
merely regards it as a fact.

Hedda says to Brack that she does not think Tesman
can be called ridiculous. But in reality she finds him so.
Later on she finds him pitiable as well.

Tesman: Could you not call me by my Christian
name?

Hedda: No, indeed I couldn't—unless they had
given you some other name than the one you have.

Tesman puts Lövborg's manuscript in his pocket so
that it may not be lost. Afterwards it is Hedda who, by
a casual remark, with tentative intention, gives him the
idea of keeping it.

Then he reads it. A new line of thought is revealed to
him. But the strain of the situation increases. Hedda
awakens his jealousy.

*

In the 3rd act one thing after another comes to light
about Lövborg's adventures in the course of the night.
At last he comes himself, in quiet despair. "Where is
the manuscript?" "Did I not leave it behind me here?"
He does not know that he has done so. But after all, of
what use is the manuscript to him now! He is writing of
the "moral doctrine of the future"! When he has
just been let out of the police cells!

Hedda's despair is that there are doubtless so many
chances of happiness in the world, but that she cannot

discover them. It is the want of an object in life that torments her.

When Hedda beguiles T. into leading E. L. into ruin, it is done to test T.'s character.

It is in Hedda's presence that the irresistible craving for excess always comes over E. L.

Tesman cannot understand that E. L. could wish to base his future on injury to another.

Hedda. Do I hate T.? No, not at all. I only find him boring.

Brack. But nobody else thinks so.

Hedda. Neither is there any one but myself who is married to him.

Brack. . . . not at all boring.

Hedda: Heavens, you always want me to express myself so correctly. Very well then. T. is not boring, but I am bored by living with him.

Hedda: . . . had no prospects. Well, perhaps you would have liked to see me in a convent (home for unmarried ladies).

Hedda: . . . then isn't it an honourable thing to profit by one's person? Don't actresses and others turn their advantages into profit? I had no other capital. Marriage—I thought it was like buying an annuity.

Hedda: Remember that I am the child of an old man—and a worn-out man too—or past his prime at any rate—Perhaps that has left its mark.

Brack: Upon my word, I believe you have begun to brood over problems.

Hedda: Well, what cannot one lapse into when one has gone and got married.

Miss R. (*walking about the room*). There. Now we can see all the finery. Yes, yes—it looks well, Berta. Flowers everywhere.

Berta. They were all sent in last night. So that they might keep fresh of course. But this a lady brought herself—just before you came, Miss.

Miss Rising. Yes, that is as it ought to be. When a young couple come home from their honeymoon——

FROM THE FIRST ACT

Miss Rising. Oh well—just at first. You must do as well as you can.

Berta. Most like she'll be terrible grand in her ways.

Miss Rising. Well, you can't wonder at that. Think of the sort of life she was accustomed to in her father's time.

Berta. Yes, and if I only had to do with Master Axel, it would be easy enough.

Miss Rising. No, Axel is not difficult to please. If he only has what he has always been accustomed to, he's satisfied. But by-the-bye, you mustn't call him Master Axel any more. In future you must say Dr. Tesman.

Tesmen. Yes, you may be sure I have.

Miss Rising. And what do you think of it?

Tesman. I'm delighted. This is the very house Hedda wanted to live in. She said often and often, before

we were engaged, that she would never care to live anywhere but in Secretary Falk's villa.

MISS RISING. And how lucky it was that this very
house should be to let [for sale].

TESMAN. Yes, you may be sure I was glad to hear of
it. And Hedda too—when you wrote about it. And
how comfortably you have arranged it all.

MISS RISING. So you really think that, dear Axel?

TESMAN [(rising)]. Yes, it is simply splendid, I think.

MISS RISING. So do I. And Judge Brack says
the same.

TESMAN (looking round). [(feeling the chairs.)] Fancy
—carved furniture! What I have always been wanting.

MISS RISING. Well, you see, now you will be made
professor, and then you will at once have your own salary
to depend upon——

TESMAN. That is a matter of course. But in any
case I am not yet appointed.

MISS RISING. Oh, you may be sure they will be
quick about appointing you—as soon as they hear you
are home again.

TESMAN. Yes, that may be so. But just suppose that
to-morrow I fall down in the street and lie there!

MISS RISING (laughing). Oh, there is no fear of that.
A man who is born to make a noise in the world, he
doesn't fall down in the street, you may be sure. The
people who want to stand in your way, they fall. Holger
Lövborg—his fall was the worst. And now he has to
lie on the bed he has made for himself—poor [unfortu-
nate] creature.

TESMAN. Have you heard anything of him? Since I
went away?

Miss Rising. Only that he has published a new book——

Tesman. What! Recently?

Miss Rising. Yes, but heaven knows whether it can be worth much? Ah—when *your* new book appears, Axel! That will be another story, won't it!

Tesman. Yes, it won't be long now, Auntie. For now it will be very easy for me—I feel that.

(Hedda, *in a morning gown, enters by the corner door on the left.*)

Miss Rising (*going to meet her*). Good morning, my dear Hedda! Good morning!

Hedda (*holds out her hand*). Good morning, dear Aunt! So early a call! That is kind of you.

Miss Rising. Well—has the bride slept well in her new home?

Hedda. Oh yes, thanks—passably. But of course one has always to accustom one's self to new surroundings. Little by little. (*Looking towards the left.*) Oh— there the servant has gone and opened the veranda door, and let in a whole flood of sunshine.

Miss Rising (*going towards the door*). I will shut——

Hedda. No, no, not that. Tesman, please let down the Venetian blinds. That will give a softer light.

Tesman (*goes to the door*). All right—all right— There now, Hedda, now you have both fresh air and shade.

Hedda. Yes, fresh air we certainly must have, with all these stacks of flowers— (*At the table.*) H'm,—we shall never get on with this servant.

Miss Rising. Not get on with Berta——!

Tesman. You don't know how good Berta is.

Hedda. Well, but just look here. She has left her

old bonnet lying about on a chair. Just fancy, if any one should come in and see it!

TESMAN. Why Hedda! That's Aunt Jane's bonnet!

HEDDA. What! No really——

MISS RISING (*taking up the bonnet*). And, what's more, it's not old, Mrs. Hedda.

HEDDA. No, of course—I can see that now.

MISS RISING (*half in tears*). And I only bought it in honour of your coming home.

HEDDA. But my dear good Miss [Aunt] Rising——

MISS RISING (*tying on the bonnet*). Yes, indeed I did.

HEDDA. No, but look here, Aunt Jane——

TESMAN. Hedda is a little short-sighted, you know, Auntie——

MISS RISING. Well, well, I'm sure it isn't worth saying any more about such a trifle.—But now I must see about getting back into town. And to Sister Rina, poor dear.—My parasol? Ah, here it is. For this is mine too. (*Mutters.*) Not Berta's. (*Cordially to them both.*) Well, good-bye, good-bye, dears! Good-bye, Axel! Heaven be thanked that everything is well with you.

HEDDA. Good-bye, Aunt Jane!

TESMAN. And mind you come and see us again soon.

MISS RISING. A thousand thanks, my boy. You may be sure I shall. (*She goes out by the hall door.*)

HEDDA. Do you think she was angry with me about that bonnet?

TESMAN. No, not angry. But I think she was a little annoyed.

HEDDA. Well, but what an idea, to pitch her bonnet about in the drawing-room? When she comes to call. How can she think of such a thing? No one does it.

TESMAN. Well you may be sure Aunt Jane won't do it again.

HEDDA. In any case, I shall manage to make it up with her.

TESMAN. Yes, my dear Hedda, please do that.

HEDDA. I will ask a few good friends to spend the evening with us to-morrow. And then I can ask her at the same time.

TESMAN. Yes, do, Hedda! For remember what she has been to me ever since I was a boy.

HEDDA. And besides, it may be useful to keep her about us. For this servant—we evidently can't depend upon her.

TESMAN. And there's one thing more you could do that would delight her heart.

HEDDA. What is it?

TESMAN. If you could only prevail on yourself—. For my sake, Hedda! If you could say *du* to her in future.

HEDDA. No no, Tesman—you really mustn't ask that of me. I have told you so already. I shall call her "Aunt"—and you must be satisfied with that. I have never said *du* even to my own uncles and aunts.

TESMAN. No no—if you're not used to it—. What are you looking at, Hedda?

HEDDA. Oh, I'm only looking at my old pianoforte. It doesn't go at all well with all the other things.

TESMAN. The first time I draw my salary, I'll see about exchanging it.

HEDDA. No, no—no exchanging. I don't want to part with it. I would rather have it in my own little room, and then get another here in its place. When it's convenient, I mean.

TESMAN. Yes, of course we could do that.

HEDDA (*takes up the bouquet from the piano*). These flowers were not here last night when we arrived.

TESMAN. Aunt Jane must have brought them.

HEDDA (*examining the bouquet*). A visiting-card (*Takes it and reads.*) "Shall return later in the day." —Can you guess whose card it is?

TESMAN. No. Whose?

HEDDA. Mrs. Elfstad's. An old flame of yours.

TESMAN. Is it really? So Mrs. Elfstad is in town!

HEDDA. It's odd that she should call upon us. I have scarcely seen her since we left school.

TESMAN. I haven't seen her either for—heaven knows how long. I wonder how she can endure to live in such an out-of-the-way hole.

HEDDA (*with sudden animation*). But look here— isn't it somewhere in those parts that he—that—Holger Lövborg is living?

TESMAN (*smiling*). *Your* old flame, Hedda? Yes, he is somewhere in that part of the country.

(BERTA *enters by the hall door.*)

BERTA. That lady, ma'am, that brought some flowers a little while ago, is here again. (*Pointing.*) The flowers you have in your hand, ma'am.

HEDDA. Ah, is she? Well, show her in at once.

(BERTA *opens the door for* MRS. ELFSTAD, *and goes out herself.*)

HEDDA (*receives her warmly*). How do you do, my dear Mrs. Elfstad? How delightful to see you again!

MRS. ELFSTAD (*nervous, but self-controlled*). Yes, it's a very long time since we met.

TESMAN (*gives her his hand*). And we too.

[Thanks, thanks, I hardly knew whether I might call.]

HEDDA. And a thousand thanks for these lovely flowers——

———————

TESMAN. His book? Then he has really published a new book?

MRS. ELFSTAD. Yes, a big book called "Sociology." Haven't you heard of it, Mr. Tesman?

TESMAN. No, how should I have heard of it?

HEDDA. You see, we've been roving about all over the place——

TESMAN. My aunt did say something about it just now— When did the book come out?

MRS. ELFSTED. About a fortnight ago. And since it has sold so well, and been so much read—and made such a sensation——

HEDDA. Has it indeed?

TESMAN. It must be something he has had lying by since his better days.

MRS. ELFSTED. Here it is.

(She hands him a slip of paper.)

TESMAN. Good, good. Then I'll go in——

HEDDA. Be sure you write him a cordial letter. And a good long one too.

TESMAN. Yes, I will.

MRS. ELFSTED. But please, please don't say anything about me!

TESMAN. No, no—if you don't want me to.

[H. Look there. Take those with you.

T. What are they?

H. Your slippers.

T. Oh yes, I forgot.]

(He goes out by the door in the corner on the right.)

HEDDA. No, that's clear.

MRS. ELFSTED. And then my husband sometimes made use of him in his office.—You see. Lövborg was to be had for—for a small salary.

HEDDA. Did Holger Lövborg have to sit writing in an office!

MRS. ELFSTED. Chiefly when my husband was away on official business.

HEDDA. And your husband—perhaps he is often away from home?

MRS. ELFSTED. Yes. Being sheriff, you know, he has to travel about a good deal in his district.

HEDDA (*leaning towards her, with both hands on her shoulder*). Thea—my poor, sweet Thea—now you must tell me everything—exactly as it stands.

MRS. ELFSTED. Well then, you must question me. Question me about anything you please! And I will try to answer.

HEDDA. What sort of a man *is* your husband, Thea?

MRS. ELFSTED. What sort of a man?

HEDDA. Well, I mean—you know—in everyday life. Is he kind to you?

MRS. ELFSTED. I am sure he means well in everything. And no doubt everyone else thinks so too. I mean, the few people who visit us.

HEDDA. Then you don't see much society.

MRS. ELFSTED. No.

HEDDA. But can you endure it, year after year?

MRS. ELFSTED. No, I cannot. Nor can I endure *that* any more—after this.

HEDDA. Not *that*, you say? Then is there something else?

MRS. ELFSTED. Everything!

HEDDA. Your husband must be much, much older than you. There is at least twenty years' difference between you, is there not?

MRS. ELFSTED. Yes, that is true, too. Everything about him is repellent to me! We have not a thought in

common! We have never had a single point of sympathy
—he and I.

HEDDA. But is he not fond of you all the same?
At heart? In his own way?

MRS. ELFSTED. Oh no—please don't think that.
He regards me simply as a useful property. And then
it doesn't cost much to keep me. I am not expensive.

HEDDA. That is stupid of you.

MRS. ELFSTED (*shakes her head*). It cannot be otherwise—not with *him*.

HEDDA. No, no—if you can't make him really care
for you——.

MRS. ELFSTED. He can't care for any one but himself—and perhaps a little for the children.

HEDDA. And for Holger Lövborg, Thea.

MRS. ELFSTED (*looking at her*). For Holger Lövborg!
What puts that into your head?

HEDDA. Well, my dear—when he lets you go—.
When he sends you after him all the way to town.

MRS. ELFSTED (*smiling nervously*). Oh, of course.
Yes, yes— (*Vehemently, but not loudly.*) No—I may
just as well make a clean breast of it! I can't sit here
telling lies any longer. For it must all come out in any
case.

HEDDA. Lies! Why, dear Thea——!

MRS. ELFSTED. Well, to make a long story short—.
My husband did not know that I was coming.

HEDDA. What! Your husband didn't know it!

MRS. ELFSTED. No, of course not. For that matter,
he was away from home himself—he was travelling. I
could bear it no longer. I couldn't indeed—so utterly
alone as I should have been in future.

HEDDA. Well? And then?

MRS. ELFSTED. So I put together a few little things—
what I needed most—as quietly as possible. And then
I left the house.

HEDDA. Without a word?

MRS. ELFSTED. Yes—and took the steamer first.
And then the train to town.

HEDDA. Why, my dear, good Thea——!

MRS. ELFSTED. What else could I possibly do?

HEDDA. But what do you think your husband will
say when you go home again?

MRS. ELFSTED (*looks at her*). Back to *him?*

HEDDA. Of course.

MRS. ELFSTED (*rises and moves about the room*). I
shall never go back to him again.

HEDDA (*turns on the sofa and follows her with her eyes*).
Then you have—left house and home—for good and all?
Left everything?

MRS. ELFSTED. A thing of that sort cannot be undone.

HEDDA (*rises from the sofa and goes towards her*). But,
Thea, did you think well over this?

MRS. ELFSTED. I thought over nothing. I only did
what I thought I *had* to do.

HEDDA. And what are your plans now? What do
you think of doing?

MRS. ELFSTED. I don't know yet. I only know this,
that I *must* live where he is—if I am to live at all.

HEDDA. Sit down a moment—then you will be calmer.
(*They seat themselves at the table.*) How did this—this
understanding—between you and Holger Lövborg come
about?

MRS. ELFSTED. Oh, I suppose it grew up gradually.
As I saw that I had gained a sort of influence over him.

HEDDA. So you had that?

MRS. ELFSTED. He gave up his bad habits. Not because I asked him to, for I never dared do that. But of course he saw that they were repulsive to me; and so he dropped everything of that sort.

HEDDA (*with slight mockery*). Then you have reclaimed him—as the saying goes.

MRS. ELFSTED. And he ha*s* made a real human being of me—taught me to think, and to understand so many things.

HEDDA. Did he give *you* lessons too, then?

MRS. ELFSTED. No, not exactly lessons. But he talked to me—talked about such an infinity of things.

HEDDA. Scientific things, I suppose.

MRS. ELFSTED. Yes, that sort of thing. Why do you smile? Remember,—up there I was not situated as you are here. You have your husband to explain so much to you.

HEDDA (*dryly*). Yes, I have. But do you think it amusing to sit and listen to explanations?

MRS. ELFSTED. Yes, indeed I do. Don't you think so too?

HEDDA. No, most certainly I don't. I think it horribly boring. (*Glances towards* TESMAN's *door*.) But that's between ourselves, of course.

MRS. ELFSTED. Everything must be between ourselves. For heaven's sake—all that I've been telling you just now.

HEDDA. Oh, I suppose Tesman may——

MRS. ELFSTED (*struggling with herself*). Hedda—there is—*one* thing more.

HEDDA. And what is that?

MRS. ELFSTED. I don't feel at all sure what will be the end of it—between Holger Lövborg and me. Whether it will be nothing but close friendship—on his side.

HEDDA. What? Are you not sure of him, then?

MRS. ELFSTED. Yes, I think I ought to be now. Now that I have left house and home for his sake. But —but—oh, Hedda, there is *some one* that stands between us.

HEDDA. What do you mean by that?

MRS. ELFSTED. Some one who has hurt him and injured him so profoundly— But whom I don't believe he can ever forget in spite of that.

HEDDA (*rises slowly, rests her hands on the table and fixes her eyes upon her*). Who is it you mean?

MRS. ELFSTED. Yourself, Hedda.

HEDDA. Can this be—! Hush! (*Glances towards* TESMAN'S *door.*) Hush, he's coming! (*Whispers.*) For God's sake, Thea—let all this be between ourselves!

(AXEL TESMAN, *with a letter in his hand, comes from his room.*)

TESMAN. There now; the letter is finished.

HEDDA. That's right. Mrs. Elfsted and I were thinking of going out.

TESMAN. Good. Then perhaps you will post this when you go.

HEDDA (*takes the letter*). I will tell the maid to.

TESMAN. Yes, of course; that is what I meant.

(BERTA *enters from the hall.*)

BERTA. Judge Brack wishes to know if Mrs. Tesman will receive him.

HEDDA. Yes, ask Judge Brack to come in. And look here—put this letter in the post.

BERTA (*taking the letter*). Yes, ma'am.

(*She opens the door for* JUDGE BRACK *and goes out herself.*)

BRACK. May one venture to call so early in the day?

HEDDA. Of course you may.

TESMAN. Welcome at any time. (*Introducing him.*) Mrs. Elfsted—Judge Brack.

BRACK. Ah, delighted——

HEDDA. It's nice to see you by daylight, Judge.

BRACK. And I think it's nice to see you and your husband in your home. Where I have been arranging the empty rooms and putting them into shape.

TESMAN. I can't thank you sufficiently.——

BRACK. Oh, pray don't——

HEDDA. Yes, you are a friend indeed——

BRACK. And is Mrs. Hedda tolerably satisfied?

HEDDA. Yes, indeed I am. Of course—there will have to be a little re-arrangement here and there.

BRACK. Oh, we only arranged things just for the present.

HEDDA. And one or two things are still wanting. We shall have to buy some additional trifles.

BRACK. Indeed!

HEDDA (*laughing*). Don't be alarmed! You shall not be troubled with them. I shall see to them myself.

BRACK. Oh, I didn't mean that. (*To* TESMAN.) By-the-bye, I really called on business——

TESMAN. Indeed? Business——?

HEDDA. That's good of you! You want to turn me out.

BRACK. I!

HEDDA. Yes, aren't you threatening to talk about business?—Come along, Thea! (*To* TESMAN.) I shall not be out long.

TESMAN. Just as you please, dear.

HEDDA (*to* BRACK). *Au revoir*, then—when you have done your business.

BRACK. *Au revoir*, Mrs. Hedda.

(HEDDA *and* MRS ELFSTED *go out by the hall door.*)

TESMAN. There. Now we can have a talk. Won't you sit down?

BRACK (*seats himself beside the table*). Thanks, for a moment.

TESMAN (*seating himself*). Then it's business——?

BRACK. Yes, in a way.

TESMAN. I understand. It's the serious part of the frolic that is coming now.

TESMAN. It was Holger Lövborg we were talking about.

HEDDA (*glancing at him rapidly*). Ah——!

TESMAN. And I really can't see what is to become of him.

BRACK. Perhaps I can give you some information on that point.

TESMAN. Indeed!

BRACK. You must not forget that he comes of a powerful family.

TESMAN. He can't count upon those people.

BRACK. Are you so sure of that?

TESMAN. I know that among themselves he is known as the stain on the family.

BRACK. At one time they called him the hope of the family.

TESMAN. At one time—yes. But he has put an end to all that.

HEDDA. He has recovered himself, though.

BRACK. And then this book that he has published—

TESMAN. Well well, I hope to goodness they may find something for him to do. I have just written to him. Asked him to come to us to-morrow evening.

HEDDA. You come too, Judge Brack. We will have an amusing time.

BRACK. My dear Mr. Tesman—and you too, Mrs. Hedda—I think I ought not to keep you in the dark about something that—that——

TESMAN. That concerns Holger?

BRACK. Both you and him.

TESMAN. Well, my dear Judge, out with it!

BRACK. You must be prepared to find your appointment deferred longer than you desired or expected.

TESMAN. What? Is there some hitch?

BRACK. The nomination may perhaps be made conditional on the result of a competition——.

TESMAN. Competition!

HEDDA. With whom? Ah——!

TESMAN. Surely not——?

BRACK (*rises*). Yes, precisely—Holger Lövborg.

TESMAN (*springs up*). No, no—it's quite inconceivable! Quite impossible!

BRACK. Perhaps that is what it may come to, all the same.

TESMAN. But that would be the most shameful injustice towards me. They had as good as promised me the appointment!

BRACK. Well, and no doubt you will get it in the end; only after a contest.

HEDDA. Fancy—! There will be a sort of sporting interest in that.

TESMAN. Why, Hedda, how can you be so indifferent about it!

HEDDA. I am not at all indifferent. I am most eager to see who wins.

BRACK. In any case, Mrs. Hedda, it is best that you should know the position, before you—before you set about the little purchases that you were threatening just now.

HEDDA. This can make no difference.

BRACK. Indeed. Then I have no more to say. Good-bye for the present.

HEDDA. Good-bye, Judge; and be sure you call to-morrow!

BRACK. Many thanks. Good-bye, good-bye.

TESMAN (*accompanying him to the door*). Good-bye, Judge!

(JUDGE BRACK *goes out through the hall.*)

TESMAN. Well, Hedda—you and I must have a serious talk.

HEDDA. Not now, Tesman. I assure you, I haven't time.

TESMAN. No time!

HEDDA. No. I must go and change my dress before lunch.

(*She goes towards the door on the left.*)

TESMAN. But you take this as if it didn't matter at all.

HEDDA (*turns in the doorway*). Why should I not? You are so fond of saying that the strongest always wins.

(*She goes out.*)

TESMAN (*grasps the back of a chair and gazes uneasily before him*). The strongest, yes——

SECOND ACT

The room at the TESMANS' *as in the First Act, except that the piano has been removed, and an elegant little writing-table and an* étagère *put in its place. Some of the bouquets have been removed from the table and placed in the inner room. It is afternoon.*

HEDDA, *dressed in a tasteful afternoon gown, is alone in the room. She stands by the open door of the veranda, loading a revolver. The other lies in an open case on a chair by her side.*

HEDDA (*looks down the garden and calls*). So you are here again, Judge!

JUDGE BRACK (*is heard calling from below*). As you see, Mrs. Hedda!

HEDDA (*raises the revolver and points*). Now I'll shoot you, Judge Brack.

JUDGE BRACK (*calling unseen*). No, no, no! Don't stand aiming at me!

HEDDA (*fires*). Bang!

BRACK (*outside*). Are you out of your senses——!

HEDDA. Did I hit you?

BRACK (*still outside*). I wish you would let these pranks alone!

HEDDA (*lays the revolver in the case*). Come in then, Judge.

(JUDGE BRACK *enters by the door of the veranda.*)

BRACK. What the deuce are you shooting at?

HEDDA. Thrushes.

BRACK. But the thrushes haven't come yet.

HEDDA. Oh, then I'm firing in the air.

BRACK. What is the good of that?

HEDDA. Then what in heaven's name would you have me do with myself?

BRACK. Have you had no visitors?

HEDDA (*closing the door of the veranda*). Not one. I suppose all our set are still out of town. I have to be content with their flowers and visiting-cards.

BRACK. And is Tesman not at home either?

HEDDA. No, he rushed out of the house as soon as I took up the pistol-case.

BRACK. Really, Mrs. Hedda!

HEDDA. Oh, you mustn't take it so literally. Though, for that matter, he is almost as much afraid of these things as you are.

(*She takes the case and locks it up in a drawer of the writing-table.*)

BRACK (*standing behind her, still with his overcoat on his arm and his hat in his hand*). So he's not at home.

HEDDA. No—he didn't expect you so early. And then it struck him that he had to go into town and get some new books.

BRACK. Of course. It was stupid of me not to have thought of that before.

HEDDA (*turning her head to look at him*). Why stupid?

BRACK. Because if I had thought of it I should have come—a little—earlier.

HEDDA (*puts the key of the writing-table in her pocket and walks across the room*). Then you would have found no one to receive you; for I have been in my room changing my dress ever since lunch.

BRACK. And is there no sort of a little chink that we could talk through?

HEDDA. Not for you in any case, my good Judge.— But let us sit down and wait. Tesman is not likely to be back for some time yet.

———

BRACK. Yes and no. To speak frankly, I never imagined that engagement would lead to anything.

HEDDA (*smiling*). The wish was father to the thought.

BRACK (*laughs*). Yes, yes, yes, Mrs. Hedda, so they say.

———

HEDDA (*jestingly*). Oh, I assure you I have never cherished any illusions with respect to *you*.

BRACK. All I require is a pleasant and intimate interior, where I can be of assistance in every possible way——

HEDDA (*raising her forefinger*). Not with money though!

BRACK. No, *that* would at once destroy the understanding. That is why, you see, I prefer those houses where there is no question of anything of that sort, and where I am free to come and go as a friend——

HEDDA. Of the mistress of the house?

BRACK (*bows gallantly*). Of the mistress first of all, of course. But of the master too, in the second place. Such a triangular friendship—if I may call it so—is really a great convenience for all parties, let me tell you.

TESMAN. I think it shows quite remarkable soundness of judgment. He never wrote like that before.—   But haven't you been down into the garden and had a look round, Hedda? Eh?

HEDDA. No, I have only been out on the veranda a little.

TESMAN. Ah, isn't the view lovely? Over the fiord and the islands? (*Goes nearer to her.*) Well, isn't it nice to find yourself established as mistress of the house it had always been your dream to live in?

HEDDA. Yes, wasn't it a strange piece of luck?

TESMAN (*putting the books together*). Now I shall take all these into my study. I'm longing to——! And then I must change my clothes. (*To* BRACK.) I suppose we needn't start just yet?

BRACK. Oh, dear no—there is not the slightest hurry.

TESMAN. Well then, I can take my time. (*Is going with his books towards the inner room, but stops and turns*

in the doorway.) By-the-bye, Hedda—I looked in on
the aunts.

HEDDA (*by the door of the veranda*). Yes, I've no
doubt you did.

TESMAN. Aunt Jane is not coming to-day.

HEDDA (*turns towards him*). Not coming? Is it
that affair of the bonnet that keeps her away?

TESMAN. Oh, not at all. How could you think such
a thing? But Aunt Rina is very ill now.

HEDDA. She always is.

TESMAN. Yes, but to-day she was much worse.

HEDDA. Oh, then it's only natural that her sister
should remain with her. I must bear my disappoint-
ment.

TESMAN (*a little disappointed*). Of course this does
not affect you so nearly. But I thought I would tell you,
all the same.

(*He goes through the inner room and out to the right.*)

HEDDA (*goes over towards the stove*). Oh, those ever-
lasting aunts!

BRACK. What bonnet were you talking about?

HEDDA. Oh, it was a little episode with Miss Rysing.
She has such extraordinary manners at times. This
morning she had pitched her bonnet down here in the
drawing-room. (*Looks at him and smiles.*) And I pretended to think it was the servant's.

BRACK (*shaking his head in disapproval*). Now my
dear Mrs. Hedda, how could you do such a thing? To
that excellent old lady, too!

HEDDA (*moving nervously about*). Well, you see—
these impulses come over me all of a sudden; and I *cannot* resist them. And then to suffer torments of remorse
—there seems to be a kind of pleasure in it. A real—

refinement of pleasure. Oh, I don't know how to explain it.

> (*She has thrown herself into the easy-chair by the stove.*)

BRACK (*behind the easy-chair*). You are not really happy—that is at the bottom of it.

HEDDA (*looking before her*). I know of no reason why I should be—happy. Perhaps you can give me one?

BRACK. Well—amongst other things, because you have got exactly the home you had set your heart on.

HEDDA (*looks up at him and laughs*). Do you believe in that legend?

BRACK. Is there nothing in it, then?

HEDDA. Oh yes, there is *something* in it. I'll tell you the story.

BRACK. Well?

HEDDA. Some time ago, when there were evening parties at the Consul General's country house, Tesman used often to contrive to see me home——

BRACK. Yes, yes, he was very attentive. I remember that.

HEDDA. And you always had one of the younger ladies to look after.

BRACK. And then I had to go quite a different way—

Hedda. That's true. I know you were going a different way last summer.

BRACK (*laughing*). Oh fie, Mrs. Hedda! Well, then —Tesman——?

HEDDA. Well, it happened one evening. We were just passing here. And Tesman was writhing in the agony of having to find conversation, poor fellow. So I took pity on him——

BRACK (*smiles doubtfully*). *You* took pity?

HEDDA. Yes, I really did. And so—to help him out

of his torment—I happened to say, in pure thoughtlessness, that I should like to live in this villa. And, thank heaven—that loosened his tongue.

BRACK. No more than that?

HEDDA. Not *that* evening.

BRACK. But afterwards?

HEDDA. Yes, my thoughtlessness had consequences, my dear Judge.

BRACK. Unfortunately that too often happens, Mrs. Hedda.

HEDDA. Thanks! But all through the winter, whenever we met, he sat down and talked about this blessèd villa. How nice it must be to live in Secretary Falk's villa.

BRACK. But then you contradicted him, of course? As you always do.

HEDDA. No, I said just the same as he. For Tesman is not one of the men that it is any pleasure to contradict.

BRACK. And you really cared not a rap about it all the time?

HEDDA. No, heaven knows I didn't.

BRACK. But now? Now that it has been made so homelike for you!

HEDDA. Uh, the rooms all seem to smell of lavender and dried rose-leaves.—But perhaps it's Aunt Jane that has brought that scent with her.

(GEORGE TESMAN, *dressed in black, with his gloves and hat in his hand, enters from the right through the inner room.*)

TESMAN. No answer from Lövborg, Hedda? Eh?

HEDDA. No. I don't suppose he'll send any answer. He'll come himself.

TESMAN (*to* BRACK). .Well then, I must wait for him as long as possible.

BRACK. We have plenty of time yet. None of my guests will arrive before seven or half-past.

TESMAN. Well then, that's all right.

(*He places his hat and gloves on a chair on the right.*)

HEDDA (*placing* BRACK's *hat and overcoat on the same chair*). And at the worst Mr. Lövborg can remain here with me.

BRACK (*offering to take his things*). Oh, allow me.— What do you mean by "At the worst"?

HEDDA. That he won't go with you and Tesman.

TESMAN (*looks dubiously at her*). But, Hedda dear— do you think it would quite do? Remember, Auntie can't come.

HEDDA. No, but Mrs. Elfsted is coming. We three can have a cup of tea together.

BRACK. Yes, that would perhaps be the safest plan for him.

HEDDA (*rather sharply*). Why so?

BRACK. You were saying this morning that you knew what my bachelor parties were like.

(BERTA *appears at the hall door.*)

BERTA. There's a gentleman asking if you are at home, ma'am——

HEDDA. Well, show him in.

(BERTA *goes out.*)

TESMAN (*softly*). Hedda—you'll see, this is he.

(EILERT LÖVBORG *enters from the hall. He is slim and lean; of the same age as* TESMAN, *but looks older and somewhat worn out. His hair and beard are of a blackish brown, his face long, delicately*

*shaped and pale, but with spots of colour on the
cheek-bones. He is dressed in a well-cut black
visiting-suit, quite new, the frock-coat rather long.
He has light brown gloves and a silk hat. He
carries under his left arm a small portfolio with
papers in it. He stops near the door and makes
a slight bow, seeming somewhat embarrassed.)*

TESMAN *(goes up to him and gives him his hand)*.
My dear Lövborg! Well, so we see each other again at
last!

EILERT LÖVBORG *(speaks in a subdued voice)*. Thanks
for your letter, Tesman. *(Approaching* HEDDA.*)* May
I shake hands with you too, Mrs. Tesman?

HEDDA *(giving him her hand)*. I am glad to see you.
(Introducing him with a motion of her hand.) I don't
know whether you two gentlemen——?

LÖVBORG *(bowing slightly)*. Judge Brack, I think.

BRACK *(bows)*. Oh yes—we have often met.

TESMAN *(with his hand on* LÖVBORG'S *shoulder)*. Well,
now you must make yourself at home! *(Bringing him
further forward.)* So I hear you are going to settle in
town again.

LÖVBORG. Yes, I am.

TESMAN. Quite right, quite right. Let me tell you,
I have got hold of your new book.

LÖVBORG *(indifferently)*. Oh, *that* one.

TESMAN. But I haven't had time to read it yet.

LÖVBORG. Oh, my dear fellow, you may spare yourself the trouble.

TESMAN. Why so?

LÖVBORG. Why, because there is very little in it.

TESMAN. Very little in it!

BRACK. But, good gracious, it has been very much
praised, I hear.

Lövborg. Just so. That was what I wanted. What served my purpose. So I put nothing into the book but what every one would agree to.

Brack. Very wise of you.

Tesman. Well but, my dear——

Lövborg. I had to win myself a position again—to make an absolutely fresh start.

Tesman (*a little embarrassed*). Yes, yes, I suppose you had to do that.

Lövborg (*smiling, lays down his hat, and taps the portfolio, which he holds out*). But look here—when *this* one appears—! For this—this is the real book. The one with something in it.

Tesman. Indeed? And what is it?

Lövborg. It is the continuation.

Tesman (*looks dubiously at him*). The continuation? Of what?

Lövborg. Of the book.

Tesman. Of the new book——?

Lövborg. Yes, of course.

Tesman. But, my dear fellow—does it not come down to our own days?

Lövborg. Certainly it does; and this one deals with the future.

Tesman. But, my dear Lövborg—we know nothing of the future. And so there is nothing to be said about it.

Lövborg (*smiling*). Oh yes, perhaps there is a thing or two to be said about it all the same.

Brack. But there can't possibly be anything—really scientific.

Lövborg. I don't trouble myself about that either. (*To* Tesman, *showing him the papers*). Look here— you see. I have divided it into two sections. The first section deals with "The civilising forces of the future."

And here is the second—(*running through the pages towards the end*)—here—forecasting the probable line of development.

TESMAN. How odd now. (*Shakes his head.*) I should never have thought of writing anything of that sort.

HEDDA (*at the glass door, drumming on the pane*). H'm! I dare say not.

LÖVBORG (*shutting up the portfolio*). I brought it with me, thinking I might read you a little of it this evening.

TESMAN. That was very good of you, Lövborg. But this evening—? (*Looking at* BRACK.) I don't quite see how we could manage it——

LÖVBORG. Well then, some other time. There is no hurry at all.

BRACK. I must tell you, Mr. Lövborg—there is a little gathering at my house this evening. In honour of Tesman, you understand. A few friends are coming.

LÖVBORG (*looking for his hat*). Oh—then I won't detain you——

TESMAN. No, no, there's time enough.

BRACK. No, but listen. Will you not do me the favour of joining us?

LÖVBORG (*with slight uneasiness*). I? No, no! Thank you very much.

BRACK. Oh, nonsense—do! We shall be quite a select little circle. And I assure you we shall have a "lively time," as Mrs. Hed—as Mrs. Tesman says.

LÖVBORG. Yes, I can believe that. But nevertheless——

BRACK. And then you might bring your manuscript with you, and read it to Tesman there. I could give you a room to yourselves.

TESMAN. Yes, why shouldn't you?

HEDDA (*interposing*). But, Tesman, if Mr. Lövborg

would really rather not! I am sure Mr. Lövborg is much more inclined to remain here and have supper with me.

LÖVBORG (*with a rapid look at her*). With you, Mrs. Tesman!

HEDDA. And with Mrs. Elfsted——

LÖVBORG. Ah——!

HEDDA. —for she has promised to come this evening. So you see you are almost bound to remain, Mr. Lövborg, or she will have no one to see her home.

LÖVBORG. That's true. Many thanks, Mrs. Tesman —in that case I shall be very glad to remain.

HEDDA. Then I have one or two orders to give——
    (*She goes to the hall door and rings.* BERTA *enters.* HEDDA *talks to her in a whisper, and points towards the inner room.* BERTA *nods and goes out again.*)

TESMAN (*at the same time, to* EILERT LÖVBORG). Tell me, Lövborg—is it this new subject—the future—that you are going to lecture about?

LÖVBORG. Yes.

TESMAN. I have heard that you are thinking of delivering a course of lectures this autumn.

LÖVBORG. That is my intention. I hope you won't take it ill, Tesman.

TESMAN. Take it ill! No, not in the least.

LÖVBORG. You see, I can quite understand that it must be disagreeable to you——

TESMAN. Oh, I can't expect you, out of consideration for me, to——

BRACK. And then it is not the first time in your lives that you two friends have met as rivals——

LÖVBORG (*looking rapidly at him*). Rivals?

HEDDA (*doing likewise*). How?

BRACK. In generous, friendly contest, of course.

For prize medals and for scholarships and for—many other things.

TESMAN. Yes, in those days you carried off many a victory, my dear Lövborg.

LÖVBORG. Oh yes—at first. But latterly—. I have fallen a long way behind, Tesman.

HEDDA. But now you can catch him up again, Mr. Lövborg.

LÖVBORG. I hope to be able to.

TESMAN (*in suspense*). To win?

LÖVBORG. Yes. If not, I should not engage in a contest——

BRACK. Oh, when a man has such good backing as you have——

LÖVBORG. Backing? Aha—you refer to those relatives of mine, who run about and give themselves so much trouble——

BRACK. Ah, then you have heard of it at any rate?

LÖVBORG. Yes, I was told about it to-day. But I will have nothing to do with those people. I decline to see them!

TESMAN. But, my dear Lövborg——

HEDDA. Will you reject all help?

LÖVBORG. Yes, Mrs. Tesman, I will.

BRACK. But why in the world—! Why do you do that?

LÖVBORG. Because I wish to owe the victory to myself. To my own powers.

TESMAN. And—and do you think you will win?

LÖVBORG. Yes, I am sure of it.

TESMAN. And that—it will be you who—who will get the appointment?

LÖVBORG (*looks at him in astonishment*). Appointment?—Is it that professorship you are talking about?

TESMAN. Yes, of course.

Lövborg. Is *that* what you think I am competing with you for?

Tesman. But, bless my soul, what else should it be? If it isn't the appointment, why——

Lövborg. I wouldn't accept that appointment at any price. Such a position is not the thing for me. I have found that out while I was in the country.

Brack. Then it is only the honour and glory you will compete for?

Lövborg (*softly, with diffidence*). Honour and glory mean much to a man with—well—with a past like mine.

Tesman (*pressing his hands*). Yes, yes, Lövborg, I can quite understand. Thanks—now I recognise your old self. (*Joyfully, to* Hedda.) Well, what do you say to that! Only the honour and glory! He is not going to stand in our way.

Hedda (*curtly, looking at him*). *Our* way? Pray leave *me* out of the question.

(*She goes up towards the door of the inner room, where* Berta *is placing a tray with decanters and glasses on the table.* Hedda *nods approval, and comes forward again.* Berta *goes out on the right of the inner room.*)

Tesman (*at the same time*). And you, Judge—what do you say?

Brack. Well, I say that honour and glory are fine things. And an old friendship—is an exceedingly lasting bond——

Tesman. Yes, certainly it is; but all the same——

Lövborg. What I can't understand is that you could think so ill of me.

Tesman. Yes, think of my being able to do that!

Hedda (*looking at* Tesman *and smiling*). You [stand there] look[-ing] as if you were thunderstruck.

TESMAN. Yes, so I am——

BRACK. Don't you see, Mrs. Tesman, a thunderstorm has just passed over?

TESMAN. But tell me, Lövborg—what are you thinking of doing?

LÖVBORG. I am going to live as a free man.

BRACK. A pleasant occupation. But it doesn't bring in much.

LÖVBORG. I don't want much either. Not now.

TESMAN. No, and besides—when one is alone. With no one but one's self to look after. I should think you would get on quite well.

HEDDA (*pointing towards the inner room*). Will you not [go in and] take a glass of iced punch, gentlemen?

BRACK (*looking at his watch*). A stirrup-cup? Yes, it wouldn't come amiss.

TESMAN. A capital idea, Hedda! A capital idea! Now that the weight has been lifted——

HEDDA. Won't you go in? You too, Mr. Lövborg.

LÖVBORG (*with a gesture of refusal*). No, thank you. Nothing for me!

TESMAN. Oh yes, do! Come and join us.

LÖVBORG. No, no, many thanks. Nothing at all.

BRACK. Why bless me—iced punch is surely not poison.

LÖVBORG. No, perhaps not for every one.

HEDDA. I will keep Mr. Lövborg company in the meantime.

TESMAN. Yes, yes, Hedda dear—do.

(*He and* BRACK *go into the inner room, seat themselves at the table, drink punch, smoke cigars, and chat during what follows.* EILERT LÖVBORG *remains standing beside the stove.* HEDDA *goes to the writing-table.*)

HEDDA (*turns her head and says in a rather loud voice:*) Now I will show you some photographs, Mr. Lövborg. You know Tesman and I made a tour in the Tyrol on our way home?

    (*She brings an album, and places it on the table beside the sofa, in the further corner of which she seats herself. LÖVBORG approaches, stops, and looks at her. Then he takes a chair and seats himself to her left, with his back towards the inner room.*)

HEDDA (*opening the album*). Do you see this range of mountains? It's the Ortler group. Tesman has written the name underneath. Here it is: "The Ortler group near Meran."

LÖVBORG (*who has never taken his eyes off her, says softly and slowly:*) Hedda—Gabler!

HEDDA (*glances hastily at him, and says softly:*) Ah! —Hush!

LÖVBORG (*repeats softly, in a pained voice:*) Hedda Gabler!

HEDDA (*looking at the album*). That was my name in the old days—when we knew each other.

LÖVBORG. And now—as long as I live—I must teach myself to say Mrs.—Tesman——   .

HEDDA (*still turning over the pages*). Yes. And I think you ought to practise in time. The sooner the better, I should say.

LÖVBORG. Married. Married to another——!

HEDDA. Yes—so the world goes.

LÖVBORG. Oh, Hedda—Hedda—how could you do it!

HEDDA (*looks sharply at him*). What! I can't allow this!

LÖVBORG. What?

    (TESMAN *comes from the inner room and goes towards the sofa.*)

HEDDA (*calmly, in her usual voice*). And this, Mr. Lövborg—is a view from the Val d'Ampezzo. Look at these peaks. (*Looks up at* TESMAN.) What's the name of these curious peaks?

TESMAN (*looking more closely*). Those? Oh, those are the Dolomites.

HEDDA. Yes, that's it.—Those are the Dolomites, Mr. Lövborg.

TESMAN (*to* HEDDA). I only wanted to ask whether I shouldn't bring you a little punch? Or wine, perhaps? For yourself at any rate.

HEDDA. Yes, please. And a few biscuits.

TESMAN. No cigarettes?

HEDDA. No [, many thanks].

TESMAN. Very well.

(*He goes into the inner room and out to the right. BRACK sits in the inner room, and keeps an eye from time to time on* HEDDA *and* LÖVBORG. *Soon after,* TESMAN *again appears and seats himself at the table with* BRACK.)

LÖVBORG (*softly, as before*). Answer me, Hedda—how could you go and do this?

HEDDA (*apparently absorbed in the album*). If you say *du* to me I won't talk to you.

LÖVBORG. May I not say *du* even when we are alone?

HEDDA. No. You may *think* it; but you mustn't *say* it.

LÖVBORG. Why not—exactly?

HEDDA. Because I should look upon it as a sort of unfaithfulness towards Tesman. And I won't hear of that.

LÖVBORG. Is it really possible that such a trifle offends your love for him?

HEDDA (*glances at him and smiles*). Love? What an idea!

LÖVBORG.   I don't understand you, Hedda.

HEDDA.   Do you believe that anything so wonderful exists?

LÖVBORG.   As love?

HEDDA.   Yes.   For *I* don't.   I believe it's only something that people have invented.   And that they go about discussing.

(*In the meantime* BERTA *has entered from the right in the inner room, bringing a smaller tray with punch, wine and biscuits, which she places on the table of the inner room, going out again on the same side.* TESMAN *takes up the tray and brings it into the drawing-room.*)

TESMAN.   Here you are!   Isn't this tempting?

HEDDA.   Why do you bring it yourself?

TESMAN (*filling the glasses*).   Because I think it's fun to wait upon you, Hedda.

HEDDA.   But you have poured out two glasses.   Mr. Lövborg said he wouldn't have any——

TESMAN.   Mrs. Elfsted will soon be here, won't she?

HEDDA.   Yes, by-the-bye—Mrs. Elfsted——!

TESMAN.   Had you forgotten her?

HEDDA.   Oh, we were so absorbed in these photographs.—Tesman—what is the name of this little village?

TESMAN (*goes round to her*).   Which?   Let me see.— Oh, that's Gossensass, by the Brenner Pass.   It was there we stayed *more* than a day——

HEDDA.   Yes, and met that lively party.

TESMAN.   Yes, of course it was *there*.

(*He returns to the inner room and sits beside* BRACK.)

LÖVBORG.   Not in *our* friendship either?

HEDDA.   What?

LÖVBORG. Was there no love in it? Not a single spark—not a tinge of love in the whole of it?

HEDDA. I wonder?

LÖVBORG. None at all on your side then?

HEDDA. To me it seems as though we were two good comrades—two intimate friends. You especially were frankness itself.

LÖVBORG. I fear I was too frank. But it was you that made me so. Oh, Hedda—why should not that, at any rate, have continued, as it was then!

HEDDA. The fault was yours that it could not. Yours—and that of the life you were leading.

LÖVBORG. Yes, I know. I know that well enough.

HEDDA (*looking at him*). I think there was something beautiful—something almost fascinating—in—in that secret intimacy which no living creature so much as dreamed of.

LÖVBORG. Yes, yes, Hedda! Was there not? (*Pauses for a moment and looks before him.*) When I used to come to your father's in the afternoon—and the General sat over at the window reading his papers—with his back towards us——

HEDDA. And you and I on the corner sofa——

LÖVBORG. With the illustrated magazines, Hedda——

HEDDA. Just as we are now with this album.

LÖVBORG. Yes, and when I made my confessions to you—told you about myself, things that at that time no one else knew. Told you of my escapades—my days and nights of devilment.—Oh, Hedda—what was the power in you that drove me to confess these things?

HEDDA (*starts, and looks at him*). Do you think it was any power in me?

LÖVBORG. How else can I explain it? And all those —roundabout questions—you used to put to me——

HEDDA. Which you understood so particularly well——

LÖVBORG. But how could you sit and question me like that? Question me about—all that sort of thing?

HEDDA. And how could you answer, Mr. Lövborg——?

LÖVBORG. Well, a man—. But tell me now, Hedda —was there not love at the bottom of this? On your side? Was it not all because you felt as though you might purge my stains away—if I made you my confessor? Was it not so?

HEDDA. No, not quite.

LÖVBORG. But what was your motive, then?

HEDDA (*with slight hesitation*). Do you think it so strange that a lady—when it can be done—without any one knowing——

LÖVBORG. Well?

HEDDA. —should be glad to have a peep, now and then, into a world which——

LÖVBORG. Which?

HEDDA. —which she is forbidden to know anything about? [To me you were like a messenger from a forbidden country.]

LÖVBORG (*looking at her*). So that was it?

HEDDA. Partly. Partly—I almost think.

LÖVBORG. But why could not things go on between us? As they were then? Why did you break it all off so suddenly?

HEDDA. Do you need to be told that?

LÖVBORG. Certainly. Tell me!

HEDDA. Have you forgotten your abominable behaviour—on a certain occasion? The last time we were alone.

LÖVBORG. Oh, don't remind me of that! But I have an impression that it was not *that* which caused the rupture.

HEDDA. No, not exactly. But from such a person as you were then, I might expect—I was going to say—anything.

LÖVBORG. Oh, you certainly had no need to fear a repetition.

HEDDA. The worst of it was that the whole town got to know what kind of a life you were leading. What kind of company you had got into.

LÖVBORG. I don't think, though, that I took any pains to conceal it. I did it in defiance!

HEDDA. And that is why all the best houses were closed to you.

LÖVBORG. Yes, the others. But that *you*—you, Hedda——!

HEDDA. Of course we had to do as the others.

LÖVBORG. Yes, but—*that* is precisely what I had never imagined.

HEDDA. Well—fortunately you soon consoled yourself in the country.

LÖVBORG. Not so soon as you think.

HEDDA. No?

LÖVBORG. But as I never heard any more from you —never had a word in answer to my letters——

HEDDA. It is imprudent to put things in writing. And besides—I ended by giving you a sufficiently plain answer—in deeds.

LÖVBORG. Yes, you went and married another. When I heard *that*, it was quite natural that I should try to console myself, as you call it.

HEDDA. I'm sure I quite agree.

LÖVBORG. But, by-the-bye, how do you know all this? Mrs. Elfsted must have told you something.

HEDDA. Mrs. Elfsted has told me—most of it— Ought she not to have done so?

LÖVBORG. Yes, to you, Hedda—with all my heart.

HEDDA. But—now that—happily—you are on your feet again—. Do you know what I think so very strange in you?

LÖVBORG. Well?

HEDDA. That you should sit here lamenting over an old story like this. Over something which *now*, I should think, must be—what shall I call it?—a sort of exercise of your memory.

LÖVBORG. Then do you too labour under the prejudice that a man can only feel love for one woman—at a time?

HEDDA (*looking before her for a moment*). Well—perhaps you're right in—(*half turned towards him*). What is one really to believe—if that be so?

LÖVBORG. Oh, I entirely forgot that you don't believe there is such a thing as love.

HEDDA (*turning over the pages of the album*). You mustn't take everything I say so literally, either.

LÖVBORG (*looks at her a moment, and whispers passionately*). Oh, Hedda! Hedda Gabler! Now I begin to see a hidden meaning beneath all you have been saying.

HEDDA (*softly, with a glance*). Take care! Believe nothing of the sort!

(*The hall door is opened from without by* BERTA.)

HEDDA (*closes the album with a bang and calls smilingly*). Ah, at last! My darling Thea—come along!

(MRS. ELFSTED *enters, without her cloak. She is in evening dress. The door is closed behind her.*)

HEDDA (*on the sofa, stretches out her arms towards her*).
Oh, Thea—you can't think how I have been longing for
you all this time!

(MRS. ELFSTED *goes up to the table and gives* HEDDA
her hand. LÖVBORG *has risen from his chair.*
He and MRS. ELFSTED *greet each other with a*
silent nod.)

MRS. ELFSTED (*who remains standing*). Ought I not
to say good evening to your husband too?

HEDDA. Oh, leave those two where they are. They
are going soon.

MRS. ELFSTED. Are they going out?

HEDDA. Yes, to a bachelor party.

MRS. ELFSTED (*involuntarily*). Not *you*, Mr. Lövborg?

LÖVBORG. No.

HEDDA. No, Mr. Lövborg remains with you and me.

MRS. ELFSTED (*takes a chair and is about to seat her-*
self). Ah, how nice it is here!

HEDDA. No, thank you. Not *there!* You'll be good
enough to come over here to me. I will sit between you.

MRS. ELFSTED. Yes, just as you please.

(*She goes round the table and seats herself on the sofa*
on HEDDA'S *right.* LÖVBORG *also seats himself.*)

LÖVBORG (*after a short pause, to* HEDDA). Is not she
lovely to look at?

HEDDA. Only to look at?

MRS. ELFSTED (*anxiously to* HEDDA). Oh, but does
he know——?

HEDDA. Of course he knows——

LÖVBORG. You were quite right to tell Hedda everything.

MRS. ELFSTED. Thank heaven! I was so afraid you
would not like it.

HEDDA. You afraid! When you have such power over him?

MRS. ELFSTED. Oh, I have no power in reality. If we share our thoughts and opinions, it is purely voluntary on both sides.

LÖVBORG (*to* HEDDA). Yes. *We* two—she and I— we are two good comrades. Frank, trusty comrades. A man and a woman who have absolute faith in each other—though our fellowship is one of perfect freedom. And then she is so brave, Hedda!

MRS. ELFSTED. Good heavens—am I brave?

LÖVBORG. Perhaps not in other ways. But exceedingly, where your comrade is concerned.

HEDDA. Ah, courage—courage. If one only had that.

MRS. ELFSTED. There was nothing so very courageous in coming away when——

LÖVBORG. Oh yes, dear friend, it takes a good deal of courage to leave one's husband. To leave house and home. And all to throw in one's lot freely with another.

HEDDA. Yes, I certainly think so too, Thea. (*Lightly stroking her hair.*) I can't imagine—no, I don't understand how you could do it. How you could dare actually to set about it.

MRS. ELFSTED. But there was nothing else to be done. I could not possibly stay up there alone—with —with——

HEDDA. —with the other?

MRS. ELFSTED (*hides her face in her hands and leans her head on* HEDDA'S *shoulder*). Oh, Hedda—Hedda!

HEDDA. And then the worst part of it all! It will be impossible to keep this a secret for long.

LÖVBORG. That she has left her home, yes. That will soon be common property. But no one except you will know that she did it to be with me.

MRS. ELFSTED (*to* HEDDA). No, that must not come out for the world! You won't say anything to Tesman, will you?

HEDDA. Not to any living soul, Thea dear.

LÖVBORG. For I have to make a fresh start. And a man with a past like *mine*—. H'm! One knows pretty well how people would interpret such a connection. She too would be dragged in the mire.

HEDDA (*looking before her*). Yes, if only we could be free of—of what people think——

(*There is a general leave-taking.* JUDGE BRACK, LÖVBORG *and* TESMAN *go out by the hall door. At the same time,* BERTA *brings in two lamps through the inner room, places them on the tables in the drawing-room, and goes out again through the inner room.*)

MRS. ELFSTED. Hedda—Hedda—what will come of all this?

HEDDA. We shall see about ten o'clock.

MRS. ELFSTED (*rises and crosses the room*). I only hope we may. But you don't know him so well as I do.

HEDDA. Can he be so pitiful as that! With such a thirst, such a devouring thirst for all that he calls the joys of life, and then—not daring to take even a sip of them!

MRS. ELFSTED. Ah yes, Hedda, unhappily it is true.

HEDDA (*rising*). It is not true! You may doubt him as long as you please. I believe in him! Now we will try——

MRS. ELFSTED. You have some hidden motive in this, Hedda!

HEDDA. Yes, I have. I want for once in my life to have power over a human mind.

MRS. ELFSTED. Have you not the power?

HEDDA. I have not and have never had it.

MRS. ELFSTED. Not your husband's?

HEDDA. His! Do you think that is worth the trouble? Oh, if you could only understand how poor I am.

(*Clasps her passionately in her arms.*)

MRS. ELFSTED. Let me go! Let me go! I am afraid of you, Hedda!

BERTA (*from the inner room*). Tea is laid in the dining-room, ma'am. (*Goes out again.*)

HEDDA. Very well! Come along to tea, you little— you lucky little stupid!

(*She drags* MRS. ELFSTED *almost by force towards the door at the back.*)

FROM THE THIRD ACT

HEDDA (*goes towards her*). There there there! There's nothing to be so alarmed about. I know quite well what has happened.

MRS. ELFSTED. Well, what do you think? Won't you tell me?

HEDDA. Why—of course it has been a pretty late affair at Judge Brack's. These bachelors generally make things rather lively.

MRS. ELFSTED. Yes, yes, yes—that is clear enough!

HEDDA. And Tesman hasn't cared to come home and ring us up in the middle of the night. He didn't want to disturb me. (*Laughing.*) Perhaps he wasn't inclined to show himself either—immediately after a jovial party.

Mrs. Elfsted. But in that case—where can he have gone?

Hedda. Of course he has gone to those blessed Aunts' and slept there. They have his old room ready for him.

Mrs. Elfsted. No, he can't be with *them;* for a letter has just come for him from Miss Rysing. There it lies.

Hedda. Indeed? (*Looks at the address.*) Why yes, it's addressed in Aunt Jane's own hand. Well then— he is staying behind at Judge Brack's—he too.

Mrs. Elfsted. He too? Do you mean that Lövborg——?

Hedda. Yes, Lövborg is certainly there still. Otherwise he would have come to fetch you.

Mrs. Elfsted. Oh Hedda, you are just saying things you don't believe a bit.

Hedda. Well, bless me—even if it's as bad as you think? What of it? Once doesn't count.

Mrs. Elfsted. Oh, that's just what does not apply here. Here least of all!

Tesman (*sits down heavily to the left of the table*). Enjoyed myself? Oh, Hedda—I'm afraid it will take me a long time to get over to-night.

Hedda. You! But you are always moderate——

Tesman. Yes, of course. I didn't mean *that*——

Hedda (*in suspense*). What became of Eilert Lövborg? Why didn't he come back?

Tesman. Well, you see, Hedda, that is just it. And I can't get rid of the distressing thought that it was all my fault.

Hedda. But what was your fault?

TESMAN. I must tell you the whole story.

HEDDA. Yes, yes, do.

(*She seats herself on the other side of the table.*)

TESMAN. It began well enough. Nobody chaffed him. And nobody tempted him either. He and I were able to sit by ourselves in one of the side rooms. And then he read to me. Long extracts from the new book that is coming out.

HEDDA. Well?

TESMAN. You can't imagine what a book that is going to be, Hedda! So grand both in design and execution——

HEDDA. Yes, yes, I don't care about that. And it has nothing to do with the story either.

TESMAN. Yes, it has. It is the very kernel of it, you see.

HEDDA. How?

TESMAN. As I sat listening to him—. It seemed as if a rustling flight of ideas were darting over my head. I felt myself filled with a wealth of intuition, which I only half understood.

HEDDA. Could you not understand it?

TESMAN. Not altogether, I say. And then came that gnawing thought, that has haunted me and that I have thrust away from me—ever since our school-days.

HEDDA. 'What thought?

TESMAN. That Eilert Lövborg is really my superior.

HEDDA. But what if he is? He has no intention of competing with you for the appointment.

TESMAN. Every one who reads his new book will say that he was the right man. And therefore I could not resist it. Oh, Hedda, what evil may lie hid in a man'

HEDDA. Tell me more about this!

TESMAN. Then some more lively companions joined us. They had been to a big dinner-party. Came straight from table.

HEDDA. And then it began?

TESMAN. Yes, then came the orgie. I saw it was coming. And I saw too that it seemed to carry Eilert Lövborg away.

HEDDA. Could he not resist?

TESMAN. Neither could nor would. I saw what it would lead to. And—just think—I did nothing to save him.

HEDDA. Oh, I suppose there was nothing to be done.

TESMAN. Yes, I might have tried to get him home with me. Might have reminded him of his promise to Mrs. Elfsted.

HEDDA. Oh yes. Do you think *that* would have been any use?

TESMAN. Yes, I think so. For *she* has a power over him that nobody else has.

HEDDA. How do you know that?

TESMAN. I could understand that from all he said.

HEDDA. What did he say!

TESMAN. That the whole of his new work came to him as an inspiration from her.

HEDDA. And in spite of that—he wallowed in these orgies——

TESMAN. Deeper than you have any idea of.

HEDDA. What became of him?

TESMAN. He went off with a lot of the others. But where they went I don't know. Both Brack and I went to his rooms and rang. But he hadn't come home.

HEDDA. That was to be expected. And you don't know any more?

TESMAN. No. Brack and I separated, so as to inquire in different directions. But they knew nothing about him, where I went. He must have gone by himself——

HEDDA. And Brack——?

TESMAN. I haven't seen him since. Oh, that unhappy fellow—! Now he is down again. And then after all—Hedda—to think that——

HEDDA. What? What do you mean?

TESMAN. That I let him go. That I could sit there secretly wishing that he would go and ruin himself for ever.—Am I better than he? In my inmost heart! If this is the end of him, that question will never leave me any peace.

HEDDA. I don't think there's any use in brooding over things of that sort.

TESMAN. But his conduct last night cannot possibly have been more than a passing aberration. There was such profound sincerity in the way he spoke of her.

HEDDA. Was there?

TESMAN. I don't understand him. Can't conceive how it is with him.

HEDDA. Let him fall, Tesman. He is irretrievable after all.

TESMAN. Oh, don't let us think that.—I was able to do him *one* service.

HEDDA. Last night?

TESMAN. Yes. (*Taking* LÖVBORG'S *portfolio out of his coat pocket.*) I rescued this for him.

HEDDA. His new book!

TESMAN. Yes; as we were leaving. He and some of the others were a little way in front. I heard him shouting and making a noise. And as I was hurrying after them to try to quiet him, I found the portfolio lying by the wayside. He had lost it.

HEDDA. Let me see it.

TESMAN (*handing her the portfolio*). Here it is. Just think if that had been lost. And it might have been so easily.

HEDDA (*turning over the papers*). This is not Löv-borg's handwriting.

TESMAN. Mrs. Elfsted wrote parts of it for him. From loose notes, he said.

HEDDA. So that is how they sat working together. (*Shuts her eyes.*) I seem to be able to see them.

TESMAN. You too might work with me in the same way, Hedda. Might help me—if you cared to.

HEDDA. You!—(*Looking at him and tapping the portfolio with her finger.*) Well, Tesman—what are you going to do with this?

TESMAN. Do with it, dear? Give it him back, of course.

HEDDA. Yes, yes, I suppose that is what you will do.

TESMAN. But he shall have a good fright first. Put it away in the writing-table drawer. And say nothing.

HEDDA. You said nothing to him about having found it?

TESMAN. No, of course not. In the unmanageable state he was in.

HEDDA. Did any of the others see you find it?

TESMAN. No, none of them.

HEDDA. And you didn't tell any of them afterwards either?

TESMAN. No, I wouldn't do that for his sake.

HEDDA. So no one knows what has become of it?

TESMAN. No. And he shall wait a little while before he is told.

HEDDA (*goes to the writing-table and places the portfolio underneath some books*). There. He shall never get this back.

TESMAN (*springing up*). But, Hedda—what are you thinking of! What do you mean!

HEDDA. This must be got rid of. [Were you not thinking of getting rid of this?]

TESMAN. What has come over you?

HEDDA. Do you think he would be able to write it over again?

TESMAN. Impossible. The inspiration would be lacking the second time.

HEDDA. Take it and burn it. Then it will be done with.

TESMAN. But you must be mad.

HEDDA. You must do it. I must see whether I have any power over you.

TESMAN. Oh, you know quite well you have.

HEDDA. Not altogether. I know I have over him.

TESMAN. Over him!

HEDDA. It was I who made him go to Judge Brack's drinking-party.

TESMAN. Oh, Hedda, but how could you do that!

HEDDA. It came over me with such force. So irresistibly. I had to see whether I could tempt him to his fall.

TESMAN. And it turned out that you could.

HEDDA. Yes. But this must be the end of it. He must go away from here.

TESMAN. Away! For your sake!

HEDDA. Yes. If not, I can't answer for anything.

TESMAN. Hedda!

HEDDA. Not on any pretext must he be allowed to come here!

TESMAN. Oh, I see what it is. You have never really been able to forget him altogether!

HEDDA. I don't know myself. Only get him out of the way. I will not have my thoughts fixed on anything but—what is coming.

TESMAN. What is coming!

HEDDA. Yes.

TESMAN. Oh, Hedda—if I understand you aright.

HEDDA. Yes, you do.

TESMAN. Oh, Hedda, Hedda! And Aunt Jane! Think how happy Aunt Jane will be.

HEDDA. Ugh, don't be so ridiculous!

TESMAN. Ridiculous?

HEDDA. Yes, isn't it ridiculous and absurd that the first thing you do is to cry out for—Aunt Jane?—By-the-bye, there is a letter from her here.

TESMAN. For me?

HEDDA. Yes. (*Handing it to him.*) It came early this morning.

TESMAN (*opening it*). What can it be?

HEDDA. Perhaps she has heard something about him.

TESMAN (*runs his eye through it*). Oh, Hedda—she says that Aunt Rina is dying.

HEDDA. Well, we were prepared for that.

TESMAN. She says that if I want to see her again, I must make haste. I'll run in to them at once.

HEDDA (*suppressing a smile*). Run!

TESMAN (*takes his hat and throws his overcoat over his arm*). I do hope I mayn't come too late.

HEDDA. Oh, if you run——

(BERTA *appears at the hall door.*)

BERTA. Judge Brack is here, and wishes to know if he may come in.

TESMAN. Judge Brack! No, I can't possibly see him.

HEDDA. But I can. (*To* BERTA.) Ask Judge Brack to come in.

(BERTA *opens the door to* JUDGE BRACK, *and goes out herself.*)

BRACK. Oh, are you starting again to hunt for him—the bird of ill omen?

TESMAN. No, I must rush off to my aunts'. The invalid one is lying at death's door.

BRACK. Dear me, is she indeed?

TESMAN. And did you find any trace of him?

BRACK. No. And you?

TESMAN. I didn't either.

BRACK. I didn't think you would. But don't let me detain you. At such a critical moment——

TESMAN. Yes, I must really hurry—Good-bye! Good-bye! (*He goes out by the hall door.*)

HEDDA. Well, you seem to have had quite a lively night.

BRACK. I have not had my clothes off a moment, Mrs. Hedda.

HEDDA. And yet you have heard nothing.

BRACK. Oh yes, I have. Practically everything.

HEDDA. But you said——

BRACK. Tesman was on tenterhooks to get away, you see.

HEDDA. Yes, aren't you sorry for poor Tesman? Just think, Aunt Rina—! Well, where did you get hold of Lövborg?

BRACK. I didn't get hold of him at all. But I heard that he was being well taken care of.

HEDDA. Where?

BRACK. At the police station.

HEDDA. Ah—but what has he done?

BRACK. H'm—I think we had better not go into details.

HEDDA. Oh yes. Details above all. They are what I want to hear about.

BRACK. Well, you must really excuse me all the same, Mrs. Hedda. I was not present, you know.

HEDDA. You! No, I know that.

BRACK. I have only heard that he fell in with a lot of other revellers.

HEDDA. Not any of yours?

BRACK. Of mine?

HEDDA. Yes, of your guests then.

BRACK. Oh, can you think that! No, they always behave themselves out-of-doors. They go home to bed like good boys.

HEDDA. Yes, yes. We well-behaved people——

BRACK. No, unfortunately it was some of his old acquaintances he came across.

HEDDA. Well, and then?

BRACK. Then the usual thing happened. They paid a visit to some—singing girls, I think.

HEDDA. Or something of the sort, yes. And afterwards?

BRACK. An orgie, presumably. Followed by the customary free fight with resultant ejection. Then a street row outside. Windows smashed. Police called. And so to the lock-up.

HEDDA. It must be curious to be present at such a scene.

BRACK. Would you like to be, Mrs. Hedda?

HEDDA. Oh yes, once in a way. If nobody saw one. And nobody heard anything of it afterwards.

BRACK. No, I should think not.

HEDDA. For there must be something untameable among all this coarseness and vulgarity—. But this is a thing that I keep for your ears alone, my dear Judge.

BRACK. I should certainly advise you to do so. But what annoys me beyond measure is that this person could be so inconsiderate as to go straight from my party and——

HEDDA. Do you think it will get about that he came from your house?

BRACK. Yes, of course it will come out at the police-court.

HEDDA. Will the matter come into court!

BRACK. Yes—when the police get hold of an affair—. But I had a suspicion that something of this sort was coming. And therefore, Mrs. Hedda, I will give you a friendly piece of advice. After this. you must not allow this person into your house.

HEDDA. What do you say!

BRACK. Yes, and there is another person that you ought not to receive either.

HEDDA. I can see that you mean Mrs. Elfsted.

BRACK. Of course. Those two have been plotting together.

HEDDA. Do you know anything definite!

BRACK. No, but it is not difficult to guess a thing of that sort. She, a woman who as a rule never sets foot in town, arrives here simultaneously with him. It was all arranged between them, Mrs. Hedda.

HEDDA. What do you mean?

BRACK. Their meeting here in your house.

HEDDA. I don't believe it. You are mistaken.

BRACK. Well, wait and see which of us is right. I don't believe she will go home just at present.

HEDDA. No, that she will not do.

BRACK. There, you see. Yes, of course I am right. You are to serve as a blind.

HEDDA. A blind!

BRACK. Now, of course, he will try to win you over. Just watch whether he doesn't strike the melancholy note. Whether he doesn't begin talking of bygone days. Of disappointed hopes——

HEDDA. —of what might have been so beautiful—but was not to be. Ah yes, one has heard all that.

BRACK. Perhaps that was the line that was taken yesterday, when you were sitting here with the album?

HEDDA. But now you are getting altogether too suspicious, my dear Judge.

BRACK. Well, I confess I am on my guard against that gentleman. It would be terrible to me to think that an intruder was coming into——

HEDDA. —into the triangle.

BRACK. Yes, precisely. Don't laugh at it. It would simply mean that I should find myself homeless.

HEDDA. Oh, come, I am sure you have plenty of other comfortable homes about town.

BRACK. No, unfortunately. Not now. In the last six months I have lost no fewer than three. And those among the best.

HEDDA. Oh—did intruding cocks come into those baskets too?

BRACK. No, but other intruders arrived——

HEDDA. Of what kind?

BRACK. Children.

HEDDA. Indeed? But what have those children to do with you?

BRACK (*laughing*). They have nothing at all to do with me. That is why I call them intruders.

HEDDA. Then I don't at all see——

BRACK. But, bless me, you must know that I can't endure children——

HEDDA. And why not?

BRACK. Because the little angels occupy the whole attention of the mistress of the house. Old friends are nothing to her when an event of that kind takes place.

HEDDA. Egoist!

BRACK. Happily no such danger is threatened here. (*Laughing.*) Although—I won't deny that—it would be worth anything——

HEDDA. Worth anything? What?

BRACK. To see—a certain specialist in his new dignity.

HEDDA. Do you think *that* would make him so supremely ridiculous?

BRACK. Well, you mustn't be offended, Mrs. Hedda—but I can't deny——

HEDDA. I won't listen to you any more, Judge——

BRACK. Ah—indeed! Well, put that gentleman out of your thoughts; for I assure you he doesn't care a scrap for you.

HEDDA. Only for her, you mean.

BRACK. For his fellow-worker, yes. (*Looking at his watch.*) But now I must be getting back. Good-bye, Mrs. Hedda. (*He goes towards the glass door.*)

HEDDA. Are you going through the garden?

BRACK. Yes, it's a short cut for me.

HEDDA. And then it is a back way, too.

BRACK. Quite so. I have no objection to back ways. At times. They may be piquant enough.

HEDDA. When there is ball practice going on, you mean.

BRACK (*in the doorway*). Oh, people don't shoot their own poultry, you know. And the stork—is inviolate——

HEDDA. —and is not to be found in these parts.

BRACK. No, no, that's true.

(*He bows, and goes out by the glass door.*)

HEDDA. You and she!

LÖVBORG. You can be of no more service to me. Thea!

MRS. ELFSTED. Oh, how can you speak so! No more service to you! Am I not to help you? Now, most of all! Are we not to work together?

LÖVBORG. It is all over. I shall never do any more work. Least of all with you.

MRS. ELFSTED. But what can have come between us!

LÖVBORG. Let that be as it may. But the comradeship between us is now at an end.

MRS. ELFSTED. Oh, but this is so utterly inconceivable. What am I to do with my life?

LÖVBORG. You must try to live your life as if you had never known me.

MRS. ELFSTED. But you know I cannot do that! How can you think it possible!

LÖVBORG. Try if you cannot, Thea. You must go home again——

MRS. ELFSTED (*with a shriek*). Ah—you can say that! Go home again! Leave you!

LÖVBORG. It will be best for you. And besides— there is nothing else to be done.

MRS. ELFSTED. Never in this world will I go back there. Where you are, there will I be also. And what would happen to you then?

LÖVBORG. I think you can see what will happen to me.

MRS. ELFSTED. Oh, but I must be able to give you some support. I could before. Up there.

LÖVBORG. For a time, yes. But it wanted nothing but a stormy night to blow all that we had built up into fragments.

MRS. ELFSTED. Well, that cannot be helped.—But I will not let myself be driven away like this. You have no right to do it.

LÖVBORG. No, I know that.

MRS. ELFSTED. Well, and therefore I will not put up with it! I will not submit to it on any account! Do you hear, Lövborg! I tell you that. I will remain here. I will be with you when the book appears.

HEDDA. Ah, the book——!

LÖVBORG. My book and Thea's, Mrs. Tesman; for that is what it is.

MRS. ELFSTED. Yes, that is what it is. You have said that so often. And in my inmost self I feel that it is true. I have my share in its existence.

LÖVBORG. You have.

MRS. ELFSTED. Yes, and that is why I have a right to be present when it appears. I must see with my own eyes how respect and honour are showered upon you. Now more than ever, Lövborg. And the happiness— the happiness—oh, I must share it with you!

LÖVBORG. Thea—our book will never appear.

HEDDA. Ah——!

MRS. ELFSTED. Never appear!

LÖVBORG. *Can* never appear.

MRS. ELFSTED. Lövborg—what have you done with the manuscript?

HEDDA (*breathlessly*). The manuscript——!

MRS. ELFSTED. Where is it?

LÖVBORG. Oh Thea—don't ask me about it!

MRS. ELFSTED. Yes, yes, I *will* know. I demand to be told at once.

LÖVBORG. The manuscript—. Well then—I have torn the manuscript into a thousand pieces.

MRS. ELFSTED. Oh no, no——!

HEDDA (*involuntarily*). But that's not true!

LÖVBORG (*looks at her*). Not true——!

HEDDA (*collecting herself*). Oh well, of course. But it sounded so incredible——

LÖVBORG. It is true, all the same, Mrs. Tesman.

MRS. ELFSTED. Just think, Hedda—torn his own work to pieces.

LÖVBORG. Tore it into a thousand pieces—and scattered them on the fiord—far out. There there is cool sea-water at any rate—let them drift upon it—drift with the current and the wind. And then presently they will sink—deeper and deeper—as I shall, Thea.

MRS. ELFSTED. Oh, Lövborg, Lövborg—this is terrible to think of.

LÖVBORG. Yes. Therefore you must go away in time.

MRS. ELFSTED (*without listening to him*). Do you know, Lövborg, that to my dying day I shall think of what you have done now as though you had killed a little child.

LÖVBORG. Yes, you are right, Thea. It is a sort of child-murder.

MRS. ELFSTED. How could you then—! Did it not belong to me too?

HEDDA. Ah——.

Lövborg. That is why I would rather part from you now. After this, you understand.

Mrs. Elfsted. Yes, oh yes, I can understand. But it seems impossible that we *can* part nevertheless! Well well, now I will go, Hedda.

Hedda. But you are not going away from town?

Mrs. Elfsted. Oh, I don't know. I see nothing but darkness before me.

(*She goes out by the hall door.*)

Hedda. So you are not going to see her home, Mr. Lövborg?

Lövborg. I? Through the streets? In broad daylight?

Hedda. No, no—. Though, after all—! Is it then so utterly irretrievable—this that happened last night?

Lövborg. It will not end with last night—I know that perfectly well—it is all over with me now.

Hedda. But *can* you never learn to control yourself?

Lövborg. No—that is just what I cannot do. And that is the desperate part of it. It is not with me as with so many others. They have it in their power to pull themselves up, when they find it running away with them. I shall never be able to learn that. I have brought myself down to be a bondman. Lost the power over my own will.

Hedda. Yes, yes. But how could you treat poor Thea so heartlessly?

Lövborg. Oh, don't say that it was heartless!

Hedda. To go and destroy what has filled her whole soul day and night—for months and years. You do not call that heartless!

Lövborg. To you I can tell it, Hedda——

Hedda. What can you tell?

LÖVBORG. First promise me—give me your word— that what I now confide to you neither she nor any one else shall ever know.

———————

LÖVBORG. Beautifully?

HEDDA. For once in a way. Good-bye, you must go now. And do not come here any more.

LÖVBORG. Good-bye, Mrs. Tesman. And give George Tesman my love.

HEDDA. No, wait. I must give you a memento to take with you.

(*She goes to the writing-table, opens the drawer and returns to* LÖVBORG *with one of the pistols.*)

LÖVBORG. This? Is this the memento?

HEDDA. Do you remember—you asked me for it once before.

LÖVBORG. You would not give it me then.

HEDDA. Take it. Now it is yours.

LÖVBORG (*puts the pistol in his breast pocket*). Thanks.

HEDDA. And beautifully—promise me that.

LÖVBORG. Good-bye—Hedda Gabler.

(*He goes out by the hall door.*)

(HEDDA *listens for a moment. Then she goes up to the writing-table, takes out* LÖVBORG'S *manuscript, goes with it and seats herself in the armchair beside the stove, opens the packet and sorts the blue and white quires separately, lays the white quires in the wrapper again and keeps the blue ones in her lap.*)

HEDDA (*opens the stove door; presently she throws one of the blue quires into the fire and whispers to herself*). Now I am burning your child, Thea! (*Throwing one or two more quires into the stove.*) Your child and Eilert Lövborg's. (*Throws the rest in.*) I am burning—I am burning your child.

FOURTH ACT

The same room at the TESMANS'. *It is evening. In the drawing-room a lighted lamp stands on the table in the corner to the right. The hanging lamp in the inner room is also lighted.*

(HEDDA *walks to and fro in the inner room and disappears for a moment to the left. She is heard to strike a few chords on the piano. Presently she comes in sight again, and enters the drawing-room.*)

(BERTA *enters from the right, through the inner room, with a lighted lamp, which she places on the writing-table. Her eyes are red with weeping, and she has black ribbons in her cap. She goes quietly and circumspectly out to the right.*)

(*A little while afterwards,* MISS TESMAN, *in mourning, with a bonnet and veil on, comes in from the hall.*)

MISS TESMAN. Yes, Hedda—now my poor sister has at last found peace.

HEDDA (*pressing her hand*). I have heard the news already. Tesman sent me a card.

MISS TESMAN. He said he would do so. But I thought nevertheless I ought myself to bring the tidings.

HEDDA. That was very kind of you. She died quite peacefully, did she not?

MISS TESMAN. Oh, she went so calmly, so beautifully. And then she had the great happiness of seeing George once more—and bidding him good-bye. Has he not come home yet?

HEDDA. No; he wrote that he might be detained. But won't you sit down?

MISS TESMAN. No, thank you. I have so much to do. I must prepare my dear one for her rest as well as I can.

(GEORGE TESMAN *enters by the hall door.*)

HEDDA. How long you have been.

TESMAN. You here, Aunt Julia!

MISS TESMAN. I was just going. Well, have you seen to what you promised?

TESMAN. No, I clean forgot it. My brain is in a whirl. I can't keep my thoughts together.

MISS TESMAN. Why, you mustn't take it so much to heart.

TESMAN. Not take it to heart!

MISS TESMAN. You ought to have expected it. And was it not best for her to be at rest?

TESMAN. Oh yes! Of course——

MISS TESMAN. And now you have other things to think of.

TESMAN. Yes, yes, so I have——

MISS TESMAN. That is the way of the world, Hedda. My home is the house of death, and this—this is the house of life.

HEDDA. Life! Here!

MISS TESMAN. At home we shall be sewing a shroud; and here there will soon be sewing too, I suppose—but of another sort, thank God!

HEDDA. Oh, has he gone and told her!

MISS TESMAN. Yes, therefore we must rejoice. For one thing as well as the other.

HEDDA. You will feel lonely now.

MISS TESMAN. That will not last long. I shall find an occupant for poor Rina's little room.

TESMAN. Who do you think will take it?

MISS TESMAN. Oh, there's always some invalid body in want of nursing—unfortunately.

HEDDA. Would you really take such a burden upon you again?

MISS TESMAN. A burden! Heaven forgive you, child—it has been no burden to me.

HEDDA. Well, but if you had a stranger on your hands.

MISS TESMAN. Oh, one soon makes friends with the sick; and it's such an absolute necessity for me to have some one to live for. Well, heaven be praised, there will soon be something in this house, too, to keep me busy.

HEDDA. Oh, don't trouble about that.

TESMAN. Oh yes, how nice everything might be——

HEDDA. If——?

TESMAN. Oh, nothing. It will all come right.

MISS TESMAN. Yes, yes, I daresay you two have a great deal to say to each other. Good-bye. I must go home to Rina.

(*There are leave-takings.* MISS TESMAN *goes.*)

HEDDA. I can't make it out. It seems as though this affected you more than it does her.

TESMAN. Oh, it is not that. It's Eilert Lövborg I am so uneasy about.

HEDDA. Is there anything new about him?

TESMAN. I met Mrs. Elfsted this afternoon.

HEDDA. Yes!

TESMAN. And she told me that he had been here early this morning.

HEDDA. Yes, directly after you had gone.

TESMAN. He wanted to see me, I suppose.

HEDDA. No, it was Mrs. Elfsted he asked for.

TESMAN. Did he not inquire about the manuscript too?

HEDDA. No, it never occurred to him that you had found it.

TESMAN. I can't make it out. I hear he said that he had torn it to pieces.

HEDDA. Yes, so he told us.

TESMAN. But did you not tell him that I had found it? That you were keeping it?

HEDDA. No.

TESMAN. But, good heavens—! Just think of the desperate state he must have been in.

HEDDA. Desperate! What makes you think that?

TESMAN. Of course it was shame and humiliation that made him say that. That he had wilfully destroyed it.

HEDDA. Yes, perhaps so.

TESMAN. He naturally did not want to confess that he had been in such a state. That he did not know what he had done with his own belongings.

HEDDA. And you did not tell her that you had the packet?

TESMAN. No, I was ashamed on his account.

HEDDA. Be sure you don't say anything.

TESMAN. Well, but it must come out all the same. He must have it back, the sooner the better. Where is it?

HEDDA. I have not got it.

TESMAN. Have not got it? What in the world do you mean? What have you done with it?

HEDDA. I have burnt it.

TESMAN. Burnt! Burnt his manuscript.

HEDDA. Don't scream so. The servant might hear you.

TESMAN. Burnt! Why, good God—! No, no, no, it's impossible.

HEDDA. It is so, nevertheless.

TESMAN. Do you know what you have done? It's unlawful appropriation of lost property. Just ask Judge Brack, and he'll tell you what it is!

HEDDA. Don't speak of it to any one. Neither to Judge Brack nor to any one else.

TESMAN. But your reason, Hedda! I must know your reason! For I feel that you are concealing something from me. Answer me.

HEDDA. Yes. I did it for your sake.

TESMAN. For mine!

HEDDA. When you came home and spoke so highly of what he had read to you.

TESMAN. Yes yes—what then?

HEDDA. I could not bear the idea that he should throw you into the shade.

TESMAN. Hedda! Is this true?

HEDDA. You must remember that—at this time—. I am not like my usual self——

TESMAN. Oh, great heavens—! It was for love of me!

HEDDA. Don't shout so. The servant might hear.

TESMAN. Well, let her. I'll tell Berta myself.

HEDDA. Oh, it will be the end of me, all this.

TESMAN. What will?

HEDDA. All this—absurdity.

TESMAN. Absurdity. Well well, then. Perhaps it won't do to say anything to Berta.

HEDDA. Oh—why not?

TESMAN. No, no, I see that. But I must certainly tell Aunt Julia. Oh, she will be so happy, so happy——

HEDDA. When she hears that I have burnt Eilert Lövborg's manuscript?

TESMAN. No, by-the-bye—that affair of the burning —nobody must know about that. But that your love for me has awakened in this way——

HEDDA. Say nothing about that.

TESMAN. Oh yes—Aunt Julia must share in *that*. Oh, I am so happy—so proud——

HEDDA. Well, be so. But keep it to yourself.

TESMAN. I cannot, Hedda. That would take away half the pleasure of it. I wonder, now, whether this sort of awakening is usual in young wives?

HEDDA. You had better ask Aunt Julia that question too.

TESMAN. I will, some time or other. For she knows all about such things.

(MRS. ELFSTED, *with her cloak on, enters by the hall door. She appears to be much agitated.*)

MRS. ELFSTED. Oh, dear Hedda, forgive my coming again——

HEDDA. What is the matter with you, Thea?

TESMAN. Something about Eilert Lövborg again?

MRS. ELFSTED. Oh, I am so dreadfully afraid some misfortune has happened to him——

HEDDA. Ah—do you think so?

TESMAN. But, good Lord—what makes you think so, Mrs. Elfsted?

MRS. ELFSTED. I heard them talking of him at my boarding-house, just as I came in——

TESMAN. Well? What did they say?

MRS. ELFSTED. Oh, I couldn't make out anything clearly. Either they knew nothing definite, or else—. They stopped talking when they saw me.

TESMAN. You surely misunderstood them——

MRS. ELFSTED. No, no; I am sure it was of him they were talking. And I heard something about the hospital——

TESMAN. About the hospital!

HEDDA. Surely that cannot be.

MRS. ELFSTED.   I was in such mortal terror.   And then—just think——

TESMAN.   Yes?

MRS. ELFSTED.   I went to his lodgings and asked for him——

HEDDA.   How could you make up your mind to do such a thing!

MRS. ELFSTED.   Oh, because I couldn't endure it.

TESMAN.   But you didn't find him?

MRS. ELFSTED.   No.   And the people knew nothing about him.   He hadn't been home since yesterday afternoon, they said.   Oh, I am sure something has happened to him!

TESMAN.   Hedda—how would it be if I were to go and get Brack——

HEDDA.   No, not in this affair.

(JUDGE BRACK, *with his hat in his hand, enters by the hall door, which* BERTA *opens, and closes behind him.   He looks grave.*)

TESMAN.   Oh, is that you, my dear Judge?

BRACK,   Yes.   It was imperative I should see you.

TESMAN.   I can see you have heard about Aunt Rina.

BRACK.   Yes, that among other things.

TESMAN.   Isn't it sad—eh?

BRACK.   Oh, that depends on how you look at it.

TESMAN.   Has anything else happened?

BRACK.   Yes.

MRS. ELFSTED (*in suspense*).   Anything sad, Judge Brack?

BRACK.   That, too depends on how you look at it, Mrs. Elfsted.

MRS. ELFSTED.   Oh! it is something about Eilert Lövborg?

BRACK. What makes you think that? Have you already heard something?

MRS. ELFSTED. No, no, but——

TESMAN. Oh, for heaven's sake, tell us!

BRACK. Eilert Lövborg has been taken to the hospital. He is lying at the point of death.

TESMAN. At the point of death! In the hospital.

HEDDA. Ah——!

MRS. ELFSTED. Oh God! oh God——

HEDDA (*whispers*). Thea—be careful.

MRS. ELFSTED. I must go to him! I must see him alive.

BRACK. It is useless. No one will be admitted.

MRS. ELFSTED. Oh, at least tell me what has happened to him?

TESMAN. You don't mean to say that he has himself——!

HEDDA. Yes, I am sure he has.

TESMAN. Hedda, how can you——!

BRACK. Unfortunately you have guessed quite correctly, Mrs. Tesman.

MRS. ELFSTED. Oh, how horrible!

TESMAN. Himself, then——!

HEDDA. Shot himself!

BRACK. Rightly guessed again.

MRS. ELFSTED. When did it happen?

BRACK. This afternoon—between three and four.

TESMAN. And where did he do it?

BRACK. Where? Well—I suppose at his lodgings——

MRS. ELFSTED. No, that is not so; for I was there between seven and eight.

BRACK. Well then, somewhere else. I don't know precisely. I only know that he was found——. He had shot himself—in the breast.

MRS. ELFSTED. Oh, how awful!

HEDDA. Was it in the breast——?

BRACK. Yes.

HEDDA. Not in the temple?

BRACK. No, it was in the breast.

HEDDA. Well, well, the breast is a good place, too.

BRACK. How do you mean?

HEDDA. Oh, nothing—nothing.

TESMAN. And the wound is dangerous?

BRACK. Absolutely mortal. The end has probably come by this time.

MRS. ELFSTED. Yes, yes, I feel it! And then not to see him.

TESMAN. How have you learnt this?

BRACK. Through one of the police. A man I had some business with——

HEDDA. At last a deed worth doing!

TESMAN. Hedda—what are you saying?

HEDDA. I say there is beauty in this!

BRACK. H'm—Mrs. Tesman——

MRS. ELFSTED. Beauty! Oh, Hedda—how can you——

TESMAN. But, great heaven—Hedda——

HEDDA. He has passed judgment on himself, and has had the courage to do—the one right thing.

TESMAN. And you can speak thus of something so reprehensible! Fancy—a suicide———

MRS. ELFSTED. Oh yes, yes. But do not condemn him. He did it in delirium——

HEDDA. No, no, that he did not. I am certain of that.

MRS. ELFSTED. Yes, he did. In delirium. Just as when he tore up our manuscript.

BRACK. The manuscript? Has he torn that up?

Mrs. Elfsted. Yes, last night.

Tesman (*softly*). Oh, Hedda—Hedda.

Brack. H'm—very extraordinary.

Tesman. To think of his going out of the world without leaving behind him anything that would have immortalised his memory.

Mrs. Elfsted. Oh, but think, if it could be put together again!

Tesman. Yes, if it only could. I don't know what I would not give, if it only could——

Mrs. Elfsted, Perhaps it can, Mr. Tesman.

Tesman. How!

Mrs. Elfsted. Look here. I have kept all the loose notes he used to dictate to me from.

Hedda. Ah——!

Tesman. You have them!

Mrs. Elfsted. Yes, here. I brought them with me. I was going to ask you or Hedda to keep them.

Tesman. Oh, let me see. Let me see!

Mrs. Elfsted. But they are in such disorder—so mixed up.

Tesman. If we could make something out of them. Perhaps if we two put our heads together.

Mrs. Elfsted. Yes, let us try.

Tesman. We will manage it. I will dedicate my life to this.

Hedda. You? Your life?

Tesman. Yes, or all the time I can spare. My own collections must wait in the meantime. Hedda—you understand. I owe this to my friend.

Hedda. Perhaps.

Tesman. And so, my dear Mrs. Elfsted, we will give our whole minds to it. We will control our grief. Will you promise me that?

MRS. ELFSTED. I will try to do that.

TESMAN. Come here. I can't rest until we have looked through them. A thing of this sort—arranging other people's papers—is just the work for me. Where shall we sit—here? No, in there, in the back room. Excuse me—my dear Judge. Come along, Mrs. Elfsted.

MRS. ELFSTED. Oh, if only it were possible.

(TESMAN *and* MRS. ELFSTED *go into the back room, sit at the table under the hanging lamp, and are soon deep in the papers.* HEDDA *crosses to the stove and sits in the armchair. Presently* BRACK *goes up to her.*)

HEDDA. Oh, what a sense of freedom this gives one.

BRACK. Freedom?

HEDDA. Yes, to know that a deed is still possible in this world—a deed of beauty.

BRACK. H'm—my dear Mrs. Hedda——

HEDDA. Oh, I know what you are going to say. For you are a kind of specialist too, like—you know. You are neither able nor willing to see what there is in this deed of Eilert Lövborg's.

BRACK. Mrs. Hedda—this man was more to you than perhaps you are willing to admit— Is that not so?

HEDDA. I don't answer that. But now I can see him as he used to be. And I may say this to you. To me his reckless life was not aberration. There was spirit in it. Defiance of public opinion. It was not expiation of faults that he intended. He ended his life in freedom and courage.

BRACK. I am sorry, Mrs. Hedda, but I fear I must dispel an amiable illusion——

HEDDA. Illusion?

BRACK. Which could not have lasted long in any case.

HEDDA. What do you mean?

BRACK. The thing did not happen exactly as I told it.

HEDDA. How then?

BRACK. Eilert Lövborg did not shoot himself!

HEDDA. Is he not shot?

BRACK. Yes. But it is not a case of suicide.

HEDDA. Now you are belying him!

BRACK. And it was not at his lodgings——

HEDDA. That makes no difference.

BRACK. Eilert Lövborg died of an accidental shot in the same low tavern where he made a disturbance last night.

HEDDA. Impossible! He cannot have been there again to-day.

BRACK. He was there. He went to look for something. Talked wildly. Accused them of having stolen a child from him——

HEDDA. Ah——!

BRACK. I thought he meant his manuscript; but he destroyed that himself, didn't he? So I suppose it must have been his pocket-book.—Then there was a fight. He was thrown downstairs. Had a loaded pistol in his pocket. It goes off, and the ball lodges—not in the breast, but in the bowels.

HEDDA. Oh, what curse it is that makes everything I touch turn ludicrous and mean?

BRACK. There is another disagreeable feature in the affair, Mrs. Hedda.

HEDDA. And what is that?

BRACK. The pistol he carried——

HEDDA. Well—what of it——

BRACK. He must have stolen it——

HEDDA. Stolen it! That is not true!

Brack. No other explanation is possible—hush——

(Tesman *and* Mrs. Elfsted *have risen from the table in the back room, and come into the drawing-room.*)

Tesman (*with the papers in both his hands*). Impossible to see under that lamp. Do you mind our sitting at your writing-table, Hedda?

Hedda. If you like. No, wait. Let me clear it first.

Tesman. Oh, there is plenty of room.

Hedda. No, no, let me clear it. I will take these things in and put them on the piano. There.

(*She takes a case out of the shelf, places sheet music over it and carries it into the inner room, to the left.* Tesman *lays the papers on the writing-table, and moves the lamp there from the corner table. He and* Mrs. Elfsted *sit down and become engrossed in the papers.* Hedda *returns.*)

Hedda. Well, are you getting on?

Tesman. It will be terribly hard to put in order.

(Hedda *goes over to the stove, and seats herself in the armchair.* Brack *stands beside her.*)

Hedda (*whispers*). What did you say about the pistol?

Brack. That he must have stolen it.

Hedda. Why do you think so?

Brack. Eilert Lövborg was here this morning.

Hedda. Yes.

Brack. Were you alone with him?

Hedda. Part of the time.

Brack. Were you out of the room whilst he was here?

Hedda. No.

Brack. Try to recollect. Were you not out of the room a moment?

HEDDA. Yes—perhaps just a moment.

BRACK. And where was your pistol-case during that time?

HEDDA. It stood there on the shelf of the writing-table.

BRACK. Have you looked since, to see whether both the pistols are there?

HEDDA. No.

BRACK. Well, you need not. I saw the one found in his pocket, and I knew it at once.

HEDDA. Have you it with you?

BRACK. No; the police have it.

HEDDA. What will the police do with it?

BRACK. Search till they find the owner.

HEDDA. Do you think they will succeed?

BRACK. Not so long as I say nothing.

HEDDA. And if you do not say nothing?

BRACK. Well—Mrs. Hedda—then comes the scandal.

HEDDA. The scandal!

BRACK. The scandal, of which you are in such mortal terror. You will be brought before the court. Will have to give evidence. Was it stolen? Or did you give it to him? And what conclusions will people draw from that?

HEDDA. That is true. I did not think of that.

BRACK. Well, fortunately, there is no danger, so long as I say nothing.

HEDDA. So I am in your power.

BRACK. I shall not abuse my advantage, Hedda.

HEDDA. I am in your power none the less. A slave! a slave then! Oh, that intolerable thought. I cannot endure it! Never! (*Rises.*) Well, are you getting on, Tesman?

TESMAN. Heaven knows. It will be the work of months.

HEDDA (*passes her hands softly through* MRS. ELF-STED'S *hair.*) Doesn't it seem strange to you, Thea? Here are you sitting with Tesman, just as you used to sit with Eilert Lövborg.

MRS. ELFSTED. Ah yes, if I could only inspire your husband in the same way.

HEDDA. I am sure you can.

TESMAN. Yes, I really think I begin to feel something of the sort. But won't you go and sit with Brack again?

HEDDA. Is there nothing I can do to help you two?

TESMAN. Nothing in the world. You will have to keep Hedda company, my dear Brack.

BRACK. With great pleasure.

HEDDA. Thanks. But now I am going to lie down on the sofa.

TESMAN. Yes, do.

(HEDDA *goes into the back room and draws the curtains. There is a pause. Suddenly* HEDDA *is heard playing a wild dance on the piano.*)

MRS. ELFSTED. Oh—what is that?

TESMAN (*goes to the curtains*). But, Hedda dear—don't play dance-music. Just think of Aunt Rina——

HEDDA (*in the inner room*). And Aunt Julia. Yes, you're right. But after this, I will be quiet.

TESMAN. It's not good for her to see us at this distressing work. You shall take the empty room at Aunt Julia's, Mrs. Elfsted, and then I will come in the evenings and we can work there.

MRS. ELFSTED. Yes, let us do that.

HEDDA (*calls from the inner room*). I hear what you are saying, Tesman. But how am *I* to get through the evenings?

TESMAN (*at the writing-table*).   Oh, I daresay Judge Brack will be so kind as to look in now and then.

BRACK (*calls loudly*).   Every blessèd evening, with all the pleasure in life, Mrs. Hedda.   We shall get on capitally together, we two.

HEDDA (*is heard to say*).   Thanks for your kindness, Judge.

(*A shot is heard in the inner room.   TESMAN, MRS. ELFSTED and BRACK leap to their feet.   TESMAN throws back the curtains.   HEDDA lies on the sofa, lifeless.   Screams and cries.   BERTA appears from the right in the inner room.*)

TESMAN (*shrieks*).   Shot herself!   Shot herself in the temple!

BRACK (*half-fainting in the armchair by the stove*).   Good God!—people don't *do* such things!

THE MASTER BUILDER
A PLAY IN THREE ACTS
BY
HENRIK IBSEN
1892

FROM THE FIRST ACT

SOLNESS. Well then. I daresay you know that I took Knut Brovik and his son into my employment. About seven or eight years ago. When the old man's business had gone to the dogs.

DR. HERDAL. Yes, so I have understood.

SOLNESS. They are really clever fellows, these two. That is, when they are not working on their own account. But then, a couple of years ago or more, the son took it into his head to get engaged, and the next thing, of course, was that he wanted to begin to build on his own account. That is always the way with these young people.

DR. HERDAL (*laughing*). Yes, they have a bad habit of wanting to marry.

SOLNESS. Just so. Of course that did not suit my plans. H'm—for I needed them for calculating bearing-strains and cubic contents—and all that sort of devilry, you know.

DR. HERDAL. Oh yes, no doubt that's indispensable.

SOLNESS. Yes, it is. But Alfred was absolutely bent on setting to work for himself.. No matter what increase of salary I offered him, it was no use.

DR. HERDAL. Oh no, when young fellows get *those* ideas into their heads——

SOLNESS. But one day this girl came to see them on some errand or other. And when I saw how utterly infatuated they were with each other, the thought occurred to me: if I could only get her into my employment, then perhaps he would stay too.

461

DR. HERDAL. That was not at all a bad idea.

SOLNESS. Yes, but I did not say a word to her on that subject. Only talked to her a little, in a friendly way, about one thing and another. And she did not know me then. Nor I her either——

DR. HERDAL. Well?

SOLNESS. Well then, the next day, pretty late in the evening, when the other two had gone home, she came here again, and began to talk as if I had made an arrangement with her. About the very thing I had fixed my mind on, but hadn't said a single word about.

DR. HERDAL. That was most extraordinary.

SOLNESS. Yes, was it not? She wanted to know what she would have to do—whether she could begin the next day—and so forth.

DR. HERDAL. Don't you think she did it in order to be with her sweetheart?

SOLNESS. That was what occurred to me at first. But no, that was not it. She seemed to drift quite away from him, when she came here to me.

DR. HERDAL. She drifted over to you, then?

SOLNESS. Yes, entirely. Cannot take her eyes off me. Feels it, when I look at her. Trembles and shakes the moment I come near her. What do you think of *that?*

DR. HERDAL. H'm—that's not very hard to explain.

SOLNESS. Well, but what about the other thing? That she believed I had said to her what I had only wished and willed—silently?

DR. HERDAL. Yes, that is most extraordinary.

SOLNESS. Can you explain that, Doctor?

DR. HERDAL. No, I won't undertake to do that.

SOLNESS. I felt sure you would not; and so I have never cared to talk about it till now. But it's a cursed nuisance to me in the long run, you understand.   Here have I got to go on day after day pretending—.   But I *cannot* do anything else.   For if *she* runs away from me —then Alfred will be off too.

FROM THE SECOND ACT

SOLNESS.   Yes, thanks to the fire.   For then I got money in my hands to build with.   To build after my own heart, you understand.

HILDA.   For yourself, then?

SOLNESS.   No, not at once.   But I laid out the big garden in villa lots, and built four or five houses there—. To begin with, you see.

HILDA (*ardently*).   Yes, yes, that was very sensible of you.   For then the stupid people could see what they were like.

SOLNESS.   Yes, they could.   And so I came to the front with a rush.   Every one who was at all able to, would have a house from me.   Since that time I have raised building after building round the outskirts of the town.   And far down the fiord too.   And right up in the country.   And now at last they have begun to talk of me abroad — (*Breaking off.*)   Well, who knows — who knows——?

SOLNESS (*with a slight smile*).   After all, why shouldn't one play a little with the impossible?

HILDA (*with animation*).   Yes, indeed, *that* I can understand very well.

SOLNESS.   For, you see, there are some people who are always expecting to win in the lottery.   Even when they never have a ticket.

HILDA (*looking serious*). Oh yes, there must be such trolls in the world, too.

SOLNESS. Why trolls?

HILDA. What would you call it, then?

SOLNESS (*confidentially*). Don't you agree with me, Hilda, that there are certain people who have the power and faculty of *desiring* a thing, *craving* for a thing, *willing* a thing—so persistently and so—so inexorably—that at last it *has* to happen?

HILDA. Of its own accord?

SOLNESS. Yes. Don't you believe that?

HILDA. No, I certainly don't. I think that, if you want to carry anything through, you have got to put your hand to it yourself.

SOLNESS. Pure imagination. It is not one's self alone that does it.

SOLNESS. Why did you not write to me now and then?

HILDA. Oh, because it was so thrilling, not to know when you would come.

SOLNESS. Then you were sure I should come?

HILDA. I expected it every single day, from early in the morning. It was so gloriously thrilling.—But we were going to write on the drawings, Mr. Solness.

MRS. SOLNESS. Oh—I can see what I can see, Halvard.

SOLNESS. Well, after this we shall have nothing more to do with these people. And *that* is a good thing.

MRS. SOLNESS.   Are you really dismissing them?

SOLNESS.   Yes.

MRS. SOLNESS.   Her as well?

SOLNESS.   Was not that what you wished?

MRS. SOLNESS.   But how can you get on without *her*—? (*stops and throws a glance at Hilda.*)   Oh, perhaps you have another one in reserve, Halvard?

SOLNESS.   But, my dear, good Aline——!

HILDA (*playfully*).   No, indeed, Mrs. Solness.   You needn't be afraid of me.   I am not the person to stand at that desk.

MRS. SOLNESS.   But Halvard must have somebody with him——

SOLNESS (*changing the subject*).   Never mind, never mind—don't let us think about it.   It will be all right, Aline.   Now all we have to do is to think about moving into our new home—as quickly as we can.   This evening we will hang up the wreath—(*Turns to* HILDA.)—right on the very pinnacle of the tower.   What do you say to that Miss Hilda?

HILDA (*looks at him with sparkling eyes*).   It will be splendid to see you so high up once more.

SOLNESS.   Me!

MRS. SOLNESS.   For Heaven's sake, Miss. Wangel—don't imagine such a thing.   When my husband always gets so dizzy.

HILDA.   *He* get dizzy!

SOLNESS (*vehemently*).   I *don't* get dizzy!   It is only your imagination!   I don't!

MRS. SOLNESS.   Oh, how can you say so, Halvard?   Why, you can't even bear to go out on the second storey balcony here.

SOLNESS.   You are wrong, I tell you——

MRS. SOLNESS. Oh, but you always have been so, dear. Why will you never admit it?

SOLNESS. You are wrong, Aline. Perhaps you will see that this evening.

MRS. SOLNESS. No, please God I shall never see that. I will write to the doctor—and I am sure he won't let you do it.

SOLNESS. Why, Aline——!

MRS. SOLNESS. Oh, but you're ill, Halvard! Oh God—Oh God! (*She goes out to the right.*)

FROM THE THIRD ACT

HILDA. All these ten years I have stayed at home, believing in you. Simply believing in you. And every day I have seen you in my thoughts, free and high up.

SOLNESS. Oh, Hilda, it is not every day that one can be so.

HILDA (*imploringly*). Just once more, Mr. Solness.

SOLNESS. I cannot. Have I not told you that what I did then was the impossible?

HILDA. Well then, do the impossible once again!

SOLNESS. Such a thing can never be done again.

HILDA. *You* can do it.

SOLNESS (*looking at her*). How have you become what you are, Hilda?

HILDA. How have you made me what I am?
[Well how?
By willing and daring the impossible.]

SOLNESS. The princess shall have her castle.

HILDA [*jubilant, clapping her hands*). Oh, Mr. Solness——!

SOLNESS.   Her castle in the air the princess shall have. [The one with a firm foundation.]

[If I ever try it, H., I will stand up there and say to him: Hear me, Mighty Lord, thou may'st judge me as thou wilt. But hereafter I will build nothing but the loveliest thing in the world. Build it for a princess, whom I love. H. You would say that! S. Yes. And then I will say to him: Now I shall go down and throw my arms round her and kiss her. H. Many times. S. Many, many times. H. And then—. S. Then I would wave my hat and come down and do as I said to him. H. Do the impossible once again!

Now I see you again as I did when there was song in the air.]

LITTLE EYOLF

CHARACTERS

HARALD BORGHEIM.
JOHANNE, his wife.
RITA, his sister.
ALFRED, his son, eleven years old.
EIVIND ALMER, a road engineer.
MISS VARG, Johanne's aunt.

(*The action takes place on* BORGHEIM'S *property, on the fiord.*)

FROM THE FIRST ACT

Well, but that can only be good for him.

RITA. Do you really think so?

MRS. SKIOLDHEIM. I don't think one way or the other. Hakon himself is the best judge of such things.

> (HAKON SKIOLDHEIM *enters by the door on the left, leading little* ALFRED *by the hand. He has a slim, slight figure and a serious expression. Thin dark hair and beard.* ALFRED *is undersized, and looks somewhat delicate.*)

HAKON SKIOLDHEIM. Well, have you come, Rita?

RITA. Yes, I felt I must—. Welcome home again.

SKIOLDHEIM. Thank you.

MRS. SKIOLDHEIM. Doesn't he look well?

RITA. Splendid! Quite splendid! His eyes are so much brighter! And I suppose you have done a great deal of writing on your travels? I shouldn't wonder if you had finished the whole book, Hakon [Alfred]?

SKIOLDHEIM [ALF]. The book——?

471

RITA [A].   Yes, I was sure you would find it go so easily when once you got away.

SKIOLDHEIM.   The truth is, I have not written a line of the book.

RITA.   Not a line——?

MRS. SKIOLDHEIM.   Oho! I wondered when I found all the paper lying untouched in your bag.

RITA.   But, dear me, what have you been doing for these two months [all this time]?

SKIOLDHEIM (*smiling*).   Only thinking, thinking, thinking.

MRS. SKIOLDHEIM (*putting her arm round his neck*). And thinking a little, too, of those you had left at home?

SKIOLDHEIM.   Yes, you may be sure of that. I have thought a great deal of you.

MRS. SKIOLDHEIM.   Oh, how nice of you.

RITA.   But you haven't even touched the book. And yet you can look so happy. And so contented with yourself. That is not what you generally do—I mean when your work is going badly.

SKIOLDHEIM.   You are right there. For I have been such a fool hitherto, Rita. All the best that is in you goes into thinking. What you put on paper is worth very little.

RITA.   Worth very little!

MRS. SKIOLDHEIM.   Oh but, Hakon——!

ALFRED.   Oh yes, Papa, what *you* write is worth a great deal!

SKIOLDHEIM (*smiling, stroking his hair*).   Well, well, since *you* say so— But I can tell you, some one is coming after me who will do it better.

ALFRED.   Who can that be? Oh, tell me!

SKIOLDHEIM.   Only wait—you may be sure he will

come, and let us hear of him.   But next summer, when I go to the mountains again, I will take you with me, Alfred.

ALFRED.   Take me!

MRS. SKIOLDHEIM.   Oh fie, Hakon—are you thinking of deserting me again?

RITA (*to Alfred*).   Would you not like to go with him, little boy?

ALFRED (*considering*).   Oh, yes—I think I should. If it is not very dangerous——

SKIOLDHEIM.   Dangerous?   How do you mean?

ALFRED.   Well, might I not easily fall and be crippled?

SKIOLDHEIM (*decisively*).   You must and shall come with me to the mountains, my boy.

RITA.   And then you must ask your father to let you learn to shoot, and hunt, and swim—and all that sort of thing.   Would you not like that, Alfred?

ALFRED.   Yes, I should like that very much.—Well —I should only have to be rather careful——

SKIOLDHEIM.   Yes, you would have to be, of course. But now you can run down into the garden and amuse yourself.

ALFRED.   Shall I not take some books with me?

SKIOLDHEIM.   No, no, no books.

ALFRED.   Well then, I'll just go down and amuse my-self.

(*He is going out on to the veranda, but stops and comes back.*)

ALFRED.   Oh, no—I dare not!

SKIOLDHEIM.   Why daren't you?

ALFRED.   Because Aunt Ellen is coming that way!

SKIOLDHEIM.   Are *you* so afraid of her too?

MRS. SKIOLDHEIM.   What can she want here?

ALFRED.   Papa, do you think it is true that she is a were-wolf at night?

SKIOLDHEIM. Oh, not at all. What put that into your head?

ALFRED. I don't know, but that's what I think.

SKIOLDHEIM. She has had a lot of trouble. And it has made her rather strange. That is all.

(MISS VARG *comes up the steps on to the veranda. She is old and grey-haired. A thin little shrunken figure. Old-fashioned flowered gown. Black hood and cloak. She has in her hand a large red umbrella, and carries a black bag over her arm.*)

MISS VARG. Good morning, good morning to you all! It is long since I set foot here.

MRS. SKIOLDHEIM. Yes, it is a long time. Won't you sit down and rest a little?

MISS VARG. Yes, indeed! Thanks! (*Seats herself on a chair by the sofa*). I have been out at my work. And must go out again. And it takes your strength out of you.

SKIOLDHEIM. So you have been out this morning——?

MISS VARG. Yes, over on Grönö. (*Laughing to herself.*) The people sent for me last night, to be sure. They didn't like it a bit. But at last they had to bite the sour apple—. (*Looks at Alfred, and nods.*) The sour apple, my boy. The sour apple.

ALFRED (*involuntarily, timidly*). Why did they have to——?

MISS VARG. What?

ALFRED. To bite it?

MISS VARG. Why, because they couldn't keep body and soul together.

ALFRED (*turns a doubtful and questioning look upon his father*).

SKIOLDHEIM. Why could they not keep body and soul together?

Miss Varg. Because of the rats and mice, of course.

Alfred. The rats and——!

Mrs. Skioldheim. Ugh! Poor people! Have they so many of them?

Miss Varg (*laughing*). Yes, it was all alive and swarming with them. Both indoors and out. They came creepy-crawly up into the beds all night long. They plumped into the milk-cans, and they went pattering all over the floor, backwards and forwards. But then *I* came.

Alfred. How can any one dare [I could never dare] go there——! [I shall never go there, Auntie.]

Miss Varg. I dare. And then I took them with me —every one. The sweet little creatures! I made an end of every one of them.

Alfred (*with a shriek*). Papa—look! look!

Skioldheim. What is it?

Mrs. Skioldheim. Good heavens, Alfred!

Alfred. There's something wriggling in the bag!

Mrs. Skioldheim (*shrieks*). Ugh!

Miss Varg (*laughing*). Oh, you needn't be afraid of such a little thing.

Skioldheim. But what *is* it?

Miss Varg (*loosening the string of the bag*). Why, it's only little Mopsëman. Come out, my little friend!

(*A little dog with a broad black snout pokes its head out of the bag.*)

Miss Varg (*to* Alfred). Come a little nearer. He won't bite. Come along!

Alfred. No, I dare not.

Miss Varg (*stroking the dog*). Don't you think he has a gentle, friendly countenance, my young master?

Alfred [(*pointing*)]. That thing *there?*

Miss Varg. Yes, this thing here.

ALFRED [(*staring fixedly at the dog*)] (*almost under his breath*). I think he has the horriblest—countenance I ever saw.

MISS VARG (*closing the bag*). Oh, it will come—it will come, right enough.

ALFRED ([*drawing nearer,*] *involuntarily strokes the bag*). But he is lovely—lovely all the same.

MISS VARG (*in a tone of caution*). But now he is so tired, so utterly tired out, poor thing. For it takes the strength out of you,—that sort of work.

SKIOLDHEIM. What sort of work?

MISS VARG. Luring.

SKIOLDHEIM. Then is it the dog that lures the rats?

MISS VARG. Mopsëman and I. I slip a string through his collar, and then I lead him three times round the house [,and play on my Pan's pipes]. And then they have to come out of their hiding-places—every one of them. [All the blessed little creatures.] Whether they like it or not.

ALFRED. And then does he bite them?

MISS VARG. Oh, not at all. No, we go down to the boat, he and I do—and then they follow after us [,—both the big ones and the little children].

ALFRED (*eagerly*). And what then——?

MISS VARG. Then I take my seat in the stern. [And play on my Pan's pipes.] And Trond pushes out from the land. And Mopsëman swims behind. And I hold him by the string. And all the rats and all the mice, they follow [and follow] us. Ay, for they *have* to.

ALFRED. Why do they have to?

MISS VARG. Just because they want not to. [Because they are so deadly afraid of the water—that is why they have got to plunge into it.]

ALFRED. Are they drowned, then?

MISS VARG. Every blessed one. [And then they are at peace, the lovely little things. Down there they sleep sweetly and securely.] (*She rises.*) In the old days, I can tell you—I didn't need any Mopsëman. For then I did the luring myself—in another way.

ALFRED. And what did you lure then?

MISS VARG. Men. One most of all. One in particular.

ALFRED (*eagerly*). Oh, who was that one? Tell me!

MISS VARG (*laughing*). It was my own sweetheart, it was [, little heart-breaker].

ALFRED. And why did you lure him?

MISS VARG. Because he had gone away from me [I loved him so dearly]. Far, far away over the salt sea waves. But I drew him and drew him home to me again. I almost had him.—But then my grasp failed. He was gone—for ever.

ALFRED. Well, where is he now, then?

MISS VARG. Down where all the rats are.—But now I must really be off and get to business again. Have you any use for me here? I could finish it all off while I am about it.

MRS. SKIOLDHEIM. No, thank you, Miss Varg—I don't think we require anything.

MISS VARG. Well, well, you can never tell—. If there should be anything, just send for Aunt Ellen. (*Laughs.*) Isn't it strange that everybody calls me Aunt Ellen? And yet I have no living kinsfolk—neither in heaven or earth. Well, good-bye, good-bye to you all.

(*She goes out by the door on the right. Shortly afterwards, ALFRED slips cautiously and unnoticed out into the garden.*)

RITA. To-day she was almost horrible.

MRS. SKIOLDHEIM. I think she is so always.

SKIOLDHEIM. I can very well understand the sort of spellbound fascination that she talked about. Nature among the glaciers and the great waste places has something of the same magic about it.

RITA (*looks attentively at him*). [What is it that has happened to you—] Something seems almost to have transformed you, Hakon.

MRS. SKIOLDHEIM. Yes, don't you think so too?

SKIOLDHEIM. Something *has* happened, that has transformed me. It has happened within me. For in external reality I have had no adventure on my journey.

MRS. SKIOLDHEIM (*seats herself on the sofa*). You must tell us all about it.

SKIOLDHEIM. Yes, let us sit down, too, Rita—then I will try.

(*He seats himself on the sofa at his wife's side.* RITA *on a chair by the table.*)

SKIOLDHEIM (*after a brief pause*). The journey has really made me so happy and light-hearted. But there has been a tinge of melancholy with it, that I cannot shake off.

MRS. SKIOLDHEIM. That must be because you have not been able to work——

SKIOLDHEIM (*smiles rather sadly*). Yes, you know me. You know that hitherto it has been so with me.

MRS. SKIOLDHEIM (*smiles*). Very cross and fretful. Quite out of humour when there was now and then a difficulty with your writing.

SKIOLDHEIM. Well, you see, my dear Andrea—I have now got over those vexations.

MRS. SKIOLDHEIM. While you were in the mountains?

SKIOLDHEIM. Yes, up in the great solitude.—Well I can't say I have not been a happy man hitherto. But I have lived my life far too much in the study. Without cares, without troubles of any kind. Abundance on every side.—(*Giving them his hands.*) And then you two to flatter me and spoil me.

RITA. All we have done is to understand you, Hakon.

MRS. SKIOLDHEIM. We have believed in you. And tried to go with you.

SKIOLDHEIM. When I look back—. Book after book I have sent out into the world. They were well done, I believe. And they have been well received too. And now the masterpiece was to come out. The work on the spiritual [psychological] doctrine of life——

MRS. SKIOLDHEIM. Yes, but it will come out—it will come out, Hakon. Now that you are at home again——

SKIOLDHEIM. It will never come out, dear—. Must never come out.

MRS. SKIOLDHEIM. Good heavens, but why not?

SKIOLDHEIM. Because there is a fundamental defect in it.

RITA. A fundamental defect? But can you not remedy it?

SKIOLDHEIM. No, it is irreparable, Rita.

MRS. SKIOLDHEIM. Yes, but now that you have discovered it——

RITA. But what can this fundamental defect be?

SKIOLDHEIM. I have not taken renunciation into account.

MRS. SKIOLDHEIM. Renunciation?

SKIOLDHEIM. Renunciation, yes. Self-denial. The desire—the joy of self-sacrifice. All that should be the inmost core of one's conduct.

RITA.   Well, but why not include all this now?

SKIOLDHEIM (*shakes his head*).   It shall not be put into any book.   What I have learnt to see—shall be made part of my own life's conduct.

MRS. SKIOLDHEIM.   What do you mean by that?

SKIOLDHEIM.   You   see—every   family—that   has breeding, be it observed—has its ascending series of generations: it rises from father to son, until it reaches the highest point the family is capable of attaining.   And then it goes down again.

RITA.   You are destined to attain the highest, Hakon.

SKIOLDHEIM.   My belief in that has been the great delusion of my life.

MRS. SKIOLDHEIM.   You don't believe it any longer!

SKIOLDHEIM.   No.   Now I know that it is not so. I have usurped a throne.   Now I resign it.   I abdicate——

MRS. SKIOLDHEIM.   In whose favour should you abdicate?

SKIOLDHEIM.   In favour of the rightful one.

MRS. SKIOLDHEIM.   Yes, but who, who, in Heaven's name, is the rightful one?

SKIOLDHEIM.   Alfred [Eivind].

RITA.   Alfred [Eivind]!

MRS. SKIOLDHEIM [MRS. ALMER].   Alfred [Eivind]! Do you think that?

SKIOLDHEIM [ALMER].   I see it.   He will be the summit and crown of the Skioldheim stock.

MRS. ALMER.   Ah, do you believe that, Alfred?

ALMER.   I believe it confidently.   I will devote all my powers to it.   I will be his teacher——

MRS. ALMER.   Oh, but why burden your life so?   We have no need of that.

ALLMER. It is not any technical knowledge that I want to cram him with. It is the art of life itself that I will try to make him understand. Make the art of life his very nature.

MRS. ALLMER. But, Alfred, what is the 'art of life'? There is no art in living, I should think.

ALLMER. Don't you think so?

MRS. ALLMER. No, it is the simplest thing in the world. Living! When one has enough to live on, as we have. And when one can live exactly as one pleases. And need do nothing but what one thinks right and proper.

ALLMER. Yes, you have a bright and happy disposition, Andrea.

MRS. ALLMER. You ought to cultivate the same.

ALLMER. It will come to me through the fulfilment of my duty.

MRS. ALLMER. What duty?

ALLMAR. My highest duty. The duty of making every side of Eivind's individuality attain its highest, fullest development.

MRS. ALLMER. Do you hold that to be your highest duty?

ALLMER. Yes, for a father there is none higher.

MRS. ALLMER. Nor for a mother either, I suppose?

ALLMER. No, that is understood. If I say *I*, it is only an instance, a relic, of my old egoism. Such things are not so easy to tear up by the roots. I mean, of course, *we*. We two in fellowship, Andrea.

MRS. ALLMER. No, my dearest Alfred, I really cannot be altogether with you in this.

ALLMER. You cannot devote your existence to perfecting our child! As far as we are able.

MRS. ALLMER. Oh, you talk about existence. Existence—that is life—one's sense of happiness, I think it might be called.

ALLMER (*seriouly, almost severely*). I know of no deeper sense of happiness than that of seeing Eivind grow under my hands.

MRS. ALLMER. But you used only to occupy yourself with him in such a very desultory way.

ALLMER. I am sorry to say you are right there. I have been too much taken up by myself and by——

MRS. ALLMER. —and by——?

ALLMER. —by all these morbid, distorted, baseless fancies that I, myself, had some special mission in the world. Something of extreme importance and moment —something that concerned myself alone.

MRS. ALLMER. Is this all that has occupied you? Occupied your life, Alfred?

ALLMER. Yes.

MRS. ALLMER. Nothing else at all?

ALLMER. Nothing worth mentioning, as far as I can see.

MRS. ALLMER. No *person* either? No other person?

ALLMER. Other person? What do you mean? Who should *that* be?

MRS. ALLMER. Myself, I suppose.

ALLMER. Oh, you, yes. But, my dearest Andrea, that is a matter of course——

MRS. ALLMER. No, no, no! I won't hear of anything that is a matter of course. I will have it to be because I am myself. And because you are yourself.

ALLMER. But, dearest Andrea, that's just as it was in the days of our honeymoon——

MRS. ALLMER. Yes, and so it must continue.

ALLMER. No, but look here—we must begin to be reasonable some day.

MRS. ALLMER. Never in this world will you get me to be reasonable. Not on this point. This talk about being reasonable—it is nothing but excuses—when one doesn't care any more.

ALLMER. No, but listen to me——

MRS. ALLMER. I have one thing to say to you, Alfred —I will not consent to give up my place—the first place in your heart. Not even for my own little boy.

RITA. Alfred must always have some one to devote himself to. He has always been so. Towards me too. As early as I can remember.

MRS. ALLMER. Is it only this that has put you in such wild spirits to-day?

BORGHEIM. Yes, and all the brightness and hopeful-ness [bright and hopeful prospects] that is being showered upon me [that are opening out before me].

MRS. ALLMER. Is there still something more?

BORGHEIM. Yes, there is! There is—. No, I can't keep it in any longer. (*Turns to* RITA.) Shall we——?

RITA (*quickly and softly*). No, no—! Oh, take a little walk in the garden, you mean?

BORGHEIM. Walk—? Yes, that is just what I meant.

RITA. Yes, I should like to.

ALLMER. And [while you are there] you can see what Eivind is doing. He is playing down there.

BORGHEIM. Oh, then Eivind has begun to play now? He used always to be sitting over his books.

ALLMER. There is to be an end of that now. I am going to make a regular open-air boy of him.

BORGHEIM. Ah, now, that's right! Out into the open air with him. Good Lord, what can we possibly

do better than play in this blessed world? For my part,
I think all life is one long playtime!

(*He and* RITA *go out on the veranda and down
through the garden.*)

ALLMER (*looking after them*). Is there anything between those two?

MRS. ALMER. I am beginning almost to think so.
Would it displease you if there were?

ALLMER. It would not exactly displease me. But of
course, I am in a way responsible for Rita. And it is
always a precarious thing when two people form an
attachment of this sort.

MRS. ALLMER (*looking at him*). You mean that it does
not last?

ALLMER. One can never tell. Even those who engage themselves cannot tell that.

MRS. ALLMER. For my part, I don't think at all ill of
Borgheim.

ALLMER. No, dear—ill? Who is saying anything of
the sort? But I am so afraid that those two have no
right to undergo transformation together.

MRS. ALLMER. Transformation? Must they do that?

ALLMER. Or develop—if you prefer it. Mature.
Grow. You must remember that in married life new
situations are formed. Little by little, you understand.
New duties assert themselves. The children, too, claim
their rights. They *have* the first claim, Andrea.

MRS. ALLMER (*close to him, almost wildly*). Do you
say that! The first. Do you say that, Alfred!

ALLMER. Yes, for that is how I have come to look at
things.

MRS. ALLMER. Then you don't love me any more?

ALLMER. Andrea, how can you say such a thing?
For it is impossible that you can mean it!

MRS. ALLMER. Oh yes, I am not far from meaning it now. You are no longer the same to me as you used to be. Not as you were the first year.

ALLMER. Never have you been dearer to me than you are now, Andrea.

MRS. ALLMER. But not in the same way. You have begun to divide yourself between me and your work. And I will not endure that. I want you entirely to myself. (*Throwing her arms round his neck.*) Oh, Alfred, Alfred, I cannot give you up!

———

(*Engineer* BORGHEIM *and* RITA *come up from the garden.*)

BORGHEIM. There! Hurrah! Now I have permission to tell the news!

MRS. ALLMERS. It is scarcely necessary, is it, dear Mr. Borgheim?

BORGHEIM. Ah? Is it not? Have you really been able to notice anything in us?

MRS. ALLMERS. Oh yes, indeed.

BORGHEIM. Well, now she has surrendered. To me— unconditionally. She hesitates no longer——

MRS. ALLMERS. Then she did before?

BORGHEIM. I can't say she did not.

ALLMERS. I hope this may mean happiness to you, dear Rita.

RITA (*kissing his hand*). Thanks, thanks for all you have been to me.

ALLMERS. Rita! My little Rita!

BORGHEIM. And now she is going with me. To share my work. We may have mountain passes enough to overcome. And abrupt precipices that might make one dizzy.

ALLMERS.   Oh, if you but keep together in sympathy
—all will be well.

MRS. ALLMERS.   And let no evil eye [come between
you] and take him from you, Rita.

RITA.   Evil eye?

———————

SECOND ACT

A little, open place by the side of the fiord, on ALLMERS'S
*property.   Mostly fir-trees, but with birches among
them.   A bench, a round table, and one or two
chairs, all made of tree-trunks and boughs with the
bark on, are set up on the right.   Some large boul-
ders lie on the beach and out in the water.   It is
about noon, on a sunny day.   The fiord lies as still
as a mirror.*

(ALFRED ALLMERS, *in his grey summer clothes, but
with a mourning band on the arm, sits on the bench,
resting his arms on the table.   His grey felt hat,
also with a mourning band, lies on one of the
chairs.   He sits still for a while, and gazes absently out over the water.   Then* MISS ANDREA
ALLMERS, *dressed entirely in mourning, comes
down a little wooded hill on the left, and goes
quietly up to him.*)

MISS ANDREA.   Are you sitting down here, Alfred?

ALLMERS (*nods slowly without answering*).

(ANDREA *moves his hat to the table and sits down
on the chair.*)

ANDREA.   I have been searching for you such a long
time.   Have you been sitting here all the time?

———————

ANDREA.   Oh, but it is not at all certain that it happened so——

ALLMERS. Yes, it is. I am sure of it. It must have happened so. The people down below—they say that Miss Warg rowed out. She sat in the stern of the boat and the dog swam behind on a string——

ANDREA. Yes, yes, but all the same—that doesn't——

ALLMERS. And, you know, there are some who saw Eyolf standing at the end of the steamboat pier. A moment later he was gone. No one saw any more of him——

ANDREA. Yes, they say so, I know, but——

ALLMERS. She has drawn him down, Andrea—there is no doubt about it.

ANDREA. But, Alfred, why should she do it?

ALLMERS. Yes, that is just the question. Why should she—? —Eyolf certainly never did her any harm. He never called names after her; he never threw stones at her dog. Why, he had never seen her till yesterday. Nor would it be like Eyolf to do such things. So meaningless. So utterly meaningless. And yet the order of the world requires it.

ANDREA. Have you spoken to Rita of this?

ALLMERS. I feel as if I can talk better to you about it.

ANDREA. Alfred, you should talk to Rita too.

ALLMERS. I will do so. Both to you and to her.— But now you will soon be leaving us.

ANDREA. That will not make a separation between you and me, I hope.

ALLMERS. No, I don't think I could imagine such a thing.

ANDREA. We shall still be near to each other, however far away I may go.

ALLMERS. But it will be lonely for Rita and me. When *you* go away from us too.

ANDREA. I believe Rita would rather have it so.

ALLMERS (*looking at her*).   She would rather——?

ANDREA.   She would rather have you entirely to herself.

ALLMERS.   Have you noticed that?

ANDREA.   Yes, now and then.

ALLMERS.   But I don't think that applies to you, Andrea.

ANDREA.   No, perhaps not so much to me as to others.

ALLMERS.   For she knows, of course, what we two have been to each other all our days.

ANDREA.   Oh, Alfred—say rather, what you have been to me.   You have been everything to me.   No sacrifice has been too great for you.

ALLMERS.   Oh, nonsense, sacrifice.   Oh, I have loved you so, ever since you were a little child.   And then it seemed to me that I had so much injustice to make up for.

————————

ANDREA.   You were generally away from home at that time..   For I am thinking more particularly of the years when you were at the University.

ALLMERS.   Yes, but, dearest Andrea—I was often at home on visits.

ANDREA.   But all the same——

ALLMERS.   You have never hinted at such a thing before now.   I thought the fault must be all on father's side.   If there *was* any fault.

ANDREA.   Oh, I don't think the fault is ever entirely on one side——

ALLMERS.   You may be right there.   But tell me——

ANDREA.   Oh, please, Alfred—say no more about this!   (*Looks into the wood on the right.*)   Here come Rita and Bergheim.

ALLMERS.   Shall we go and meet them?

ANDREA. They can see us. They are coming this way.

ALLMERS. Have you loved Bergheim long?

ANDREA (*with a rapid glance at him*). Loved him?

ALLMERS. Yes?

ANDREA. I have only known him such a short time.

ALLMERS. And now you are going away with him. So far, far away. I never thought that we two should be parted.

ANDREA. Nor I either.

ALLMERS (*looking before him*). Where is Eyolf now? Can anyone tell me that? No one in all the world. I know only that he is gone from me. And soon you will be gone from me too, Andrea. No one, no one of my own kin.

ANDREA. You have Rita.

ALLMERS. Rita is no kin to me—it isn't like having a sister——

ANDREA (*eagerly*). Do you say that, Alfred?

ALLMERS. Yes. The Allmers family is a thing apart. We have always had vowels for our initials. And we have all the same colour of eyes.

ANDREA. I too, do you think?

ALLMERS. No, that's true. Not you. You are not like father. You take more after your mother. But all the same——

ANDREA. All the same——?

ALLMERS. Living together, I believe, has stamped us alike—formed us in each other's image. Mentally and outwardly.

ANDREA. Do you feel it so, Alfred?

ALLMERS. Yes, that is just how I feel it.

ANDREA. Then you force me to tell you——

ALLMERS. What? What is it? Tell me!

ANDREA (*looking out to the right*). Presently. Here they are coming.

(MRS. RITA ALLMERS *and Engineer* BORGHEIM *come forward through the trees.*)

ALLMERS. Yes, do so.

BORGHEIM (*to* ANDREA). Andrea—shall we go a little way along the road meanwhile?

ANDREA. With pleasure.

(*She and* BORGHEIM *go off along the shore to the left.*)

(ALLMERS *wanders about for a little; then he seats himself on the bench on the left.* RITA *goes over to him.*)

MRS. ALLMERS. Can you think the thought, Alfred —that we have lost him!

ALLMERS. We must accustom ourselves to think. it

MRS. ALLMERS. I cannot. I cannot. But is it so certain that he is gone—for ever?

ALLMERS. But people say they saw him lying down on the bottom. And then the current came and carried him away.

MRS. ALLMERS. Yes, yes, I know that. But it is not that I mean.

ALLMERS. What then?

MRS. ALLMERS. He seems to be about me just the same. More, a thousand times more than before.

ALLMERS (*bitterly.*) He seems so now?

MRS. ALLMERS. Yes, yes. But that is not enough. I must see him. Hear him. Feel him——

ALLMERS. You were so well able to do without him before—for half a day at a time——

MRS. ALLMERS. Yes, for then I knew I had him all the same.

ALLMERS (*sadly*). Now we have him no longer. Things have come about, as you wished——

MRS. ALLMERS. What did I wish?

ALLMERS (*looking severely at her*). That little Eyolf were not here.

MRS. ALLMERS. That little Eyolf should not stand between us. That was what I wished!

ALLMERS. Well, well, he does not stand between us any more, poor boy.

MRS. ALLMERS (*looking at him*). Perhaps now more than ever.

ALLMERS. You never really and truly loved him.

MRS. ALLMERS. Eyolf would never let me take him really and truly to my heart.

ALLMERS. Because you did not want to.

MRS. ALLMERS. Oh yes, I did. I did want to. But some one stood in the way [—even from the first].

ALLMERS. I, do you mean? [Do you mean that I stood in the way?]

MRS. ALLMERS. Oh, no—not at first.

ALLMERS. Who, then?

MRS. ALLMERS. Andrea.

ALLMERS. Andrea? Can you say that, Rita?

MRS. ALLMERS. Yes; Andrea took him to her heart from the time when he was quite a little child.

ALLMERS. If she did so, she did it in love.

MRS. ALLMERS. That is just it. I cannot endure to share anything with others. Not in love.

ALLMERS. We two should have shared him between us in love.

MRS. ALLMERS. We? The truth is you have never had any real love for the child.

ALLMERS (*looks at her in surprise*). *I* have not—I How can you say—how can you think such a thing!

MRS. ALLMERS. No, you have not. You used to be so utterly taken up by your work.

ALLMERS. Yes, and I sacrificed it for Eyolf's sake——

MRS. ALLMERS. Yes, but not out of love for him.

ALLMERS. Why then? Tell me what you suppose!

MRS. ALLMERS. You had begun to be consumed with mistrust of yourself. All the happy confidence—all the hope that you had a great task to perform, had begun to desert you. I could see that.

ALLMERS. Oh yes, you may be right there. But all the same——

MRS. ALLMERS. Then you went away. Up into the great, free waste places. And that must have exalted your mind——

ALLMERS. It has. It has. Be sure of that, Andrea!

MRS. ALLMERS. But not exalted it to love——

ALLMERS (*eagerly*). It was up there in the vastness and solitude that I gave up my place in life for little Eyolf's sake.

MRS. ALLMERS. But why—why did you give it up?

ALLMERS. Why?

MRS. ALLMERS. [I will tell you.—ALLMERS. Well?] Because you needed something new to fill up your life. Andrea had so often talked to you of Eyolf's great abilities, of all the possibilities there were in him—and that sort of thing——

ALLMERS. Yes, she took most interest in him. But it was for that reason, you think——?

MRS. ALLMERS. You wanted to make a prodigy of him, Alfred. Because he was *your* child. But you never really loved him. Never cared for him sincerely for his own sake.

ALLMERS. Do you think that?

Mrs. Allmers. Yes. If I had known that you loved him sincerely, I might perhaps have been resigned to sharing you with him. Although—no, perhaps not, after all.

Allmers (*looking thoughtfully at her*). But if it is so, Rita, then we two have never really possessed our own child.

Mrs. Allmers. No, not in perfect love.

Allmers. And now we are sorrowing so bitterly for him.

Mrs. Allmers. Yes, isn't it curious that we should grieve like this over a little stranger boy?

Allmers (*pained*). Oh, don't call him a stranger!

Mrs. Allmers. We never won the boy, Alfred. Not I—nor you either.

Allmers (*wringing his hands*). And now it is too late! Too late!

Mrs. Allmers. And no consolation. No hope anywhere—in anything!

Allmers (*in quiet emotion*). I dreamed about him last night. I thought I saw him standing in the garden. I felt so glad. So rich. So he was not lost to us. We had him. And the terrible reality was nothing but a dream. Oh, how I thanked and blessed——

———————

Mrs. Allmers (*moaning softly*). I could not. I could not [never could]!

Allmers. Not if I went there at the same time?

Mrs. Allmers. No, no! Not for all the glory of heaven!

Allmers. Nor I.

Mrs. Allmers. No, you feel it so, too, don't you— you could not either, could you?

ALLMERS.   For here we are at home—for the present.

MRS. ALLMERS.   Yes, for here is [the] happiness [we can understand].

ALLMERS.   Happiness?

MRS. ALLMERS.   Yes, we *must* find happiness again. Without happiness I cannot live.

ALLMERS.   Where are we to find it now?

MRS. ALLMERS (*shaking her head*).   No, no, no—you are right there.   We shall never find it, while we do nothing but grieve over little Eyolf.   (*Looks inquiringly at him.*)   But——?

ALLMERS.   But——?

MRS. ALLMERS (*quickly, as though in terror*).   No, no. I dare not say it!   Nor even think it.

ALLMERS.   Yes, say it!   Say it, Rita!

RITA (*hesitatingly*).   Could we not try to—?   Would it not be possible to forget him?

ALLMERS.   Forget Eyolf!

MRS. ALLMERS.   Forget our grief for him, I mean.

ALLMERS.   Can you wish it?

MRS. ALLMERS.   Yes, if it were possible.   (*With an outburst.*)   For I cannot bear this for ever!

ALLMERS.   But the memory, Rita?   We cannot escape that.   And the memory brings remorse.

MRS. ALLMERS.   The memory of little Eyolf will soften with time.   Oh, don't you think so, Alfred?

ALLMERS.   May be—some day, perhaps.   But the sense of void—can that ever be deadened?

MRS. ALLMERS (*looking before her*).   No, *there* it is. The void—the void.   Every day, every hour—it will assert itself in the smallest trifle.

ALLMERS.   Even the empty chair at table.   Even the fact that his coat is not hanging in its usual place in the hall——

Mrs. Allmers. And happiness will not grow in the void. Neither you nor I are capable of bearing this, Alfred. We must try to think of something that will bring forgetfulness.

Allmers. Oh, what could that be?

Mrs. Allmers. Could we not see what travelling would do—far away from here?

Allmers. From home? When you know you are never really well anywhere but here.

Mrs. Allmers. Well, then, let us have crowds of people about us! Keep open house! Try something of that sort that might deaden and dull our thoughts——

Allmers. But such a life would be impossible for me—you know that. I simply could not endure it. No, rather than that, I would try to take up my work again.

Mrs. Allmers. Your work—the work that has been like a wall between us?

Allmers. It has not, Rita. You are wrong there.

Mrs. Allmers. No, I am not! But I will not consent to share you. I want you utterly and entirely as you used to be. You must give me your love again, unaltered—I will have it, I tell you.

Allmers. That love was an intoxication, and it is dead [quenched].

Mrs. Allmers. And you can say that——!

Allmers. It is dead. But in what I now feel for you there is a resurrection——

Mrs. Allmers. I don't care a bit about any resurrection——

Allmers. Rita——!

Mrs. Allmers. I am a warm-blooded being. I have not fishes' blood in my veins.—And now to be imprisoned for life! Imprisoned in grief and bereavement.

ALLMERS (*looking thoughtfully at her*).   Ah, can this be properly called grief and bereavement—this that we feel?

MRS. ALLMERS.   What else?

ALLMERS.   Despair.

MRS. ALLMERS.   Despair!

ALLMERS.   Yes—despair.   I believe that is the right name for it.

MRS. ALLMERS (*looking at him with anxious inquiry*). Why should we——!

ALLMERS.   Have you no inkling of the reason?

MRS. ALLMERS.   No.   Yes.   No.   Tell me!

ALLMERS.   You say it first.

MRS. ALLMERS.   No, you must——

ALLMERS.   Little Eyolf was really rather in our way——

MRS. ALLMERS.   Oh, Alfred—how can you——!

ALLMERS.   You were never a real mother to him. And I was never entirely a father.

MRS. ALLMERS.   What else then?

ALLMERS.   It sounds so paltry when I say it.

MRS. ALLMERS.   I don't understand you, Alfred.

ALLMERS.   But it is not paltry.   I don't think it can be called so.

MRS. ALLMERS.   No, no—but what in the world——?

ALLMERS.   You were rich and I was poor, Rita.

MRS. ALLMERS (*takes a step towards him*).   I don't believe that!

ALLMERS.   So it came about, nevertheless.

MRS. ALLMERS.   Paltry, then!

ALLMERS.   I had a sister to provide for.   Remember that.

MRS. ALLMERS.   Then it was for her sake——!

ALLMERS.   We were alone in the world.   She and I.

I worked for her, so long as I was able. Till I was
ready to drop——

MRS. ALLMERS. And you can stand here and avow
all this afterwards!

ALLMERS. It seemed to me I ought to free you of the
anguish of self-reproach. Now I think you know the
reason of your never being able really to love Eyolf.

MRS. ALLMERS. Oh, but I have loved him.

ALLMERS. You always looked upon him as though an
insoluble riddle lay behind.

MRS. ALLMERS. You have interpreted it wrongly. I
was always trembling at the prospect of his taking you
away from me. (*With a wild outburst.*) And now you
tell me yourself that I have never possessed you.

ALLMERS. You have! I found you and won you so
entirely when Eyolf was born.

MRS. ALLMERS (*scornfully*). Yes, I daresay. For he
belonged to the family, of course. The child—and the
sister! They are something apart.—Oh, how I hate—
how I hate her!

(ANDREA *and* BORGHEIM *come forward along the
path by the shore.*)

ALLMERS. Well, here we are still, Andrea.

ANDREA. And you have been talking things over.
We will not disturb you.

MRS. ALLMERS. No, let us all walk together. We
must have company about us in future. Alfred and I
cannot get on alone.

ALLMERS. Yes, go on, you two. I have something
to say to you, Andrea!

MRS. ALLMERS. Oh! Very well, will you come, Mr.
Borgheim?

(MRS. ALLMERS *and* BORGHEIM *go up through the
wood on the right.*)

ANDREA.   You have something to say to me, Alfred?

ALLMERS.   Yes, I want to ask you something.

ANDREA.   Well?

ALLMERS.   Tell me, is there anything between you and Borgheim?

ANDREA.   Oh, I don't know how to answer you.

ALLMERS.   What? You don't know——

ANDREA.   I have no right to answer.

ALLMERS.   We two must remain together.

ANDREA.   But we are together.

ALLMERS.   Not here.   I do not feel that I am at home here any longer.

ANDREA.   Alfred!

ALLMERS.   Rita and I cannot share the same love.

ANDREA.   Oh, don't say that!

ALLMERS.   Yes, yes, I see it now.   And that is why I come to you.

ANDREA.   Oh, but I cannot help you in this.

ALLMERS.   Yes, you can.   You and no one else.   It is a sister I need——

ANDREA (*almost in a whisper*).   A sister!

ALLMERS.   A sister's love.   Something pure!   Something holy.   I feel I shall grow wicked here.

ANDREA.   Alfred! Alfred!

ALLMERS.   Since you were a little child we have kept together.   We two alone.   In those days you needed me. And I did what I could for you.

ANDREA.   All that I am I owe to you.

ALLMERS.   Not so much to me.   But to our beautiful, holy companionship.

ANDREA.   Every fibre of my mind has received its stamp from you.   By you.   Through you.

ALLMERS.   No, no.   This has come about through the calm, inscrutable mystery.——

ANDREA. What, Alfred?

ALLMERS. The mystery of the love of brother and sister. The inexplicable attraction of sister to brother and brother to sister.

ANDREA. Have you felt *that?*

ALLMERS. And you too. You too, Andrea. I am certain of that.

ANDREA. And now? What do you wish now?

ALLMERS. I wish that you and I should return to each other.

ANDREA (*trembling*). You and I!

ALLMERS. In the past you needed me. Now I need you. Do not let any one come between us. Promise me to continue being a sister to me.

ANDREA. I cannot, Alfred.

ALLMERS. You cannot!

ANDREA. No, not now. Not as you now are. I can no longer be like a sister to you.

ALLMERS. And why can you not?

ANDREA. Because I *am* not.

ALLMERS. What does that mean!

ANDREA. That I have no right to bear the name of Allmers.

ALLMERS. Andrea!

ANDREA. I have known it a long time. Now you know it too. And now we must part.

ALLMERS. No right to bear—! Tell me—! Explain——!

ANDREA. Not a word more! That is how it is.

ALLMERS (*sadly*). Oh, how unspeakably poor this makes me.

ANDREA. You might be so rich—so rich, Alfred.

ALLMERS. I! I rich!

ANDREA. Yes, dear. For you have Rita, and you have the treasures of both sorrow and loss. (*She goes up the wood-path to the right.*)

ALLMERS (*to himself*). No sister, then.—And little Eyolf is at the mercy of the currents of the fiord.

(*He goes slowly up the path.*)

THIRD ACT

An elevation in ALLMERS'S *garden.   At the back, a sheer cliff, with a railing along its edge.   An extensive view over the fiord.   A flag at half-mast, by the railing. A table, bench and garden chairs on the elevation. On the right, a summer-house.   It is a late summer evening.*

(MISS ASTA ALLMERS *is sitting on a bench on the left, and appears to be waiting for some one.   Her hands in her lap.   After a while Engineer* BORGHEIM *comes up the slope at the back.*)

BORGHEIM.   So I have found you at last!

ASTA.   I have been sitting here waiting—

BORGHEIM.   Not for me, have you?

ASTA.   Yes.   I have been waiting for you.

BORGHEIM (*coming nearer*).   I may come, then?

ASTA.   Yes, if you like.

BORGHEIM.   And talk to you—once more?

ASTA.   Yes.   Or first—let me say something to you.

BORGHEIM (*standing before her*).   Well?

ASTA.   Are you going this eveinng?

BORGHEIM.   I am going to-night.   By the steamer.   I must.

ASTA. Yes, yes, I suppose you must. But you must understand me, Borgheim.

BORGHEIM. That is what I want so much to do.

ASTA. Oh, if one could divide one's self! Be in two places at the same time.

BORGHEIM (*with a subdued outburst*). If you could— what would you do?

ASTA. I should go with you——

BORGHEIM. You would——!

ASTA. With you. By the steamer to-night.

BORGHEIM. You would do that! Then after all——!

ASTA. But I *cannot* divide myself! I cannot let my brother go.

BORGHEIM. No, you have already told me that twice, Asta.

ASTA. And least of all now, when he has lost little Eyolf. For think of what he has been to me all my life——

BORGHEIM. Yes, of course I understand that, Asta. You consider it your duty——

ASTA. Oh no, it is not for that. Not because it is my duty——

BORGHEIM. But——?

ASTA. But because I love him, as—well, as I believe only a sister can love a brother.

BORGHEIM. And you think that is the deepest kind of love?

ASTA. Yes, I am almost sure it is. Because it is the purest—the most sacred.

BORGHEIM. Then what have you to say about a mother's love for her child?

ASTA. I have never known much of that.

BORGHEIM. What of a father's then?

ASTA. That I know nothing about. Do you?

BORGHEIM. Yes, both a mother's and a father's. And I believe that is what has made me so light-hearted and happy. But then——?

ASTA. Then——?

BORGHEIM. Then I must make my roads alone.

ASTA. Oh, if I could be with you. Help you——

BORGHEIM. Would you, if you could?

ASTA. Yes, that I would.

BORGHEIM. But you cannot.

ASTA. Would you be content to have only half of me, Borgheim?

BORGHEIM No, you must be utterly and entirely mine.

ASTA. Then I cannot.

(ALFRED ALLMERS *comes up from below.*)

ALLMERS (*stops and looks at them*). Aha, are you both here, you two!

BORGHEIM. You know that *I* am going to start to-night.

ALLMERS. Well, what then? Are you going alone?

BORGHEIM. Yes, I am. And I shall have to remain alone, too—hereafter.

ALLMERS. Alone. There is something terrible in being alone.

ASTA. Oh, but, Alfred, you are not!

ALLMERS. Am I not! I, who no longer have a child. —Nor a sister either.

ASTA (*anxiously*). Alfred, Alfred, you must not——

BORGHEIM. How can you say so? Have you not heard—your sister is not going away with me.

ALLMERS. It is all the same. Oh, Asta, I have you no longer. Not as I had before.

BORGHEIM (*looking at them in astonishment*). But I don't understand——

ASTA. Yes, you have Alfred. Believe me—I shall always be the same to you as I have been.

ALLMERS. But I shall not!

ASTA (*shrinking back*). Ah——!

ALLMERS. Never bind yourself, Borgheim! There may come a time when you will regret it. But then it will be too late.

BORGHEIM. Never in this world could I regret anything here.

ALLMERS. Oh, it is incredible what changes a human being can undergo.

ASTA. Could not two people change together? Then they would none the less be one.

ALLMERS. Never rely upon that, Asta. That would be lifelong happiness.

(MRS. RITA ALLMERS *comes up the hill.*)

RITA. Oh, are you up here too, Alfred?

(*She is going again.*)

ALLMERS. No, stay, Rita. What did you want?

RITA. Only to walk and walk. I have no rest anywhere.

ALLMERS. Nor I either.

RITA. And then, we cannot even walk together.

ASTA. Oh, but cannot you? Try to.

RITA. That seems to be so utterly impossible now. We must each take our own way in future.

ALLMERS. I cannot bear the loneliness——

RITA. I see that. I know it. Feel it. Asta, you must never leave him.

ASTA. I!

BORGHEIM. Never!

RITA. No, he must have some one to lean upon.

ASTA. Oh, but you, Rita!

RITA. Not now. Something stands between us.

ALLMERS. It must be got rid of—if we are to live.

RITA. It will never be got rid of. You thrive in the shade. And I must have sunshine. Stay with us, Asta.

ALLMERS. Do you wish it!

RITA. Yes, everything for your sake. Stay with him. And if I am a hindrance, I will give way.

ALLMERS. You shall never give way.

RITA. I have given way once before. Made way for my own child. Must not that be right?

ALLMERS. Oh, but—Rita!

RITA. You shall be our child, Asta. We will take you in the place of Eyolf. For we must have a child to draw us together.

ASTA *(looking at him)*. What do you say, Alfred?

ALLMERS *(doubtfully)*. I——?

RITA. You must! You must! What you need is a tranquil, warm, passionless feeling. A child or a sister.

ALLMERS *(with a glance at* ASTA*)*. Ah, a sister——

ASTA. Do you wish me to remain here, Alfred?

ALLMERS. No, you must go.

RITA. You cannot!

ASTA. I will and must go away. This very evening.

RITA. Where are you going?

ASTA. At first only in to town. But afterwards——

BORGHEIM. Afterwards——?

ASTA. Far, far from here. *(Looks at* BORGHEIM *and gives him her hand.)* I am going with you.

BORGHEIM *(in radiant joy)*. Will you, after all!

ASTA. To-morrow you shall hear everything. And then you must make your choice.

BORGHEIM. Oh, I care for nothing else if I have you, Asta!

RITA. Ah! That is how it is——!

Asta. Good-bye, Rita. (*Throwing her arms round her neck.*) And thanks for all your goodness. (*Offering her hand.*) Good-bye, Alfred.

Allmers (*opens his arms to her*). Asta——

Asta (*shrinking back timidly*). Good-bye—good-bye! (*To* Borgheim.) Come, come. We must hurry.

(Borgheim *silently presses* Allmers's *and* Rita's *hands, and follows* Asta *down from the hill.*)

Allmers (*standing at the railing and looking over the fiord*). There comes the steamer. Soon they will be gone.

Rita. And we two alone.

Allmers. It must be so.

Rita. Can we bear it?

Allmers. We must.

Rita. Yes, for Asta's sake.

Allmers (*looking at her*). For Asta's—? What do you mean?

Rita. She could not stay here. She, too, wished to be everything to you. As I did.

Allmers. For her own sake there was no need for her to go. But——

Rita. But——?

Allmers. For mine.

Rita. Alfred! You could think—desire—something criminal! Never!

Allmers (*shaking his head*). Oh no, nothing criminal. But there is a secret in the family——

Rita. In your family?

Allmers. Yes. Asta and I are free in every way.

Rita. And you have concealed this from me!

Allmers. I only learnt it to-day.

Rita. From her?

Allmers. Yes.

RITA. And then she goes away.

ALLMERS. Yes, then she goes away.

RITA. And you did not ask her to remain——?

ALLMERS. It was better for us all that Asta should go.

RITA. How could you do it, Alfred? I should never have been able to do such a thing. Oh, but it is, as I was saying—the fishes' blood—. No, no—I don't mean it. It is what is great and pure in you that has gained the victory!

ALLMERS. Oh, it is a long way yet to the victory.

RITA. Then let us help each other.

ALLMERS. To find happiness again?

RITA. Not the happiness we have lost. We shall never find that again. But——

ALLMERS. But——?

RITA. Oh, I don't know, Alfred. But there must be something to put in its place.

ALLMERS. Something that would counterbalance the loss of happiness, do you mean?

RITA. Nothing that would equal happiness. But something that might make life livable.

ALLMERS. Then you will live your life by main force? At any price?

RITA. Yes, Alfred—I will. In spite of all! In spite of all.

ALLMERS (*after a short silence*). Rita—I wrote a few little verses this afternoon.

RITA. Could you do that?

ALLMERS. Yes, to-day I could. Would you like to hear them?

RITA. Yes, I should like to. Is it something about me?

ALLMERS.   About you as well.   (*Seats himself on the bench.*)   Come and sit down, and I will read them to you.

(*She seats herself on a chair by the table, opposite to him.   He takes a piece of paper out of his breast pocket.*)

ALLMERS (*reads*).

They dwelt, these two, in so cosy a house
In autumn and winter weather.
Then came the fire—and the house was gone.
They must search the ashes together.

For down in the ashes a jewel lies hid,
Whose brightness the flames could not smother,
And search they but faithfully, he and she,
'Twill be found by one or the other.

But e'en though they find it, the gem they lost,
The enduring jewel they cherished—
She ne'er will recover her vanished peace—
Nor he the joy that has perished.

(*He looks questioningly at* RITA.)   Did you understand that, Rita?

RITA (*rises*).   Yes.   And I understood, too, that you did not write those verses about me.

ALLMERS.   About whom else——?

RITA.   You wrote them about yourself and Asta.

ALLMERS.   About little Eyolf in the first place——

RITA.   Oh, not at all about the little Eyolf who lies out there, deep, deep down.

ALLMERS.   Rita, Rita, how can you——

RITA.   You wrote them about the other one.   About her whom you used to call little Eyolf when she was a child.

ALLMERS. Both for the big one and the little one. And for you too, Rita. I had to give expression to something that I can no longer bear in silence.

RITA. Would it help you if you were free of me?

ALLMERS. No.

RITA. And we cannot live together as man and wife either.

ALLMERS. No.

RITA. For little Eyolf might see it, perhaps. Who knows? And he must not see us living in happiness without him.

ALLMERS. Nor could we do so, Rita. Even if we wished.

RITA. No, we could not. (*Stops.*) But if we could call him to life again, Afred!

ALLMERS. What do you mean by that?

RITA. If we could make him live within us, I mean.

ALLMERS. Oh, he does live within us. In sorrow and heartache—and in remorse too.

RITA. Oh, sorrow and heartache and remorse—that is not life at all. They are not for Eyolf's childish soul. We must think of something that may fill him with quiet joy.

ALLMERS (*shaking his head with a sad smile*). As if he could see what we are about here!

RITA. Perhaps he can see, though—in his own way. We must live and act as though he were behind us. Looking at us. Seeing everything and understanding everything. All our actions and all our thoughts.

ALLMERS (*wringing his hands*). Oh, if he could have lived with us. Lived his own life. Now it is as though he had never existed. What was he doing here in the world, if he was not to——

RITA. He did not live in vain, nevertheless.

ALLMERS. Oh, phrases, Rita. (*Pointing down over the railing.*) But listen to them down below. All the shrieking, yelling children. All those who let him go to destruction. And who did not help him.

RITA. They will all go to destruction too, Alfred. Go to destruction in their unhappy homes.

ALLMERS. Yes, I daresay you are right.

RITA. And we stand up here on our height and look on. And do not help them.

ALLMERS. We——?

RITA. We could help them, if we wished. But we do not.

ALLMERS (*looking before him*). That would be little Eyolf's revenge. To repay death with life.

RITA. Then he would not have lived in vain.

ALLMERS. Nor died in vain either.

RITA. If you will—we will do it, Alfred. Stand by one another like two faithful friends.

ALLMERS. Little Eyolf shall continue to live through us.

(*He goes to the flagstaff and hoists the flag to the top.*)

RITA. No more sign of death. That is a relief, Alfred. Oh, what a relief!

ALLMERS. Thanks for rousing me to this.

RITA. Thank little Eyolf.

ALLMERS. Yes, him first.—In deeds.

RITA. If only one does not demand happiness—at any price—I do not see why one should not be able to live one's life.

ALLMERS. Eyolf's memory will teach us how to live our lives.

RITA. Yes, yes, Alfred. And he himself will live in them.

RITA. Yes, he is living with us. We will never more look for him down in the deep, dark, turbid current.

ALLMERS. He is not down there. He is up here on earth with us, unseen. Taking part in our daily life. Helping us to protect our uncertain, changeable human destinies.

RITA. And if now and then a mysterious Sabbath peace descends on our souls——?

ALLMERS. What then, Rita?

RITA. Do you not think it might be a visit from some one who is gone?

ALLMERS. Who knows? We will look for those who are gone. Perhaps we shall catch sight of them.

RITA. Little Eyolf. And big Eyolf. Where shall we look for them, Alfred?

ALLMERS. Upwards.

RITA (*nods in approval*). Yes, yes, upwards!

ALLMERS. Upwards—towards the stars. And towards the great silence.

RITA (*giving him her hand*). Thanks!

JOHN GABRIEL BORKMAN

FROM THE FIRST ACT

MRS. BORKMAN. He thinks, what is the truth, that you are ashamed of us—that you despise us. And do you pretend that you don't? Were you not once planning to adopt him? To make him change his name? Call himself Rentheim. Erhard Rentheim.

MISS RENTHEIM. That was at the height of the scandal—when the case was before the courts.

MRS. BORKMAN. Yes, then you wished me to lose my boy too. As I lost everything—everything else. I was only to be left with the dishonoured name. I alone. It was good enough for me to be called Borkman.

MISS RENTHEIM. I have no such designs now.

MRS. BORKMAN. And it would not matter if you had. For in that case what would become of his mission? No, thank you. Erhard no longer needs you. And therefore he is as good as dead to you—and you to him.

MISS RENTHEIM (*with an outburst*). Can you say that, Gunhild!

MRS. BORKMAN. He has promised me that. He has sworn it to me. Now you know it.

MISS RENTHEIM (*firmly, with resolution*). We shall see. For now I shall remain out here.

SECOND ACT

The great gallery on the first floor of the Borkman house. The walls are covered with faded tapestries, representing hunting-scenes, gods, shepherds and shepherdesses, all in faded colours. A folding-door to the

*left, and further forward a piano. In the left-hand
corner, at the back, a door, cut in the tapestry, and
covered with tapestry, without any frame. Against
the middle of the right wall, a desk, with books and
papers. Further forward on the same side, a sofa
with a table and chairs in front of it. The furniture
is all of a stiff Empire style. A lighted chandelier
hangs from the ceiling.*

(JENS BORKMAN *stands by the piano, with a music-stand
in front of him, playing the violin.* FRIDA FOLDAL
sits at the instrument, accompanying him.)

(BORKMAN *is a slender man of middle height, well on in
the sixties. His appearance is distinguished, his
profile finely cut; he has white hair and is clean-
shaven. He is in evening dress, with a black coat
and a white necktie.* FRIDA FOLDAL *is a girl of seventeen, pretty, pale, with a somewhat weary and overstrained expression. She is cheaply dressed in dark
clothes.*)

(*They are playing the last bars of a piece of Beethoven.*)

BORKMAN (*lowers the violin and remains standing at
the music-stand.*) It went passably well this evening.
You are getting on, Miss Foldal.

FRIDA. Oh, I have had so little practice as yet, unfortunately. I am so badly wanting in proficiency.

BORKMAN. You have the fire of music in you. And
to have fire in one's soul—that is the decisive thing.
The decisive thing in every relation of life. (*Turning
over the pages of the music book.*) Let me see—. What
shall we take next——

FRIDA (*looks at her watch*). I beg your pardon, Mr.
Borkman—but I am afraid I must go.——

BORKMAN. Are you going already?

FRIDA (*rises*). I really must. I have an engagement this evening.

BORKMAN. Are you to play for dancing?

FRIDA. Yes, there is to be a dance after supper.

BORKMAN (*places his violin and bow on the piano*). Do you like playing dance music—in private circles, I mean?

FROM THE THIRD ACT

BORKMAN. But it does not know *why* I did it; why I *had* to do it. And that is what I want to explain.

MRS. BORKMAN. Reasons acquit no one.

BORKMAN. They may acquit one in one's own eyes.

MRS. BORKMAN. Oh, let all that alone. I have thought over that business enough and to spare.

BORKMAN. I too. During those six years in my cell I had time to think it over. And during the eight years up there in the gallery I have had still more ample time. I have gone over the whole case again—by myself. I have turned every one of my actions upside down and inside out. Backwards and forwards. And the final judgment I have come to is this: the one person I have sinned against is—myself.

MRS. BORKMAN. And what about me? What about your son?

BORKMAN. You and he are included in what I mean when I say myself.

MRS. BORKMAN. And what about the hundreds of others, then—the people they say you have ruined?

BORKMAN. I had power in my hands. And these others did not concern me.

MRS. BORKMAN. No, no, there may be something in that.

Borkman. If the others had had the power, do you think they would not have acted exactly as I did?

Mrs. Borkman. They would not—most of them.

FROM THE FOURTH ACT

Ella Rentheim. A long sleep, I think!

Mrs. Borkman. Ella! (*To* The Maid.) Go for help. Men and horses.

(The Maid *goes out to the right.*)

Mrs. Borkman (*behind the bench*). The night air has killed him.

Ella Rentheim. So it appears. Will you not look at him?

Mrs. Borkman. No, no, no. He could not stand the fresh air.

Ella Rentheim (*nods slowly*). It must be so. The cold has killed him.

Mrs. Borkman. Oh, Ella, the cold had killed him long ago.

Ella Rentheim. Us too.

Mrs. Borkman. You are right.

Ella Rentheim. We are three dead beings—we three here.

Mrs. Borkman. We are. And now I think we two may hold out our hands to each other, Ella.

Ella Rentheim (*quietly*). Over the third. Yes.

(Mrs. Borkman *behind the bench, and* Ella Rentheim *in front of it, take each other's hand.*)

WHEN WE DEAD AWAKEN

NOTES AND DRAFT

The first act passes in the summer. Fashionable bathing establishment on the sea coast.

Second act up at a health resort, high in the mountains.

Third act among glaciers and precipices on the western slope.

He is a sculptor. Elderly. Famous. Newly married. Returning from honeymoon. He has taken her "up into a high mountain and shown her all the glory of the world." And so he won her. She is young, bright and joyous. They are both radiantly happy. Now he will begin to enjoy life.

Then it is that he meets "his first love" at the bathing establishment. The one he has forgotten. She who has never forgotten. Clad in white. Accompanied by her nurse. She was of rich family. Left her home and went away with him, the young, poor, unknown future artist. Became his model. Then she broke with him and left him. Has since been married to another and divorced. Then married again. He committed suicide. All this happened abroad.

CHARACTERS

The DOCTOR at the Baths, an intelligent man, still young.

The INSPECTOR at the Baths. Fussy. Goes about among the visitors, spreading gossip.

The GOSSIPING LADY from the capital. Has the reputation among the visitors of being extremely amusing. Malicious from thoughtlessness.

519

MANY VISITORS at the Baths, with their CHILDREN.
A Waiter at the Bath Hotel.
Waitresses.
The Sportsman from the mountains.
Stubow.   Rambow.
Professor Erik Stubow, famous sculptor.

SCENARIO

Stubow and Maia.

The former and the Inspector.

The former and the strange lady in white with her nurse.   They go into the pavilion.

The former, the lady from the capital and other ladies. The ladies go off after a short scene.

The mountain sportsman arrives with his servant and dogs from the steamer.   Servant and dogs out to the right.

Stubow, Maia, the Sportsman and the Inspector.

The Sportsman and Maia out to the right.

The strange lady in from the left.

The Inspector goes into the hotel.

The lady and Stubow alone.   Dialogue.

Maia comes back.   The lady off.

Stubow and Maia decide to go to the mountain health resort.

In this country only the mountains give an echo, not the men and women.

He was a diplomatist, a distinguished Russian [Bulgarian] diplomatist.   Him I managed to drive out of his mind, mad, incurably mad.   It was great sport while it was in the doing.   I could have laughed within me.   If I had anything within me.

So that was Herr von Satow.

No, my second husband was called Satow. He was a Russian.

And where is he

I have killed him.

Killed!

Killed him with a fine sharp dagger which I had with me in bed

[Don't believe you

Indeed you may believe it]

Have you never had children.

Yes, many children

And where are they now

I killed them.

Now you are telling lies, Irene. [All this.]

Killed them [murdered them pitilessly] as soon as they came into the world. [Long, long before.] One after the other.

Religious brooding?

No, I have never——

Some of the strings of your nature have broken.

Does not that always happen when a human being dies?

————————

First became famous through Irene—Now he will live and enjoy his youth over again with another. Then he alters the statue into a group. Irene becomes a secondary figure in the work that made him famous——

First a single statue; then a group. Then she left him.

Our life was not that of two human beings

What was it then

Only that of artist and model.

2nd ACT.

Children playing on the upland.
Professor Rubek is sitting on the bench and looking at their play.
Maia comes to look for him.   Scene between them.
Irene with a band of children advances over the upland.
The bear hunter comes and fetches Maia.
Irene and Rubek.   Great scene.
Something is locked up in me
You took the key with you

> When we dead awaken——
> What do we see then?
> We see that we have never lived.

> U.   Come down again as fast as you can
> The mist is upon us
>
> We will go up above the mists.
> But you must pass through them first

Oh, how I shall rejoice and sing, if I get down with a whole skin

The hut by the Lake of Taunitz.   There it lies
Great, white swans are dipping their necks in the water.

THE RESURRECTION DAY

A PLAY IN THREE ACTS

BY

HENRIK IBSEN

1899

FROM THE THIRD ACT

MAIA (*interrupting*). Was it not a strange chance that we four should meet here on the wild mountain side?

PROFESSOR RUBEK. You with an eagle-shooter, and I with—(*to* IRENE)—well, what do I come with?

IRENE. With a shot eagle.

MAIA. Shot?

IRENE. Shot in the wing, Mrs. Rubek.

MAIA. Rubek—there seems to be something good and reconciling in our meeting here for the last time.

PROFESSOR RUBEK. Never to see each other again. If you wish the same as I do.

MAIA. With all my heart I do.

ULFHEIM. Then all is well. I would rather have carried her off—by force—violently—but let that be——

MAIA. Then I will say good-bye to you, Rubek.

PROFESSOR RUBEK. I have done you a great wrong. I, too, have taken you by force——

MAIA. Yes, when you bought me——

PROFESSOR RUBEK (*nods*). —bought you, in spite of all the ferment of open-air life in you.

MAIA. And if you now set me free so easily [and cheerfully], it is because you want to be free yourself.

PROFESSOR RUBEK. Yes, I could not bear it any longer.

MAIA. If we had not been joined together in wedlock, as it is called, you would have borne it longer.

PROFESSOR RUBEK. You too! You too, Maia. You have spent days and nights regretting it.

ULFHEIM. Don't think of that now. Here we meet and here we part. Here we will hold our feast.

MAIA. A feast here? Where will you get the champagne from, Mr. Ulfheim?

ULFHEIM. Champagne? *Must* there be champagne?

MAIA. Nothing less will do!

ULFHEIM. Then, upon my soul, you shall have it!

(*He takes a key from his pocket, opens the door of the shooting hut and goes in.*)

MAIA (*looking after him*). What is he doing now?

PROFESSOR RUBEK. He is making a clatter with knives and forks. And with glasses. He is preparing the feast for us.

(ULFHEIM *comes out, bringing a tray covered with a cloth, with bottles of wine and cold meats, and puts it down on the stone table.*)

MAIA. But what in the world——!

ULFHEIM. You will have to take pot luck, ladies and gentlemen. This was really intended only for two. But our guests are welcome. (ULFHEIM *opens a bottle of champagne.*) [(*softly.*) Lars is a good fellow. He knows me. Looks after everything.]

MAIA (*in a half whisper*). Oh, you base criminal!

ULFHEIM. No reproaching your comrade. (*Pouring out the wine.*) Only intended for two, as I said. We men must make shift with beer glasses. (*Hands the glasses round and raises his glass.*) Your health, ladies and gentlemen! (*To* MAIA.) What shall the toast be, Madam?

MAIA. Freedom shall be the toast!

(*She empties her glass at one draught.*)

PROFESSOR RUBEK. Yes, let freedom be the toast.

(*He empties his glass.*)

IRENE. And a toast for those who have the courage to use it.

(*She sips at her glass and throws the rest on the ground.*)

ULFHEIM. Thanks for the toast, Madam. I take it for myself. For *I* have never lacked courage to use my freedom! (*He drinks and fills the glasses again.*) And now a toast to the hunt for the new life! I have a castle to offer her who follows me——

MAIA. No castle! I won't own it!

ULFHEIM. You may want it in time. In a year or two perhaps all the rest will be done with.

MAIA. Hurrah! Then we shall be altogether free.

(*Empties her glass.*)

ULFHEIM. Then we shall only have this hut left.

MAIA. We can set fire to that. Burn it down any day we like.

ULFHEIM. But first live—live in it!

MAIA. Live the new life, yes!

ULFH. And now we take our leave.

PROF. R. No doubt we shall meet down at the hotel.

ULF. Scarcely. Before you come down, I shall be gone.

PROF. R. Are you going with him, Maia?

M. Yes, I am going with him.

PROF. R.   And we are going further over the mountains.

ULF.   Shall we not warn him?

M. (*struggling for a moment with herself*).   No.   Let him choose his own way.

ULFH. (*raising his hat*).   A pleasant trip among the mountains.

> (*Silent leave-takings are exchanged.   ULFHEIM and MAIA begin to descend the precipice at the back.*)

ULFH.   Take care.   It is a deadly dangerous way we are going.

M. (*between jest and earnest*).   You must take the responsibility for us both.

> (*They continue to climb down and are no longer seen.*)

PROF. R.   [(*with a breath of relief*).   Now I am free!] So lightly and cheerfully could she leave me.

IRENE.   She is awakened.

PROF. R.   Awakened?

IRENE.   From life's deep, heavy sleep.   Even as she descends into the ravine, she is being carried upwards towards her bright native heights—without her knowing it.

PROF. R.   To me she is dead.   Then let her live [—or rest].

IRENE.   Did you not murder her a little every day —when you were living together?

PROF. R.   I?

IRENE.   As you murdered me a little every day. Sucked her blood too—to support yourself——

PROF. R.   Never!   Against you I have sinned.   But never against her.   Never against any other.

IRENE.   Then perhaps that very thing was death to her.

PROF. R.   No one else in the world concerns us.   We can now be everything to each other.

IRENE.   Now!

PROF. R.   Yes, now.   Come, Irene, before we go home we will climb up on yonder peak and look far out over the country and all its glory.

IRENE.   Driving clouds are sweeping up the mountain side.

PROF. R.   But the peak rises clear of them.

IRENE.   And you will go up there?

PROF. R.   With you.   I will live the resurrection day and reshape it in a new image—in your image, Irene.

IRENE.   In mine——?

PROF. R.   In yours, as you now are.

IRENE.   And do you know what I am now?

PROF. R.   Be what you please.   For me, you are what I see in you.

IRENE.   I have stood on the turn-table [in the glare of electric lamps, amid the blaring of trumpets], naked, and made a show of myself to hundreds of men—after you.

PROF. R.   It was I that drove you to the turn-table— blind as I then was—I, who placed the dead clay-image above the happiness of life—of love—not a hairsbreadth has this lowered you in my eyes.

IRENE.   Nor in my own.   But the desire of life is dead in me.   Now I have arisen, and see that life lies dead. All life lies on its bier—(*The clouds sink slowly down like a damp mist.*)   See how the shroud is closing in on us!   But I *will* not die again, Arnold!—Save me!   Save me, if you can and will!

PROF. R.   Up above the mists I have a glimpse of the mountain peak.   It stands there glittering in the sunrise

—there it is we must go—through the mists of night up into the light of morning.

> (*The mists close in thicker and thicker over the scene. R. and* IRENE *step down into the veil of mist and are gradually lost to sight.*)
>
> (*The head of the* SISTER OF MERCY *appears, searching, in a rift in the mist.*)
>
> (*High up above the sea of mist the mountain peak shines in the morning sun.*)